Charles I and the Making
of the Covenanting Movement

'Our main fear to have our religion lost,
our throats cutted, and our poor countrey
made an English province.'

Robert Baillie,
Minister of Kilwinning,
1637

Charles I and the Making of the Covenanting Movement
1625–1641

ALLAN I. MACINNES

Department of Scottish
History, University of
Glasgow

JOHN DONALD PUBLISHERS LTD
EDINBURGH

To Mairead

ISBN 0 85976 295 5

British Library Cataloguing in Publication Data
Macinnes, Allan I.
  Charles I and the making of the Covenanting movement,
  1625–1641.
  1. Scotland. Covenanters, history
  I. Title
  285.2411

Phototypeset by The Midlands Book Typesetting Co.
Printed and bound in Great Britain by Billings and Sons Ltd., Worcester

Acknowledgements

This book owes much to colleagues, students, family and friends. As supervisors of my thesis on which this book is based, Professors I. B. Cowan and A. A. M. Duncan have to be thanked for their advice, assistance and, above all, for their forebearance. For constructive dialogue, professional support and academic guidance I would especially like to thank two other colleagues in the Department of Scottish History, University of Glasgow — namely, Mr J. B. S. Gilfillan (now retired) and Dr J. F. McCaffrey. Students in my special subject provided immense feedback throughout the 1980s. Their collective wit, individual insights and occasional derisory humour allowed me to define, sharpen and refocus innovatory as well as revisionary ideas on Charles I and the Covenanting Movement. A debt of gratitude, which can only be acknowledged rather than repaid, is owed to family and friends for their continuing support, exhortations and fortifying of spirits. My wife Mairead has quite simply proved the most positive influence in my life.

In conducting my research, I received magnanimous assistance from the ducal family of Hamilton, most notably from Lord Hugh Douglas-Hamilton. Not only was I afforded access to the family muniments at Lennoxlove, but a considerable quantity of documents was placed on temporary deposit with the Scottish Record Office for perusal at my convenience. The staff in the Scottish Record Office — at Register House and West Register House, Edinburgh — merit my appreciation for their unstinting assistance despite the deplorable managerial drive for stultifying bureaucracy in recent years; a trend from which the Strathclyde Regional Archives, Glasgow, remains mercifully free. The librarians and archivists at the National Library of Scotland and the British Museum, as at the Universities of Edinburgh and Glasgow, must especially be thanked for allowing me courteous and prompt access to original sources in manuscript and print. Particular mention must be made of Mr N. Higson, archivist at the Brynmor Jones Library, for furthering my research by constructive guidance through the Scottish material lodged at the University of Hull.

Last, but by no means least, I should like to thank John Tuckwell, publishing director of John Donald Publishers Ltd., for his supportive advice and editorial comments. Needless to say, I am solely responsible for all sins of omission and commission.

Contents

Abbreviations and Conventions

Ancrum & Lothian	*Correspondence of Sir Robert Kerr, first earl of Ancrum and his son William, third earl of Lothian*, D. Laing ed., 2 vols, (Edinburgh, 1875).
APS	*Acts of the Parliaments of Scotland*, T. Thomson & C. Innes eds, vols II–VI(ii), (1414–1660), (Edinburgh, 1814–72).
BM	British Museum
Burnet, *Memoirs*	Burnet, G. *The Memoirs of the Lives and Actions of James and William, Dukes of Hamilton and Castleherald*, (London, 1838).
CSP, Domestic	Calendar of State Papers Domestic Series, of the reign of Charles I, J. Bruce & W. D. Hamilton eds., 17 vols, (1625–41), (London, 1858–82).
CSP, Ireland	*Calendar of State Papers relating to Ireland, of the reign of Charles I, 1625–32*, R. P. Mahaffey ed. (London, 1900).
CSP, Venice	*Calendar of State Papers and Manuscripts relating to English Affairs existing in the Archives and Collections of Venice, and in other Libraries of Northern Italy*, A. B. Hinds ed. vols XIX–XXIV, (1625–39), (London, 1913–23).
EUL	Edinburgh University Library
GUA	Glasgow University Archives
GUL	Glasgow University Library
Hailes, *Memorials*	*Sir D. Dalrymple, Lord Hailes, Memorials and Letters relating to the History of Britain in the reign of Charles I*, (Glasgow, 1766).
Hamilton, I	HMC, Eleventh Report, appendix, *The Manuscripts of the Duke of Hamilton*, (London, 1887).

Hamilton, II	HMC, *Supplementary Report on the Manuscripts of the Duke of Hamilton*, (London, 1932).
HUL	Hull University Library
HMC	Historical Manuscripts Commission
Laing MSS	HMC, *Report of the Laing MSS preserved in the University of Edinburgh*, (London, 1914).
Large Declaration	(W. Balcanqual), *A Declaration concerning the Late Tumults in Scotland*, (Edinburgh, 1639).
Macinnes, Thesis	A. I. Macinnes, The Origin and Organization of the Covenanting Movement during the reign of Charles I, 1625–41; with particular reference to the west of Scotland, 2 vols, (University of Glasgow, Ph.D. thesis, 1987).
Mar & Kellie, I	HMC, *Manuscripts of the earls of Mar and Kellie*, (London, 1904).
Mar & Kellie, II	HMC, *Supplementary Manuscripts of the earls of Mar and Kellie*, (London, 1930).
NLS	National Library of Scotland
RCRB, Extracts	*Extracts from the Records of the Convention of Royal Burghs*, J. D. Marwick ed. 2 vols, (1616–1711), (Edinburgh, 1880–98).
RKS	*Records of the Kirk of Scotland, containing the Acts and Proceedings of the General Assemblies, 1630–54*, A. Peterkin ed. (Edinburgh, 1843).
RMS	*Registrum Magni Sigilli Regum Scotorum*, J. M. Thomson ed. vols VIII–IX, (1620–51), (Edinburgh, 1894–97).
Rothes, *Relation*	John Leslie, earl of Rothes, *A Relation of Proceedings Concerning the Affairs of the Kirk of Scotland, from August 1637 to July 1638*, J. Nairne ed., (Bannatyne Club, Edinburgh, 1830).
RPCS	*Records of the Privy Council of Scotland*, D. Masson & P. H. Brown eds., first series, vols VI–XIV, (1599–1625), (Edinburgh, 1884–98); second series, 8 vols, (1625–60), (Edinburgh, 1899–1908).
Scot, *Narration*	*An Apologetical Narration of the State and Government of the Kirk of Scotland since the Reformation*, D. Laing ed., (Wodrow Society, Edinburgh, 1846).

SHR	*Scottish Historical Review*
SHS	Scottish History Society
Spalding, *Troubles*	*J. Spalding, The History of the Troubles and Memorable Transactions in Scotland and England, 1624–45, 2 vols, J. Skene ed., (Bannatyne Club, Edinburgh, 1828–29).*
SR	*The Earl of Stirling's Register of Royal Letters, Relative to the Affairs of Scotland and Nova Scotia from 1615 to 1635, C. Rogers ed. 2 vols, (Edinburgh, 1885).*
SRA	Strathclyde Regional Archives
SRO	Scottish Record Office
Traquhair MSS	*HMC, Ninth Report, part ii, appendix, Traquhair Muniments*, (London, 1887).
TRHS	*Transactions of the Royal Historical Society*
Dates:	Old Style dates used in contemporary Britain are retained throughout. The new year is taken to begin on 1 January according to Scottish usage, not 25 March (English usage).
Money:	The merk was valued at two-thirds of the pound Scots (£), twelve of which were equivalent to a pound sterling. All monetary values are Scots unless otherwise stated.
Numerals:	All monetary quantities, like page references in the notes at the end of each chapter, are expressed in arabic numerals. Roman numerals capitalised are used to denote volumes of printed works, lower case for volumes of manuscripts (MS) or muniments (MSS). Folio references (fo) revert to arabic numerals.
Quotations:	All abbreviations in manuscripts, pamphlets and broadsheets and other printed texts are extended, but otherwise the original spelling and punctuation are retained.

1

The Political Nation and Scottish Identity

Introduction

James VI and I died on 27 March 1625. His son, Charles I, succeeded to the thrones of Scotland and England. Standing no more than 5 feet [1.52 metres] from his buckled shoes to his manicured wig, the new monarch was intent on changing radically the style, pace and direction of royal authority. Unfortunately, Charles's dogmatic conviction in his own rightness was not grounded in personal experience of Scottish politics prior to his accession in his twenty-fifth year. Indeed, Charles set out to rule his Scottish inheritance ill equipped politically — other than with an authoritarian conviction in his own rightness. His remorseless promotion of conformity to English practice took no account of Scottish fears of provincial relegation inflamed by the union of the Crowns since 1603. His relentless pursuit of administrative, economic and religious uniformity not only provoked constitutional opposition, but fanned the flames of nationalism that was to terminate his personal rule by 1638. Charles was thus the principal architect in the making of the Covenanting Movement whose rigorous imposition of constitutional checks on absentee monarchy fulfilled the worst fears of the diminutive king that in Scotland by 1641, 'He had no more Power than the Duke [doge] of Venice'.[1]

The Unprepared Prince

Although born in Dunfermline on 19 November 1600, Charles was thoroughly anglicised. A rather unloved upbringing as the second son and third surviving child of James VI and Anne of Denmark made Charles an intensely private and secretive individual, much given to duplicity and incapable of bestowing lasting trust on his political associates or inspiring unstinting loyalty from his subordinates.[2]

Charles had not been schooled by James to succeed him as monarch. Other than to act as a spur to his elder brother Prince Henry, Charles had not been encouraged to take an interest in affairs of state. Although the death of Henry in 1612 shattered his reclusive life at Court, Charles remained the product of a narrow environment in which the politics of power were dominated by

1

personal rivalry and factional intrigue. Unlike his father, Charles had never faced aristocratic rebellions, vituperative denunciations from the pulpit or angry mobs in the streets of the Scottish capital. Conversely, he had no appreciation of the ready familiarity between Scottish monarchs and their leading subjects prior to 1603. Charles's concern that order, seemliness and decency should prevail undoubtedly served to make his Court a model of decorum. But such concerns entailed the deliberate distancing of the king from his subjects and, simultaneously, compounded his remoteness from Scotland.

Having been befriended by his father's last favourite, George Villiers, duke of Buckingham, who acted as a surrogate elder brother from 1618 until his assassination ten years later, Charles was included in the triumvirate which grappled with the diplomatic, constitutional and religious problems that beset James I's final years in England. But Charles was never involved in the government of Scotland prior to 1625. Charles did not actually visit Scotland from his departure as an infant in 1604 until his coronation visit in 1633. He had been pointedly excluded from the state visit of 1617. When he acceded to the Scottish throne, Charles possessed an unparalleled lack of understanding of the mechanics of government and the underlying social structure of Scottish politics, notably the pervasive ties of kinship and local association between the nobles, gentry, burgesses and clergy who composed the political nation.[3]

In the directives which streamed from Court during his thirteen-year personal rule in Scotland, Charles repeatedly referred to 'our ancient and native kingdom',[4] not so much to promote Scottish interests as to preclude English councillors interfering in Scottish affairs which he came to regard as his own special preserve. The anglicised absentee failed to grasp that government in Scotland depended less on long-established central institutions than on the consensus provided by co-operation between the Crown and the political nation. Each of the four political estates represented a social class with separate privileges and vested interests.[5] On the one hand, the orientation of government was decentralised, following more the practice of Germanic States than the centralised conformity expected in England. On the other hand, the particularist interest of each social class contained variations of group and individual status definable not only on political but also on feudal, judicial and ecclesiastical grounds.

The Nobles

The most important estate within the political nation was that of the nobility. In Scotland, as in England, the designation of noble was reserved for the peerage and did not encompass untitled members of landed society as elsewhere in Europe. Every duke, marquis, viscount, earl and lord was summoned individually to parliament to give counsel and consent to royal policy. From the fifteenth century, the new rank of parliamentary lord emerged to broaden this basis of consultation. The feudal complement to the giving of advice was the nobles' recognition of the Crown, not only as the ultimate superior over all estates in Scotland, but as the upholder of justice and the source of all temporal government. Heritable grants of lands and judicial privileges by charter from the Crown had the twofold effect of decentralising government and providing an objective definition of status based on heritable jurisdictions, not gradations of rank.

Each territorial lordship was bounded by a heritable jurisdiction, usually that of a barony court. By the seventeenth century, the main concern of such courts was estate management. The barony court administered and interpreted the customary relationships on which the rural economy operated. The baron was no more than an ordinary litigant in cases affecting his own interest and was expected to attend regularly at the sheriff court in whatever shire his barony lay. The primary responsibility of the Crown was not to run local government, but to harmonise divergent baronial interests through sheriff courts and justice-ayres (judges on circuit) to hear appeals on the grounds of partial justice or deal with civil and criminal cases beyond the competence of the barony court. However, this framework of local government was complicated from the later middle ages by the heritable annexation of the office of sheriff by leading noble families and the infrequency with which judicial circuits were conducted. Civil litigation was as a result attracted to the Court of Session (alternatively known from its reconstitution in 1532 as the College of Justice). The Privy Council, as the central intelligence agency in Scotland, took cognizance of serious crimes — though trials for capital offences were usually before tribunals appointed specifically by the Crown.

A regional alternative existed. Higher rights of public justice encompassed within a regality court had been bestowed heritably on leading nobles since the later middle ages. In addition to the usual baronial privileges, such nobles had the same civil jurisdiction as sheriffs and the criminal competence of justice-ayres: namely, the right to try the four pleas of the Crown — rape, murder, arson and robbery. Only charges of treason were reserved for the Crown. Lords of regality could be given judicial rights over lands and baronies outwith their own estates. Such baronies, though losing their judicial autonomy, continued to operate within the hierarchical framework of the regality. Thus, lords of regality acquired extensive powers of judicial recall: that is, the right to repledge from the local and central courts of the Crown not only cases affecting their tenantry, but also those citing neighbouring barons and other landlords within their territorial spheres of influence. In return for the exclusion of royal officials, the exercise of regalian privilege demanded the development of procedural and administrative sophistication. Apart from annexed baronial courts, ordinary courts within the regality were presided over by bailies — occasionally the office was heritable within another landed family — and higher jurisdiction was implemented through the establishment of judicial circuits.[6] Regalian administration was continually evolving in co-operation with the Crown. Ordinary taxation was traditionally assessed on the landed resources of the four estates and was collected by government agents within every shire.

When James VI decided to impose an extraordinary tax on the interest arising from financial loans (annual rents) in 1621, regalities as well as shires were accountable to the Exchequer as distinct fiscal units.[7]

The secularisation of church property provided the major extension of land-ownership during the sixteenth century. The main beneficiaries among traditional noble families were those who had acquired, as lay commendators, a life interest in the landed resources of the late medieval Church. When James VI annexed the temporal property of the pre-Reformation Church to the Crown by an enactment of 1587, he inserted the provision that church property already in the hands of lay commendators should be erected heritably into temporal lordships. The king was also given parliamentary approval to make heritable grants from the considerable portion of annexed kirklands. Although James had an act passed in 1606 which removed episcopal temporalities from the scope of the 1587 enactment, he reserved the right to create temporal lordships from secularised monastic property. As a result, temporal lordships remained the most important avenue for elevation into the peerage. By using temporal lordships to reward officers of state, James was able to draw lesser members of the landed classes into the service of the Crown. Within the ranks of the peerage he built up a nobility of service with a vested interest in the maintenance and intensification of royal government. At the same time, by delegating baronial and regalian rights to temporal lords, James continued to underwrite the decentralised orientation of government in Scotland. However, James did withhold the power of repledging from justice-ayres when conferring regalian jurisdiction on temporal lords from 1587, thereby diminishing aristocratic opportunities for the maintenance of kinsmen, local associates and tenants in serious criminal actions.[8] At James's death in 1625, 21 abbeys, 11 priories, six nunneries and one preceptory, either separately or conjointly, had been erected into temporal lordships. Indeed, of the 54 major ecclesiastical foundations in Scotland, only one — Dunfermline Abbey — had been retained, but not wholly preserved, by the Crown.[9]

Before an appraisal can be made of the pervasive territorial influence of the nobility, distinction must be drawn between lands directly managed as property and those perpetually tenanted (or subinfeudated) as superiority. The lands which composed the property were worked and leased by the peasantry as removable tenants. The superiority consisted of lands bestowed irredeemably to feuars who, as heritable tenants, were deemed members of the landed classes. Although the heritable as well as the removable tenants came within the jurisdiction of the barony or regality, the feuars were not bound to observe the dictates of estate management from either court. Rigorous exploitation of landed resources or judicial privileges on the part of the nobility was diluted by ties of kinship and local association, the longstanding affinities towards neighbouring families and communities manifested as relationships of kindness. This was particularly evident in the designation kindly-tenant applied to possessors whose families had enjoyed long and continuous settlement. Conversely, kinship and local association reinforced social and political deference towards the nobility.

The secularisation of the kirklands affords particularly striking testimony to the continuing importance of kinship and kindness to the political nation.

Secularisation primarily augmented the territorial influence of the nobility rather than their economic resources. Prior to the annexation act of 1587, nobles who had acquired church property as lay commendators sought to protect their interests by apportioning about a third of all kirklands within their control among their families and local associates. Kindness was further cultivated among the longstanding tenants of ecclesiastical foundations by wholesale feuing. Around 65% of all charters to kirklands were granted to existing possessors.[10] The general expectation that lay commendators, and subsequently temporal lords, would retain superiority but feu their kirklands left little for their own immediate exploitation as property. Moreover, the feuing of kirklands coincided with a period of persistent inflation which depreciated, but not necessarily decimated, the value of landed incomes. This combination of feuing and inflation has been interpreted as promoting a collective transfer of wealth away from the nobility — as also the Crown — towards the rest of landed society by the early seventeenth century. Although the traditional equation of landed wealth and landed power was undoubtedly distorted, a temporal lord still retained the largest share of actual income generated on his estates — individual estimates vary from a fifth to a third.[11]

Furthermore, although the feuing of kirklands in alliance with inflation eventually eroded customary social relationships, there was no immediate restructuring of customary expectations. Land was still regarded as a source of political and social clientage as much as a commercial asset. Thus, the territorial spheres of influence of James Hamilton, third marquis (later first duke) of Hamilton, during the 1640s were encompassed by a fivefold classification of kinship and kindness: 28 household men, of whom all but nine were Hamiltons, responsible for the routine management of his extensive estates in the central Lowlands, particularly in the shires of Lanark (including Lesmahagow Priory), Stirling and West Lothian as well as the isle of Arran; 123 of his surname, neighbours and feuars, none of whom were Hamiltons, cited as gentlemen and loyal dependants; 50 removable tenants associated by kindness not kinship; and 17 retainers who actually ran his household.[12]

Undoubtedly, inflation, manifested by the marked rise in prices from the mid-sixteenth century, compounded the financial problems of nobles and other landlords who lived conspicuously beyond their means. The nobles were not in a state of collective crisis at the outset of Charles I's reign, however. Nor was their position as the natural leaders of society under threat even though the economic position of several became parlous and indebtedness was an established characteristic of their class.[13] Indebtedness certainly served to maintain the buoyancy in the land market stimulated by the secularisation of the kirklands. But, nobles and other impecunious landlords were suffering less from a diminution of landed resources than from a shortage of ready cash: a perennial problem given the inelastic nature of estate revenues limited by seasonal yields and customary obligations. For most nobles in most localities their debts remained manageable.

The few families that suffered terminal decline were nobles of the second rank lacking the resources of kinship and local association readily available to the magnates, resources particularly useful to mobilise credit, secure loans and ensure against judicial apprisings of rent or even expropriation.[14]

In assessing the impact of inflation, too much should not be made of apparent differences in farming practices leading to social instability in areas, such as the west of Scotland, which, in turn, created a ready constituency for political insubordination.[14] Certainly, the money rents yielded by pastoral farming were less able to keep pace with inflation than the provendar rents yielded by arable farming. Within most Scottish localities, however, differences in farming were simply a matter of emphasis rather than of kind. In the west no less than the east of Scotland, nobles and other landlords primarily through the agency of their barony courts made significant commercial adjustments in estate management without causing wholesale removal, relocation or alienation among their tenantry. By the outset of Charles I's reign, the marked upsurge in money rents in mixed farming areas like the west of Scotland should be attributed less to rack-renting than to the composition of grassums (entry-fines on the renewal of leases), provendar rents and work services. Such composition of rents was but part of the general reorientation of estate management, along with the consolidation of tenant holdings and the gradual replacement of multiple-tenant by single-tenant farms, instigated by nobles and other landlords as part of a more flexible and remunerative managerial response to inflation than recourse to feuing. Conspicuous consumption was in turn sustained and expanded through the commercial reorientation of estate management as evident from the enthusiasm with which younger members of the nobility undertook the European 'grand tour', from the increasing architectural emphasis on domestic style and comfort and, not least, from the fashionable pursuit of landscaping through the creation of parks, woodlands, orchards and gardens.[16]

Inflationary pressures on landed resources certainly contributed to the controversy surrounding the disposal of the teinds — the nominal tenth (tithe) of all revenues produced within the bounds of each parish — a lucrative social no less than economic asset. During the middle ages, the teinds had been grossly appropriated by ecclesiastical foundations. Any church whose parsonage (or major) teinds were appropriated invariably had its right of patronage annexed. The creation of temporal lordships had led to the secularisation of these parochial rights. Temporal lords thus acquired ecclesiastical status as titulars of the teinds in the parishes where they exercised the right of patronage — that is, in parishes where they assumed the responsibility of nominating the minister as well as underwriting his stipend. This prescriptive development apportioned the same parochial rights to titulars as were already possessed heritably by the Crown and some landlords in their capacity as lay patrons in the minority (14%) of parishes where teinds had remained unappropriated.[17]

However, there were significant divergences between lay patrons and titulars in the exercise of parochial rights. Lay patrons tended to exercise their ecclesiastical superiority over single parishes where, not infrequently, the geographic bounds of the parish and that of the barony court coincided. Titulars tended to exercise their ecclesiastical superiority over a large number of parishes which were not always grouped together; nor did temporal lords necessarily have exclusive jurisdiction within these geographic bounds. Within every parish, the lay patron or titular controlled the disposal of the teinds of other landowners, designated ecclesiastically as heritors. Within parishes where control was vested in the lay patron the heritors were usually feuars. Thus, the patron to whom they paid teind was also the feudal superior to whom they paid feu-duties. Even where heritors held lands directly from the Crown as freeholders, they were usually tied to the lay patron by kinship or local association. In parishes which either contained or lay adjacent to the domain of the temporal lord, a similar social nexus prevailed between the lord as titular and the heritors. However, where a temporal lordship was dispersed geographically and titularship was not exercised over consolidated groupings of parishes, a considerable portion of heritors were neither bound to the titular as feudal superior nor tied by kinship or local association. Indeed, some heritors were not only freeholders, but held baronial rights and even headed their own local nexus of kinsmen and associates. The temporal lords in their capacity as titulars thus exercised control over other landlords of substance, a control which was perennially contentious. As a measure of appeasement, titulars continued the practice of the ecclesiastical institutions which they had replaced by farming the teinds to tacksmen, a speculative group of middlemen. In return for the security afforded by long leases, the tacksmen — who were often prominent local landowners — guaranteed the temporal lord a definite income from the teinds.[18]

The Gentry

After the nobility, the most influential estate within the localities, though the most recently established in terms of national politics, was the gentry. This collective term, as applied to members of landed society designated individually as lairds, was coming into common usage in the early seventeenth century, Charles I being among its most active promoters. Feudally, the gentry consisted, on the one hand, of the lesser or untitled barons and freeholders who held their lands directly from the Crown and, on the other, of the feuars who held their lands within the superiority of other landlords. Judicially, the lesser barons as well as the freeholders were expectd to give regular attendance at the sheriff or regality court within whose bounds their estates were located. Feuars were not necessarily required to give such regular attendance. Ecclesiastically, all the gentry — apart from a select few lay patrons — were committed to paying teinds as heritors.

The political entitlement of the gentry to parliamentary representation grounded in an enactment of 1428, reiterated in 1587, was not only inequitable and inflexible but anachronistic and fraught with anomalies. Unlike the nobility, the gentry were not summoned individually to parliament, but had to suffice with the election of commissioners — usually two from each shire — to represent their estate. Each of the thirty-three shires was only allowed one vote. Although the shire commissioners can be regarded as representing a distinct political estate, this estate neither encompassed nor directly represented the gentry as a distinct social class. The parliamentary franchise was restricted to lesser barons and freeholders whose estates were rated at no less than 40/– old extent for the purpose of paying the traditional land tax to the Crown. Freeholders whose lands were rated at less than 40/– old extent, together with all feuars who paid taxes indirectly as reliefs to their feudal superiors, were unenfranchised, not eligible for election as shire commissioners and had to rely on the virtual representation of their interests through ties of kinship and local association.[19]

The restriction of the franchise to freeholds of 40/– old extent was based on a land rating distinct and long distanced from the current income, rents and feu duties of estates by the early seventeenth century. Electoral participation was effectively confined to gentry who held their lands from the Crown by traditional tenures of ward and relief or blench. Tenure by ward and relief entailed the payment of incidental casualties arising from delays in heritable succession (non-entry) and minorities (wardship) and for the marriage of heirs. A more commercial variant of this tenure was taxed ward which replaced these incidental casualties by a fixed annual composition. Tenure by blench also involved the payment of a fixed annual composition which was often nominal or even idiosyncratic. The tenure coming into vogue from the later fifteenth century and given particular prominence by the feuing of kirklands in the sixteenth century was feu-ferme, which marked a further commercialisation of the relationship between feudal superior and feuar. The feuar, as heritable tenant, had his annual feu-duty fixed in perpetuity in return for an initial payment to his superior of an entry-fine (grassum), which was usually a direct multiple of his feu-duty. Debarring of gentry holding by feu-ferme from electoral participation was particularly anomalous and inflexible in the case of feuars of kirklands whose landed resources often matched and occasionally outstripped the freeholds of gentry holding by ward and relief or blench. Enfranchisement of the feuars of kirklands would have required the overhaul of the distinctive conventions for levying taxation in Scotland, a massive task which neither James VI nor Charles I was prepared to undertake.

By medieval convention, the barons and freeholders had paid a third of all taxation levied by the Crown, the ecclesiastical foundations paid half and the royal burghs the remaining sixth. Only the barons and freeholders were rated according to old extent. Thus, the first ordinary taxation of Charles I in 1625 rated the estates of barons and freeholders and 30/– for every £1-land of old extent. But the secularisation of the kirklands in the sixteenth century meant that fiscal distinctions could no longer be rigidly maintained between secular and ecclesiastical landowners. Moreover, increased feuing of Crown lands to sitting tenants from the fifteenth century created freeholds from leaseholds which were not rated to old extent. In like manner, the Crown's annexation of ecclesiastical estates in 1587 converted feuars of annexed kirklands into freeholders. Although James VI instructed that notional old extents were to be devised for the estates of these synthetic categories of freeholders, the tax rolls revised in 1621 remained loaded against landowners rated to old extent. The first land tax levied by Charles I in 1625 was designed to raise £400,000. Ecclesiastical landowners (including temporal lords) were assessed at 42.6% of the total levy rather than their customary half, while the secular landowners (including synthetic freeholders) were rated at 43.3% rather than their customary third: an imbalance in tax quotas which went uncorrected in the further levies of the personal rule in 1630 and 1633. Despite the relative shift in tax burdens in favour of ecclesiastical foundations, temporal lords as well as bishops were increasingly experiencing opposition when exacting reliefs from their feuars for the land tax.[20] This reaction against indirect taxation was growing testimony both to the political frustration provoked by the restricted franchise and to the social assertiveness of feuars of kirklands, who included among their considerable numbers individual lairds whose traditional landed resources had been enhanced significantly by secularisation.

The feuars of kirklands can be regarded as the main beneficiaries of feu-ferme tenure.[21] Their superiors had initially profited from high entry-fines and the opportunity to increase rents formerly paid by removable tenants. In the longer term, however, the feuars had gained not only heritable security of tenure but fixed feu-duties and their estates were exempt from the managerial dictates of barony and regality courts. The feuars were thereby provided with a valuable hedge against inflation and, simultaneously, with an opportunity to profit personally from the steady increase in grain prices which, for almost forty years, characterised the rule of James VI. Moreover, though neither as powerful nor cohesive as the nobility, the gentry as a whole did not lack social assertivenesss or political initiative as evident from the regular appearance of shire commissioners in parliament from the outset of the seventeenth century.[22]

The leading social position of the gentry within the localities had been tapped productively by the Kirk since the Reformation. In particular, since the nobles were reluctant to undertake administrative duties outwith their heritable jurisdictions, the gentry were encouraged to serve as elders on kirk sessions. In every parish, the elders along with the ministers were responsible for the collective exercise of discipline. Moreover, as the State increasingly underwrote the commitments of the Kirk to social welfare and education, the gentry, in their capacity as heritors, were held financially accountable for the efforts of kirk sessions to apportion relief to the deserving poor in times of dearth, like the famine of 1623, and to establish schools in every parish from 1633. Participation as elders, or less routinely as heritors in association with the kirk session on an augmented parochial executive, was not restricted to the enfranchised. Feuars as well as freeholders and lesser barons were not only offered greater opportunities for official employment in the Kirk than in the State, but also gained experience of a more centrally orientated structure of government uncluttered by heritable jurisdictions. In turn, the Kirk can be regarded as more responsive to the vast expansion in the ranks of the gentry effected by the secularisation of kirklands. The State seemingly remained thirled to the feudal privileges of the nobility.[23]

The Crown conspicuously failed to harness the administrative energies of the gentry to the reform of local government. In 1609, James VI had launched a scheme for justices of the peace which, though based on his English experience, had been first projected in 1587. 'Some godlie, wyse and vertuous gentilmen of good qualitie' were commissioned to oversee, prevent and try all incidents which disrupted the peace within every shire. After meeting initial hostility from the barons and the royal burghs, James re-launched the scheme in 1612 as a local supplement rather than an alternative to heritable jurisdictions. So constricting was the scope of their revised powers that the justices complained that they were 'bot as sejeandis and officearis to the uther judgeis in the countrey'. Despite further parliamentary ratification for peace commissions in 1617, the scheme met with so little enthusiasm from the gentry that less than half of the Scottish shires had commissions still functioning by 1625.[24]

The landed classes were not wholly composed of nobles and gentry. Secularisation of the kirklands had provided the major avenue of upward mobility throughout the sixteenth century. Over half the feuars who gained ownership of kirklands came from the ranks of the removable tenantry, the vast majority of whom acquired no more land than that which they already occupied and cultivated. This social movement resulted in a diverse and dispersed grouping of portioners and 'bonnet-lairds' whose status was that of lesser proprietors but whose respective agricultural holdings were indistinguishable from those of tenant-farmers. By the seventeenth century, the two most prevalent forms of agricultural holdings were the multiple-tenant and the single-tenant townships. The holding of the portioner was equivalent to a share in the former, that of a 'bonnet-laird' may be identified with the latter. Indeed, some tenant-farmers who lacked the security of tenure of the portioner or 'bonnet-laird' possessed considerably more land as a virtual aristocracy within the ranks of the peasantry.[25] This amorphous class of lesser proprietors and substantial tenant-farmers on the fringe of the political nation presents a particular problem of social definition. After the Union of 1603, no doubt fortified by a growing awareness of English social divisions, a certain currency was gained for the term yeoman in relation to this amorphous class within official circles. By mid-century, it was the Kirk rather than the State which was promoting recognition of the yeoman as a distinct social class. Their active support was sought as elders in rural parishes where there was either a shortage of resident gentry or a reluctance among local lairds to serve on kirk sessions.[26]

Moreover, although their political interests were to be given no special consideration during the personal rule of Charles I, commercially astute yeomen along with the gentry and some ministers were the major sources of credit outwith the leading towns. As evident from the detailed inventories of sums loaned and borrowed compiled for the extraordinary taxes on annualrents between 1625 and 1633, the emergence of Glasgow as Scotland's secondary money market (after Edinburgh) cannot be solely attributed to the city's mercantile community. Indeed, gentry, yeomen, and ministers in surrounding rural districts were responsible for the circulation of a greater volume of money as credit than the other towns in the west. Over the nine years covered by the inventories, the money market in the rural districts was consistently above 20% more active than in western towns. Such profitable working of surplus capital reveals the existence of a commercial interest which cut across class divisions between landowners and leaseholders as across geographic divisions between town and country.[27]

The Burgesses

Commercial exchange still tended to be concentrated within the towns in the early seventeenth century. The more important towns had been erected into burghs during the middle ages. As corporate feudal entities, the burghs held their privileges of self-government and trade either directly from the Crown or by royal licence within the superiority of a secular or ecclesiastical landlord. Burghs which held from the Crown were reclassified as royal burghs from 1400: a process which led to the dependent burghs being reclassified either as burghs of barony from the mid-fifteenth century or as burghs of regality from the later sixteenth century. Dependent burghs had tended to evolve from the estate management of barony courts, their marketing privileges being located at a convenient town within the bounds of the barony, and their areas or trading monopoly were usually confined within baronial precincts. The proliferation of the burghs of regality coincided with the creation of temporal lordships from 1587 and marked a desire among lords of regality to create larger market monopolies within their jurisdictional bounds. The small rural communities within the burghs of barony and regality were concerned primarily with the communal pursuit of agriculture, however, whereas the corporate communities within the royal burghs tended to organise their commercial life around both foreign and local trade. It was their greater capacity to generate wealth rather than different tenurial conditions which in practice distinguished the royal from the dependent burghs.

Since the late thirteenth century, burghs holding directly of the Crown had paid fixed annuities, the burgh-fermes for corporate privileges. At the end of the sixteenth century, the Crown had sought to counter the depreciation in burgh-fermes by successfully demanding increased annuities from the royal burghs. Despite the doubling of some annuities, the revenues retained by the royal burghs — such as land rents, court fees, petty customs and burgess fees — continued to appreciate for their common good funds. The Crown's endeavours to establish a right of supervision over these funds were resisted collectively by the royal burghs throughout the seventeenth century. The Crown's major source of regular income from the burghs remained the great customs exacted from exported staple wares and imported commodities and the imposts levied on wines. The Crown also exacted contributions from the burghs towards extraordinary expenditure incurred in the national interest. Such assiduous tapping of commercial wealth had resulted in the commissioners from the burghs becoming established as a parliamentary estate during the fourteenth century. Burgh commissioners were neither assigned nor expected a decisive influence in the formulation of royal policy. But in return for their contribution of a sixth of all taxes levied by the Crown, a monopoly over foreign trade was vested in the leading burghs who enjoyed parliamentary representation — notably the royal burghs from 1400, supplemented by the ecclesiastical burghs of St. Andrews, Glasgow and Brechin, because of their capacity to make a meaningful contribution to the fiscal quota apportioned to the burgess estate.

Partly to protect their monopoly of overseas trade, but primarily to defend their local trading precincts from the occasionally formidable competition generated by dependent burghs, the burgess estate sought greater formulation and promotion of their common interests through the Convention of Royal Burghs from 1552. The conservator of the Scottish staple in the Netherlands, which traditionally acted as the main overseas agency for the wholesale distribution and purchase of merchandise, was appointed by and became accountable to the Convention. Whenever taxation was levied by the Crown, the Convention assumed responsibility for allocating the amount each burgh was to be assessed to meet their estate's fiscal quota. Any royal burgh excluded from the Convention's stent-roll was effectively denied parliamentary representation and could no longer be guaranteed access to foreign trade. Conversely, positive discrimination was continuously — albeit sparingly — practised in favour of the more prominent and prosperous dependent burghs which had the commercial capacity to participate in overseas trade. The addition of a dependent burgh to the stent-roll helped curtail smuggling and spread the burden of fiscal liabilities. Contribution to the tax quota of the burgess estate served as the precursor to parliamentary representation and ultimately to the dependent acquiring the status of royal burgh.[28]

The other estates were each able to meet and consult on national issues when authorised by the Crown. Nonetheless, only the burgesses met formally on a regular basis several times a year to legislate and impose stents in furtherance of their collective interests. As well as fending off the efforts of the Crown nationally and of nobles and other landlords locally to influence internal government by the town councils, the Convention both facilitated the formulation of common policy and ensured a continuing momentum behind every issue brought before parliament by the burgess estate. From 1590, the Convention had appointed an agent to lobby parliament and the privy council, a practice extended to the Court from 1613 in the wake of the Union of the Crowns. Elections of parliamentary commissioners by the town-councils of every royal burgh were conducted under the auspices of the Convention which also monitored the attendance of commissioners at parliament. From the late sixteenth century, no royal burgh sent more than one commissioner to the Convention other than Edinburgh, the capital, which was allowed two on account of its unrivalled commercial prosperity and its watching brief over the interests of the royal burghs during the intervals between Conventions. In the interests of internal harmony, the practice was adopted as standard for parliamentary representation by 1621. Normally the commissioners attending a Convention went on to attend parliament. In contrast to England which lacked any comparable institution to the Convention, the influence of the burgesses estate in parliament was not diluted by 'carpet-bagging'. All commissioners (usually around fifty) were drawn from the ranks of the burgesses and answerable to the Convention.[29]

In essence, the royal burghs were corporate pockets of vested interests. The Crown had permitted town-councils to become self-perpetuating oligarchies from the later fifteenth century. The retiring town-council chose their successors and the magistrates in every royal burgh were chosen by the combined old and new councils. The principal magistrates, who exercised jurisdiction over the burgh courts, were the bailies. Normally only merchants and craftsmen, the freemen of the burghs, who promoted and defended their vocational interests through the cellular organisation of their guilds, were eligible for the status of burgess and for election as town-councillors, magistrates or burgh commissioners. All other inhabitants were classified as indwellers and, like strangers, were either denied any marketing privileges or subjected to specially onerous tariffs. Because of their superior capacity to accumulate capital from their trading ventures, the merchants aspired to dominate the town-council as well as monopolise the overseas trade of each royal burgh. A rigid social divide between merchants and other burgesses was usually maintained by the entry requirements for the merchant guild: notably, an apprenticeship of at least eight years accompanied by high entry fees beyond the resources of most craftsmen. In most leading burghs by the sixteenth century, the defence of mercantile privileges was personally entrusted to the dean of guild, the magistrate for the merchant community, whose court was subject to no other jurisdiction save the Court of Session.

Notwithstanding the domination of town-councils by mercantile oligarchies, craft guilds proliferated as protective institutions. The craft guilds were primarily concerned to safeguard the vocational monopoly of their members against competition from rural artisans and indwellers and to act as mutual assurance societies against pauperism. Entry into the craft guilds was restricted by entry fees, by limiting numbers of apprentices and by long periods of training — up to thirteen years as apprentices and journeymen — before full acceptance into a guild. By assiduous organisation in the course of the fifteenth century, crafts began to acquire seals of incorporation from burgh courts which bestowed on the deacon of each craft disciplinary authority over the activities of his guild. The deacon convener of all the crafts was accepted as a burgh magistrate able to try any case affecting the general privileges of craftsmen. Inflation during the sixteenth century occasioned an element of social insubordination in the royal burghs which the craft guilds exploited, with varying degrees of success, to exact economic and political concessions from the mercantile oligarchies. The town-councils' fixing of market prices was increasingly relaxed and usually only exercised after consultation with the appropriate craft. Commencing with Edinburgh in 1583, local accords or setts were negotiated within the leading burghs whereby craftsmen were assured of minority representation on the town-councils though magisterial positions other than the deacon convener were normally reserved for the merchants. By the early seventeenth century, the craft guilds in the leading burghs were organising themselves within Trades Houses to articulate their common interests and mount a continuous lobby on town-councils.[30]

The commercial activities of urban communities, allied to the general thrift and frugality of their lifestyles and their amenability to discipline would seem in Scotland, as elsewhere in Europe, to have afforded a special affinity for Calvinism. Yet, the burghs cannot necessarily be regarded as the domicile of 'the most modern and progressive elements' within Scotland in so far as their support for Calvinism, from its inception at the Reformation of 1560, was not necessarily accompanied by the promotion of a capitalist mentality.[31]

The unique feature of Calvinism among Christian theologies was that it allied the individual believer's striving for assurance of salvation to a strict adherence to worldly asceticism and the diligent exercise of his lawful calling. In particular, the Calvinist doctrine of predestination has been seen as a psychological sanction for the modern capitalist ethos. For the elect were constantly required to demonstrate their perseverance in the faith and self-confidence in their own assurance by the productive pursuit of their chosen vocations as well as by formal attendance to their religious obligations. Neither prosperity nor poverty were especially deemed distinguishing marks of the elect. However, Scottish Calvinists did not condemn the accumulation of wealth as inherently evil. Indeed, prosperity was seen as a trial for the truly pious. The elect were distinguished from the reprobate by their attitude towards prosperity, in that their piety was manifest by their productive use of worldly wealth. Anyone who acquired wealth through asceticism and diligence was actively discouraged from dissipating his prosperity by conspicuous consumption. Yet, he was not actively exhorted to give away a large proportion to charity. Calvinism, in short, laid stress not so much on good works as on hard work. For the prosperous there was apparently little alternative to the investment of wealth to promote the further accumulation of capital.[32]

Nonetheless, however much the accumulation and investment of capital was sanctioned by Scottish Calvinists in the seventeenth century, the creation of a capitalist mentality was at best a piecemeal and gradual development. The commercial activities of the mercantile community may still be depicted as traditionalist in the century after the Reformation. Rather than maximise individual profits, merchants preferred to share trading ventures in order to minimise risks. Moreover, although partnerships tended to last only as long as each venture, co-operative inclinations were strengthened by family ties. Habitual and informal alliances between relatives and friends served as a surrogate for the lack of consolidated commercial firms and insurance societies. Furthermore, burgesses in public office were not noted for their progressive spirit. Those who served as elders on kirk sessions tended to be drawn from the oligarchic town-councils. The Convention of Royal Burghs was more concerned to preserve and perpetuate privilege than to advocate social and political reform. Characterised by a persistent lack of ready money, the finances of the burghs were not managed on particularly modern principles even though most common good funds were appreciating at a greater rate than the coinage was being debased by inflation.[33]

Strong social affinities existed between town and country notwithstanding the commercial propensities of urban communities. Most burgesses outwith the commercially specialised confines of Edinburgh possessed crofts and small-holdings. As in the dependent burghs, some of the smaller royal burghs placed as great an emphasis on agriculture as trade. Kinship and local association as well as marriage played an important part in securing burgess status. Fines for admission were viewed less as a source of revenue than as a means of regulating entitlement to the privileges of a burgess. The prospect of gainful employment in trade and commerce attracted a steady flow of recruits from the countryside to the guilds. Whereas the crafts tended to attract apprentices from outwith the landed classes, the superior potential to accumulate capital drew younger sons of the gentry to the mercantile community.

The material resources of the merchants were generally on a par with all but the richest nobles, but they consciously refrained from the high levels of expenditure and conspicuous consumption prevalent within landed society. As a result, their frugality facilitated a degree of social mobility and intercourse between town and country. On the one hand, the prospect of handsome dowries induced lairds to marry merchants' daughters. On the other hand, merchants moved on to the land through marriage, through direct purchase of estates and, most frequently, through the provision of mortgages for nobles and gentry: a steadier, if indirect, means of social advancement also open to lawyers and wealthy craftsmen from the leading burghs. The relaxation of usury in the wake of Reformation had allowed the profitable working of money, interest being exacted at the rate of 10% at the outset of Charles I's reign. Sums lent in mortgage to impecunious nobles and gentry were secured usually by heritable bonds. As the creditor, the merchant, lawyer or craftsman would be assigned a portion of the borrower's estate until sufficient revenue was exacted to repay the capital sum and interest — both components being known respectively as the wadset and annualrent. Failure to repay the debt within the specified time — normally varying from seven to thirteen years — led to the title as well as the revenues of the estate, or at least that portion which remained unredeemed, passing permanently into the hands of the merchant or other creditor.

The acquisition of estates by merchants and other affluent burgesses rarely led to their withdrawal from commerce. Instead, their affinities with landed society were strengthened. Traditionally, nobles and other politically committed members of landed society had maintained prestigious lodgings in the leading towns. In turn, several burghs bestowed the title of provost — an office which normally carried no fiscal responsibilities — on a powerful neighbouring lord or laird. By the outset of Charles I's reign, it had become fashionable among the landed to erect houses of modest character in smaller towns in order to retain a watching brief over the commercial as well as the social life of their localities. At the same time, nobles and gentry were induced to supplement their rather inelastic landed incomes through partnerships in trading ventures.[34]

The Clergy

Material acquisitiveness as much as spiritual zeal characterised the clergy, the remaining political estate, by the later middle ages: a condition which promoted the secularisation of the kirklands as well as the Reformation during the sixteenth century. Carried out in defiance of the Crown, the Reformation confirmed the clergy's ideological influence over the political nation. As elsewhere in Europe, the Scottish Reformation was a response to a general desire for spiritual nourishment, a concern for the more efficacious cure of souls. Yet, the success of the movement had depended on and was shaped by political rebellion. In their justification of the Reformation, clerical polemicists like John Knox had appealed for support not just from the nobility as the natural leaders of society, but from the political nation as a whole. In essence, this was achieved by emphasising a minor aspect of Calvinist teaching: the qualified duty of lesser magistrates to resist tyranny in the head of state which was broadcast as the right to take arms against an ungodly Crown. Thus, the Reformation provided the political nation with an ideological basis for resistance to monarchy in order to correct or repress any deviation from godly government.[35]

Moreover, since the Reformation was not maintained by princely dictate, the new Kirk was able to mould its own government according to its own conceptions of best scriptural warrant, jettisoning medieval precepts and practices which were deemed contrary to the founding spirit of the apostolic church. Whereas the government of the Church of England from the time of Elizabeth Tudor can be regarded as both royal and episcopal, that of the Kirk has best been described as 'conciliar and anti-erastian'. Its ecclesiastical authority was vested separately in a hierarchical structure of representative courts which culminated nationally in the general assembly.[36]

Although the Scottish Reformation had marked a distinct break in polity as well as doctrine between the medieval Church and the Kirk, the clerical estate continued to be represented in parliament — albeit technically. Despite secularisation, abbacies and priories continued to be represented by lay commendators until 1621, even though their presence as clerical commissioners was gradually rendered redundant from 1587 by the creation of temporal lords who sat with the nobility. The right of parliamentary attendance of the pre-Reformation prelates was assumed by Protestant administrators in the guise of bishops. Even when episcopacy was eclipsed within the Kirk — following the annexation of their property by the Crown in 1587 and the initial establishment of presbyterianism in 1592 — titular bishops continued to sit in parliament. Indeed, the Kirk during the presbyterian hegemony was not altogether averse to the idea of parliamentary bishops to represent clerical interests. Thus, James VI had a ready-made excuse in 1597 when he proposed to increase the number of titular bishops in parliament. Nine years later, he passed an act restoring their landed resources and jurisdiction in order to maintain their parliamentary status.[37]

This programme of restoration, though piecemeal, was highly contentious. Where James VI believed that ecclesiastical policies could be resolved by parliament, with the bishops representing the clerical estate, a vociferous minority within the Kirk, led by Andrew Melville, sought supreme ecclesiastical authority to be vested in general assemblies. Where James conceived an erastian framework of government for the Kirk, with the bishops as agents of the Crown, the Melvilleans preferred to adhere to a presbyterian framework of courts, structuring government from local kirk sessions through district presbyteries and regional synods to national general assemblies. Where James believed ultimately that supreme government in Kirk and State was part of his prerogative, the Melvilleans believed that the Kirk and State were two distinct kingdoms, the former exercising moral supervision over the latter.

However, this ecclesiastical controversy was governed more by empirical than ideological considerations. The authorising of presbyterianism by the 'golden act' of 1592 was essentially a compromise between the aspirations of the Crown and the Melvilleans. Though weighted in favour of the latter, no recognition was accorded to the Melvillean resurrection of theories of Church independence first advocated by the papacy in the early middle ages. The supremacy of general assemblies in ecclesiastical affairs was licensed by parliament. Lay commissioners attended general assemblies in the early seventeenth century as representatives of the whole membership of the Kirk, drawn from the political estates, rather than as nominees of the synods and presbyteries. Although there were to be annual general assemblies, the Crown retained the right to appoint the time and place of their meeting. No contingency provisions were adequately established if the Crown, when present at an assembly, declined to appoint its next meeting. James, therefore, retained an effective lever for insinuating royal control over the Kirk and restoring episcopal authority. Accordingly, he followed up his nomination and endowment of parliamentary bishops by tampering with assemblies which successively frustrated and isolated the Melvilleans. The way was paved for the full spiritual restoration and reconsecration of the episcopate by 1610. Episcopal authority was further fortified by the creation of Courts of High Commission which provided civil sanctions for ecclesiastical censures. Nonetheless, presbyterianism was not totally abolished. James VI had preferred to graft diocesan control on to the existing framework of government. The parliamentary ratification of the king's ecclesiastical policy in 1612 omitted any reference to the bishops being subject to the censure of general assemblies. Nevertheless, the assembly was not formally superseded as the highest legislative authority for the national affairs of the Kirk. In turn, a spirit of moderation and co-operation characterised the subsequent relationships of synods and presbyteries with the bishops.[38]

Contention between Kirk and State was not designed to produce a system of political apartheid. Protagonists on both sides were essentially advocating alternative means of governing the Christian Commonwealth, not the separation of the Scottish people into adherents of the Kirk or the State. Underlying the whole controversy was a basic co-operation between laity and clergy within local communities, as manifest in the running of kirk sessions by lay elders and ministers. Religious leadership within the parishes was further consolidated by ties of kinship and local association between the ministers and the landed classes; by ministers marrying into the families of the gentry and burgesses; and by their acceptance of lay patronage and titularship of the teinds for both parochial placement and stipend provision. All ministers had a minimum landholding within their parishes of a manse and glebe — a house with four acres of kirkland provided by their patrons. The increasing level of personal income and assets recorded in ministers' testaments during the opening decades of the seventeenth century suggests a growing involvement in landholding, primarily as purchasers and creditors rather than as heirs. Landed affinities were especially prevalent among the episcopacy. Most bishops were men of property independently acquired or inherited prior to the restoration of their temporal estates in 1606. Like prominent families among the gentry, the bishops were linked to the nobility either as cadets or as local associates. Their Protestant persuasions notwithstanding, they exhibited the traditional characteristics of the 'somewhat ancestral type of Scottish churchmen'.[39]

Regardless of the particular ascendancy of episcopacy or presbyterianism, all ecclesiastical courts exercised a moral oversight of family life with the aim of fostering and encouraging the household as the basic unit of religious worship. The household, however, was viewed more in terms of the nuclear family than that of the extended family traditionally associated with the retinues of the nobility. Hence, the Protestant appeal to the political nation was patently more suited to the gentry, yeomen and burgesses. Nonetheless, the willingness of nobles to employ chaplains in their households not only indicates a measured accommodation with Protestantism, but also suggests that in transforming traditional expectations, Calvinism in Scotland went hand in glove with the commercial reorientation of estate management.

The gentry, yeomen and burgesses were certainly more amenable to the Kirk's exercise of discipline. Acceptance of and adherence to Protestantism, however, was made relatively painless for the nobility in particular and the political nation as a whole by James VI's emasculation of excommunication; the ultimate ecclesiastical sanction that carried the civil consequence of outlawry. From 1605, no excommunication of a noble could proceed without the consent of the Privy Council. By 1610, the general assembly was moved to agree that no sentence of excommunication could proceed without episcopal approval. The incidental power of outlawry was thus effectively denied to ministers.[40]

A Chosen People

The maintenance of spiritual welfare, like the enhancement of material prosperity, was not just the respective preserve of the clerical and burgess estates but the special concern of the political nation as a whole. Indeed, with Scotland's political interests formally subordinated to those of England after 1603, the religious aspirations of the national Kirk become the most distinctive means of promoting Scotland internationally. The Kirk of Scotland was the only national church in Europe uncompromised by the need to tolerate other religious groups in the interests of political expediency. The national standing of the Kirk was not unqualified at the outset of Charles I's reign, however. Kirk polity was a compromise between presbyterianism and episcopal authority, albeit the latter was in the ascendancy. Although its influence was pervasive throughout the Lowlands where parishes tended to be small in area and settlements nucleated, the Kirk's operations in the Highlands and Islands, where parishes tended to be large and communities dispersed, were at no more than missionary level. The Kirk had no clear or unequivocal standard of worship. Edward VI of England's *Second Prayer Book* had initially been adopted by the Scottish reformers. But the distinctly less liturgical, Genevan-inspired *Book of Common Order* was generally commended from the 1560s for the conduct of prayers and sacraments. The *Second Prayer Book* was never totally displaced, finding renewed favour with supporters of episcopacy, especially those forming close contacts with Anglican clergy after 1603. However, ministers of pronounced presbyterian sympathies, influenced by the Puritan minority who rejected the use of the *Second Prayer Book* within the Church of England, tended to deviate from if not ignore the *Book of Common Order*.[41]

Differences on polity, geographic impact and worship notwithstanding, the Protestant doctrine of the Kirk of Scotland remained staunchly Calvinist. The Arminian challenge, first aroused within the Dutch Reformed Kirk before spreading to the Church of England, had gained no foothold in Scotland by 1625. Arminianism accepted Calvinist orthodoxy with regard to original sin and justification by faith, but rejected its absolute belief in predestination which offered salvation only for the elect and eternal damnation for the reprobate. For the Calvinist, the Christian's assurance of salvation through membership of the elect depended on the effectiveness of his or her calling. Whereas all believers who attended the visible church on earth to hear the preaching of the word and receive the sacraments were partakers of an outward calling, only the true believers, as the elect members of the invisible church, had an inward calling from God to the communion of the saints. For the Arminians, because of their belief in God's universal bestowal of divine grace, salvation was obtainable for all, not just the elect, through the exercise of free will. Hence, the Calvinist teaching that the grace of God was irresistible for the elect, who as the true believers could not fall from grace, was renounced in favour of universal atonement. This precept offered salvation to every individual prepared to repent his or her sins. For the Arminian, therefore, the assurance of salvation was freely available for all believers but conditional on human endeavour. The true believers chose their own salvation. For the Calvinist, who believed in absolute and exclusive salvation for the elect, the Arminian doctrine of free will was an unwarrantable limitation on the sovereignty of God.[42]

The Kirk of Scotland, however, was concerned not only to promote the salvation of the elect, but to identify the national interest with a dutiful dedication to the godly life: that is, every member of every congregation striving to attain a state of grace as the precondition for election must adhere systematically to a Calvinist code of ethics for everyday conduct. Doctrinal precepts, moreover, underwrote the international responsibilities of the Reformed Kirk which retained a watching brief over the fate of Protestantism in general and of Calvinist minorities in particular. This special concern was intensified by the course of the Counter-Reformation and the political alignments brought about by the Thirty Years' War. For militant Catholicism, allied to the autocracy of the Spanish and Austrian Habsburgs, was ranged against and initially triumphant over Protestant and particularists interests within the Holy Roman Empire.[43]

Regardless of endemic Protestant hostility within Scotland, Catholicism maintained no more than a peripheral presence in the households of nobles and gentry in the Lowlands. While the relative spiritual neglect of the Highlands and Islands offered the greatest prospects for its entrenchment as the faith of whole communities, Catholicism was only sustained in isolated pockets among the clans. Undoubtedly, the penal laws against Catholic recusancy promulgated in the wake of the Reformation were draconian in tenor. But their regular reissue and amplification during the reign of James VI served primarily to encourage Catholics to exercise circumspection and not to flaunt their faith. The guiding spirit for their implementation by the Privy Council was to apply civil sanctions pragmatically, not dogmatically, in order to eradicate popery in succeeding generations rather than inflict irreparable material damage on prominent Catholic families.[44]

Albeit the actual profession of Catholicism was a minority pursuit, Scottish fears of Counter-Reformation, coupled to James VI's decided preference for an erastian episcopacy in the Kirk, prompted militant presbyterians to band together locally in covenants. Banding together for the purposes of local government or political alliance was a socially established practice in Scotland by the sixteenth century and, indeed, had been adopted specifically for religious purposes prior to the Reformation. Yet, the description of a religious band as a covenant only gained common currency after 1590, as the result of federal theology spreading from the continent. Nor was the conception of the covenant particularly Scottish, being shared by evangelical Protestants in areas as diverse as Transylvania, Ireland and New England.[45]

Covenant or federal theology, as identified with the evangelical ministry and their militant presbyterian followers in Scotland from the early seventeenth century, emphasised the contractual relationship between God and man rather than the stark Calvinist reliance on election by divine decree. Predestination and thereby man's ultimate dependence on divine grace for salvation was not denied, however. No accommodation was made with Arminianism. The true believer proved his election by covenanting with God, not by exercising his free will to choose salvation. His participation in the covenant did not determine his election, but merely realised the predetermined will of God. It was only divine grace which moved man to covenant. But once man had so banded himself to God he was assured of his election. Hence, through the covenant, God gave man discernible ground for his election. Salvation became man's just due in return for such an affirmation of faith.[46]

In Scotland, as in New England, the idea of the covenant was popularly translated in the early seventeenth century not simply as an elaboration of God's compact with the elect, but as a means of revealing God's purposes towards his people. The practical vitality of the covenant was derived from the expansion of the concept to cover works as well as grace, thereby banding for spiritual purposes was allied to spiritual assurance. The covenant gave tangible forms to the cardinal precepts of the Kirk's Confession of Faith: specifically to the assurance of salvation of which all members of congregations should be persuaded and to the necessity of doing good works for the glory of God, for confirmation of the elect and as an example to others.[47]

In using the concept of the covenant to propagate gospel truths among their congregations, the evangelicals were able to draw upon the dominant ideal of a national Kirk as well as the prestige and social influence all ministers acquired from the reformed emphasis on the preaching of the word. At its most potent, the covenant could be interpreted as a divine band between God and the people of Scotland. Such a covenant had a comprehensive rather than a sectional appeal, for Scottish society as a whole not just the political nation. However, anticipation of divine favour through the covenant cannot necessarily be equated with the imminence of a divine event or the revelation of a people's manifest destiny.[48] Covenanting was still a minority activity for presbyterians in the opening decades of the seventeenth century. After the exhortation of the general assembly in 1596 for a mutual band among ministers and within their congregations, no national renewal of the religious band occurred until 1638. In essence, covenanting was a new liturgical form associated especially with militant presbyterianism, an alternative religious standard which kept alive evangelical dissent from an erastian establishment in the Kirk.[49] The political potential of covenanting was still latent in 1625.

Conclusion

The Calvinist principles which inspired the Scottish Reformation have been depicted as politically and socially 'subversive', supplementing the 'silent havoc' wrought by the price rise of the late sixteenth and early seventeenth centuries.[50] Undoubtedly, Protestantism and inflation were the two major influences shaping the development of the political nation, challenging the traditional dominance of the nobility in the country and the mercantile community in the towns. Nevertheless, despite the growing assertiveness of the gentry and the craftsmen and even the emergence of the yeomen as a distinct social class, the political nation did not break up under the strain of competing vested interests or frustrated aspirations. The four estates remained interdependent, both traditionally and commercially. Protestantism was not just a means of promoting commercial acumen, of cultivating an alternative form of government to the decentralised structure of the State or of providing an ideological check on the ungodly exercise of royal authority. The profession and exercise of the Protestant faith constituted the cement which consciously bound together the political nation and justified its control over the rest of Scottish society.[51] Protestantism was to be of paramount political importance in projecting and preserving national identity. For Scotland at the accession of Charles I was faced by an international shift in economic power in favour of northern Europe and, simultaneously, was confronted by the threat of provincial relegation following the union of the Crowns in 1603.

NOTES

1. Burnet, *Memoirs*, 46.
2. C. Carlton, *Charles I: The Personal Monarch*, (London, 1984), 4–21.
3. D. Mathew, *Scotland under Charles I*, (London, 1955), 26.
4. *SR*, 2 vols, *passim*.
5. Class within this context, and especially when applied to landed society, is to be viewed more in the vertical terms of feudal title, kinship and social deference, than in the horizontal terms of material resources and cultural consciousness.
6. R. S. Rait, *The Parliaments of Scotland*, (Glasgow, 1924), 176–77, 183–85. The best guide to charters and the operation of heritable jurisdictions in town and country is to be found in *An Introduction to Scottish Legal History*, G. C. H. Paton ed., (Stair Society, Edinburgh, 1958).
7. SRO, Accounts of Compositions for concealed Rents — Taxations Ordinary and Extraordinary, 1621 & 1625, E 65/12.
8. *APS*, III, (1567–92), 431–37,c.8; IV, (1593–1624), 281–84,c.2.
9. *RPCS* second series, I, (1625–27), cxlv–cxlvii; G. Donaldson, *Scotland: James V to James VII*, (Edinburgh & London, 1965), 219–21. Of the remainder, two abbeys were still in the hands of lay commendators; six abbeys and four priories were annexed

to bishoprics; one priory and one preceptory were secularised as tenandries (freeholds) rather than as lordships.

10. M. H. B. Sanderson, *Scottish Rural Society in the sixteenth century*, (Edinburgh, 1982), deals comprehensively with the feuing of kirklands.

11. W. Makey, *The Church of the Covenant, 1637–51*, (Edinburgh, 1979), 4–6, 181–82.

12. SRO, Hamilton Papers, TD 76/100/3/109.

13. K. M. Brown, 'Aristocratic Finances and the Origins of the Scottish Revolution', *English Historical Review*, CIV, (1989), 46–87.

14. Macinnes, Thesis, II, 443–45.

15. Makey, *The Church of the Covenant*, 5–6, 167–68.

16. Macinnes, Thesis, II, 448–55.

17. *APS*, III, 433,c.8; IV, 64,c.10, 614,c.15; I. B. Cowan, 'The Development of the Parochial System in Medieval Scotland', *SHR*, XL, (1961), 50–55. The right of patronage with the titularship of at least the parsonage teinds of any parish could be transmitted as heritable property and, indeed, even mortgaged. The vicarage (or lesser) teinds were also transmitted on the land market. Control over vicarage teinds could even be erected into a separate titularship which carried no right of parochial patronage (GUA, Beith Parish MS, P/CN, II, no. 146; A. Dunlop, *Parochial Law*, (Edinburgh, 1841), 194, 205; J. M. Duncan, *Treatise on the Parochial Ecclesiastical Law of Scotland*, (Edinburgh, 1869), 102).

18. *RPCS*, second series, IV, (1630–32), 595–96, 641–43, 645–46; V, (1633–35), 586–90; G. Chalmers, *Caledonia: An Account, Historical and Topographic, of North Britain*, 3 vols, (London, 1824), III, 500–912.

19. *Thomas Thomson's Memorial on Old Extent*, J. D. Mackie ed., (The Stair Society, Edinburgh, 1946), 78–86; Rait, *The Parliaments of Scotland* 206–11. The technicalities of old extent are examined further in Macinnes, Thesis, I, 19–20, 49–50.

20. SRO, General Taxt Rolls, 1625–33, E 59/7–9; SRO, Accounts of the Collectors of Taxations granted in 1625, 1630 & 1633, E 65/10, /13, /16. The quota for the royal burghs amounted consistently to 14.1% of the total levy — nearer a seventh than the customary sixth and testimony to creative accountancy at a time when the number of burghs liable to contribute to the quota was increasing.

21. Sanderson, *Scottish Rural Society in the sixteenth century*, 77–105, 188–90.

22. *A Source Book of Scottish History*, vol. III, (1567–1707), W. C. Dickinson & G. Donaldson eds, (Edinburgh, 1961), 227–31.

23. A. Edgar, *Old Church Life in Scotland*, 2 vols, (Paisley, 1886), II, 7, 53, 69–73; R. Mitchison, 'The Making of the Old Scottish Poor Law', *Past & Present*, 63, (1974), 64–67; Makey, *The Church of the Covenant*, 11–12.

24. *APS*, III, 459,c.57; IV, 434,c.14, 535–46; *RPCS*, second series, I, 658–60, 670–75, 677–78; VIII, (1544–1660), 297–305; *A Source Book of Scottish History*, III, 278–82.

25. I. D. Whyte, *Agriculture and Society in Seventeenth Century Scotland*, (Edinburgh, 1979), 137–45; Macinnes, Thesis, II, 484–85.

26. Cf. *RPCS*, IX, (1610–13), 29; XIII, (1622–25), 744; SRA, Glasgow Presbytery Records, (1628–41), CH 2/171/3A & 3B; SRO, Synod Records of Moray, (1623–44), CH 2/271/1.

27. SRO, Inventories given up for Taxation, 1625 & 1630, E 61/6, /34, /41, /46, /49; SRO, Accounts of the Collectors of the Extraordinary Taxes granted in 1625 & 1630, E 65/11, /14; SRO, Rests of the Ordinary and Extraordinary Taxation, 1625–30, E 65/15; Macinnes, Thesis, II, 457–59.

28. *Ayr Burgh Accounts, 1534–1624*, G. S. Pryde ed., (SHS, Edinburgh, 1937), xv–xcviii; *The Court Book of the Burgh of Kirkintilloch*, G. S. Pryde ed., (SHS, Edinburgh, 1963), xxxvii–lxxxi. Glasgow, ranked only eighth in status among the royal burghs until after the Restoration, consistently paid the second highest contribution of

the burghs to the extraordinary taxes on annualrents levied during the personal rule of Charles I (SRO, E 65/11, /14, /17).

29. Rait, *The Parliaments of Scotland*, 250–58, 269–70; M. Lynch, 'The Crown and the Burghs 1500–1625', in *The Early Modern Town in Scotland*, M. Lynch ed., (London, 1987), 55–80.

30. T. C. Smout, *A History of the Scottish People, 1560–1830*, (London, 1970), 159–60, 165–66, 172–74. Agitation in Perth can be viewed as providing a model for craftsmen to secure a representative presence on town-councils; but the economic situation in Perth cannot be taken as typical since the silting up of the River Tay was progressively drying up overseas trade (M. Verschuur, 'Merchants and Craftsmen in Sixteenth-Century Perth', in *The Early Modern Town in Scotland*, 36–54).

31. R. H. Tawney, *Religion and the Rise of Capitalism*, (London, 1969), 113–14. For a critical appraisal of the promotion of Calvinism within the royal burghs, see M. Lynch, 'Scottish Calvinism, 1559–1638', in *International Calvinism, 1541-1715*, M. Prestwich ed., (Oxford, 1985), 239–41).

32. G. Marshall, *Presbyteries and Profits*, (Oxford, 1980), 65–103.

33. *Ayr Burgh Accounts, 1534–1624*, cxii–cxxii; Smout, *A History of the Scottish People*, 159–60, 168–71, 175.

34. J. G. Dunbar, *The Historic Architecture of Scotland*, (London, 1960), 181–89; J. J. Brown, 'Merchant Princes and Mercantile Investment in Early Seventeenth-Century Scotland', in *The Early Modern Town in Scotland*, 125–46.

35. G. H. Sabine, *A History of Political Theory*, (London, 1968), 366–70; *Renaissance and Reformation 1300–1648*, G. R. Elton ed., (New York, 1968), 219–23.

36. J. Kirk, 'The Politics of the Best Reformed Kirks: Scottish achievements and English aspirations in church government', *SHR*, LIX, (1980), 22–53.

37. Rait, *The Parliaments of Scotland*, 167–68; Donaldson, *James V to James VII*, 199–209.

38. I. Dunlop, 'The Polity of the Scottish Church, 1600–37', *RSCHS*, XII, 169–70; *The Party-Coloured Mind*, D. Reid ed., (Edinburgh, 1982), 17–31; D. G. Mullan, *Episcopacy in Scotland: The History of an Idea, 1560–1638*, (Edinburgh, 1986), 74–113.

39. Mathew, *Scotland under Charles I*, 31–33; W. R. Foster, *The Church before the Covenants*, (Edinburgh & London), 43–45, 56, 133, 167–70.

40. Dunlop, *RSCHS*, XII, 167–74; Foster, *The Church before the Covenants*, 88–105.

41. G. Donaldson, *The Making of the Scottish Prayer Book of 1637*, (Edinburgh, 1954), 3–15, 27–28. For a more sanguine view of the Kirk's operations in the Highlands and Islands, see J. Kirk, 'The Jacobean Church in the Highlands, 1567–1625', in *The Seventeenth Century in the Highlands*, J. Maclean ed., (Inverness Field Club, Inverness, 1985), 24–51.

42. J. Macleod, *Scottish Theology*, (Edinburgh, 1974), 28–29; A. L. Drummond, *The Kirk and the Continent*, (Edinburgh, 1956), 110–11.

43. Marshall, *Presbyteries and Profits*, 74–77, 103–07; J. P. Cooper, 'General Introduction' in *The Decline of Spain and the Thirty Years War 1609–48/59*, J. P. Cooper ed., (Cambridge, 1970) 34–35.

44. A. I. Macinnes, 'Catholic Recusancy and the Penal Laws, 1603–1707', *RSCHS*, XXIII, (1987), 27–63.

45. S. A. Burrell, 'The Covenant Idea as a Revolutionary Symbol: Scotland, 1596–1637', *Church History*, XXVII, (1958), 338–50; J. Wormald, 'Bloodfeud, Kindred and Government in Early Modern Scotland', *Past & Present*, 87, (1980), 54–97.

46. Marshall, *Presbyteries and Profits*, 107–12; MacLeod, *Scottish Theology*, 85, 219; P. Miller, 'The Marrow of Puritan Divinity', in *Puritanism in Early America*, G. M. Walker ed., (Toronto, 1973), 54–57.

47. This was the reformed Confession of Faith approved by the parliament of 1560, ratified by that of 1567 and occasionally incorporated in the commencement of presbytery records in the early seventeenth century — not the 'Negative Confession'

subscribed by James VI in 1581 and subsequently incorporated in the National Covenant of 1638 (*APS*, II, (1424–1567), 526–34,c.1; III, 14–22; SRO, Paisley Presbytery Records, 1626–47, CH 2/294/2, fo.4; *A Source Book of Scottish History*, III, 32–35).

48. Burrell, *Church History*, XXVII, 349; A. H. Williamson, *Scottish National Consciousness in the Age of James VI*, (Edinburgh, 1979), 64–85.

49. J. A. Aikman, *An Historical account of Covenanting in Scotland from 1556 to 1638*, (Edinburgh, 1848), 65. James VI reputedly sought to allay fears about his religious policies through a declaration of intent to the general assembly of 1601, which was subsequently interpreted as a covenant with the ministry by presbyterian polemicists. Despite avowed orders for renewing the covenant, no nationwide programme of subscription ensued (D. Stevenson, *The Covenanters: The National Covenant and Scotland*, (Saltire Pamphlets, 1988), 28–34).

50. Makey, *The Church of the Covenant*, 5–11.

51. Within the context of respect for lesser magistrates, the ratio for ministers exhorting their congregations to wholehearted obedience, as against reminding masters of their obligations to their servants, has been estimated at 10:1 during the seventeenth century (Marshall, *Presbyteries and Profits*, 73).

2

The Scottish Inheritance of Charles I

Introduction

Before 1603, James VI had been an ardent propagandist of divine right monarchy. Divine right was propagated to counter dissent within Kirk and State occasioned by demands for presbyterian autonomy or by fractiousness among the nobility and, simultaneously, to promote his claims to the English throne. His polemics emphasised his preference to maintain the royal supremacy by persuasion and consensus rather than by coercive force. Indeed, his successful exercise of kingship in Scotland was based essentially on his management of affairs as a 'practical politician', not on his abilities as a propagandist. After 1603, the equilibrium of the component interests of Scottish society continued to rest upon the political entente created by his personal forbearance.[1]

The Union of the Crowns — itself a misnomer — was a purely dynastic event. James's initial schemes for closer political and economic union were little desired by the parliaments of either Scotland or England and were effectively terminated by a wrecking motion in the House of Commons in April 1607. Demands for a complete incorporating union under English law were fundamentally unacceptable to the Scottish Estates.[2] Nevertheless, the dynastic union created the most enduring political feature of the seventeenth century — that of absentee monarchy. Nor was the union without its immediate political cost to Scotland. For although the union was a demonstrable enhancement of his prestige as a monarch, there was a marked decline in James's appeals and responsiveness to public opinion within Scotland after 1603. Despite promising on his accession to the English throne that he would return to Scotland every three years, James VI did so only once — in 1617. In part, this can be attributed to James I's preoccupation with the government of England where he succeeded more in aggravating than solving inherited difficulties in matters of royal finances, parliamentary privilege and religious dissent. More particularly, James was weaned away from the familiar readiness of prominent Scottish politicians to criticise royal policies. Criticism gave way to adulation and flattery from favourites and their clients — both Scottish and English — once the Court moved south.[3]

Because Scottish interests generally tended to be subordinated to those of England, James was not always fully cognisant of Scottish fears of provincialism after 1603. The political nation's feelings of remoteness from the centre of decision making were notably heightened by English antagonism during the negotiations for closer political and economic union. James had demonstrated his sympathetic awareness of Scottish fears for continuing independence when he asserted in an emotive speech to the English parliament on 31 March 1607, that 'for want of either magistrate, law or order, they might fall into such a confusion as to become like a naked province, without law or liberty, under this kingdom'. However, when James went on to ridicule any supposition that Scotland should be garrisoned like a Spanish province he rather tactlessly made comparisons with Sicily and Naples. For the Scots the more obvious, albeit implicit, model was the English province of Ireland.[4]

The Union of the Crowns undoubtedly caused the political nation to adopt a protective stance towards Scottish independence. Scotland was effectively deprived of a foreign policy in the strategic interest of securing England's northern flank. Nevertheless, Scotland's satellite relationship with England was neither all-embracing nor necessarily irreversible from 1603.[5] The English Court was not the only channel for Scottish international relations. By faith and by trade, the Scots were especially bound to the Dutch.

The Dutch Connection

Acting on a suggestion from James VI and I, the States-General of the United Provinces summoned the Synod of Dort in the autumn of 1618 to resolve theological differences within the Dutch Reformed Kirk. The Synod unequivocally reaffirmed Calvinist orthodoxy and condemned Arminianism as heresy. Dutch membership of the Synod was manipulated by Prince Maurice of Nassau, intent on identifying the oligarchic control of the house of Orange with Calvinist orthodoxy. Nonetheless, the foreign delegates — from the Reformed Churches of Germany and the Swiss Cantons and from the Church of England — who composed about a quarter of the Synod's membership, gave Dort the international standing of a general council safeguarding the Reformation. The Synod of Dort lasted only six months, in contrast to the sixteen years of intermittent deliberations at the Council of Trent which launched the Counter-Reformation in 1543. Nevertheless, the Synod's association of Protestantism with Calvinist orthodoxy was not only a rebuttal of Arminianism but of the ultimate enemy, Roman Catholicism. Although the Kirk of Scotland was not directly represented at Dort, both its presbyterian and episcopal factions accepted the canons issued at the close of the Synod in May 1619 as the definable standards of Protestantism. After Dort, any minister who was other than an uncompromising Calvinist was suspect within the Church of Scotland.[6] For Scottish Calvinists in general, Dort underwrote the national conceit enshrined in their reformed Confession of Faith, 'that the Church of Scotland through the abundant grace of our god is one of the most pure churches under heaven this day, both in respect of trueth and doctrine and puritie of worship'.[7]

In material terms, Scottish society gained distinctly from the emergence of the Dutch as the leading European entrepreneurs of the early seventeenth century. Before assessing the commercial impact of the Dutch connection, however, several caveats must be observed. Trade, though the most geographically dispersed, was probably the most socially restricted form of international contact. Although the union of the Crowns seemingly drove a permanent wedge into the cleavage evident between Scotland and France since the Reformation, the sundering of the 'auld alliance' was not inevitable so long as Scottish wine traders continued to enjoy the same commercial immunities as the French. Popular sentiment in Scotland, alcoholic fortification notwithstanding, still manifested a distinct preference for the 'auld alliance' over Dutch no less than English contacts at the outset of Charles I's reign.[8]

The dynamic growth of the Dutch economy can be traced to the revolt of the Netherlands against Spanish domination, launched by the foundation of the United Provinces in 1579. The migration of merchants, craftsmen and capital from the provinces which remained in Spanish hands led to the replacement of Antwerp by Amsterdam as Europe's leading commercial centre. The incorporation of Portugal under the Spanish Crown in 1580 subjected the extensive empires of both countries to Dutch commercial rivalry, institutionalised from 1602 through the Dutch East India Company. By deploying their trading fleets in convoys to reduce shipping risks and maintain low rates of freight, the Dutch came to dominate not only the spice trade direct from Asia to Europe, but eventually the luxury trade from the Indian Ocean and the Levant to the Mediterranean. In northern Europe, the Dutch achieved dominance in the carriage of bulk cargoes by accepting low profits on each venture in return for a high turn-around of their *fluit* (fly-boat) convoys. Competitive pricing and prompt delivery were enhanced by the establishment of factors in most Baltic ports which enabled Dutch merchant houses to deal throughout the year in commodities with different seasonal peaks of production. A final, structural advantage promoted commercial expansion. The States-General, which loosely controlled the United Provinces, tended to favour the most commercially orientated provinces of Holland and Zeeland as the main contributors to the national coffers. Hence, a mercantile influence, unparalleled throughout Europe, influenced the formulation of government policy.[9]

The location of the Scottish staple at Campvere within the province of Zeeland, which bordered both the province of Brabant in the Spanish Netherlands and that of Holland in the United Provinces, had ensured no major disruption was experienced by Scottish merchants in the shift in commercial power from Antwerp to Amsterdam. Through Campvere, Scotland gained access to the commodities of world markets exchanged at Amsterdam. Because of its entrepot status, economics of scale dictated that wholesale trade with Amsterdam outstripped any advantages derived from direct trading in specific commodities. The export of staple commodities, defined comprehensively by the Convention of Royal Burghs in 1602 as all merchandise liable to pay customs, was enhanced by the entrepot's distribution and collection of partial cargoes. Imports of wines, luxuries and manufactured goods to Scotland were facilitated by the entrepot's packaging of mixed cargoes with respect both to cost and bulk.

From 1610, the Convention enforced the requirement that all trade with the Low Countries be directed through the staple to prevent the export of Scottish goods through England to other towns in the Netherlands. In return, the magistrates of Campvere were expected to uphold and respect Scottish mercantile interests, especially as the channelling of trade through the staple heightened rather than lessened the vulnerability of Scottish shipping to piracy. Furthermore, the rivalry among the towns of Zeeland engendered by the prosperity of the province was open to Scottish exploitation. By threatening periodically to remove the staple to neighbouring Middleburg, the location of the English staple, Scottish commercial privileges and trading facilities at Campvere were cultivated and augmented — albeit friction and misunderstandings between the Convention and the magistrates of Campvere were continuously aroused by sharp practices among Scottish factors.[10]

The strong mercantile links fostered with the Dutch were to be of particular advantage to the Scots after hostilities recommenced between Spain and the United Provinces in 1621. Spain actively sought to exact economic reprisals against the Dutch who had even come to dominate the carrying trade of the Iberian peninsula. The Dutch were obliged to deploy heavily armed convoys on their northern European trading routes as well as in the Mediterranean and the Indies. While the resultant sharp rise in freight costs benefited all competitors of the Dutch carrying trade, the Scots mainly profited from two other commercial expedients. The Dutch were increasingly obliged either to hire ships of neutral, but sympathetic, nations or to crew their vessels with reliable foreigners. Scottish crews were especially prominent in the carriage of salt from Portugal by 1623.[11]

Another profitable commercial contact with the United Provinces was the direct export of coal and salt from the Firth of Forth in Dutch convoys. The lack of indigenous supplies of coal adequate to fuel the rapidly expanding economy of the United Provinces created a steady demand from the Dutch market. The Scottish trade was bolstered by the high if not exorbitant duties imposed on English coal from 1599. Likewise, the interdependent trade in sea-salt rested on the tariff differential with English salt, not superior quality. Scottish customs were stabilised by the Book of Rates in 1612 whereas the English continued to appreciate. Accordingly, the cost advantage conceded to Scottish traders, around fivefold in the opening decade of the seventeenth century, rose to almost ninefold by the accession of Charles I. The bulk export trade to the United Provinces, which was beyond the capacity of the Scottish merchant fleet, had became a major earner of foreign currency and bullion for Scotland. These earnings were largely recycled to purchase imports at more favourable rates of exchange than the native specie; a policy which admittedly did more to raise social expectations than promote indigenous manufactures. In turn, since the *riskdaler* ('rix dollar') was guaranteed to contain a fixed quantity of silver from 1606, it won greater acceptance than native currency for commercial transactions within Scotland.

Indeed, this commercial contact with the United Provinces was a mixed blessing. The growing profitability of the Dutch trade encouraged Scottish landowners to sink shafts under the Forth, to invest in elaborate pumping machines to remove water seeping into the mines below the firth and to erect large evaporating pans on coastal sites which used up coal dross in the manufacture of salt from sea water. Moreover, while the Dutch were willing to pay more for coal than the Scottish merchant community could afford, the orientation of the Forth coal mines to the Dutch market served to stimulate the development of inland mining, notably in the Lothians to cater for the expanding domestic market in Edinburgh. As the major earners of foreign currency and bullion, however, the Scottish landowners engaging in the coal and salt trade secured official backing not only to retain prices at levels which discriminated against the domestic consumer, but also to restrict vigorously the mobility of their workforce. Serfdom was gradually imposed on colliers, coal-bearers and salters from 1606.[12]

Economy and Enterprise

Because the Dutch were the undoubted dominant partners in commercial exchange, Scotland could be regarded as having an economically dependent if not a colonial relationship with the United Provinces. Despite the fundamental economic shift in favour of North Atlantic communities Scotland, like the Baltic countries, had a comparatively low level of commercial activity and industrial development. As borne out by the Book of Rates drawn up by the Privy Council in 1612 — to impose a chargeable custom of 5% on the rated value of 47 exported and 149 imported commodities — Scottish trade was dominated by the exchange of raw materials, foodstuffs and coarse cloth for wines, luxuries and manufactured goods. The importing bias was directed more towards domestic consumption than industrial reprocessing.[13]

Indeed, the Scottish response to the general price rise — primarily stimulated by the influx into Europe of precious metals from the Americas in the sixteenth century — had seemingly much in common with that of a Baltic country like Poland than the emergent capitalist societies of the United Provinces and, to a lesser extent, England and France. Landowners in western Europe benefited indirectly from increased grain prices through the conversion of their customary rents into cash which, in turn, stimulated productivity through increased wage labour. At the same time, the greater exploitation of the soil led to dislocation among the peasantry and the formation of surplus labour pools as permanent features of the national economy. The emergent capitalist societies were able to absorb a significant portion of this surplus labour in manufactures and industry. In Scotland, as in Poland, the restricted development of a monetary economy, signified by payments in kind and work services in meeting estate dues, was allied to a lack of systematic technical progress in manufactures, a necessary prerequisite to reduce prices and stimulate consumption. Such structural deficiencies meant that the burden of inflation was largely borne by agriculture as the dominant sector of the Scottish economy. Since the increase in monetary supply could not readily be absorbed into the costs of estate management, agricultural productivity tended to fall behind the rise in prices. Landowners in Poland and other parts of eastern Europe responded to inflation by exploiting their political and social dominance to curtail the economic privileges of the mercantile community and impose serfdom on their peasantry. The Convention of Royal Burghs prevented the similar erosion of mercantile privileges in Scotland. But, commercial interests in town and country failed to broaden Scotland's manufacturing base to keep pace with the apparent, but indeterminate, population growth of the late sixteenth century, with the result that inflation had the prime effect of accelerating emigration. With the notable exception of the colliers, coal-bearers and salters Scotland, unlike Poland, generally tended to export rather than enslave its population. Moreover, although the influx of American bullion had reached its peak by 1610 and went into a steady decline after 1620, the resultant devaluation of European currencies, coupled to the strain imposed on the availability of commodities during the Thirty Years' War, meant that price stability was unobtainable for most of the seventeenth century. Scotland, therefore, continued to be a major exporter of people within Europe, especially as the decreasing incidence of famine and plague after 1600 diminished natural checks to population growth.[14]

The consistently high level of migration from Scotland throughout the sixteenth century had indicated the country's traditional incapacity to support its population. The main continental repository for these migrants at the outset of the seventeenth century was Poland. Ironically, the massive Scottish presence in a country where the conduct of trade was restricted to Jews and foreigners consolidated the landlords' dominance over the Polish economy. The Thirty Years' War — a misnomer for the conflict for hegemony within Europe which dominated the first half of the seventeenth century — provided dramatic opportunities for the employment of Scottish troops either as mercenaries or as part of national levies. Around 40,000 Scots participated, primarily in service of the Danes, the Swedes and the Protestant German princes. With regular enlistment into the Scots brigades in France and the United Provinces and mercenary service in Spain, Poland and Russia also taken into account, the numbers involved almost certainly exceeded 50,000. In excess of 100,000 people, approximately a tenth of the population, reputedly left Scotland in the early seventeenth century as soldiers or colonisers.[15]

The ill-fated venture to colonise the nebulously defined Nova Scotia, undertaken from 1621 by Sir William Alexander (later first earl of Stirling), was an attempt to divert the perennial 'swarmes' of Scots to the continent. The main opportunities for colonising, however, occurred with the plantation of Ulster in the wake of the Union of the Crowns. The plantation was integral to the promotion of political stability on the Borders with England and on the western seaboard of Scotland. Concerted government action in London, Edinburgh and Dublin rechannelled the disruptive energies of Border reivers into colonising lands devastated by a series of rebellions against the English Crown. At the same time, a permanent wedge was driven between the Gaels of Scotland and Ireland. The mercenary employment of marauding clansmen by native Irish warlords was terminated. Indeed, the proximity of the west and south-west districts of Scotland made Ulster a significant factor in James VI's efforts to curb the general propensity of landed families, their kinsmen and local associates to indulge in feuding.[16]

Ulster's significance, however, extended far beyond the social distillation of undesirable and disorderly elements in Scottish society. Migration from the Lowlands, which was underway by 1606, was indicative of the growing prosperity rather than the customary poverty of the Scottish economy. For it was only by the acquisition of capital at home that colonisers were provided with the necessary stake 'to develop the wilderness in Ulster'. Plantation, moreover, acted as an immediate boost to Scottish trade. Not only did the planters look to the home market for tools and provisions, but Scottish merchants were the main suppliers of luxuries imported from the continent. In return, Scotland provided a ready market for agricultural produce exported from Ulster. Indeed, Ulster was to become a cheaper alternative to the Baltic as an emergency granary. As well as complementing the Dutch connection which was primarily conducted through east-coast ports, the Ulster connection was of particular benefit to as many as twenty-six ports in the west and south-west. Scottish shipping came to dominate if not monopolise the province's carrying trade.

The Scottish balance of trade was adversely affected, however, when imports from Ulster began to outstrip exports thereto. Good harvests in Scotland from 1617 to 1620 meant grain imports caused a glut on the home market which threatened the profitability of domestic farming. The responses of the landed classes was to persuade the Scottish government to impose punitive tariffs on imports of Irish as well as Baltic grain from 1619. As a result, profits from farming in Ulster declined despite the continuance of the livestock trade and the smuggling of grain shipments to Scotland. Such a constriction of the agricultural market reduced immigration from Scotland to a trickle by 1622. Nevertheless, after two bad harvests in successive years which threatened to undermine the growing expectations of landowners and peasantry over the previous decade, a renewed flood of emigrants — mainly from Scotland north of the Tay — crossed to Ulster from 1635, bringing the total of Scottish settlers in the province to more than 50,000 prior to the outbreak of the Covenanting Movement.[17]

The enterprise associated with the Ulster connection further indicates that Scotland, despite the basic nature of its commerce, the structural deficiencies exposed by inflation and its traditional incapacity to support its population, may on balance be placed among the emergent capitalist societies rather than among the feudally entrenched nations of Europe. The scales were tilted by certain progressive, if gradual, facets of economic growth associated with monetarism, agricultural productivity and seaborne commerce.

A more widespread use of money would seem to be indicated by the 79% growth in locally viable burghs, either of barony or regality, in the century after the Reformation. The popularising of feu-ferme tenure during the secularisation of the kirklands led to a significant commutation of annual liabilities from the sixteenth century. By the outset of Charles I's reign, a high proportion of all rents were expected to be paid in money rather than in kind and work services tended to be minimised if not eliminated throughout the Lowlands. In shires such as East Lothian and Fife, county fiars were instituted around 1620 to allow the annual conversion of rents in kind into money. Fiars were eventually to be extended nationwide to give liquidity to rentals and contracts between landlords and tenants.[18]

Within the agricultural sector, the move towards economic individualism evident in the shift from multiple-rent to single-tenant farms was consolidated by changes in land use. Runrig, the traditional division of arable land into strips for cultivation by each family within a multiple-farm, was increasingly being fixed: that is, arable strips were being apportioned specifically to individual families rather than being reallocated periodically. Consolidation was carried a stage further by rundale, the formation of single strips into concerted blocks of arable once townships passed into the control of single-tenant farmers or were feued directly to the portioners and 'bonnet lairds' who formed the Scottish yeomanry. Such developments, though by no means universal, had gathered momentum throughout the Lowlands during the sixteenth century with the spread of feu-ferme which would also seem to have stimulated a significant improvement in agricultural productivity. Imports to Scotland from Baltic granaries fell appreciably between 1590 and 1620, while substantial amounts of grain were exported annually from Scotland during the second decade of the seventeenth century. Admittedly, the re-exportation of Baltic as of Ulster grain at increased prices was an attraction for merchants which cannot be overlooked. Nor can the improvement in agricultural productivity be considered to have kept pace with the natural growth in population. Nevertheless, cultivated land was expanded through the paring and burning of lowland peat-mosses. More intensive farming was facilitated by the sporadic use of lime to improve the fertility of soils, particularly heavy clays, in localities with plentiful supplies of fuel to reduce the limestone. Aided by outward migration, Scotland was moving towards self-sufficiency in victuals by 1625.[19]

The outset of Charles I's reign was also characterised by a marked upsurge in the direct importation of Norwegian timber and Swedish iron and an increased, if fluctuating, traffic in iron, textiles, fibres, tar and pitch from the Baltic. As in the United Provinces, such imports opened up possibilities for the expansion of shipbuilding. Indeed, shipbuilders in the south-west of England were regularly supplied with masts from Scotland. While there is little supporting evidence for a shipbuilding industry outwith Leith on the east coast and probably Ayr on the west, there is scant corroboration for the notion that Scottish merchants had sufficient funds — even when costs were relatively low — to purchase ready-made ships from countries where construction techniques were more advanced. The Scots placed a similar emphasis to the Dutch on shipping for mercantile rather than martial purposes. As recognised by the mobilisation of English commercial opinion against closer economic integration following the Union of the Crowns, the Scottish preference for lightly crewed cargo vessels, instead of heavily manned armed cruisers, ensured lower capital costs in shipping. This advantage in carrying bulky commodities was allied to lower expectations of wages and diet among the crewmen and to the practice of Scottish merchants minimising commercial risks by sharing the costs of trading ventures. Within a British context, therefore, the Scots could offer the lowest freight rates. The complaints of English merchants testify to the psychological if not the actual material impact of such competitive costing. The diplomatic dubiety about Scotland's international status after 1603 even worked to commercial advantage. Scottish ships were employed with relative impunity by both England and France in waters where warfare imperilled their own nationals.[20]

Unsound Money

Growing confidence in the nation's economic prospects as much as English hostility was probably behind the Scottish aversion to closer commercial integration following the Union of the Crowns. The Scottish Estates had given their conditional assent to draft proposals for freedom of trade between both countries in 1607, confidently aware that vested commercial interests, who feared the efficiency of the Scottish carrying trade, would ensure that any economic treaty would founder in the English parliament.[21] Although common nationality for all born within Scotland and England was eventually conceded in 1608, the abandonment of wholesale commercial integration meant that no access to English markets or imperial ventures was freely afforded or guaranteeed to Scottish domiciles. Furthermore, Scottish wares were still regarded as foreign imports though Scottish merchants were no longer considered aliens from Christmas 1604, following their exemption from the discriminatory tariffs levied on aliens importing merchandise into England. While this concession was to be of particular value to Scottish exports of livestock and salt, it had to be reaffirmed in 1615 owing to the reluctant compliance of English customs officials.[22]

The truculence of English customs officials notwithstanding, the Scottish economy remained especially vulnerable to shifts in Crown fiscal policy in the aftermath of union. Royal endeavours to gain a greater return from the customs on staple commodities or, as in the case of coal and salt, to narrow tariff differentials between Scotland and England threatened to undermine the cost advantage enjoyed by Scots in continental markets. Not only would Scottish goods become less competitive, but the Scottish economy was becoming dangerously exposed to international fluctuations in the rates of exchange. Scottish commercial interests were prepared to lobby vigorously to ensure customs rates remained unchanged after 1612 and to render ineffectual all embargoes placed on overseas sales of coal and salt from 1608. But other than to complain about the manifest lack of sound money circulating within Scotland, there was no agreed internal response to correct the domestic impact of international debasement and devaluation.[23]

Indeed, the most pressing but least tractable economic problem confronting Charles I in 1625 — and throughout his personal rule — was the state of the currency. At the root of this problem was the international shortage of bullion. Coin — silver predominantly, then gold — was still the prevailing medium for settling trading balances between nations and underwriting the credit system necessary for commercial growth. More specifically, the expansion of the monetary economy in Scotland as elsewhere in northern Europe meant a growing demand for coin. Yet, the supply of silver and gold from the New World was irreversibly on a downward spiral by 1625. Moreover, the preponderance of silver in commercial exchange had led to a marked appreciation of gold since the outset of the seventeenth century, a trend compounded by hoarding. The widening gap between the supply of bullion and the commercial demand for coin resulted inevitably in price instability, debasement and devaluation of national currencies and disruption to international trade.

As the costs of central government escalated because of increasingly voracious bureaucracies and the recurrence of war on the continent, European powers were generally tempted to tamper with native currency and to convert foreign specie in order to stretch out the use of silver. In particular, the debasement and clipping of coin warranted by German princes from the outbreak of the Thirty Years' War ushered in a period of hyper-inflation throughout the Holy Roman Empire during the 1620s which pushed back the attainment of price stability throughout Europe. Arguably, an international monetary crisis was only averted because of the marked reluctance of mercantile communities to disrupt established trading relationships. Thus, silver and gold coins were allowed to retain their customary values for international trade but were circulated at inflated rates in domestic markets. Nonetheless, as prices continued to spiral upwards as the supply of bullion began to dwindle, employment prospects were jeopardised internationally which, in turn, coupled the threat of economic recession to widespread social dislocation.[24]

Scotland's strong trading links with England and the United Provinces, while not guaranteeing price stability, helped foster economic resilience and fend off recession. Within fifteen days of his accession to the English throne, James VI and I had standardised exchange rates between Scotland and England. The Scots pound and mark were fixed at a twelfth of their English equivalents. The subsequent circulation of gold and silver coins of the common monarchy as legal tender on either side of the Border had served not only to stabilise Anglo-Scottish trade but to promote international acceptance of Scottish currency. Furthermore, the paramount economic importance of the Dutch connection, particularly the trade in coal and salt as Scotland's major currency earner, had led to the regular supply and nationwide circulation of the 'rix dollar', the silver coin most acceptable for international trade. Though protected against the worst ravages of inflation, Scotland was not insulated against the international bullion shortage.[25]

At the same time as the Germanic states were devaluing and tampering with silver coin, the recurrence of dearth between 1622 and 1624 — and especially the threat of endemic famine in 1623 — obliged Scottish merchants to lay out native specie to purchase grain in continental markets. In turn, this run on the stock of Scottish coin occasioned the massive influx of debased foreign dollars to serve the needs of domestic exchange. Moreover, sectional interests within the mercantile community were profiteering from the chronic shortage of silver coin on the continent — notably in France, the Spanish Netherlands and Eastern Europe. In order to acquire Scottish specie for conversion into their own native currencies, Scottish merchants were offered large discounts on various commodities for payments in cash, discounts which were not passed on to the Scottish consumer since the merchants sold the imported commodities at inflated prices — as much as double the purchase price — in domestic markets. The net effect of such profiteering was to drain off native specie and provoke repeated public outcry 'for want of exchange'.

The shortage of native specie was compounded by declining administrative standards following the migration of the Court to London. Hitherto, foreign money was only allowed to circulate in Scotland according to the weight and silver content of each coin at rates set by the Privy Council, tabulated in the Mint and distributed to designated exchangers in the leading burghs. Foreign money brought to these exchangers was either revalued at the prescribed rates or despatched as bullion to the Mint in return for Scottish coin of equivalent value. Such central direction had lapsed by 1619. Thereafter, foreign currency was allowed to circulate at face value or rather at rates determined diversely and haphazardly by the mercantile community, a practice which exploited lack of public knowledge on international exchange, deprived the Crown of a steady supply of bullion and denied the country sound money.[26]

Much has been made of the detrimental economic effect of the removal of the Court to London in transferring a considerable amount of purchasing power which could have stimulated not only the local commerce of Edinburgh, but the national trade and manufacture of luxuries, consumer goods and fashionable garments.[27] But the most critical effect, in terms of political economy, was the Crown's failure to maintain control over the rates at which foreign coin was allowed to circulate within Scotland. Economically, the attainment of sound money was postponed indefinitely after 1619. England had no comparable experience of foreign dollars circulating at rates far in excess of equivalent native coin. The Scottish Mint had particular difficulty in acquiring and transporting gold to Scotland. By 1625, the gold coin of the common monarchy, notwithstanding the standardisation of Scots money at a twelfth of the value of sterling in 1603, was actually circulating in Scotland at rates 30–40% above its standardised value. In effect, while the official exchange rate of Scots to English pounds remained at 12:1, actual exchange of gold coin in the London money markets pushed up the rate to 16:1, 'to the great loss of all the noble and gentlemen and utheris having occasions to repair to the court of Ingland'. Politically, such unfavourable rates made no small contribution to the isolation of the Court from the most influential leaders of the political nation — a situation which Charles I failed to comprehend, far less correct.[28]

A Government Losing Touch

The most immediate political impact of the removal of the Scottish Court was in the conduct of executive government after 1603. Scotland was ruled though not administered from what was essentially the English Court. James VI and I made his celebrated claim concerning the ease with which he governed Scotland in 1607: 'Here I sit and govern it with my pen: I write, and it is done and by a clerk of the Council I govern Scotland now — which others could not do by the sword'. His facile claims were prompted by the resentment and suspicions aroused among English politicians by the initial influx of Scots to positions of prominence at Court. In reality, the government of Scotland after 1603 did not depend simply on the royal word.[29]

Certainly, James retained definite ideas on the ruling of Scotland and implemented them from the Court through his prompt establishment of a postal service between London and Edinburgh in 1603. His copious and didactic ideas were conveyed speedily to the Privy Council and their administrative diligence was duly monitored. Neither effective decision-making nor administrative initiative was totally surrendered by the Privy Council, however. For the efficacy of royal government in Scotland depended upon the personal initiatives of leading civil servants no less than the maintenance of the postal service. In particular, James was well served by two political managers whom he rewarded with temporal lordships — namely, George Home, earl of Dunbar and Alexander Seton, earl of Dunfermline. From 1603 until his death in 1611, Dunbar combined his office as treasurer within the Scottish administration with his position at Court as master of the wardrobe and member of the English Privy Council. Through continuous travel and liaison between Edinburgh and the Court, Dunbar uniquely influenced the implementation of royal policy, dominating the Privy Council in Scotland while retaining the confidence of the king. Dunfermline's dislike of travel led to a decisive shift in political management after 1611. As chancellor, Dunfermline chaired the Privy Council. At the same time, he used the postal service to maintain regular correspondence with royal favourites until his death in 1622. His assiduous cultivation of allies at Court enabled him to draw up proposals for government which the king found acceptable. Nonetheless, reliance on the postal service and clientage at Court led Scottish government after 1603 to become increasingly the preserve of a cabal of leading civil servants and courtiers.[30]

The last decade of James's reign witnessed a marked decline in the responsiveness of royal government to the aspirations of the political nation. The landed classes became increasingly disillusioned with absentee kingship, the mercantile community was growing restless, clerical faction was again unsettling the Kirk, central government was less receptive to directives from the Court and Scotland was inexorably committed to costly intervention in the Thirty Years' War.

In 1617, James had instituted the public register of sasines to give uniformity and security of title in the transfer of landownership. At the same parliament, he declared that all rights of title to land, held without quarrel for forty years, were to be incontrovertible. But, he included the provision that lands which had already been held within the one family for forty years could still have their ownership contested over the next thirteen years — regardless of any case history of untroubled possession. In the short term, this act of prescription encouraged litigation over the ownership of lands which, however unsubstantiated, prejudiced longstanding rights of property.[31] In 1617 also, James appointed a commission to augment ministers' stipends to a yearly minimum of 500 merks or 5 chalders of victual where payment was made in kind. This was to be achieved by the redistribution of teinds, the majority of which were appropriated as a secular resource, controlled mainly by nobles as titulars and leased to other nobles and affluent gentry as tacksmen. The commission made no attempt to challenge directly the proprietary rights of the titulars to the teinds. The obstructiveness of the tacksmen considerably restricted the success of the commission, however. A measure of redistribution was only effected after the tacksmen were compensated for their loss of revenue from the teinds by extending the duration of their leases. The initial commission lasted barely a year. A renewed commission of 1621 never functioned.[32]

In 1620, a convention of the nobility had forwarded a resolution to Court that any attempt to raise money by voluntary contribution in preference to a compulsory, but constitutionally authorised, levy would prove abortive. Moreover, as the burden of taxation was felt by the nobility to fall inequitably on secular landowners, parliament in the following year supplemented an ordinary tax on landed resources with an extraordinary tax on financial transactions, the tax on the annualrents. As this tax was to be levied yearly for the next four years and required all creditors and borrowers to submit inventories of money loaned, regular inquiries were instituted into the financial competence of landowners as estate managers. At the same time, as the fiscal liability of each individual was assessed on free income — after money borrowed was deducted from that loaned — the tax on annualrents acted as a disincentive to the working of capital and was thus disliked even more by the mercantile community than by the landed classes. The burgess estate complained in the parliament of 1621 that an individual's financial standing, in particular his worthiness as a creditor, would be undermined by the revelation of his debts in tax inventories.[33]

Furthermore, the mercantile community considered that their ability to accumulate capital was already being undermined by the readiness of James VI to grant patents and monopolies, a policy accelerated since the Union of the Crowns. In theory, the objectives of monopolies were to free Scotland from dependence on imports of such commodities as linen and soap, to raise the quality of native manufactures, most notably the tanning of leather, and to promote new industries like the making of paper and glass. In practice, monopolies were usually sold to courtiers and speculators concerned less to manufacture than to market and profiteer from products under patent. James was primarily concerned with the fiscal benefit the royal finances derived from the purchase of monopolies rather than the technical promotion of native manufactures. In the short term, the development under patent of alternative products to foreign imports necessarily entailed a drop in revenues from customs, a drop which the Crown was unwilling to bear. For James, therefore, monopolies became a means of farming out a value added tax on to commodities which had been marketed exclusively by the merchant community.[34]

Although not considered as serious a grievance in Scotland as in England, monopolies nonetheless remained an economic irritant. Hence, when James rather insensitively designated a noted monopolist, Nathaniel Udward, as the next conservator of the Scottish staple at Campvere, the outcry raised within the Convention of Royal Burghs in 1623 was hardly surprising. The Convention, moreover, was determined to retain a decisive voice in the appointment of the conservator. In making the previous appointment in 1598, James had outmanoeuvred the Convention by creating a courtier, Sir Robert Denniston, as ambassador to the Netherlands as well as conservator. In return for compensation of £4,000, the Convention induced Udward to resign by July 1624. In recommending the well connected, but relatively innocuous, Patrick Drummond for the post of conservator that November, James did seek the approval of the Convention. Accordingly, Drummond was obliged to subscribe lengthy and specific articles of appointment in January 1625. In July, the Convention reminded the new monarch, Charles I, that its acceptance of the royal candidate was a 'meir favour' which in no way prejudiced its rights to present and discharge conservators in future.[35]

On the religious front James had, at a managed assembly of the Kirk at Perth in 1618, intruded a liturgical programme which laid stress on the observance of holy days, kneeling at communion, episcopal confirmation and private ceremonies for both baptism and communion. The most controversial aspect of this programme was undoubtedly the requirement to kneel for all members participating in communion. Indeed, the touchstone for presbyterian nonconformity became the failure of members of congregations to kneel for the elements of communion received solely from the hands of ministers who had dispensed with the assistance of elders in the distribution of the bread and wine. More immediately, resistance to kneeling provided the common ground to unite opposition to the ratification of ecclesiastical innovations in the parliament of 1621.[36] To prevent the royal programme being compromised by the issue of kneeling, James insisted, as he had done at the general assembly in Perth, that the vote should be taken on all Five Articles in a block rather than separately. Against the grain of parliamentary subservience to royal directives, the packaged passage of the Five Articles provoked a substantial dissenting minority. To achieve their parliamentary ratification, James had to guarantee that he would not attempt any further liturgical innovations. Plans for a draft litury, which would have brought closer conformity between the Scottish and Anglican churches, were expediently shelved.[37]

The most striking political feature of the parliament of 1621 was the ability of the opponents of the Five Articles to draw substantial support from the nobility, and the shire and burgh commissioners. It is, perhaps, only with the advantage of hindsight that direct correlation can be made between opposition to the Five Articles and the rejection of the liturgical innovations of Charles I, leading ultimately to the overthrow of episcopacy at the general assembly in Glasgow in 1638.[38] Certainly, the promulgation of the Five Articles had awakened and galvanised a new generation of radicals within the ministry who had hitherto acquiesced in an erastian episcopate. But, of greater significance than the revival of the erstwhile moribund presbyterian faction was the continuing disquiet expressed by nobles, such as John Leslie, sixth earl of Rothes, a prominent member of the parliamentary opposition in 1621. Within three weeks of the death of James VI, Rothes was taking soundings at Court about Charles I's attitudes to the policies of his late father, which 'did bread greit greif and miscontentment amongst the best both in plac and knawledg'. In his letter of 14 April 1625, to Sir Robert Kerr (later first earl of Ancrum), Rothes specified that the two most controversial aspects of James's dotage had been 'the imposing of certain nouations upon the Kirk' and 'the impairing of the libertys of the Nobility both in Counsell and Parliament'. Minds which should have been united for the good of Scotland had become 'jangled with changes bothe in kirk and ciuil Stat'.[39]

Although the opposition in the Kirk and State was neither concerted nor sustained in the wake of the parliament of 1621, a loss of confidence was precipitated within the governmental framework of absentee kingship. Representing the king as his parliamentary commissioner was James Hamilton, second marquis of Hamilton, James's chief confidant at Court for Scottish affairs. As a result of bearing the brunt of public opprobrium for the passage of the Five Articles, Hamilton's interest in Scottish affairs was 'much lessened'. The death of Chancellor Dunfermline in 1622 removed the one politician based in Scotland able to exercise a commanding influence at Court.[40] Simultaneously, the confidence of James in his Scottish administration was being eroded by rumours manufactured at Court principally by Robert Maxwell, first earl of Nithsdale, an egregious spendthrift. Much was made of the reputed venality of John Erskine, seventh earl of Mar, as treasurer and of the reported omniscience of Thomas Hamilton, first earl of Melrose (later of Haddington) as secretary of state and president of the Council. Nithsdale's campaign against the 'old guard' at Edinburgh was supported by the new chancellor, Sir George Hay of Kinfauns (later viscount Dupplin, thereafter earl of Kinnoul), by William Douglas, sixth earl of Morton and by Robert Kerr, first earl of Roxburghe.[41]

Borrowing an Irish precedent for disciplining officers of state, Nithsdale promoted a commission of grievance as an effective means of reforming the lamentable condition of the Scottish administration. James duly authorised a

Scottish commission in March 1623, but its remit accorded priority to the resolution of grievances aroused by the multiplication of monopolies and patents. Immediately, the Scottish commission became a forum for the mercantile community to protest against monopolies and customs rates. The commission failed to accomplish the political objective of its initiator, namely the unchallenged establishment of Nithsdale's faction in control of Scottish government. As a result, no effective channel of liaison was restored between the Court and Edinburgh in the wake of the parliament of 1621. No less ominously for absentee kingship, a precedent had been created for factional attempts to achieve dominance over Scottish affairs through the creation of a review procedure at Court. Though the commission of grievance had operated merely as a sub-committee of the Privy Council, its implementation was hardly conducive to furthering the confidence of the Scottish administrators in directives from the Court or their desire to uphold the monarchical position within Scotland on their own initiative.[42]

There was no immediate prospect of a collapse of royal government. Yet, Charles I ascended the throne against a background of diminishing confidence in absentee kingship which his Scottish administration in Edinburgh shared with the political nation. This confidence was further dented by the imminent prospect of costly intervention in the Thirty Years' War. Charles's financial position in Scotland was deceptively solvent. He inherited a total expenditure of £159,091 11/8 for the ordinary running of Scottish government. The routine income available to the king in the last year of James VI's reign, 1 March 1624 to 1 March 1625, amounted to £259,878 19/–, a surplus over expenditure of £100,787 7/4. Although this level of profitability was not maintained in the financial year after 1 March 1625, when the ordinary income of the Crown fell to "223,930 7/4, a surplus of £64,838 15/8 remained. However, surplus Scottish income — the sterling equivalent of £8,398 19/– in the financial year 1624 and £5,403 4/7 in that of 1625 — was not going to ameliorate drastically the financial predicament of the Crown in England. Nevertheless, as an English diplomatic satellite, Scotland was expected to help finance the foreign policy of the Crown over which the Scottish administration exercised no meaningful influence.[43]

Diplomatic Embroilment

Aggravating the financial position of the Crown in England was the cost of maintaining the traditional English diplomatic aspiration, the pursuit of premier league recognition as a European power. Yet, the Crown lacked a national bank or any financial institution similar to the Bank of Amsterdam (founded in 1609) or the Banco Giro of Venice (founded 1619) to provide long-term credit. Charles was to inherit an English Crown not only perennially short of funds, but approaching a state of chronic insolvency. The financial legacy of James

I was commitment to expenditure well in excess of £1,000,000. Essentially this situation was brought about by militant changes in foreign policy.[44]

Any attempted symmetry in the foreign policy of James as king of England was sundered by 1621. The marriage of his daughter Elizabeth to the influential German prince, Frederick, the Elector Palatine, in 1613 was still to be balanced by the betrothal of Charles, as Prince of Wales, to the Spanish Infanta. The Elector Palatine, however, headed the opposition of the Protestant states within the Holy Roman Empire to the reconciliation of the Austrian and Spanish Habsburgs on a common plan of action in central Europe. By the treaty of Onate in 1617, Ferdinand, the Austrian archduke, was promoted as king of Bohemia and Hungary, and thereby as successor to the Emperor. In return, Spain was to be given sufficient imperial fiefs to link its provinces in Italy and the Netherlands. By 1620, the Elector Palatine's efforts to secure election as king of Bohemia had been overturned by force. Ferdinand II annexed Bohemia as a hereditary possession of the Austrian Habsburgs. His determination to suppress Protestantism within his imperial estates led him to move against the Palatinate. Outwith the Empire, only the Dutch had actively supported Frederick with troops and money. Commercial tensions between the Dutch and the English, particularly over fisheries, served to excuse James's refusal to participate in a diversionary attack on the Spanish Netherlands.

By the expiry of the truce between United Provinces and Spain in 1621, however, Europe was faced with the imminent realisation of Habsburg hegemony. As a result, war within the Empire continued to be waged against the imperial and Spanish forces by Protestant contingents supported by English and Danish as well as Dutch money and diplomacy. The Spanish Crown's patent lack of enthusiasm for a marriage alliance meant that James, following the eventual breakdown of negotiations in 1623, was drawn increasingly by established family ties towards direct involvement in the Thirty Years' War. His son-in-law Frederick, deprived of his electoral dignity by an imperial diet at Ratisbon and languishing in the United Provinces as a pensionary of the Dutch, required help to repulse imperial assaults on the Palatinate. His brother-in-law, Christian IV of Denmark, had territorial ambitions in northern Europe. Christian's desire for armed support of the German princes was compounded by the attachment of Poland, in permanent conflict with its Baltic neighbours, to the Habsburg alliance. English intervention in the Thirty Years' War, which commenced in January 1625, committed James to a tripartite alliance with the United Provinces and France — albeit this anti-Habsburg coalition was not formalised until the Hague Convention that December, nine months after his demise.[43]

The formalising of the triple alliance, which had entailed large financial outlays on diplomatic embassies, opened the door to massive military expenditure — the employment of forces against Ferdinand II, the equipping and manning of the English navy and the fortification of coastal defences around the British Isles in anticipation of a seaborne offensive from Spain or the Spanish Netherlands. Hardly had Charles incurred the considerable expense of the state funeral of his father in Westminster Abbey on 7 May 1625, when his marriage by proxy to Henrietta Maria, sister of Louis XIII, occasioned further lavish ceremonial costs once the new queen arrived in London on 16 June 1625. Scotland, though neither affected territorially nor embroiled diplomatically by the course of the Thirty Years' War, was not regarded as exempt from contributing manpower and finance to any British military venture. James VI, when imposing the tax on annualrents in 1621, had claimed that such an extraordinary levy was exceptional, being necessitated for the relief of the Palatinate. Nonetheless, by playing on the threat to British interests inherent in the European escalation of the Thirty Years' War, Charles had Scotland placed on a war footing by the autumn of 1625. At the same time, a Convention of Estates — an attenuated parliament with the right to vote supply — was summoned to meet the cost of this alleged emergency.[46]

In his inaugural meetings to the Convention on 27 October 1625, Charles stressed his need for sufficient taxation not only to honour his Scottish commitments, especially his impending coronation, but 'likewayes suche designes as we haif in hand bothe at home and abroade for the weele of our kingdomes'. The Estates dutifully responded, awarding an ordinary taxation of £400,000 and renewing the extraordinary tax on the annualrents (exacted as the twentieth penny — 5% — of free income), both levies to run concurrently for four years. Royal pleas for financial assistance, though rewarded, were far from universally respected by the Estates. An alternative proposal from Charles — to discharge all taxation save for an amount sufficient to cover the costs of his coronation in return for the outfitting and supply of 2000 men and shipping to defend the country for three years from foreign invasion — was rejected summarily. Blissfully unaware that he had overplayed his hand, Charles continued to adhere to the dictum publicly professed at the commencement of his reign, 'that the welfare of England is inseperable from [that of] Scotland'.[47]

Iberian Analogies

The prospect of war and the resultant increased burden of taxation, which we cannot afford to overlook as significant precipitants of Scottish discontent with absentee kinship,[48] suggest close but by no means linear, Iberian analogies to the political situation unfolding in Scotland during the personal rule of Charles I. The strained relationships of Catalonia and Portugal to the Castilian-dominated Spanish throne culminated in separate revolts in 1640, at the same time as the Scottish Covenanters were resorting to arms against Charles I. Catalonia was a dominion of Aragon whose dynastic unification with the kingdom of Castile in the late fifteenth century laid the foundation of the Spanish state. The kingdom of Portugal was annexed to Spain in 1580. While Scotland had provided the king of England and separately supported a national Reformed Kirk, neither Catalonia nor Portugal had provided a monarch for the Spanish throne, and both shared, with the rest of Iberia, a common Catholicism. Like Scotland, however, both were afflicted by absentee kingship. Though formally supervised by viceroys, both had retained a large measure of independence through nationally disparate agencies of government and constitutional assemblies.

Moreover, although Catalonia and Portugal lacked the Scottish ideological tradition of resistance to kingship, like Scotland they do not apparently conform to the conventional interpretation of the 'general crisis' in western Europe during the mid-seventeenth century. Revolts in England, France and the United Provinces, marked reputedly by a rift between Court and Country, have been viewed as the culmination of almost a century of mounting crisis in the relationship between state and society. Within each country, an increasingly voracious Court allied to the steady dominance of government by a centralised bureaucracy transformed resentment in the Country into revolution. Although intervening events and political errors divergently affected the movement from a revolutionary situation to actual revolution, each revolt was the product of the same general grievance: specifically, the character and cost of the state.[49]

Neither Catalonia nor Portugal contributed to the upkeep of the Castilian Court nor to the centralised bureaucracy of the Spanish state in the early seventeenth century. In like manner, the Scottish Exchequer, apart from sundry pensions to Scottish courtiers, was not expected to contribute directly to the upkeep of the English Court or the English government. Arguably, the crisis of government was not solely or even primarily financial, but essentially and immediately that of counsel — the failure to seek or secure the consent of the political nation.[50] After the termination of the twelve-year truce between Spain and the United Provinces in 1621, Olivares, the chief minister of Philip IV of Spain, was resolved to renew war as both a commercial and a military exercise. Faced with mounting and recurrent costs, Olivares determined to restructure the Spanish fiscal system. Not only were the resources of the kingdoms of Aragon and Portugal to be exploited financially, but the authority of the Spanish monarchy was to be made uniformly effective throughout its constituent kingdoms by the imposition of the style and laws of Castile. Hence, Catalonia and Portugal rebelled primarily because of a Castillian-imposed threat to their separate national identities as well as their economic resources.[51]

War and taxation were not the main precipitants of the Scottish revolution. This international aspect of Scottish subordination to English political interests, however galling, was secondary to the main domestic irritants caused by the anglophile policies of an absentee monarchy. Scottish national identity was to be substantially challenged and undermined not by the corporate importation of English laws and customs, but by the imposition of administrative, economic and, ultimately, religious uniformity solely on the strength of the royal prerogative. Unlike the Catalan and Portuguese revolts against forcible assimilation to the style and laws of Castile, which took the form of movements of national separation from the Spanish state, the emergence of the Covenanting Movement in Scotland was to mark a concerted effort at national consolidation in defiance of

Charles I. The Covenanters reacted against an innovatory monarchy, not against the English nation.

Conclusion

As evident from the Dutch connection in religion and commerce, Scotland's satellite relationship with England was by no means comprehensive nor were the country's economic prospects poor or lacking in enterprise following the union of the Crowns. The failure to maintain sound money notwithstanding, the dotage of James VI and I did not presage an imminent collapse of royal government. The loss of his sure grip over Scottish affairs in his later years was critical, nonetheless. Charles I inherited a kingdom in which the Crown had failed to maintain consensus within the political nation. As the opposition to the personal rule of Charles I made manifest, the Scottish revolt, like that of the Catalans and the Portuguese, was the product of growing tensions, not just between the Court and the Country, but between absentee kingship and the political nation. Accordingly, the nationalist impulses motivating the revolts in Scotland, Catalonia and Portugal should be viewed as integral not peripheral facets of the general European crisis in the mid-seventeenth century. The Revocation Scheme, the first sustained initiative of Charles I, was to drive home the clear message of his personal rule: the alternative to revolution was provincialism.

NOTES

1. J. M. Brown, 'Scottish Politics, 1567–1625', in *The Reign of James VI and I*, A. G. R. Smith ed., (London, 1977), 22–39; W. Ferguson, *Scotland's Relations with England: a Survey to 1707*, (Edinburgh, 1977), 106–07.

2. *APS*, IV, 263–64, c.1; B. P. Levack, *The Formation of the British State: England, Scotland, and the Union 1603–1707*, (Oxford, 1987), 32–44; B. Galloway, *The Union of England and Scotland 1603–1608*, (Edinburgh, 1986), 103–30.

3. Donaldson, *James V to James VII*, 215–16.

4. *APS*, IV, 366–71, c.1; *RPCS*, (1604–07), 534–37, 537–38 note 1.

5. Ferguson, *Scotland's Relations with England*, 105.

6. G. D. Henderson, *Religious Life in Seventeenth Century Scotland*, (Cambridge, 1937), 72–73; Drummond, *The Kirk and the Continent*, 112–17.

7. Cf. SRO, Paisley Presbytery Records, 1626–47, CH 2/249/2, fo.1–5.

8. *CSP, Venetian*, XX, (1626–28), 77, 615; XXI, (1628–29), 143; S.G.E. Lythe, *The Economy of Scotland, 1550–1625*, (Edinburgh & London, 1960), 171–72.

9. R. Davis, *The Rise of the Atlantic Economies*, (London, 1973), 89–90, 181–82; C. T. Smith, *An Historical Geography of Western Europe before 1800*, (London & New York, 1978), 430, 435, 443–44, 447–48, 458–61.

10. J. Davidson & A. Gray, *The Scottish Staple at Veere*, (London, 1909), 179–81; M. P. Rooseboom, *The Scottish Staple in the Netherlands*, (The Hague, 1910), 96, 118–19, 132–33, 136–41. Scots were given the same judicial privileges as the citizens of Campvere and legal assistance to pursue commercial actions and seek compensations for victims of pirates. In addition, Scottish merchants were afforded extensive hospitality rights by the town, including a furnished lodging house — a conciergery — and a kirk was provided for the worship of the resident Scottish community.

11. J. L. Israel, 'A Conflict of Empires: Spain and the Netherlands 1618–1648', *Past & Present*, 76, (1977), 34–74.

12. Lythe, *The Economy of Scotland, 1550–1625*, 47–51, 245–46; J. U. Nef, *The Rise of the British Coal Industry*, 2 vols, (London & Edinburgh), I, 46–48, 84, 92–93, 108; II, 219–27; C. A. Whatley, *The Scottish Salt Industry 1570–1850*, (Aberdeen, 1987), 39–40, 80, 98.

13. *RPCS*, IX, (1610–13), lxvii–lxxiii.

14. S. Hoszowski, 'Central Europe and the Price Revolution', in *Economy and Society in Early Modern Europe*, P. Burke ed., (London, 1972), 85–103; W. Abel, *Agricultural Fluctuations in Europe*, (London, 1980), 147–57. Makey's reassessment of the social causation of the Covenanting Movement is not helped by his blatant assertion that 'the price rise was much greater in Scotland than anywhere else' (*The Church of the Covenant*, 6). No reference is made to any comparative statistics for the rates of inflation in other European countries. The estimation of a tenfold increase in prices (*Ibid.*, 3) during the century which culminated in the revolution against Charles I relies on the indexing of agricultural commodities — consumables noted more for their volatility than reliability as price indicators — not the more accurate measurement provided by consumer durables.

15. T. A. Fischer, *The Scots in Germany*, (Edinburgh, 1902), 32–33, 73; M. Perceval-Maxwell, 'Sir William Alexander of Menstrie (1567–1640)', *Scottish Tradition*, XI/XII, (1981–82), 14–25; J. A. Fallon, 'Scottish Mercenaries in the Service of Denmark and Sweden, 1626–32', (University of Glasgow, Ph.D. thesis, 1972), 75–76, 120, 154–57. The recomposition of regiments during campaigns and the problems of orthography in identifying the separate British nationalities among the rank and file make the numerical accuracy of any estimate of Scottish soldiers difficult to establish but easy to exaggerate.

16. K. M. Brown, *Bloodfeud in Scotland 1573–1625: Violence, Justice and Politics in Early Modern Scotland*, (Edinburgh, 1986), provides a thorough appraisal of feuding and its decline.

17. M. Perceval-Maxwell, *The Scottish Migration to Ulster in the Reign of James I*, (London, 1973), 29, 34–37, 294–308, 313–15.

18. *The Court Book of the Burgh of Kirkintilloch*, lxxx; Fife Fiars, 1619–1815, (Cupar, 1846); Smout, *A History of the Scottish People, 1560–1830*, 139; Whyte, *Agriculture and Society in Seventeenth Century Scotland*, 192–94.

19. T. M. Devine & S. G. E. Lythe, 'The Economy of Scotland under James VI: A revision article', *SHR*, L, (1971), 100–01; Smout, *A History of the Scottish People, 1560–1830*, 122, 147; Whyte, *Agriculture and Society in Seventeenth Century Scotland*, 145–52, 198–211.

20. NLS, Yule Collection, MS 3134, fo.104; Lythe, *The Economy of Scotland, 1550–1625*, 132–33, 157–58; Devine & Lythe, *SHR*, L. 101–03. The major European powers were still willing to discriminate positively in favour of Scotland, albeit as a means of embarrassing the English Crown. Thus, when Charles I initiated war with Spain in 1625, the Spaniards reciprocated by declaring war on England, Scotland and Ireland. Yet, freedom of trade was maintained with the Scots and the Irish 'as they coloured not English goods'. Likewise, after Charles opened hostilities with France in 1626, the French were sufficiently mindful of the 'auld alliance' to set at liberty the 60 Scottish ships among the 120 British vessels impounded while loading wine at Bordeaux (*CSP, Domestic*, (1625–49), 55; *CSP, Venetian*, XX, 76).

21. Galloway,, *The Union of England and Scotland 1603–1608*, 98–103; S. G. E. Lythe, 'The Economy of Scotland under James VI and I', in *The Reign of James VI and I*, 57–73.

22. Levack, *The Formation of the British State*, 147–48; Lythe, *The Economy of Scotland, 1550–1625*, 202–04.

23. Macinnes, Thesis, I, 464–519, examines in detail the internal debate provoked by unsound money and commercial disruption.

24. F. C. Spooner, 'The European Economy, 1609–50', in *The Decline of Spain and the Thirty Years War, 1609–48/59*, 78–86; Davis, *The Rise of the Atlantic Economies*, 96–98; H. Kamen, *The Iron Century, Social Change in Europe, 1550–1660*, (London, 1971), 119–25.

25. Lythe, *The Economy of Scotland, 1550–1625*, 101–02, 200–01. Prior to standardisation at the ratio of 12:1, which remained in force throughout the seventeenth century, the ratio of Scots to English currency had been considerably overvalued and difficult to sustain at 5:1.

26. *RPCS*, second series, IV, (1630–32), 63–64; *Records of the Coinage of Scotland*, 2 vols, R. W. Cochrane-Patrick ed., (Edinburgh, 1846), II, 87, 96, 111–12.

27. Lythe, *The Economy of Scotland, 1550–1625*, 212; Brown, 'Aristocratic Finances and the Origins of the Scottish Revolution', *English Historical Review*, CIV, 62–64.

28. *RPCS*, second series, I, (1625–27), 564, 628–31; *Records of the Coinage of Scotland*, II, 73–75.

29. *RPCS*, VII, 537–38 note 1; Galloway, *The Union of England and Scotland 1603–1608*, 116–17.

30. W. Taylor, 'The King's mails, 1603–25', *SHR*, XLII, (1963), 143–47; M. Lee, jr, 'James VI's government of Scotland after 1603', *SHR*, LV, (1976), 41–53.

31. *APS*, IV, 545–47, c.16; 543–44, c. 12. From 1617, all changes in heritable property, outwith the royal burghs, were to be recorded in the general registers in Edinburgh or in the particular registers for the most geographically appropriate of seventeen specified registration districts.

32. *APS*, IV, 531–34, c.3; *RPCS*, second series, I, clxviii–clxxv.

33. *RPCS*, XII, (1619–22), 379; *APS*, IV, 597–600, c.2; Rait, *The Parliaments of Scotland*, 494.

34. Donaldson, *James V to James VII*, 244–46, Devine & Lythe, *SHR, L.* 106.

35. *RCRB, Extracts*, (1615–76), 187–93, 205–06; Rosebbom, *The Scottish Staple in the Netherlands*, 110–12; Davidson & Gray, *The Scottish Staple at Veere*, 186–88, 195–97.

36. I. B. Cowan, 'The Five Articles of Perth', in *Reformation and Revolution*, D. Shaw ed., (Edinburgh, 1967), 39–40; R. Mitchison, *Lordship to Patronage: Scotland 1603–1707*, (London, 1983), 18–19; P. H. R. Mackay, 'The Reception Given to the Five Articles of Perth', *RSCHS*, XIX, (1977), 185–201.

37. D. Calderwood, *The History of the Kirk of Scotland*, T. Thomson ed., 8 vols, (Wodrow Society, Edinburgh, 1845), VII, 497–501; W. Scott, *An Apologetical Narration of the State and Government of the Kirk of Scotland since the Reformation*, D. Laing ed., (Wodrow Society, Edinburgh, 1846), 255–98.

38. Cowan ['The Five Articles of Perth', in *Reformation and Revolution*, 44] tends to adapt this standpoint to redress the over-generous estimation of Donaldson (*James V to James VII*, 211; reiterated in 'The Scottish Church 1567–1625', in *The Reign of James VI and I*, 40–56) that James VI was 'able to leave a church at peace'. Stevenson (*The Scottish Revolution*, 24) takes a middle course, though underestimating, perhaps, the infusion of new blood into the presbyterian faction after the passage of the Five Articles.

39. *Ancrum & Lothian*, I, 35–38.

40. Burnet, *Memoirs of the dukes of Hamilton*, 1; M. Lee, jr. *SHR*, LV, (1976), 44–48.

41. HUL, Maxwell-Constable of Everingham MSS, DDEV/79/H/142.

42. *RPCS*, XIII (1622–25), xv, 210–22, 239–48.

43. SRO, Treasury Accounts, 1624–25, E 19/22. Just under half the recurrent costs of royal government in Scotland — £75,717 6/8 — were taken up by pensions to courtiers and leading government officials. The shortfall in ordinary income for the financial year 1625 of £35,948 11/8 can largely be attributed to a decline in the efficiency of royal officials in central and local government. Although the impost of wine was probably collected, no attempt was made to record the amount in the Treasury before the end of the financial year (SRO, Exchequer Responde Book, 1623–38, E 1/11).

44. *RPCS*, second series, I, xxii. The English aspects of this legacy are placed firmly in their constitutional context by C. Russell, 'Parliament and the King's Finances', in *The Origins of the English Civil War*, C. Russell ed., (London, 1975), 91–116. That the English parliament had no official foreign policy to support or oppose in the last years of James I is the central theme of S. L. Adams, 'Foreign Policy and the Parliaments of 1621 and 1624', in *Faction and Parliament*, K. Sharpe ed., (Oxford, 1978), 139–71.

45. J. V. Polisensky, *The Thirty Years War*, (London, 1971), 91–136, 162–70; S. H. Steinberg, *The 'Thirty Years War' and the Conflict for European Hegemony 1600–1660*, (London, 1966), 33–43. The expeditionary force which embarked from England in January 1625, under the command of the German military adventurer, Count Ernest von Mansfeld, was still entrenched in the Netherlands by James's death at the end of March and, subsequently, failed to make any significant advance on Bohemia and Moravia before being defeated by imperial forces in April 1626.

46. *RPCS*, second series, I, 72 note 1; Sir J. Balfour, *Historical Works*, 4 vols, J. Haig ed., (Edinburgh, 1824–25), II, 117–26; J. Row, *The History of the Kirk of Scotland 1558–1637*, D. Laing ed., (Wodrow Society, Edinburgh, 1842), 340–41, 365.

47. *APS*, V, (1625–41), 166–75; *RPCS*, second series, I, 151–56; *CSP, Venetian*, XIX, (1625–26), 294.

48. M. Lee, jr, 'Scotland and the 'General Crisis' of the Seventeenth Century', *SHR*, LXIII, 136–54, is too dismissive of war and, in turn, over-assertive about the uniqueness of the Scottish revolt. However, he is on surer ground in discounting the reputed parallel with the Netherlands and Scotland. After Charles V had become ruler of Spain as well as the Netherlands in 1516, an initial influx of counsellors and favourites from the Netherlands aroused resentment at the Spanish court, souring the next forty years of his reign. But his son, Philip II, as a culturally assimilated Spaniard, provoked the revolt of the Netherlands by treating that country as a Spanish province from the commencement of his 42-year reign in 1556. However, this parallel with Scotland under Charles I benefits much from hindsight (C. V. Wedgwood, 'Anglo-Scottish Relations, 1603–40', *Transactions of the Royal Historical Society*, fourth series, XXXII, (1950), 34–35; Stevenson, *The Scottish Revolution*, 320–21). Scotland was not separated geographically from England. Edinburgh and Glasgow were less remote from London than Antwerp and Amsterdam from Madrid. Although Scottish influence at the English Court was initially weighty, neither the dominant Scottish presence nor the resultant English antagonism was to be sustained throughout the reign of James VI and I. Moreover, the secession by the United Provinces in 1579 had still left a Belgian rump as the Spanish Netherlands. In short, insufficient time had elapsed in the opening decades of the seventeenth century to suggest that Anglo-Scottish relations were going to develop along similar lines.

49. H. R. Trevor-Roper, 'The General Crisis of the Seventeenth Century', in *Crisis in Europe 1560–1660*, T. Aston ed., (London, 1974), 59–95.

50. Indeed, K. Sharpe, 'Introduction: Parliamentary History 1603–1629: In or out of Perspective?', in *Faction and Parliament*, 1–42, argues persuasively that the crisis in England was occasioned by the failure of the Privy Council and parliament to provide good counsel to the Crown.

51. J. H. Elliot, 'The Spanish Peninsula 1598–1648', in *The Decline of Spain and the Thirty Years War 1609–48/59*, 435–73; Kamen, *The Iron Century*, 318–20.

3

The Revocation Scheme

Introduction

From the outset of his reign, Charles I was to prove incapable of acknowledging that political manoeuvring within constitutional assemblies was not necessarily intended to obstruct or reverse royal initiatives. Moreover, Charles was loath to concede revisionary powers to the Convention as a less formal meeting of parliament, even though the meeting of the Estates, from 27 October to 2 November 1625, was attended by forty nobles, seven bishops, commissioners from fifteen shires and twenty royal burghs with four officials present *ex officio*. The determination of the Estates to modify the rigorous and check the incongruous implementation of royal policy went unappreciated at Court. Charles's distrust of constitutional assemblies was further fuelled by the Estates' dismissive attitude towards his proposal to finance the colonisation of the nebulously defined Nova Scotia in North America by the sale of baronetcies.[1]

Charles proposed to sell the honour of baronet for 2000 merks to gentlemen willing to act as planters. The honour, initially conceived by James VI, was to be restricted to 100 gentlemen who were to rank above the rest of their estate including other knights. At the behest of the shire commissioners, the Estates rejected such distinctions of rank among the gentry which derogated from their status as lesser barons and freeholders. Charles, nonetheless stuck obstinately to the project's confusion of rank and status, seeing a baronetcy as an alternative to grants of heritable jurisdiction.[2]

More ominously, Charles failed to appreciate that the initial enthusiasm of the Estates in consenting to the continuance of taxation was to head off reforms which the king was rumoured to be contemplating for the government of Scotland.[3] Indeed, rumours of sweeping reforms led the Estates to debate matters not encompassed within the royal agenda for the Convention. Carried unanimously was the motion that any intention of Charles to alter the existing constitution of the College of Justice should only be undertaken 'be the advise of the Estaittis of this kingdome in Parliament'. The efforts of John Spottiswood, archbishop of St Andrews, to build up a party for the Court in the wake of the convention serves to confirm that opposition to royal reforms drew support from nobles, gentry and burgesses.[4] Significantly, religion was not the major nor most pressing grievance.

Restructuring Government

The specifications for the king's proposed restructuring of Scottish government, which duly emerged in the aftermath of the Convention, effectively undermined Archbishop Spottiswood's endeavours to build up a party for the Court. Restructuring entailed the clear subordination of Scottish-based officials and councillors to those resident at Court. Moreover, restructuring could only be achieved by a substantial dilution of the traditional political leadership of the nobility. Nor was restructuring of government to be accompanied by any positive changes in administrative attitudes. The cliquish mentality which bedevilled the last years of James VI was intensified by Charles's distanced handling of his leading Scottish officials.[5]

Restructuring had been heralded by the appointment of Sir William Alexander of Menstrie as secretary for Scottish affairs in attendance at Court. Melrose was to remain principal secretary, but all correspondence between the Court and Edinburgh was to be channelled through Alexander of Menstrie. Nithsdale rather than Treasurer Mar was subsequently appointed collector-general for the taxation voted by the late Convention. A campaign of vilification was orchestrated from Court against the leading Scottish-based officials. Alexander's charges of 'unkyndness and distrust' against Melrose were compounded by Nithsdale's accusations against Mar of wilful negligence in drawing up accounts for the taxation voted in 1621. Charles was duly persuaded that factional interests in Scottish government could be repaired by the separation of executive and judicial powers.[6]

Having replaced Melrose as president of the College of Justice by Sir John Skene of Curriehill, Charles decided that all ordinary judges in the College of Justice were to be excluded from the Privy Council. Simultaneously, all councillors were barred from sitting as ordinary judges. In total fourteen councillors were affected. In terms of personnel, the seven gentry among the ordinary judges could most easily be replaced on the Council, at the cost of their professional expertise. But the removal of officers of state and other councillors from the College of Justice prejudiced the formers' customary tenure for life and diminished the status of the latter, predominantly nobles. In stressing his right to remove judges at his pleasure, Charles studiously ignored the opinion of Chancellor Hay. Since the reconstitution of the College of Justice in 1532, no ordinary judge was ever 'cheinged or depryved bott upon ether deth, demission or commission of a fault'.[7]

Restructuring of government also entailed the creation of two conciliar bodies. By July 1626, Charles had appointed a Council of War charged to administer all martial business in the kingdom. It never aspired to supersede or even to act as a separate entity from the Privy Council, being content to operate as a sub-committee for the supervision of coastal defences. Yet, as the Council of War was composed of six nobles and eleven gentry, Charles was demonstrating his patent reluctance to rely on traditional co-operation from the nobility in governing Scotland.[8] Furthermore that March, appealing to the precedent of his father's reign, Charles had constituted a Commission for Grievances with comprehensive powers to remedy malpractices in government. While the Jacobean model had only dealt with monopolies and commercial projects, this new Commission was explicitly designed to oversee all aspects of government, central and local. Perhaps the most obnoxious aspect of this prerogative court was its remit to establish a network of informers throughout the Scottish localities. The threatening nature of this Commission bred immediate fears of a Scottish equivalent of the English Court of Star Chamber, 'come doune heir to play the tyrant, with a specious vissor one its face'.[9]

Operational records of the Commission terminate in July 1626 — after only two working sessions. In no small measure, this situation can be attributed to the tumultuous lobbying of the Commission when it convened under the auspices of the Privy Council. Nithsdale had an exaggerated and uncorroborated report circulated at Court that nobles were using the excuse of military recruitment for British intervention in the Thirty Years' War to augment the numbers of their retainers. The active collusion of leading officials and councillors for the presence of Border nobles and their retainers in Edinburgh was deemed intimidatory, if not inflammatory. Nithsdale's fulminations notwithstanding, violent picketing did make a demonstrable contribution to the declining effectiveness of absentee kingship in so far as the Commission for Grievances 'evanished in itselffe'.[10]

The opponents of the king's reforming programme were certainly able to draw on aristocratic sympathies in condemning restructuring as 'unlawful and prejudicial to the liberties of the kingdom'. Although this opposition was not yet expressed by a substantial or even cohesive group, there was a growing inclination among the nobility to vote with their feet. Scottish nobles, including those serving as officers of state, comprised twenty-two out of the forty-seven members of the reconstituted Privy Council which first met on 23 March 1626. The quorum for Council meetings of eight ordinary members in addition to the officers of state was modified to any nine members and officers at the outset of 1627. Thereafter a return was made to the Jacobean quorum of seven. Indeed, it was only the administrative loyalty of experienced administrators, notably Melrose and to a lesser extent Mar, that ensured a measure of efficiency in the unenthusiastic conduct of royal business in Scotland.[11]

For the political nation as a whole, the most ominous aspect of restructuring was the rationalisation of the Exchequer. The offices of treasurer and treasurer-depute were retained, but effective control over royal rents and other revenues was vested in an Exchequer Commission. Presidency of this Commission was entrusted to Archbishop Spottiswood, whose unstinting commitment to authoritarian kingship led him to be accorded precedence over Chancellor Hay in the Privy Council. The Exchequer was not reformed simply to ensure that royal revenues were 'weele governed'. Charles was preparing the financial ground for the pursuit of his major design in Scotland, the Revocation Scheme. The Commission was established as the necessary precursor of the restoration of property and revenues which Charles conceived to be 'unjustlie withholdin from our patrimonie'.[12] Thus, within a year of his accession, Charles set the political agenda for the remainder of his personal rule by promulgating, solely on the strength of his prerogative, a scheme 'which yeilded no better fruit than the alienation of the subiectis hartes from ther prince, an layed opin a way to rebellion'.[13]

Authoritarian Sophistry

On account of the minorities which had bedevilled Stewart kingship, it had become an accepted constitutional tenet that a sovereign, between his twenty-first and twenty-fifth year, could annul all grants of royal property, pensions and offices made by any regency government prior to his majority. An act of revocation could be used acquisitively also. Thus James V, on attaining his twenty-fifth year in 1537, claimed the prerogative, both by canon law and the statutes of the realm, to revoke all grants made through 'evil and false' counsel since he effectively began to rule in person eleven years earlier. In practice this revocation, which was ratified by parliament in 1540, became a means of exacting large sums of money, by way of compositions, from all obliged to seek ratification of landed titles granted from the outset of the king's minority in 1513.[14]

Being in his twenty-fifth year at his accession, Charles I had rushed through a notice of intent on 14 July 1625, to effect a revocation of all grants from the Crown patrimony. However, a regency government had never acted in Charles's name. Less than four months had elapsed since his assumption of personal rule: hardly sufficient time for the Crown patrimony to have suffered materially from prejudicial counsel! It was only by deliberately obscuring legal and moral rights that Charles was able to claim an initial entitlement to review all gifts of any kind granted out of the principality of Scotland, either by himself in his minority, or by James VI 'as Prince of Scotland, or as father and laughful administrator to us', or by his late brother Prince Henry. The retrospective scope of such a revocation was thus extended to cover all alienations of property and revenues as far back as the birth of his father as Prince of Scotland in 1566. Charles then carried his sophistry a stage further by asserting that a revocation which affected part of the Crown patrimony could not be dissociated from the whole. Hence, specific grants 'hurtfull to the Principalitie' were to be interpreted as generally inimical to the Crown. It was therefore a general revocation of all grants of property and revenues from the Crown patrimony, for an indeterminate duration, which Charles had enacted discreetly through the privy seal on 12 October 1625.[15]

Charles's authoritarian sophistry was further amplified in his decree for the restructuring of government of 26 January 1626. A revocation was deemed necessary 'because his Majestie, not comeing to the crowne in his minoritie, and so not haveing hurt the patrimonie thairof by himself, behooved for keiping of his royall prerogative to revoke what his praedicessors had done to the hurt of the samyne'!^{16} Charles ignored remonstrances from his Privy Council on 17 November 1625, that a general revocation threatened to undermine, even annul, the security of landed title bestowed by charter. The fears aroused by revocation in Scotland were reiterated at Court during consultations between the king, leading officials and councillors on 7 January 1626. Mar warned the king that Scottish landowners were alarmed not only that titles conferred and ratified by previous monarchs were being called into question. Any grant by Charles I was now open to revocation by his royal successors. Indeed, 'no subjectt could be seur of any inheritance vithin the kingdome of Scotland doun be any of his Majesteis predicessors sen King Fergus the First' — from whom Charles was reputed to be one hundred and forty-seventh in succession.[17]

Charles was not inclined to accept informed criticism, however. His patent lack of political *nous*, his dismissive attitude to understandable apprehensions and his belittling of Scottish sensibilities, stand in marked contrast to the pragmatism of his father, James VI. Yet Charles was not entirely devoid of political sensibility. He had delayed publication of his intent to make a general revocation until the Convention of Estates had ended in November 1625. Nonetheless, as Charles had made no attempt to clarify the scope and duration of his Revocation Scheme for almost seven months, a favourable reception was prejudiced by alarmist rumours.[18] In an attempt to explain his true purpose, Charles issued two decreets to the Privy Council on 9 February and 21 July 1626. The former proclaimed his motivation and was aimed at temporal lordships, the latter elaborated the properties and revenues which were to be subject to revocation. Both decreets became the basis for his act of revocation which eventually received parliamentary ratification in 1633.

Charles remained adamant that his Revocation Scheme was to conform to the most recent model — his father's act of 1587. Yet detailed comparison with his father's act reveals not only minor and unremarkable changes in order, but subtle shifting in format and significant alterations in content. Three features are especially noteworthy. Firstly, Charles placed no retrospective timescale on the commencement of revocation. Secondly, he and his successors — not parliament — were to be the sole judges of grants inimical to the Crown patrimony. Thirdly, and most damaging politically, Charles claimed that the annexation act associated with his father's revocation of 1587 had incorporated teinds as well as kirklands; that is, the spiritualities as well as the temporalities of the Church, within the Crown patrimony. Charles's stated intent, therefore, was to equip himself with the constitutional pretext to annexe to the Crown as much of the alienated and dispersed properties and revenues of the pre-Reformation Church as possible. In so doing, Charles studiously ignored the spirit and operation of the annexation act. The underlying significance of this act rested less on its annexation of ecclesiastical temporalities to the Crown than on the exceptions to this general principle — that is, the estates of the Church in the hands of lay commendators which were erected into temporal lordships. This position was merely modified by the act for the restitution of the estate of bishops which James VI passed in 1606. Lordships erected from the estates of monasteries and priories remained unaffected. The exclusion of teinds from the annexation act had been tantamount to royal recognition of the longstanding claims of the churchmen that the teinds, as spirituality, formed the special patrimony of the Church.

Thus, Charles's appeal to the precedent of the annexation act did more to demonstrate the authoritarian sophistry of the Revocation Scheme than to confirm its legal validity. Even though Charles had modified his stated intent to make a general revocation, public confidence in the Crown was hardly restored by the technical complexities of effecting the revocation prescribed in 1626 and ratified in 1633. Charles, moreover, claimed to link economic advantage — the lessening of his dependence on taxation — to religious advancement — greater funding for ministers, education and poor relief. But his primary motivation, camouflaged by his intent to emancipate the gentry from their dependence on the nobility, was social engineering on an unprecedented scale. The vested interests of the political nation were directly affected in four main areas — not only kirklands and teinds but also heritable jurisdictions and feudal tenures.[19]

The Scope of Revocation

The vested interests affected by the proposed revocation of temporal lordships were considerable. Economically, the spiritual estates – that is, the ecclesiastical as well as the temporal lordships — accounted for over two-fifths (42.6%) of the land taxes apportioned in 1625, 1630 and 1633. Socially, Charles's assault on temporal lordships not only threatened the nexus of clientage associated with the nobility in the localities, but also the social mobility of all members of landed society who had profited from the secularisation of kirklands. Politically, leading administrators and councillors rewarded with temporal lordships by James VI were particularly discomfited. Over a fifth of his father's last Council were temporal lords, a proportion actually increased to thirteen out of forty-eight when Charles's own reconstituted Council became operative on 23 March 1626. The persons expected to implement the Revocation Scheme on behalf of the Crown were thus to be among its foremost victims.[20]

The same lack of political plausibility hallmarked his promotion of teind redistribution. Charles asserted that his first concern was to be the advancement of religion: namely, the furtherance of the ideals of the Reformation through the nationwide provision of ministers, education and poor relief. Charles did have a precedent in seeking to finance this programme through teind redistribution. The Commission for the Plantation of Kirks established by James VI in 1617 had proceeded on the principle that the teinds of each parish should maintain the minister of the parish rather than rely on stipends which combined pensions and revenues from diverse benefices. To accord with the decreasing value of money since the Reformation, the Commission of 1617 had set out to raise the stipendiary range (100–300 merks). In the event, none of the augmented stipends actually reached the revised maximum (1000 merks or 10 chalders of victual). There was a marked reluctance among the landed interest to redistribute teinds for stipends in excess of the revised minimum (500 merks or 5 chalders of victual). Yet complaints from ministers about inadequate personal provision from parochial resources, which had characterised presbytery records of the early seventeenth century, had all but disappeared by 1625.[21]

Basic provision of parochial schooling was generally regarded as a matter of 'greit necessitie'. Since the Reformation, the revenues of some chaplainries in the burghs had been directed towards the provision of salaries for masters of grammar schools. Yet this was often accomplished at the expense of parochial self-sufficiency. For such allocations could include teinds drawn from neighbouring parishes.[22] Unfortunately, Charles offered no national guidelines for educational funding to help unravel local priorities between town and country. His initial proposals for a national structure of social welfare, presented to the Convention of Estates in 1625, had been rejected not only for their untutored intervention in an area deemed the special preserve of the Kirk, but for their impracticality. The relative poverty and geographic diversity within Scotland dictated a piecemeal response to poor relief. Financial and moral assistance was designed merely to supplement the family resources available to the deserving poor.[23]

Charles's proclaimed secondary intention for teind redistribution was to 'free the gentrie', in essence the heritors, from their dependence on lay patrons, titulars, and the tacksmen. The process of leading the teinds, the annual uplifting of the crops designated as teind at harvest time, was certainly fraught with difficulties. Considerable annoyance was occasioned among heritors by delays in leading teinds at the convenience of the lay patrons, titulars and tacksmen. Claims that the leading of teinds was a perennial source of civil disturbance and blood-letting must be treated with caution, however.[24] James VI had not been oblivious to the problems of public order arising from the legal obligations of heritors to keep crops intact for twenty days after harvesting until teinds were uplifted. James shifted the burden on to the lay patrons, titulars and tacksmen to collect their teinds before crops rotted from exposure or were eaten in the fields by stray animals. From 1617, the heritor and his tenantry, upon four days' notice to the lay patron, titular or tacksman, could separate teind from the rest of the crop eight days after harvesting.[25] Nevertheless, Charles deemed it his social duty to eradicate the leading of teind by lay patrons, titulars and tacksmen. Heritors were henceforth to be allowed to lead their own teinds at their own convenience. But this task neither necessitated nor justified the wholesale redistribution of teinds proposed by Charles I. The same objective could have been expedited less fractiously by encouraging greater commutation of teinds from kind into money through the mechanism of fiars prices.

Because Charles chose to regard heritable jurisdictions as a further source of bondage for the gentry, the Revocation Scheme was directed indiscriminately against regalities and the heritable annexation of royal offices. Again, James VI had anticipated Charles in seeking to remedy abuses. Not only had the power of repledging from justice-ayres been denied to temporal lordships from 1587, but an itinerant commission had been appointed in 1617 to buy out heritable offices, especially those of sheriffs in the counties and stewarts and baillies in estates annexed to the Crown. Although limited funding was available to compensate those persuaded to surrender their heritable offices, posts were steadily being vacated by 1625. Not all the replacements, who were given yearly appointments, proved efficient. Nonetheless, the Crown was establishing an annual right of review over local government, and judicial malpractices were gradually being phased out. Not content with the pace of change, Charles failed to realise that an indiscriminate assault on heritable jurisdictions threatened to rend asunder the traditional pattern of local government in Scotland.[26]

Charles's final area of revocation was the reversion of feudal tenures converted since 1540. The increasingly commercial approach to estate management, signified by the popularising of feu-ferme tenure during the secularisation of kirklands, had induced the conversion of traditional tenures of ward and relief into blench-ferme or taxed ward during the sixteenth century. Blench-ferme, which usually entailed more nominal annual dues than feu-ferme, was more a form of patronage than a financial burden. Taxed ward, which replaced incidental dues or reliefs arising from wardship, marriage and non-entry of heirs by annual monetary compositions, enabled landowners to regularise financial demands. The reversion of feudal tenures was the area of revocation most blatantly suited to the financial convenience of the Crown. In contrast to England, reliefs in Scotland were never set at definite rates but were scaled to rentals current on individual estates. Hence reliefs, unlike fixed compositions, tended to be adjusted to monetary depreciation whenever landlords raised rents. Once an estate held by ward and relief passed into royal custody during a minority, the king could raise as well as retain rents until the heir came of age. Furthermore, the king had the right to sell or gift the wardship and marriage of an heir, a right which was not only a potentially lucrative source of income during the minorities of leading nobles, but also a cheap source of patronage. The sale or gift of custody, however, exposed estates to detrimental management for the duration of minorities, an eventuality which had enhanced conversions of ward and relief to blench-ferme and taxed ward.[27]

The time-limit of 1540 (presumably the revocation of James V) imposed on conversions from ward and relief applied only to feudal tenures — not to the Revocation Scheme as a whole.[28] No retrospective time-limit was to be placed on kirklands, teinds and heritable jurisdictions until 1630. In order to enforce compliance from the temporal lords in particular and the political nation in general, Charles determined to suspend his father's act of prescription of 1617. Under this act, the thirteen-year period for questioning heritable rights to property possessed continuously for forty years was due to lapse in June 1630. To counter this statutory defence for landlords who withheld their compliance, Charles issued a proclamation on 29 December 1629, affirming his right to suspend the act of prescription. This proclamation was presented to the College of Justice for formal ratification on 30 March 1630. In giving their assent to the king's right to suspend, the senators of the College added the proviso that the suspension applied to property claimed by the Crown as far back as 1455 but not further. In effect, by associating Charles's act of revocation with that of his ancestor James II, a retrospective time-limit of one hundred and seventy-five years was placed on the whole Scheme.[29]

Implementation by Commission

On 25 August 1626, Charles publicly unveiled his intention to resort to the legal process of improbation and reduction to nullify individual rights to temporal lordships and heritable offices. Anyone who refrained from co-operating voluntarily was to be proceeded against, 'without exception'. On the one hand, Charles intended to utilise a private summons which compelled the existing possessor to come into the royal courts and prove his title. On the other hand, the requirement that each defender produce relevant charters of temporal lordships and heritable offices was tantamount to a public inquisition.[30] Thus, Charles, in seeking to take advantage of private means to prosecute the public ends of royal government, unwittingly created a precedent for the separation of the personal conduct of the king from the office of monarch.

Although Charles was determined to enforce his revocation, he had no coherent strategy. His attempt to cover up this lack of coherence led him to oscillate between legal compulsion and voluntary co-operation. Having instructed the lord advocate, Sir Thomas Hope of Craighall, to prepare summons in June 1626, Charles in the following month offered to compensate all who would voluntary surrender their temporal lordships and heritable offices before 1 January 1627. Compensation was to be decided by a commission of sixteen members, drawn equally from the four estates. Although a commission for surrenders operated fitfully for the remainder of the year, it would appear to have functioned merely as a committee of the reconstituted Exchequer Commission, not as an independent tribunal. Only five temporal lords made approaches about surrendering their rights and titles prior to 1 January 1627. No surrenders were effected.[31]

Charles's continuing commitment to legal compulsion led the nobility to despatch a delegation to Court at the end of November 1626. The delegation was composed of two members of the traditional nobility, John Leslie, earl of Rothes, and Alexander Livingstone, second earl of Linlithgow, together with one temporal lord, John Campbell, Lord Loudoun. Their mission, which had the support of leading Scottish administrators, was to petition the king that the Revocation Scheme should not proceed further without parliamentary consultation. Having denied the delegation access to the Court for a fortnight, Charles treated their petition with disdain. Nonetheless, faced with the underwhelming response of temporal lords to the commission for surrenders and the prospect of protracted legal proceedings if obliged to serve individual summons, Charles was moved to concede a new commission to implement his Scheme by negotiation. Accordingly, he declared a six-month moratorium on legal proceedings from 17

January 1627. Charles switched tack to the extent that he went on to establish a Commission for Surrenders and Teinds as his main agency for implementing the Revocation Scheme. Yet he never renounced his right to resort to legal compulsion. Nor was he prepared to concede a parliament to allay the fears of the nobility that comprehensive implementation of the Revocation Scheme would result in 'irreperable ruin to an infinite number of families of all qualities in every region of the land'.[32]

Promulgated as an alternative to law as to parliament, the Commission for Surrenders and Teinds was duly instituted on 3 February 1627. The composition and powers of this Commission, which commenced its initial six-month operations on 1 March, served as a model for subsequent renewals. The Commission was to prove a major influence on Scottish politics for over a decade. Final notification of its suspension, on 12 July 1637, pre-dated the riots against the Service Book in Edinburgh by only eleven days.[33] Indeed, as Charles himself came to realise, the inauguration of this Commission was second only to his promotion of revocation in 'sowing the seeds of sedition and discontent' among the political nation.[34]

Intended as a practical demonstration of the king's prerogative at the expense of landed privilege, the Commission, nonetheless, did not discriminate against the nobility in terms of its original or subsequent composition. Of the sixty-eight persons drawn from the four estates, the nobles and gentry dominated, with twenty-two and twenty-four nominees respectively. The clergy were represented by ten bishops, the same number of commissioners as the burgesses. The Commission was to work with, but independently of, the Privy Council with whom it shared no more than twenty-seven members in common. Requirements for a quorum — three from each estate to be present — seem to indicate a realisation at Court that service on the Commission would prove more onerous than attractive. Indeed, the powers prescribed for the Commission were those for an administrative and deliberative body. All executive decisions concerning the surrender of kirklands and heritable offices and the redistribution of teinds were to be determined solely by Charles I. The Commission was empowered to act in three areas — compensating surrenders of kirklands, costing and quantifying teinds.

The remit of the Commission confirmed that Charles, rather than attempt a wholesale revocation, was now selectively seeking to realign and renegotiate landed titles. Kirklands were to be surrendered but temporal lords were not to be expropriated. They were to be stripped of their superiorities but allowed to retain lands directly managed as property. Compensation, based on the value of the current feu-duties paid by their feuars, was to be offered to temporal lords for the loss of their superiorities. The Commission was to devise a suitable rate for compensation in proportion to the annual sums the superiors received as feu-duty. In principle, therefore, temporal lords were to lose the feudal control they exercised over the estates of other landowners. These feuars, in turn, were to hold their lands directly from the Crown as freeholders. Charles affirmed that he did not wish 'to quarrel or annull' any title to kirklands set to feuars by abbots, priors, lay commendators and temporal lords before 12 October 1625 (the official registration date for the Revocation Scheme). Moreover, superiorities were only open to acquisition by the existing feuars 'and to none others'. In practice, if feuars did not wish to hold their own property direct from the Crown as freeholders, the temporal lords were to retain superiority. In either event, whether temporal lords were stripped of all or part of their superiorities, their own feu-duties to the Crown for their remaining lands and jurisdictions were to be renegotiated. Thus, implementation of revocation through the Commission committed the Crown neither to the wholesale annexation nor the creation of an open market in kirklands. At the same time, temporal lords, holders of regalities and other heritable offices were to be compensated for surrendering their public rights of justice. Private rights of estate management, as exercised through the barony court, were not impaired.[35]

The remit of the Commission also suggested that temporal lords and lay patrons were not necessarily to be stripped of their titularship of teinds. The Commission was required to cost the rates at which heritors could purchase control over their own teinds. However, if heritors failed to exercise their option to purchase, titulars and lay patrons were to have their existing rights to teinds confirmed but renegotiated to the advantage of the Crown. Regardless of heritors purchasing control over their own teinds, the Commission was charged to draw up guidelines for quantifying the amount of teind to be redistributed for pious and other uses. An adequate financial basis for the augmentation of ministers' stipends, the sustenance of schooling and poor relief was to be achieved not only by redistributing teinds within every parish but, if necessary, by redrawing geographical boundaries between neighbouring parishes. At the same time, Charles's intention to secure 'a competent maintenance' for the Crown that 'we may be less burdenable to our subjects' now materalised as an annuity from the teinds. As well as drawing up guidelines as to how much teind should be quantified as annuity, the Commission was instructed to exact sureties from heritors, tacksmen, titulars and lay patrons to pay the royal annuity which now assumed paramount importance in determining the redistribution of teinds. The priority accorded by Charles to his annuity not only came to be regarded as far from 'honourable' within official circles, but was deemed base and counted as 'brocage' by the political nation.[36]

Redistribution could not be effected until the teinds in every parish were evaluated. Charles wholly underestimated the technical complexity of this task — in many charters teinds were amalgamated with other landholding dues into composite feu-duties; tacks to teinds were of variable duration and could range over several parishes in disparate localities; titularship was not restricted to temporal lords and lay patrons but was also exercised by corporate bodies, notably burghs, universities and hospitals as by bishops. His assertion that landowners were neither bound to submit nor comply with the valuations of the Commission was spurious, no more than an excuse to justify his withholding of executive powers from the Commission. No final decision on costing or quantifying teinds as on compensating superiorities, regalities and heritable offices, was to be made without royal approval.

Notwithstanding the selective targeting of revocation, the compulsory evaluation of teinds in every parish entailed onerous inquisitions into landed title and contractual conditions. In the short term, the creation of the Commission for Surrenders and Teinds served to devolve opprobrium for the implementation of the Revocation Scheme. Over the next decade, however, the fitful and intermittent working of the Commission, marked by the reluctance and dilatoriness of all parties connected with its operation, helped crystallise dissent within the localities against revocation by royal prerogative. Not only did the Commission fail to establish promptly its own ground rules for surrenders and valuations, but Charles took thirty months to finalise the rates at which surrenders were to be compensated and teinds costed and quantified for redistribution.[37]

Class Antagonism

The Commission served as a forum for antagonism between the political classes, especially in its initial session from March to August 1627. The nobility were on the defensive from a combined assault by the gentry and clergy. While the burgesses pursued exemption from the Revocation Scheme, the bishops representing the clergy soon alienated the other three estates by their patent unwillingness to concede that any but churchmen had rights to the teinds as spirituality. Indeed, Charles was even moved to rebuke the bishops on 3 May, as 'men voyde of charity, bezond measure timorous without a cause'. Class antagonism fanned out from the Commission into the localities. Ministers preached that neither the king nor any lay person could lawfully enjoy any benefit from the teinds. More significantly, Charles allowed the gentry and clergy to hold separate conventions for their respective estates — similar to the standing convention for the royal burghs — to formulate a common policy towards revocation. The nobility, however, were not licensed to convene separately or permitted to elect representatives to promote their interests at Court.[38]

The concession of a convention affirmed rather than abated the uncompromising stance of the clergy on the teinds. The clergy concluded their two-day deliberations on 19 July by agreeing to finance lobbying at Court by the levy of 20/- on every 100 merks or chalder of victual from bishops' rents and ministers' stipends. In effect, the clergy set aside 1.67% of their yearly income as a political fighting fund.[39] The concession of a convention to the gentry was no more rewarding for Charles I. He was guilty of wishful thinking that he was assured of reliable backing from the gentry for his Revocation Scheme. Charles was not totally deluded, however. For a militant vanguard of gentry, organised covertly by Sir John Scot of Scotstarvit, the director of chancery, had mounted a counter-supplication in December 1626 to complain about the nobility's opposition to revocation.[40]

The principal spokesmen for this militant vanguard were Sir James Lear-mouth of Balcomie and Sir James Lockhart of Lee, from the shires of Fife and Lanark respectively. Balcomie and Lee were actually authorised by Charles on 11 April 1627 to organize — that is, manage — a convention of gentry as a public display of support for the Revocation Scheme. The Privy Council effectively sabotaged this initiative by fixing a specific date for elections to the convention, which were to be held in every shire on 29 May. The electoral meetings were to be open to all heritors interested in purchasing teinds. The fixed date meant that the managerial endeavours of the militant vanguard were overstretched. The opening up of electoral meetings meant that nobles as well as their kinsmen and local associates among the unenfranchised gentry and yeomen could intrude as heritors. In the event, the elections in the shires were affected less by intrusionists than by absentees as heritors boycotted meetings organised by the militants reputedly 'for ther privat endes'. Fresh elections on 29 August again failed to produce a convention prepared to articulate a consensus in favour of revocation.[41]

A deputation representing titulars and lay patrons as potential teind-sellers was allowed to visit Court at the outset of August, principally to be chastised by Charles. This deputation was composed of John Elphinstone, Lord Balmerino and Sir John Stewart (later lord then first earl) of Traquair. Neither Balmerino nor Traquair had voluntarily commenced negotiations with the Commission for Surrenders and Teinds. Consultations with this deputation, as also with members of the militant vanguard representing potential teind-buyers and with the clerical lobby, convinced Charles of the necessity of drawing up a general submission to which all interested parties were to subscribe their assent to royal arbitration in finalising rates of compensation, costing and quantifying. As these rates were to be proclaimed subsequently by legal decreet, subscribers to the general submission were effectively being asked to write a blank cheque.[42]

The format of the general submission did not find approval at Court until 17 January 1628. Charles only despatched the approved version north on 12 February, after securing the subscription of courtiers and commanding that his Scottish-based councillors stage an exemplary subscription on receipt. Rather than condone a convention of nobles in Edinburgh to implement the general submission, Charles commissioned select nobles to receive the subscriptions of teind-sellers within the shires. Of the twenty-two copies of the general submission despatched to the shires, only nine were returned to the Privy Council by 22 April, and only three contained unqualified subscriptions. Moreover, as the general submission applied to all potential teind-sellers, the bishops were required to subscribe on behalf of the clergy. The signal failure of the episcopate to comply by 22 April served to fortify the resolve of defaulting temporal lords and other teind-sellers. Despite claims by Charles at the end of June that copies had been subscribed by the most influential as well as the majority of potential teind-sellers, defaulters and those who qualified their subscription to the general submission were twice threatened with prosecution by 10 September.[43]

The gentry were not prepared, in their capacity as potential teind-buyers, to turn informers against the temporal lords and other teind-sellers who refused to subscribe the general submission. Having on the advice of Lord Advocate Hope extended subscription to heritors as well as titulars, Charles had commissioned select gentry, mainly from the militant vanguard, to convene meetings of potential teind-buyers in the shires. Instead of requiring individual subscription to copies of the general submission, teind-buyers in every shire were to elect two of their number to appear before the Privy Council and subscribe on behalf of their shire. From the twenty-eight electoral meetings convened in the shires, twenty-five despatched delegates to Edinburgh on behalf of potential teind-buyers by the end of April 1628. Only the enfranchised gentry, not all the heritors, in the shires had selected the delegates. Many enfranchised gentry had either absented themselves from the meetings or refused to endorse warrants electing delegates. Over half the warrants for delegates were found to be incomplete. Few delegates provided any information about defaulting temporal lords and other lay teind-sellers. Albeit the delegates were returned to their shires with instructions to complete their warrants or to submit lists of gentry refusing their endorsement by 25 July, subscriptions of teind-buyers to the general submission remained less than wholehearted. Charles was moved to complain on 11 November that delegates for the teind-buyers were still failing to report defaulting teind-sellers.[44]

The only tangible advance made by Charles during 1628 was to secure the compliance of the royal burghs, after agreeing to pay special regard to their corporate rights as titulars. Lands and teinds traditionally devoted by the burghs for the sustenance of the ministry, schools, hospitals and other pious uses were to continue to be employed exclusively for these purposes. On 28 June, Charles even conceded that his annuity would only be exacted from the burghs in the event of a surplus, when the income each burgh derived from teind was greater than its expenditure for pious uses. In turn, the Convention of Royal Burghs on 2 July affirmed that heritors would be allowed to purchase their own teinds once the tacks of teinds granted by the burghs had expired. The burgesses thus effectively extricated themselves from the Revocation Scheme.[45]

Because no wholesale redistribution of teinds could be accomplished without prior evaluation, Charles determined on 21 July 1628 that the task of valuation be devolved from the Commission for Surrenders and Teinds to sub-commissions operating within the bounds of every presbytery. Although the remit of the sub-commissions was restricted, their implementation was delayed for almost a year. Particular difficulties were experienced in defining the relationship of the sub-commissions to the Commission on the matter of appeals; in establishing ground rules for valuations; and in appointing willing sub-commissioners, drawn from the ranks of potential teind-buyers, whose nomination was entrusted to the clergy within each presbytery.[46]

Charles unilaterally resolved the first difficulty by granting the sub-commissioners on 15 January 1629 'full and absolute pouare' to conduct valuations. No appeals were allowed to the Commission for Surrenders and Teinds, though mistaken or partial valuations would be referred to the next parliament for remedy. The second difficulty was to become a running sore. Sub-commissions were not only to evaluate teinds paid separately to titulars, lay patrons and tacksmen, but were also to disentangle teind from other landholding dues in composite feu-duties. Separate payments tended to be made by heritors in their capacity as barons or freeholders, while composite feu-duties were paid by feuars. The proving of valuations — requiring the exaction of oaths, the citing of witnesses as well as the production of landed titles and rent rolls — was loaded in favour of the teind-sellers over the teind-buyers. If the titular or lay patron, directly or through his tacksman, had led the teinds of the heritor for seven years in the last fifteen, his 'oath of verity' was all that was required to uphold the accuracy of a disputed valuation. Valuations of teinds in relation to other landholding dues were inherently contentious as each estate was assessed in terms not only of feu-duties to the Crown, temporal lord or other landed superior. Because inflation had eroded the relative value of feu-duties paid in money, a valued or constant rent was to be ascertained from the current rents paid to each heritor by his tenantry. But no simple formula was applied nationwide to establish the proportion of current rents that was to be assessed as the valued rent.[47]

The third difficulty — persuading sub-commissioners to serve in every presbytery — was certainly not alleviated by the prospects of a technically exacting workload and anomalous as well as contentious valuations. As many as fifteen out of the fifty-nine presbyteries had no sub-commissions appointed by 24 February 1629 — albeit only that of Banff remained unfilled by 9 June, when sub-commissioners in diverse presbyteries were chastised for having 'undewtifullie and unworthillie shunned' employment in the service of the Crown. In practice the sub-commissioners were drawn usually but not exclusively from the ranks of the gentry. Each presbytery tended to appoint seven to nine lairds, chosen for their local prominence, not as parochial representatives. In the west of Scotland, however, yeomen were appointed as sub-commissioners for the presbytery of Lanark and Glasgow. Indeed, the latter presbytery actually appointed up to two commissioners for every parish within its bounds. The subsequent performance of the sub-commissions nationally was at best patchy.[48]

Expectations that the sub-commissions would meet at least twice weekly were not regularly fulfilled despite the imposition of fines ranging from 6 to 40 merks for unwarranted and persistent absenteeism. The Commission for Surrenders and Teinds minuted on 27 January 1632 that few sub-commissions had submitted reports of their diligence. Conveners of fifteen sub-commission were actually outlawed for their failure to provide reports by 1 March. Deadlines for the submission of reports went largely unheeded. On 9 January 1633 the Commission made a general attack on 'the slouth and negligence' of the sub-commissioners. Reports submitted from 22 presbyteries were deemed informal, while those that were accepted as formal contained significant undervaluation of teinds. Indeed, by the final deadline for reports on 1 March 1634, ministers were being requested to forward current details of teinds and other landholding dues in composite feu-duties in order to correct incomplete or inaccurate valuations.[49] In effect, the sub-commissions, instead of expediting valuation, had actively engaged in collusion with local vested interests to restrict the amount of teind available for redistribution: a situation that can be traced directly to the hostile reception accorded to Charles's legal decreet of 18 September 1629.

Class Collusion

The legal decreet can be separated into five major components affecting the future disposal of superiorities and teinds under the general headings of compensation for surrenders, costing of teinds, limitations on purchase, quantification of teinds and redistribution for pious and other uses. Other than costing and quantification where the Commission for Surrenders and Teinds was empowered to make empirical revisions, Charles was content to ratify recommendations already made by the Commission.[50]

Compensation to the temporal lords for loss of their superiorities was confirmed as 1000 merks for every chalder of victual or 100 merks of free rent: that is, ten times the feu-duties hitherto paid by their feuars less the feu-duty paid by the temporal lords themselves to the Crown. Superiorities were to be purchased at a price specified as ten years' rental (that is, free rent), an offer initially made to John Maitland, first earl of Lauderdale, but regarded as prejudicial to the nobility when upheld by the Commission on 29 June 1627. The actual mechanism of sale, suggested by the militant vanguard on 10 November 1628, was not approved formally until 17 July 1630. Feuars who advanced the purchase price for superiorities to temporal lords were to hold their kirklands directly of the Crown as freeholders. Their feu-duties, which were now owed to the Crown, were to be retained for up to ten years to recoup monies advanced to temporal lords. Thus, by mortgaging the kirklands to existing feuars, temporal lords were to be compensated for their superiorities at no cost to the Crown. Not every feuar, however, had a sum equivalent to ten years' rental readily available. Nor were all feuars prepared to combine to strip temporal lords of their superiorities. Moreover, no change was proposed in apportioning taxation. Feuars who bought out superiority were still to pay reliefs to temporal lords who remained responsible for uplifting taxes from kirklands.[51]

The price at which heritors could acquire control of their own teinds was costed at nine years' purchase for every 100 merks paid annually in money: that is, a purchase price equivalent to nine years' valued rent. Where teinds were paid in kind, the same costing applied once the valuations were commuted into monetary sums — allowance having been made for regional variations in the quality and quantity of crops designated as teind. However, not every heritor was entitled to purchase control over his own teinds. Charles ratified his agreement of the previous summer with the royal burghs that teinds assigned to ministers' stipends, educational provision and social welfare could be led by but not sold to heritors — a prohibition on purchase extended to the teinds of universities and hospitals in 1633. Moreover, heritors had to await the expiry of existing tacks before purchasing their teinds from clerical titulars. When Charles eventually abrogated this provision on 20 May 1634, churchmen not heritors were given the first priority to buy out tacksmen and secure the whole teinds of parishes for the permanent use of the Kirk. Heritors were also required to pay teinds to tacksmen of temporal lords and lay patrons with no immediate prospect of leading, far less of purchasing, their own teinds. For valuations could not be concluded until current tacks — usually long leases — had expired.

While the right to purchase their own teinds was neither guaranteed nor immediate for some heritors, it was not practicable for others. The right to purchase was not so much a standing concession as a singular option. The coronation parliament of 1633 went on to impose specific time-limits on this option. All heritors whose teinds had already been valued were obliged to make an offer to purchase by the autumn of 1635. Those heritors awaiting valuation of their teinds were given no more than two years to make an offer on the completion of valuation. Because of a lack of ready cash, few heritors outwith the ranks of the nobility and leading gentry were able to exercise their option to purchase within two years. Heritors were not entirely quit of superiority if they purchased their own teinds. The formal contract of sale issued from 1631 required heritors to provide the titular of every parish with a written undertaking not only to pay reliefs for taxation, but to meet their share of parochial teinds apportioned to ministers' stipends, other pious uses and the king's annuity.[52]

Where the teinds were intermingled with other landholding dues and were thus to be valued conjointly, Charles determined that the quantity to be assessed as teind should be the fifth part of the valued or constant rent: that is, a fifth of composite sums paid as feu-duty was to be accounted teind when determining the valued rent of each estate. Where the teinds were assessed separately, Charles allowed a deduction of one-fifth of their estimated value to be retained as a personal allowance for the heritor. Basically, this personal allowance from the valued rent was afforded because teind quantified separately tended to carry a higher valuation than that where teind was intermingled with other landholding dues. The personal allowance was thus a practical corrective to titulars profiteering from the loading of valuation in their favour. This personal allowance primarily benefited barons and freeholders who were now guaranteed a minimum share of their own teinds whether or not they exercised their option to purchase.

Indeed, the personal allowance was the only guaranteed portion of the heritors's teinds not liable to redistribution. The legal decreet upheld the revised minimum for ministers' stipends raised by the Commission from 500 merks or 5 chalders of victual to 800 merks or 8 chalders on 30 May 1627. While the amount requiring redistribution within each parish varied, the national minimum was an identified target. However, the contribution towards pious uses was not limited by national ratings or current demands, but was elastically geared to future local aspirations for schooling and social welfare. Contributions to the king's annuity were fixed nationally but variably in accordance with the Commission's recommendation of 29 May 1627. The rating of 6 per cent to be exacted as annuity applied only to payments of teind in money, not in kind where exactions varied according to the type and quality of victual and fluctuated annually according to local rates of commutation.[53] Given that a significant if indeterminate proportion of teind was to be redistributed, the heritors' inducement to purchase was not so much financial as managerial.

Reflecting on the legal decreet on 24 October 1629, Charles affirmed that he had provided the necessary guidelines for the surrender of superiorities and teind redistribution 'that non of our subjectis interested can have just caus to complain'. The presentation of the legal decreet before a Convention of Estates in July 1630 provided no ringing endorsement from the political nation, however. The resistance encountered over teind redistribution was such that leading officials were initially averse to moving its ratification 'for feir of repulse'. Only adroit presentation of the legal decreet as a composite package by the lord president, William Graham, seventh earl of Menteith, ensured acceptance. Nonetheless, the gentry, as spokesmen not just for the shires but for the political nation as a whole, called upon the Convention to petition the king to take account of 'the great feare' aroused by his efforts to compel compliance with the Revocation Scheme.[54]

While Charles remained unresponsive to such petitioning, he had already provided the touchstone for the furtherance of class collusion. His quantification of teind as a fifth of the valued rent, when intermingled with other landholding dues, was open to manipulation by titulars and lay patrons with the active support of heritors. Taking advantage of ties of social deference and the loading of proof against heritors, titulars and lay patrons concocted valued rents that devalued the amounts apportioned as teind. The coronation parliament pointed out that valued rents were undervalued by as much as a third in relation to feu-duties where teinds and other landholding dues were paid as composite sums. Undervaluing could not be accomplished, however, without the connivance of the sub-commissions who were empowered to scrutinise all landed titles and contractual conditions. Thus, collusion was a community enterprise designed to diminish the amount of teind available for redistribution for ministers' stipends, pious uses and, above all, the king's annuity. By 1 July 1635, collusion had become so prevalent that the Commission for Surrenders and Teinds was itself censured by Charles for its routine acceptance of valuations from sub-commissions in which valued rents had been diminished by a third in relation to composite feu-duties. An official committee of inquiry into the operation of the Commission reported to Court by the end of December 1636 that 'the great ill of undervaluing' was the foremost impediment to comprehensive teind redistribution. Moreover, 'the farr greater sort' of the teinds were 'not yet valued'.[55]

Limited Accomplishment

No more than seven temporal lords had commenced negotiations with the Commission prior to the Convention of Estates in July 1630, which served to expose the critical weakness of the Revocation Scheme — notably, the king's lack of financial resources to implement the surrender of kirklands, regalities and heritable offices. Prior to the implementation of his legal decreet, Charles was already committed to expenditure of around £250,000 for the compulsory purchase of four regalities and twelve heritable offices. Yet the annual income ordinarily available to the Crown during the first four years of his reign had dropped by £27,321-14/4 (from £223,930-7/4 to £196,608-13/-) and his expenditure had moved from a modest surplus of £64,838-15/8 to an accumulating deficit of £137,640-7/6. Furthermore, the revenues raised from the land tax of £400,000 and the 5% tax on annualrents voted by the Convention of Estates in 1625, were earmarked for British expeditionary forces on the continent, national defence and the maintenance of the Scottish establishment at Court and in Edinburgh. Although both taxes were renewed by the Convention of 1630, military and establishment expenditure was still accorded priority.[56]

Charles's continuing financial embarrassment obliged him to rely on feuars to buy out their own superiorities, a policy impeded partly by legal loopholes arising from transfer of title, but primarily because feuars were unprepared to advance the requisite lump sums. Charles took four years to clear up the loopholes arising from his legal decreet. As well as prohibiting temporal lords questioning their feuars' titles at law, feuars were obliged to produce documentary evidence that compensation, including any arrears of feu-duty, had been paid in full before they received a charter for their kirklands direct from the Crown. Actual, as against threatened, legal action between temporal lords and their feuars was rare. Conversely, bands of suspension raised between August 1632 and January 1634 reveal that only the most prominent gentry among feuars of kirklands had sufficient local standing or independent resources to enforce their right to buy out superiority. The tendency among most feuars was to collude actively with temporal lords in exploiting legal loopholes. Thus, feuars resigned their kirklands in favour of their temporal lords who then registered the resigned lands as their property with the Commission for Surrenders and Teinds. On the lands being declared exempt from revocation, they were granted back to the feuars.[57]

The financial embarrassment of the Crown — which led Charles to suspend negotiated surrenders of regalities and heritable offices in October 1634 — was compounded by temporal lords withholding payments of their feu-duties for over seven years. Only eleven temporal lords, less than a third of the total number, had made any meaningful effort to negotiate with the Crown. Although no temporal lord was exempted from the scope of revocation, Charles had not enhanced prompt compliance by his blatant favouring of courtiers. No more than two temporal lords, both anglicised absentees — James Stewart, fourth duke of Lennox and James Colville, Lord Colville — were prepared to make unconditional surrenders. The remaining temporal lords negotiated with the Crown essentially to win concessions. Their lordships were to continue, but their rights and privileges were realigned.[58]

In reality, Charles's bargaining position was compromised from the conclusion of a package deal for 32,000 merks with Lord Loudoun on 5 August 1630. After three years of intricate negotiations, Loudoun was persuaded to surrender his heritable sheriffship of Ayr for 14,000 merks, to be paid in ten annual instalments. His regalian privileges over the lordship of Kylesmure (erected from the Ayrshire estates of Melrose abbey) were downgraded to those of a barony. His superiorities were valued at 18,000 merks but not surrendered as the Crown lacked the ready cash and his feuars the inclination to purchase outright. His feu-duty was reduced to 100 merks — a third of its value prior to negotiations.[59] In only one instance did Charles actually resort to law — to compel Sir William Forbes of Craigievar to surrender the estates of Lindores abbey, estates which had been purchased as recently as April 1625. Proceedings, instigated four years later, took another six to conclude. No more than five temporal lordships were wholly revoked during Charles's personal rule. Instead of being annexed inalienably to the Crown, they tended to be gifted to the Church. Thus, lordship over their feuars was merely transferred not terminated.[60]

Individual negotiations ultimately concluded with nine nobles and four gentry, for the surrender of five regalities and thirteen heritable offices, were no less protracted and fudged. Rather than make prompt cash settlements, the Crown tended either to earmark future revenues for compensation in instalments — as was the case with Loudoun — or allow the retention of regalities and heritable offices under mortgage, that is for an indeterminate time until the Crown met the agreed compensation. Thus, the regality and sheriffship of Sutherland were regranted to John Gordon, fourteenth earl of Sutherland, in September 1631, pending the Crown finding compensation of £12,000. In essence, local government still remained a matter of hereditary private enterprise. Even where a heritable official was removed, his replacement — for one year or longer at royal pleasure — tended to be another prominent landowner.[61]

The financial constraints on the Crown did lead to the prompt shelving of one aspect of the Revocation Scheme — the reversing of tenures changed from ward and relief to taxed ward and blench-ferme since 1540. The threat of such a reversal had led to landlords pursuing legal loopholes, notably when obliged to feu portions of their estates as surety to creditors. In the spring of 1628, Charles was induced to forego reversing tenures in return for an evasion tax proposed by Sir Alexander Strachan of Thornton, a courtier of dubious repute, whose successful overtures to farm Crown revenues were to make him a leading fiscal entrepreneur over the next decade. As part of a project rather optimistically promoted to treble the revenues available to the Crown from feudal casualties, at least £24,000 was to be exacted annually in compositions from landowners who had defaulted on the payment of reliefs for wardship, non-entry and marriage or converted to taxed ward and blench-ferme without royal approval. By the second year of its operation, Thornton's commission had provoked 'so great contestatione' that its operation was suspended by the Exchequer Commission. Having been deemed a significant grievance by the Convention of Estates in 1630, the commission was discreetly withdrawn, Thornton being granted £36,000 compensation for the four years left to run. From 1631, Charles began to grant individual dispensations to prominent landowners who had inherited or acquired lands held by taxed ward. But he never entirely abandoned the concept of an evasion tax which he sought to reimpose from June 1637, when the Exchequer was instructed to exact 'ane considerable compositioun' for registering changes in tenure from ward and relief.[62]

As Archibald Napier, Lord Napier of Merchiston, had anticipated when treasurer-depute in 1630, the combination of restrictive and impracticable conditions governing the acquisition of teinds was a major cause of disenchantment among heritors, 'most of them not being able to buy there tythe, and the able not willing'. Despite the attested willingness of the Crown to support legal proceedings against obstructive titulars and lay patrons, only two heritors have been registered — both in 1634 — as having secured their own teinds by compulsory purchase: a statistic which lends little credence to the reputed oppression of the heritors. Undoubtedly, social deference and a reluctance to become entangled in legal confrontations with obstructive titulars and lay patrons contributed to an aversion to compulsory purchase among heritors.[63] Some sales did proceed by voluntary agreement between titulars or lay patrons on the one hand and heritors on the other. Among heritors classified as barons and freeholders, no more than nine — less than 3% — in the western shires of Dumbarton, Lanark and Renfrew appear to have purchased their own teinds.[64]

As was the case with their superiority over kirklands, temporal lords retained control over the bulk of the teinds comprehended within their titularship. However, renegotiation of their titles did lead to the realignment of their landed resources. Thus, in May 1634, the earl of Roxburghe's lordship of Halydean (erected from the estates of Kelso abbey) had its territorial influence contracted not revoked, a realignment that resulted in the feu-duty being reduced by a quarter to 100 merks. As well as downgrading his regalian privileges to those of a barony, his right of titularship was rescinded in twenty parishes but reserved in six, notably in the districts of Teviotdale and Ettrick Forest which mainly consisted of the earl's own lands or those of his kinsmen and local associates. In effect, the territorial influence of the titular was realigned to that of the lay patron, a process first promoted in Ayrshire in July 1631, but not implemented nationwide until March 1637.[65]

Incomplete and inaccurate valuations were undoubtedly the major stumbling blocks to the accomplishment of teind redistribution. Out of the seventy-six parishes in the western presbyteries of Dumbarton, Glasgow, Hamilton, Paisley and Lanark, valuations were completed in fifty-two, of which twenty-four required rectification on account of collusion.[66] Despite vociferous overtures from clerics intent on securing augmentations to their stipends, ministers were more concerned to appease than confront titulars, lay patrons and heritors.

The Commission for Surrenders and Teinds was by no means reluctant to implement significant augmentations of stipend as borne out by thirty decreets of locality enforced between 1634 and 1636. Yet no uniform parochial provision resulted, even for ministers within the same presbytery. Rather than impair their good standing within the local community by the protracted and fractious enforcement of a decreet of locality, ministers actually colluded in the deliberate undervaluing of teinds. Their failure to act as watchdogs for the Commission was identified on 25 March 1636 as a significant factor in the submission of inaccurate and unrectified valuations. Conversely, recourse to legal decreets served to harden attitudes against redistribution for pious uses, especially as the legislative framework for the provision of schools and social welfare continued to rely on voluntary stents by the landed interest in every parish.[67]

Inaccurate and incomplete valuations particularly prejudiced the exaction of the king's annuity. Charles had intended that his annuity would be exacted from the harvest of 1628. In the event, despite threats of outlawry to titulars, lay patrons, tacksmen, heritors, sub-commissioners and even commissioners, and despite directives for the exaction of the annuity from unvalued as well as valued teind, the processing of annuity payments remained a fringe activity in the Exchequer until 1635.[68] Charles, however, did have sufficient foresight to provide for contingency action. He declined to have his annuity annexed to the Crown as heritable income by the coronation parliament. Thus, the ground was prepared for its flexible deployment to ensure an immediate return for Charles if not a regular income for the Crown. On 28 February 1634, Charles instructed the Commission to commence negotiations with titulars, lay patrons and heritors prepared to buy out their obligation to pay annuity. Sales, which were to be completed by 1 August 1635, were restricted to heritors who had secured control over their own teinds following valuation and to titulars and lay patrons who continued to control unsold teinds. Teind apportioned as annuity was to be sold for a price costed at fifteen years' purchase: that is, a price equivalent to fifteen times the annuity liable from each estate. As a further stimulus to sales, Charles conceded on 7 November 1634 that this purchase price was to include existing arrears, amounting in most instances to seven years' annuity.[69]

Only eight landowners purchased their share of the king's annuity by 1 August 1635. The period for sales was duly extended on 6 November and effectively lasted until the end of his personal rule, by which time another eighty sales were concluded. Some landowners were obliged to pay a purchase price equivalent to sixteen years' annuity to cover mounting arrears. The total of eighty-eight sales — realising individual sums from under £100 to over £2000 — did little to alleviate the financial burdens of the Crown, but much to highlight the widespread lack of enthusiasm among the landed classes for Charles's pursuit of revocation to his own personal advantage. Even before the initial period for sales had expired, Charles had resorted to the farming of his annuity primarily to ensure a return from unvalued as well as valued teind from 24 July 1635. But the political discontent occasioned by the zealous farming of the annuity by entrepreneurs like Strachan of Thornton would appear to have outweighed the financial benefit accruing to Charles.[70]

Conclusion

In retrospect, given the decade of wrangling occasioned by its implementation, the political castigation of the act of revocation as 'a dangerous nonsense' may appear justified.[71] There were only two contemporaneous international comparisons. Charles's Scheme was certainly less sustained than the systematic attempts at social engineering undertaken by the Russian Czars who sought to perpetuate a 'service-state' by governing through landowners of a similar status to the gentry, whose holdings were regulated bureaucratically according to rank. Like the Romanovs, Charles made the political miscalculation of underestimating the atavistic desire of the nobility to preserve the privileges of their class. Charles, moreover, lacked the political pragmatism of the Holy Roman Emperor, Ferdinand II, whose Edict of Restitution of 1629 decreed that all property sequestered by Protestant princes or cities since 1552 was to be restored to the Roman Catholic Church. Ferdinand, however, had sufficient wit to rescind his Edict during 1630, after Catholic as well as Protestant German princes had formed a common front to defend their particularist interests.[72]

The authoritarian manner in which Charles strove to impose his Revocation Scheme made scant allowance for either its technical complexities — 'like the heads of Hydra, no sooner one cut off but another arises'[73] — or the exacting workloads assigned to the Commission for Surrenders and Teinds and the sub-commissions within the presbyteries. Having initially incited antagonistic interests within the political nation, his remorseless pursuit of revocation ultimately forged an accord among the landed classes to frustrate its accomplishment. Class collusion, which found expression in the widespread reluctance within the localities to fulfil central directives, gradually brought about the erosion of the Scottish administration's political will to uphold the royal prerogative.

The nobility were never more than grudging participants on the Commission. Support from the gentry could not be relied upon once that estate came to realise that the surrender of superiorities and teind redistribution were qualified by exacting financial as well as legal restrictions. The burgesses displayed their indifference by conspicuous absenteeism. Despite their initial truculence and their poor attendance record, Charles was forced increasingly to call upon the bishops to ensure that the Commission maintained weekly meetings. Such reliance, in turn, led to the clerical commissioners being identified as the common target for opposition from 21 December 1631, when the king's proposal that the work of the Commission be entrusted to a select committee dominated by leading officials was rejected by the lay commissioners. As no attempt was made in the coronation parliament to appease the constitutional apprehensions raised by the Scheme, the earl of Haddington (formerly Melrose) could still point out to the Court on 17 June 1635 that the principle of revocation had merely been affirmed not proved. The bishops were specifically implicated as barriers to the constitutional redress of grievances when they used their inbuilt majority of one on the thirteen-man official inquiry into the Commission to recommend its renewal after its tortuous proceedings had been suspended by Charles on 16 October 1636. A parliament promised to be a difficult 'and ane uncertaine event'.[74]

Yet the most contentious aspect of the Revocation Scheme was neither its aims nor its promotion through the Commission for Surrenders and Teinds, but Charles I's unstinting resolve to impose his revocation, if necessary by legal compulsion, solely on the strength of his prerogative. Although the political nation did reject his imposition of social engineering from above, the substance of the Revocation Scheme was to find support from the Covenanting Movement during the 1640s.[75] That the Scheme should be postponed rather than terminated in 1637 indicates that opposition from the political nation was neither a uniform nor necessarily a conservative reaction against social engineering, but primarily a collective vote of no confidence in Charles I.

NOTES

1. *APS*, V, 166–88; *RPCS*, second series, I, (1625–27), 80, 122–24, 173–74, 261–63.

2. *The Red Book of Mentieth*, W. Fraser ed., 2 vols, (Edinburgh, 1880), II, 14, 25–26; *Royal Letters, Charters and Tracts relating to the Colonization of New Scotland and the Institution of the Order of Knight Baronets of Nova Scotia, 1621–38*, D. Laing ed., (Bannatyne Club, Edinburgh, 1857), 120–23; T. H. McGrail, *Sir William Alexander of Menstrie*, (Edinburgh, 1940), 89–104. In July 1626, the sale of baronetcies was prolonged until 150 gentlemen had enrolled with a view to realising 300,000 merks for the Crown. By the end of 1626, only 28 Scottish lairds had purchased a baronetcy though the number did rise to 113 by 1638. Having realised 126,000 merks for the Crown by 1629, sales yielded another 120,000 merks over the next nine years. The order did not remain exclusively Scottish, however, with three French, four Irish and twelve English gentry being enrolled from 1629.

3. J. Row, *The History of the Kirk of Scotland*, D. Laing ed., (Wodrow Society, Edinburgh, 1842), 340–41.

4. HUL, Maxwell-Constable of Everingham MSS, DDEV/79/D; *The Book of Carlaverock* W. Fraser ed., 2 vols, (Edinburgh, 1873), II, 73–74.

5. NLS, Morton Cartulary & Papers, MS 80, fo. 67; HMC, *Mar & Kellie*, II, 245–49; M. Napier, *Montrose and the Covenanters*, 2 vols, (London, 1837), I, 43–52; Sir J. Scot of Scotstarvit, *The Staggering State of Scottish Statesmen, from 1550 to 1650*, C. Rogers ed., (Edinburgh, 1872), 67.

6. HUL, Maxwell-Constable of Everingham MSS, DDEV/79/H/7 & /142; *Memorials of the Earls of Haddington*, Sir W. Fraser ed., 2 vols, (Edinburgh, 1889), II, 88–90, 146–47; *SR* I, 16, 28–29; *RPCS*, second series, I, 232–34, 238–41.

7. *SR*, I, 13–14, 46; *RPCS*, second series, I, 220–21; Balfour, *Historical Works*, II, 131; HMC, *Mar & Kellie*, I, 141.

8. *RPCS*, second series, I, 337–38, 378–81.

9. Balfour, *Historical Works*, II, 131; *RPCS*, second series, I, 241, 263–65, 359–61.

10. Balfour, *Historical Works*, II, 131; HUL, Maxwell-Constable of Everingham MSS, DDEV/79/H/7; *RPCS*, second series, I, 359, 361, 402.

11. HUL, Maxwell-Constable of Everingham MSS, DDEV/79/D; *RPCS*, second series, I, 248–52, 487–88; Donaldson, *James V to James VII*, 291.

12. *SR*, I, 52, 59, 62; *RPCS*, second series, I, 265–67; HUL, Maxwell-Constable of Everingham MSS, DDEV/79/D; *Mar & Kellie*, I, 153–54. Spottiswood has also figured prominently in the last endeavour to establish an Exchequer Commission — by James VI in 1609 — which had failed through the failure of members to attend in Edinburgh.

13. Balfour, *Historical Works*, II, 138.

14. *APS*, II, 357–58, c.4; Donaldson, *James V to James VII*, 53.

15. *RPCS*, second series, I, 81–82, 150. Comparison of the revenues of the Principality with those of the Crown in the last year of James VI show that Charles receives £704–13/2 as prince, mainly fixed income from feu-duties — less than 0.6% of the £127,365-9/11 which James VI received from the Crown lands and customs. The only major alienation of property from the Principality during his father's reign would appear to have been the lordship of Dunfermline which yielded, over the same period, revenues worth £11.764-1/- for the benefit of his mother, Queen Anne (SRO, Treasury accounts, 1624–25, E 19/22).

16. *RPCS*, second series, I, 228.

17. HMC, *Mar & Kellie*, I, 135–36, 139; *RPCS*, second series, I, 193–94.

18. Row, *History of the Kirk*, 341.

19. *RPCS*, second series, I, 230–31, 351–53; *APS*, III, 281–84, c.2; 431–37, c.8; 439–42, c.14; V, 23–27. c.9–10.

20. SRO, Accounts of the Collectors of the Ordinary Taxation Granted in 1625, 1630 and 1633, E 65/10, /13 & /16. *RPCS*, second series, I, vii–viii, xlix–lii, cliv–clvii.

21. Foster, *The Church before the Covenant*, 157, 162, 164–65; *RPCS*, second series, I, clxx, clxxiii, clxxv. Impoverished ministers were afforded indirect maintenance through relief from taxation, though this benefit did depend on a recommendation from a bishop (SRO, E 65/10, /13/ & /16).

22. Cf. *Reports of the State of Certain Parishes in Scotland, 1627*, A. MacGrigor ed., (Maitland Club, Glasgow, 1835), 191, 193; *Dumbarton Common good Accounts 1614–60*, F. Roberts & I.M.M. Macphail eds., (Dumbarton, 1972), xvii, 30, 42.

23. *RPCS*, second series, I, 160–62.

24. *Ibid.*, I, 230; NLS, Morton Cartulary & Papers, Ms 80, fo. 27; M. Lee jr, *The Road to Revolution: Scotland under Charles I, 1625–37*, (Urbana & Chicago, 1985), 34.

25. *APS*, IV, 541–42, c.9.

26. *Ibid.*, III, 435–36, c.8; IV, 549–50, c.24; C. A. Malcolm, 'The Sheriff Court: sixteenth century and later', in *An Introduction to Scottish Legal History*, G. C. H. Paton ed., (The Stair Society, Edinburgh, 1958), 357–58.

27. I. A. Milne, 'Heritable Rights', in *An Introduction to Scottish Legal History*, 153–54. Although Charles in the first year of his reign increased the revenue which the Crown derived from reliefs, from £1783 to £4875-6/8, this amounted to no more than 2.2% of his ordinary revenues from Crown lands and customs (SRO, E 19/22).

28. Donaldson, *James V to James VII*, 296; Stevenson, *The Scottish Revolution*, 35; Lee Jr, *The Road to Revolution*, 16.

29. *SR*, II, 417, 439, 470; *The Acts of Sederunt of the Lords of Council and Session, 1628–1740*, (Edinburgh, 1740), 3–6.

30. SR, I, 52, 57–58, 72; Balfour, *Historical Works*, II, 138; J. A. Connell, *Treatise on the Law of Scotland respecting Tithes*, 3 vols, (Edinburgh, 1815), III, appendix, 68–71.

31. *SR*, I, 91, 102, 103, 105–06; Row, *History of the Kirk*, 342–43.

32. Sir J. Scot of Scotstarvit, 'Trew Relation of the Principal Affaires concerning the State', G. Neilson ed., *SHR*, XI, (1913–14), 187–88; Balfour, *Historical Works*, II, 151–54; *SR*, I, 109, 117, 119.

33. *APS*, V, 35–39, c.19; SRO, Sederunt Books of the High Commission of Teinds, 1630–50, TE 10/1–2; NLS, Kirklands; Laws, MS 1943.

34. *Large Declaration*, 15.

35. *RPCS*, second series, I, 509–16.

36. *Ibid.*, I, 352; Napier, *Montrose and the Covenanters*, I, 85–86.

37. *RPCS*, second series, I, cxciii; SRO, Sederunt Book of the High Commission of Teinds, 1630–33, TE 1/1; SRO, Cunninghame-Grahame MSS, GD 22/3/785.

38. *SR*, I, 174–75; NLS, Morton Cartulary & Papers, MS 80, fo. 27, 58, 64–65; NLS, Kirklands; Laws MS 1943, fo. 36; Balfour, *Historical Works*, II, 156; *Memorials of the Earls of Haddington*, 148–52.

39. 'Proceedings of the Commissioners of the Kirk at a Meeting held in Edinburgh in July 1627', in *Bannatyne Miscellany*, III, (Bannatyne Club, Edinburgh), 219–24.

40. Scot of Scotstarvit, 'Trew Relation', *SHR*, XII, (1914–15), 76; Morton Cartulary & Papers, MS 81, fo.62.

41. SR, I, 157–59, 160, 182–83, 197, 203–04, 229; RPCS, second series, I, 594–95, 598–99, 638–39; NLS, Morton Cartulary & Papers, MS 83, fo. 18; Balfour, *Historical Works*, II, 155.

42. *SR*, I, 194, 197, 205, 211–13; *Mar & Kellie*, I, 162–63.

43. *RPCS*, second series, II, (1627–28), 195–96, 245–46, 309–11, 318–21, 370–71, 478–80; *The Red Book of Menteith*, II, 3–5.

44. *RPCS*, second series, II, 247–49, 311–13.

45. *RCRB, Extracts*, (1615–76), 266–68; *SR*, I, 221–22; *RCPS*, second series, II, 318, 323.

46. *The Red Book of Menteith*, II, 94; HMC, *Mar & Kellie*, I, 170; *SR*, I, 300. In essence, Charles was relaunching a project of the previous year when the minister and two heritors in each parish had been instructed to assess ecclesiastical resources, a project which met with a rather limited response from around fifty parishes — about a twentieth of the Scottish total (*Reports of the State of Certain Parishes in Scotland, 1627*).

47. Lee jr, *The Road to Revolution*, 56, 59; *SR*, I, 300, 321–22, 324, 333; NLS, Kirklands; Laws, MS 1943, fo.40–41; NLS, Teinds, MS 2708; Connell, *Treatise on Tithes*, III, appendix, 96–101.

48. *RPCS*, second series, III, (1629–30), 53–54, 62–63, 105–06, 151, 162, 165; SRO, Notes from the Sederunt Book of the Teind Commissioners, 1633–50, TE 1/4; SRO, Reports from the Sub-Commissioners of the Presbyteries of Argyll, Dumbarton and Lanark, TE 2/1, /5 &/13; SRO, Register of the Presbytery of Lanark, 1623–57, CH 2/234/1; SRA, Glasgow Presbytery Records, 1628–40, CH 2/171/3A.

49. NLS, Kirklands; Laws, MS 1943, fo. 41; SRO, Sederunt Book of the High Commission of Teinds, 1630–33, TE 1/1, fo. 384–85, 414–15, 425–27, 434–35; SRO, Cunninghame-Grahame MSS, GD 22/3/785; *RPCS*, second series, IV, (1630–32), 416, 438; V, (1633–35), 35–36; *APS*, V, 39, c.19.

50. *RPCS*, second series, III, 293–313; *APS*, V, 32–33, c.14–15; 34–39, c.17–19; NLS, Kirklands; Laws MS 1943, fo. 37–39.

51. *Memorials of the Earls of Haddington*, II, 152–53; HMC, *Mar & Kellie*, I, 159–62; *SR*, I, 321; SRO, Copy Minutes taken from Exchequer Register, 1630–34, E 4/8; *APS*, V, 218.

52. SRO, Southesk Miscellaneous Papers, RH 2/8/13; SRO, Sederunt Book of the High Commission of Teinds, 1633–50, TE 1/2, fo. 8, 12, 26; SRO, Copy Minutes taken from Exchequer Register, 1630–34, E 4/8, fo. 2; NLS, Kirklands; Laws, MS 1943, fo. 5, 43–44, 119, 123, 125; Connell, *Treatise on Tithes*, III, appendix, 237–41; *SR*, II, 657, 796, 826.

53. Stevenson, *The Scottish Revolution*, 37–38; Lee jr, *The Road to Revolution*, 45. The Commission had specified on 29 May 1627 that the Crown was to have an annuity from the teinds rated at 10/- for each boll of wheat, 8/- for each boll of bere (barley), 6/- from each boll of oats, pease, meal and rye. Where oats were of the inferior variety, the

rate exacted was to be 3/- from each boll (NLS, Kirklands; Laws, MS 1943, fo. 37–38). Thus, the higher the rate of commutation for each crop, the lower the proportion the Crown received for its annuity.

54. SRO, Cunninghame–Grahame MSS, GD 22/3/518 &/781; *SR*, I, 387.

55. SRO, Sederunt Book of the High Commission of Teinds, 1633–50, TE 1/2, fo. 17, 23, 28, 31, 35; NLS, Kirklands; Laws, MS 1943, fo. 119; *APS*, V, 38–39, c.19; Connell, *Treatise on Tithes, III, appendix, 222–23, 232–33. Two centuries were to elapse before all teinds in Scotland were valued (A. A. Cormack, Teinds and Agriculture: an historical survey*, (London, 1930), 108).

56. SRO, Treasury Accounts, 1624–25, E 19/22; SRO, Accounts of the Collectors of the Ordinary and Extraordinary Taxations Granted in 1625 and 1630, E 65/10–11 & /13–14; SRO, Mar & Kellie Collection, GD 124/10/340; Sir W. Purves, *Revenues of the Scottish Crown in 1681*, D. M. Rose ed., (Edinburgh and London, 1897), xliv–xiv; *APS*, V, 209. Macinnes, Thesis, I, 195–263, for a full account of the intricacies of negotiations concerning surrenders and teind redistribution. Despite suggestions to the contrary (Makey, *The Church of the Covenant*, 13), Charles had no immediate prospect of diverting revenues from England to promote his Revocation Scheme (F. C. Dietz, *English Public Finance, 1558–1641*, (London, 1964)).

57. SRO, Copy Minutes taken from Exchequer Register, 1630–34, E 4/8, fo. 8–12; SRO, Hamilton Papers, TD 75/100/26/260; SRO, Southesk Miscellaneous Papers, RH 2/8/13; NLS, Kirklands; Laws, MS 1943, fo. 207–11; *SR*, II, 647, 650, 727, 790. James Hamilton, second earl of Abercorn, appears to have been the only temporal lord to instigate a summons — of reduction and improbation — not to prevent, but to regularise, the purchase of superiority by Lord John Ross of Hawkhead and Melville in 1632.

58. SRO, Sederunt Book of the High Commission on Teinds, 1630–33, TE 1/1, fo. 55, 289, 396, 429; Exchequer Act Book, 1634–39, E 4/5, fo. 21–24, 100.

59. Purves, *Revenue of the Scottish Crown in 1681*, 39–40, 50–53, 67, 85–86, 99, 109; SRO, Exchequer Act Book, 1634–39, E 4/5, fo. 3–21, 118–24; *RMS*, VIII, (1620–33), no. 1652; IX, (1634–51), no. 530. Other variants in surrendering occurred in May 1635. The marquis of Hamilton agreed to relinquish his lordship erected from the estates of Arbroath abbey once he secured his baronial rights over the estates of Lesmahagow priory and at a feu-duty reduced by a third. The earl of Abercorn agreed to surrender his right of superiority and privilege of regality over every feuar paying at least 500 merks feu-duty. In return, his lordship (erected from the estates of Paisley abbey) was to remain effective over the rest — that is, all but the most substantial feuars.

60. *RMS*, VIII, no. 780; *SR*, I, 384; II, 806, 866. The only temporal lord to claim legal exemption from the Revocation Scheme was John Sandilands, Lord Torphichen, on the grounds that his lordship had not been erected from the lands and property of any cleric, but from the estates of the Knights Hospitallers of St. John of Jerusalem. His plea was finally rejected in 1636 (*APS*, V, 50, 162–65).

61. SRO, Copy Minutes taken from Exchequer Register, 1630–34, E 4/8, fo. 2–3, 7; *RMS*, VIII, no. 1847; G. A. Malcolm, 'The Office of Sheriff in Scotland', *SHR*, XX, (1923), 305–6. The most flagrant example of protracted negotiations was that concerning the surrender of the bailiary of Kyle in Ayrshire by Sir Hugh Wallace of Cragiewallace; they were actually initiated in the reign of James VI and still not concluded at the close of 1634 (*SR*, I, 39–40; II, 809–10).

62. HUL, Maxwell-Constable of Everingham MSS, DDEV/79/D; SRO, Cunninghame -Grahame MSS, GD 22/3/582 & /777; SRO, Copy Minutes Taken from Exchequer Register, 1630–34, E 4/8, fo. 3, 6–7, 9; SRO, Exchequer Act Book, 1634–39, E 4/5, fo. 21–24, 31, 210; *APS*, V, 219. No serious effort had actually been made from the outset of the personal rule to hinder the transfer of lands held in blench-ferme.

63. Napier, *Montrose and the Covenanters*, I, 83–84; Connell, *Treatise on Tithes*, I, 462–64; NLS, Kirklands; Laws, MS 1943, fo. 118.

64. Macinnes, Thesis, II, 476.

65. SRO, Miscellaneous Ecclesiastical Records, CH 8/83; SRO, Exchequer Act Book, 1634–39, E 4/5, fo. 204, 215–17; SRO, Sederunt Book of the High Commission of Teinds, 1630–33, TE 1/1, fo. 334–35; GUA, Beith Parish MS, P/CN, II, no. 154; *SR*, II, 758–59.

66. Macinnes, Thesis, II, 477.

67. W. Guild, *The Humble Addresse, Both of Church and Poore*, (Aberdeen, 1633), 7–8; SRO, Sederunt Book of the High Commission of Teinds, 1630–33, TE 1/1, fo. 153; NLS, Kirklands; Laws, MS 1943, fo. 43–44, 123; GUA, Beith Parish MS, P/CN, II, no. 140–41; *APS*, V, 21–22, c.5; Connell, *Treatise on Tithes*, II, 279–80; III, appendix, 112–17.

68. SRO, Sederunt Book of the High Commission of Teinds, 1630–33, TE 1/1, fo. 242, 381–82; SRO, Annuity Accounts & Papers, E 52/3; SRO, Annuity of Teinds: Bonds of Caution & Consignation, 1632–35, E 50/1.

69. *APS* V, 32–33, c.15; SRO, Hamilton Papers, TD 75/100/26/998; SRO, Exchequer Act Book, 1634–39, E 4/5, fo. 21–24; *SR*, II, 724, 738, 788.

70. SRO, Disposition of Annuities, 1635–42, E 50/2, fo. 1–89; SRO, Accounts of Annuity due by Heritors, E 52/10; SRO, Exchequer Act Book, 1634–39, E 4/5, fo. 72, 74–75, 77, 101, 130, 137, 139–40, 155–56.

71. W. Ferguson, *Scotland's Relations with England: a Survey to 1707*, (Edinburgh, 1977), 112.

72. *Ibid.*, 111–12; J. Blum, *Lord and Peasant in Russia*, (Princeton, 1972), 168–69, 180–81, 184–87.

73. Napier, *Montrose and the Covenanters*, I, 82.

74. SRO, Sederunt Books of the High Commission of Teinds, TE 1/1, fo. 380–81, 420; TE 1/2, fo. 28–30; SRO, Hamilton Papers, TD 75/100/26/315; R. Baillie, *Letters and Journals, 1637–62*, D. Laing ed., 3 vols, (Bannatyne Club, Edinburgh, 1841–42), I, 7–8.

75. *APS*, V, 400, c.85; VI(i), 199, c.202; 778, c.362; VI(ii), 15, c.35; 244, c.199; 297, c.265; 300, c.274. The Commission for Surrenders and Teinds was resurrected in 1641 as the Commission for the Plantation of Kirks and Valuation of Teinds, and was to continue as the co-ordinating agency for teind redistribution over the next nine years, every heritor being guaranteed the right to purchase his own teinds. The right of every feuar to be quit of superiority and hold his kirklands directly from the Crown was reiterated in 1649; simultaneously, regalian privileges and heritable offices created since 1641 were rescinded and future creations proscribed.

4

Ramifications of the Revocation Scheme

Introduction

The Revocation Scheme did not directly precipitate the revolt against the personal rule of Charles I. Promoted and initially sustained on a basis of class antagonism, the Scheme was not an issue to rally political opposition against royal authoritarianism. Even when antagonisms among the estates gave way to class collusion, such collusion against the accomplishment of revocation was localised and unco-ordinated, being denied a national forum by the infrequency of constitutional assemblies. Nevertheless, the Revocation Scheme was of profound political significance in spreading a climate of dissent which made the management of Scottish affairs by an absentee monarch increasingly untenable. Because its political impact was diffuse rather than concentrated, the ramifications of the Revocation Scheme can primarily be held to account for the continuous disruption of channels of communication, not just between the Court and Scotland but between Edinburgh and the localities. For, the Revocation Scheme was conceived and received as a Court project, promulgated solely on the strength of the king's prerogative, imposed unilaterally on a reluctant Scottish administration and implemented cavalierly with regard to the political nation.

When Charles summoned his leading officials and councillors to Court at the outset of 1626 to discuss the Revocation Scheme and the restructuring of Scottish government, his conduct did little to allay fears about the relegation of Scotland to provincial status. Charles absented himself from the initial discussions which were chaired mainly by his English favourite, Buckingham. Although Charles was present when the Revocation Scheme was covered on 19 January, he attended merely as an observer. His right to a revocation was propagated vociferously by two anglicised courtiers, Nithsdale and James Stewart, Lord Ochiltree, both of whom in the eyes of Scottish officials, 'hes maed shipwrak of thaer awn esteeits'.[1]

Not only leading officials but other privy councillors, including courtiers not party to Charles's original designs, found the initial version of his Scheme unpalatable. Like the nobility in general, few were inclined to comply promptly with directives implementing revocation. The petition of the nobles drawn up at the close of 1626, that the Revocation Scheme should not proceed further without parliamentary consultation, appears to be the first stirring of a movement to impose constitutional checks on the monarchy during the personal rule. The presence of Rothes and Loudoun in the delegation despatched to Court suggests continuity of opposition leadership from the parliament of 1621. Indeed, George Gordon, first marquis of Huntly, felt himself obliged to reassure Nithsdale on 13 December that he was ready to mobilise those 'of my freindship' in the north-east and the central Highlands to counter any who proposed to 'rebel againis his Majestie'.[2]

Nevertheless, opposition within Scotland was not yet formed into a cohesive grouping but was basically freelance; characterised by desultory collaboration from within the Scottish administration to delay if not negate revocation in particular and government restructuring in general. Occasionally, leading officials were prepared to countenance — albeit covertly — more direct action. Charles's choice to communicate his decision to establish a Commission for Surrenders and Teinds was particularly inopportune in this respect. Although no documentary evidence has survived which implicates Nithsdale in the Scheme's conception or formulation, he was among the staunchest upholders at Court of the king's right to a revocation. He had been instrumental in prompting Charles to restructure government and he was still the main rumourmonger at Court maligning the competence of leading Scottish officials. Despite his chronic debts and uncompromising Catholicism, he enjoyed royal protection from both civil and ecclesiastical censure.[3]

News of Nithsdale's coming to Scotland had already occasioned unrest in Edinburgh and his coach was held up by a mob in Dalkeith: nobles with a vested interest in kirklands and teinds being reputedly behind such rabbling. Plans for further intimidation, including personal violence to Nithsdale on his arrival at the Privy Council, cannot be ruled out. However, allegations that his assassination was scheduled as an extramural item on the Council's agenda remain unproven.[4] Nithsdale did not actually attend the Council meetings on 30 January and 1 February 1627, when the Commission for Surrenders and Teinds was first notified and discussed. Whether or not he made any effort to attend the Council, his reception on reaching the capital sufficed to warn him about his unhealthy political prospects in Scotland. By 17 February, he had demitted office as collector-general of the taxation voted in 1625 in order to devote his energies to Charles's policy of military intervention in the Thirty Years' War.[5]

The commencement of the Commission for Surrenders and Teinds on 1 March was attended by a great influx of 'almost the wholl countrey'.[6] The stage was thus set for the continuance of tumultuous lobbying. Undoubtedly the style, direction and lack of political competence which hallmarked the personal rule was straining the credibility of absentee monarchy. Charles's stress on his prerogative, which caused him to disdain the promotion of consensus in Scotland, left him little room for pragmatic manoeuvring. His treatment of experienced administrators was dismissive. He preferred to rely on the advice of courtiers, usually anglicised, whose influence on and experience of the actual working of government was as much vacational as vocational. But relations between the Court and the political nation had not yet deteriorated to the point of constitutional breakdown. It can be contended that Charles was confronted by a more grave and less tractable political situation in England, where the problems of government, though not necessarily insuperable, were of greater order and magnitude.[7]

A British Perspective

Undoubtedly, the growth and frequency of English parliaments since the late sixteenth century had contributed to the evolution of sophisticated procedures to express constitutional dissent, procedures unrivalled elsewhere in the British Isles. Constitutional dissent in England was essentially the product of tensions between central and local government occasioned by increased financial and administrative demands of the Court. Debts inherited from Elizabeth and the rising expenditure of his own government led James I to resort increasingly to financial expedients imposed without parliamentary consent. Parliament was further irritated by James I's steadfast refusal to bargain about the scope of his prerogative. The House of Commons especially was determined to debate any aspect of royal policy which encroached on the subjects' liberties or violated rights of property. It was Charles I, however, who set the scene for the constitutional impasse between monarchy and parliament in the late 1620s by his commitment to a policy of direct intervention in the Thirty Years' War. Parliament refused to vote supply in 1625 and 1626. But Charles pressed ahead with the collection of tonnage and poundage and levied sundry impositions. Albeit Buckingham, the royal favourite, faced impeachment in the parliament of 1626, Charles's right to exact forced loans was strengthened by the Five Knights Case in the following year. Parliament countered in 1628 with the Petition of Right against arbitrary taxation, arbitrary imprisonment, compulsory billeting and resort to martial law. This attempt to define the scope of the royal prerogative was of little practical effect. Charles continued to levy impositions and quashed support in the Commons for civil disobedience by dissolving parliament in 1629, when he embarked upon his eleven-year personal rule in England.

Opposition to the Court in early seventeenth-century England did not necessarily amount to a sustained policy of parliamentary aggression, however. Indeed, the constitutional weighting of parliament's aims and achievements must not be exaggerated, given the piecemeal and particularist nature of constitutional dissent. James I's exercise of his prerogative had not threatened parliamentary enactment as the ultimate source of law in England. He was prepared to dispense and suspend, but not to replace, statute. Neither the Commons nor the Lords had any notion that the king's power should be limited by a written constitution. The Petition of Right, which sought to establish the supremacy of the peace commissions over martial law in the shires and to prevent the establishment of a standing army at parliament's expense, did not attempt a comprehensive definition of the royal prerogative. The leading procedural manoeuvres of the parliamentary opposition after 1625 — such as the appropriation of supplies and the impeachment of ministers of the Crown — were prompted from within Court circles. Counsellors temporarily out of favour viewed parliament as an alternative, but secondary, forum for the provision of correct advice: a situation not totally dissimilar to that which prevailed in Scotland where the extra-parliamentary opposition led by nobles was most potent when supported by leading officials.

Since the powers which accrued to parliament depended more on its capacity to persuade and to coerce, the constitutional impasse of the late 1620s was as much a commentary on the political incompetence of the parliamentary opposition as of Charles I. For the opposition generated in the Commons was only effective when support was forthcoming from the Lords. By 1629, however, the efforts of the Commons to stop forced loans and the levying of impositions had proved conspicuously inept. The assassination of Buckingham in August 1628 and the subsequent ending of the lavish distribution of honours — which had both diluted and distressed the traditional nobility — removed the main grounds for dissent in the Lords. Faced by a divided, disorganised and diminishing opposition, Charles was able to dissolve parliament and retain the political initiative throughout the 1630s. Far from being a strong and thriving institution through its articulation of constitutional dissent, parliament was only to be rescued from political impotence by the intrusion of Scottish Covenanters into English affairs during the Bishops' Wars.[8]

If only for its persistence throughout the 1620s, the parliamentary opposition cannot be discounted entirely in terms of constitutional impact or political principle. The frequency of parliaments during the 1620s afforded a regular national forum for blending local grievances which thus acquired a constitutional weighting that transcended their particularist origins. That there was a gulf between the governing and the governed in England may be attested from the currency of the rival polemical labels 'Court' and 'Country' during the 1620s. Admittedly, the 'Country' represented little more than a loose grouping of the disaffected, notably those displaced from or in search of office. Yet, the label did serve as a rallying point for opposition to the Court within the localities as within parliament. Adherence to the 'Country' was but one aspect — along with puritanism, legalism and even scepticism — which was undermining traditional social values and habits of obedience, such as deference towards the dictates of central government. Nonetheless, support for the 'Country' testified to the spread of a mentality distinctive in ideology, culture and lifestyle from that affected by the 'Court'. Although the 'Country' never formulated a national political programme, it did mobilise local particularism in support of a national ideal: not for parliament to share or wrest power from the Court, but to restore the equilibrium of the ancient English constitution.[9]

Local particularism also conditioned the mentality of the opponents of the Court in Scotland. But the disaffected north of the Border were able to bring into play a more potent message than adherence to the 'Country'. For opposition to the directives of absentee monarchy could be projected as a defence not just of a historical — and nebulous — constitutional equilibrium, but of the immediate national interest and future national identity. The union of the Crowns had made the Scots acutely conscious of and apprehensive about their country's status as a political satellite. Ever since 1603, the spectre of provincialism had haunted the political nation. Furthermore, leading officials as well as disaffected politicians were prepared to deploy the resentment aroused by provincialisation against a monarchy which was becoming more inclined to subordinate the welfare of Scotland to that of England. Successive Venetian ambassadors at the outset of Charles I's reign recorded sharp divisions between the desires of the new king and the pretensions of the Scottish nation. The grounds for disaffection were essentially threefold: Charles's coronation as king of Scots, his foreign policy and, above all, his Revocation Scheme.[10]

Charles's patent disinclination to be crowned first in Scotland was regarded as a slight to the royal house's native kingdom. Albeit a symbolic rather than a substantial grievance, Charles's repeated deferral until 1633 made his coronation a running sore in Scotland for over eight years. A more flagrant illustration of provincialism was afforded by Charles's foreign policy, particularly his direct intervention in the Thirty Years' War: a policy initiated and implemented without consultation north of the Border, albeit the Scots were expected to contribute financially and militarily. In the event, foreign policy was a transitory irritant, being generally discredited by the lack of success which attended British expeditionary forces on the continent. The Revocation Scheme proved the most persistent source of contention throughout Charles's personal rule in Scotland. His failure to introduce the Scheme through a parliament was especially deemed prejudicial to the privileges of the landed classes.

Yet, although nobles in, as well as out of office argued consistently that the king's promotion of revocation lacked parliamentary sanction, they remained reluctant to promote constitutional confrontation with Charles over the implementation of his Scheme. Indeed, Sir John Stewart (later earl) of Traquair doubted that a parliament could adequately safeguard the interests of the nobility. Other estates might well prove compliant to the wishes of the king. Although Traquair was seeking to ingratiate himself at Court, his counsel of 13 August 1627 — in the wake of the contentious first session of the Commission for Surrenders and Teinds — was not that of a time-server but a realist. The nobles were genuinely apprehensive about their ability to mobilise other estates in support of their class interests.[11] Over the next two years, however, the promotion of revocation on the basis of class antagonism underwent a distinct shift — if not a dramatic transformation. Charles's resort to the general submission to ensure the compliance of the landed classes and the subsequent publication of his legal decreet — specifying compensation for superiorities of kirklands, costing and quantifying teinds — confirmed that landed title depended ultimately on the discretionary powers of his prerogative, not on the security of charter. Moreover, the gentry were expected to carry the main burden of service on the sub-commissions within each presbytery from the outset of 1629; service which involved a technically exacting workload as well as anomalous and contentious valuations. The reluctance of the gentry to serve on sub-commissions, of a piece with their disinclination to coerce the nobility into participating in the Revocation Scheme, testifies to a growth of disaffection within the localities, a growth that can be further monitored through provision for parliamentary elections.

From the outset of his reign, Charles had not been averse to nominating 'weell affected' gentry whom he wished elected as shire commissioners in the event of a parliament or convention of estates. Meetings were convened in the shires every Michaelmas for such a purpose. Sheriffs, as conveners of the electoral meetings attended by lesser barons and freeholders, were directed to secure the retention or replacement of commissioners. Few sheriffs, however, had made any effort to secure the return of royal nominees as commissioners for the coronation parliament, provisionally fixed by Charles for 15 September 1628. Although the parliament was postponed, the Privy Council reported on 30 October that there had been opposition in sundry shires to royal nominees which augured 'some contestation and disordour'. In anticipation of a parliament, Haddington sent a special despatch to Court on 7 April 1629. Great numbers were amassing in Edinburgh animated by rumours that the conduct of Scottish affairs was being manipulated to the private advantage of 'some great men of this countrie at Court'. Although the coronation parliament was again postponed, the Council duly reported on 31 December that the Michaelmas elections had been wholly neglected in six out of the thirty-three shires. Such neglect could not be laid exclusively at the door of sheriffs as members of the nobility, but was more an indication of growing solidarity among the landed classes, solidarity directed against the Court in foisting the Revocation Scheme on Scotland.[12]

The Rise and Fall of Menteith

Growing solidarity among the disaffected notwithstanding, the Crown was still politically dominant at the Convention of Estates from 28 July to 7 August 1630. Charles minimised opportunities for dissent by limiting the agenda to items of legislative endorsement. He secured the renewal of ordinary and extraordinary taxation for another four years. His legal decreet of September 1629 was ratified and leading officials, councillors and bishops duly demonstrated 'thair reddiness in furthering my service'. Yet the management of the Convention — attended by forty-three nobles, thirty commissioners from the shires and thirty-two from the burghs, as well as ten bishops and eight officials — was never as untroubled as indicated in formal reports to the Court.

In no small measure, the accomplishment of royal objectives depended on the political astuteness of William Graham, earl of Menteith. The indisposition of the chancellor, viscount Dupplin (formerly Hay of Kinfauns), had allowed Menteith to chair proceedings as president of the Privy Council. On the opening day of the Convention, the thirty gentry representing nineteen shires produced a programme of reform which sought not only the redress of itemised grievances but a general improvement in the conduct of government, central and local. The shire commissioners, supported by disaffected nobles, availed themselves of the national forum provided by the Convention to articulate the widespread apprehensions aroused by the Revocation Scheme. Menteith's response was to weld the majority of councillors along with bishops, courtiers and officials into a cohesive Court party which backed his resolve that the relevance but not the substance of contentious issues was to be debated by the Estates. Once assent had been given to the renewal of taxation, all proposals to redress grievances and improve government were deferred to the consideration of the coronation parliament.[13]

The Convention of 1630 marked the zenith of Menteith's political career. He had been elevated to the presidency of the Privy Council in January 1628, a year after he was appointed a councillor. In February 1628 he was nominated to preside over the Exchequer Commission during the absences of the increasingly infirm Archbishop Spottiswood. By July he was appointed justice-general of Scotland. At the same time as he was accumulating offices, his frequent liaising with the Court won him the general respect and confidence of Charles who entrusted him with the general oversight of royal government in Scotland and a special watching brief over the Commission for Surrenders and Teinds. In essence, Menteith reinvigorated the system of shuttle diplomacy pioneered by the earl of Dunbar in the aftermath of the union of the Crowns. By commuting regularly between Edinburgh and the Court, Menteith kept Charles informed about political developments north of the Border. Conversely, he explained to Scottish-based administrators the intent behind royal directives and exercised a restraining influence when Charles periodically contemplated the purging of nobles from the Council and Exchequer Commission — because of poor attendance records. Indeed, Menteith's energy ensured that royal government in Scotland continued to function — albeit with stuttering competence — during the six years between his admission to the Council and the coronation parliament of 1633.[14]

Menteith's self-effacing claim in the aftermath of the Convention of 1630 that 'my power is small' was actually borne out by his removal from office within three years. His rise to become the most influential politician in Scotland had aroused resentment among the all but eclipsed old guard of Haddington, Mar and Dupplin. Although he had helped to secure the treasurership for William Douglas, eighth earl of Morton in April 1630 and had Traquair confirmed as the treasurer-depute in May 1631, he neglected to maintain good relations with them as with Secretary Alexander (earl of Stirling) at Court.[15] Menteith was to become the most celebrated victim of the factional strife and personal jealousies that had afflicted the conduct of Scottish affairs since the withdrawal of the Court from Edinburgh in 1603. Within the Scottish administration, the main instigators of Menteith's downfall were Sir James Skene of Curriehill, president of the College of Justice, and Sir John Scot of Scotstarvit, director of Chancery. Curriehill resented his judicial position being overshadowed by Menteith's annual appointment as chief justice. Scotstarvit's motives were more complex. He was especially aggrieved that he received little support from Menteith — whom he regarded as his protégé — when he was publicly pilloried for charging exorbitant fees for registering documents. A founder member of the militant vanguard of gentry who favoured the Revocation Scheme, he was acutely aware that Menteith sought to minimise material damage to the nobility. For Menteith, as overseer of the Commission for Surrenders and Teinds, sought to conserve the nobles' estates and resources against untoward pressures from militant lairds no less than meddling bishops.[16]

The political machinations among erstwhile allies that led to Menteith's downfall were actually triggered by his own lack of prudence. In September 1629, Menteith had put forward a claim to the earldom of Strathearn as direct heir-male of David, son of Robert II, a claim to estates held by the Crown since the early fifteenth century that also clouded the royal succession. David, earl of Strathearn, had been the eldest son of the second marriage of Robert II. However, doubts about the validity of the king's first marriage questioned the legitimacy of the current royal house. The delicacy of Menteith's claim appeared to have been settled deftly in January 1630 when he was granted the title of earl but relinquished all rights to the earldom of Strathearn — a renunciation sweetened by compensation of £36,000. Menteith's new dignity as earl of Strathearn was subject to further scrutiny from December 1632, after reports reached the Court — courtesy of Curriehill and Scotstarvit — that the new earl had boasted in his cups that 'he had the reddest blood in Scotland'. The treasonable imputations of this boast were mitigated by Menteith's own admission of imprudence and by intercessions on his behalf by Chancellor Dupplin and Treasurer Morton. Nonetheless, neither the administration in Edinburgh nor Menteith's close associates at Court made any effort to check his subsequent removal from office. In March 1633 he surrendered his title of Strathearn in return for that of earl of Airth. After he had made a submission to Court denying all utterances of having as good a right to the Crown as Charles I, the prosecution for treason initiated by Curriehill was dropped that July. Menteith formally withdrew from public life, stripped of all offices and pensions (worth £6000 annually), in November.[17]

The downfall of Menteith cannot be divorced from the antipathy aroused within the political nation to the principle and practice of revocation. Menteith's projected recovery of the earldom of Strathearn was to be accomplished by the same legal process that Charles I was threatening to use against temporal lords — the summons of improbation and reduction. Charles had been prepared not only to transfer the superiority of the earldom to Menteith, but to support Menteith in prosecuting his right to the whole property of the earldom at the expense of the existing freeholders. Whereas the Revocation Scheme promised to emancipate the gentry, Charles licensed Menteith to reduce all freeholders within the earldom to the status of feuars. The alarm occasioned among gentry well beyond the bounds of Strathearn was used by Scotstarvit as an argument to deny Menteith the earldom. Indeed, the outcry nationally persuaded Menteith to renounce his claims to the earldom while reserving his title as earl of Strathearn.[18]

Arguably, the most critical revelation arising from the downfall of Menteith was the patent incapacity of Charles to protect his leading Scottish administrator. The enforced retiral of Menteith from public life threw into stark relief the growing cleavage between the Court and the Scottish administration. Although Menteith was the only leading official removed from office on account of treasonable accusations, he was not the only counsellor to be so maligned during the personal rule. But the other celebrated victim, James Hamilton, third marquis of Hamilton, was a courtier and royal favourite, not an administrator based in Scotland.

During the spring of 1631 the marquis of Hamilton was accused of being the prime mover in a conspiracy to imprison the king and the young prince (later Charles II), cloister the queen and execute the leading royal advisers in England and Scotland. Reputedly, these objectives were to be accomplished by troops he had recruited throughout the British Isles to fight on the side of the anti-Habsburg forces under the Swedish king, Gustavus Adolphus. Hamilton's leading accuser was James Stewart, Lord Ochiltree, a courtier much given to malicious gossip and regarded as especially malignant by leading Scottish officials for his vociferous advocacy of revocation. Ochiltree's accusations, which sought to play on Hamilton's position as the leading claimant to the Scottish throne outwith the royal house, were motivated by personal jealousy and promoted by factional intrigues among courtiers. For Hamilton's influence at Court was tending to eclipse that of all other Scotsmen. In contrast to the Menteith affair, Charles was able to investigate the treasonable allegations within the confines of the Court. Hamilton was duly pronounced innocent on 29 June 1631, but Ochiltree was subsequently despatched to Scotland to face an indictment for treason. Charges had still not been pressed by June 1633, when a royal warrant confirmed that Ochiltree was sentenced to life imprisonment in Blackness Castle on the Firth of Forth.[19]

That Hamilton retained royal favour was evident from his award of all imposts on wines imported into Scotland for sixteen years from 1 August 1631. This tack of customs, to recompense Hamilton for financing the British expeditionary force under his command, was not rescinded despite persistent efforts at Court to impugn his military performance on the continent. His estates continued to enjoy the financial protection of the Crown during his fifteen-month absence abroad. Menteith, on the other hand, having been obliged to retire from public life, was left vulnerable to legal action by creditors from debts accrued largely in the course of his public service. Foremost among such creditors was John, Lord Loudoun, a prominent member of the disaffected element opposed to the Revocation Scheme as to the whole authoritarian tenor of Charles's conduct of Scottish affairs.[20]

Charles did seek to redress the financial embarrassment endured by Menteith, restoring his pension and promising him £120,000 — in instalments — to cover his arrears from November 1634. Nonetheless, the charge can be laid against Charles that he showed an utter lack of understanding of the importance of Menteith's public service. His failure to find a successor willing to undertake a similar style of shuttle diplomacy on behalf of absentee monarchy produced a hiatus in the management of Scottish affairs. But to contend that Menteith's fall from grace transformed the character of Scottish politics, paving the way for revolution, is to overstate the case.[21] Charles's capacity to govern Scotland for the rest of his personal rule certainly suffered from a lack of an accurate and reliable informant following the political eclipse of Menteith. However, the downfall of Menteith aggravated rather than instigated the growing estrangement between leading officials and the Court. The spread of class collusion within the localities to frustrate the accomplishment of revocation confirmed that government within Scotland was becoming less amenable to royal direction in the wake of the Convention of 1630. More immediately, Charles resorted to managerial overkill with respect to the composition, agenda and proceedings of the coronation parliament from 18 to 28 June 1633.

The Coronation Parliament

The composition of the coronation parliament was almost half as great again as the total number of each estate in attendance at the Convention of 1630 (and nearly double the number attending the Convention of 1625). Yet the task of political management was not to appreciate accordingly. While the voting strength of the burgesses was increased from thirty-one to fifty-one, the additional twenty commissioners merely marked an increase in numbers, not political influence. The increase in shire commissioners by thirteen was testimony more to local inertia than grassroots militancy, since only forty-five out of a possible sixty-four commissioners were actually returned from the shires. Indeed, the tendency of shires failing either to select commissioners or elect royal nominees had escalated in the run-up to the coronation parliament. Two months before its scheduled opening, elections had still to be concluded or validated by the Council in eighteen shires. In the event, nine shires entitled to send two commissioners sent only one, and six shires declined to send any. Even the pronounced increase of nobles, from forty-seven to sixty-five, did not represent a more potent challenge to the Court from the leaders of the political nation. For this rise of eighteen can be attributed entirely to proxy votes, of which at least thirteen were in the hands of leading officials and courtiers. Moreover, the twelve bishops representing the clergy provided a reliable phalanx of support for the Court.[22]

Charles was determined to exact maximum advantage from proxy voting, a medieval practice revived by James VI for nobles and bishops in the parliament of 1617. Although no proxies had been conceded for the Conventions of Estates in 1625 and 1630, all nobles seeking to be excused from the coronation parliament were encouraged to place their proxies at the disposal of the Court. The weighting of proxies in favour of the Court was further enhanced by plural voting. Between them, Traquair, Morton, Stirling and Lennox were to exercise eleven proxy votes. Charles overplayed his hand, however. Like his father before him, Charles had honoured Englishmen with Scottish lordships although they lacked estates in Scotland. Of the five Englishmen without a Scottish territorial qualification duly summoned to the coronation parliament, only one actually attended. But the proxies of the other four were divided between Traquair and Stirling. In the process, the concession of proxy votes was associated with a breach of constitutional practice. Proxies thus became a nationalist issue for the element within the political nation disaffected towards the Court.[23]

Charles was intent on getting his coronation visit over as soon as possible. Accordingly, meticulous preparation went into the packaging of the parliamentary agenda to minimise the scope for dissent. The agenda was not to be restricted to the Court's own legislative programme, completed in February 1633 after two months' drafting by Lord Advocate Hope. The intervening four months before the scheduled opening of parliament were used to establish an elaborate vetting procedure to sift out all bills and petitions critical of the Court's direction of Scottish affairs. On 30 April, the Council was advised that all bills and petitions due to be delivered to the clerk-register twenty days before the scheduled opening should be restricted to those 'as wer fitt to be exhibited or motioned in Parliament'. The role of the clerk-register was to carry out a second stage of vetting prior to the final compilation of a composite agenda by a committee of articles once parliament commenced. Adding a personal element of distrust and suspicion to this further vetting — also practised in 1621 — was the current incumbent of the office of clerk–register, Sir John Hay of Lands (later of Baro), the blatantly career-conscious, former town clerk of Edinburgh. His suppression of a petition presented by presbyterian nonconformists among the clergy led to his being described by the disaffected as 'a suorne enemy to religion and honesty and a slaue to the bischopes and courte'.[24]

The committee of articles was the most crucial vehicle for royal control of parliament. Traditionally charged to compile a composite agenda for the approval of the estates, the committee was elected according to the procedure established by James VI in 1621, which utilised the bishops as the lynchpins of royal control. On the recommendation of the king, the bishops chose eight nobles who, in turn, chose eight bishops. All the bishops owed their position to royal patronage. The eight nobles selected were predominantly, but not exclusively, courtiers. No noble associated with the disaffected element was selected. The eight nobles and eight bishops then chose commissioners from eight shires and eight burghs. Although these latter selections did provide the committee with a representative cross-section of Scottish localities, gentry with a track-record of support for the Court were specifically chosen. As added surety for royal control, Charles designated the chancellor, the earl of Kinnoul (formerly Viscount Dupplin), to preside over the committee. The other eight officers of state present were instructed to attend and vote.[25]

Not content with his inbuilt majority on the committee of articles, Charles resolved not merely to adapt but to range beyond the managerial techniques deployed by his father to minimise dissent in the parliament of 1621. Pending the compilation of the composite agenda by the committee of articles, James VI had allowed the estates to meet separately to discuss matters of common interest, contenting himself with instructions to leading officials to infiltrate these meetings and report disaffection. Contrary to customary practice, however, James had not allowed each estate to peruse the composite agenda twenty-four hours prior to its presentation in parliament. Charles preferred more drastic censorship. All separate conventions of the estates from the initial meeting of the committee of articles on 20 June, until the conclusion of its deliberations eight days later, were banned. The Convention of Royal Burghs, which customarily met when parliament was in session, was suspended. A meeting of the gentry to draw up a remedial programme for royal government was interrupted and dispersed. Intercommuning between the estates was also banned to prevent the disaffected combining. Intercommuning was practised covertly, nonetheless. Some noblemen, sympathetic to presbyterianism, attempted to lobby the king in support of the nonconforming clergy's suppressed petition. A supplication by commissioners from the shires and burghs, attacking the rumoured agenda drawn up by the committee of articles as inimical 'both to Kirk and countrey', was also suppressed.[26]

Charles's management of proceedings following the presentation of the composite agenda to parliament on 28 June was designed to overawe and, indeed, to intimidate the estates. As in 1621, only one day was set aside for the estates to approve the legislative programme. But Charles's packaging of legislation far outdid that of his father twelve years earlier. Although the Five Articles of Perth and likewise the ordinary and extraordinary taxations were presented as single enactments in 1621, the estates were at least allowed to vote specifically for or against them and the other 112 pieces of legislation. At the coronation parliament, the composite agenda was presented for acceptance or rejection as a whole. In total, the legislative programme consisted of 168 measures. No distinction for voting purposes was observed between public enactments and private bills. Thus, any of the disaffected element opposed to such contentious legislation as the ratification of acts touching religion or the extension of taxation or any of the thirteen enactments on the Revocation Scheme, was obliged to oppose such innocuous measures as the final act, the re-edification of the kirk of Beith in Ayrshire.[27]

As in 1621, the voting procedure deployed in the coronation parliament militated against any accurate assessment of the disaffected element. Votes were collected at random instead of being recorded systematically from each estate. Debate was not encouraged. Each individual was asked to shout out his assent or dissent to the clerk-register without giving reasons for his vote. Charles attended in person to reproach dissenters and note their names. Thus, the block-passage of the legislative programme was secured by the opportune use of proxies and plural voting, by dubious tallying on the part of the clerk-register and by the intimidatory presence of the king. Nonetheless, the result in favour of the Court was challenged by the earl of Rothes as spokesman for the disaffected. Although Rothes was obliged to retract on being threatened with a prosecution for treason by Charles, public rumour soon reversed the final outcome in favour of the disaffected — on the grounds that the tally of individual votes cast by persons actually present went against the Court.[28]

Charles I's heavyhanded management of the coronation parliament intensified and extended the scale of dissent within the political nation. The leadership of the disaffected element was not yet prepared to countenance direct criticism of the Crown, however. Charles's reliance on the bishops to secure control of the committee of articles, the alliance of bishops with leading officials to enforce rigorous vetting of the composite agenda and the obvious collusion between leading officials and courtiers to manipulate voting created a common constitutional platform to protest against the direction of parliament 'by the Episcopall and courte faction'.[29] Yet the fund of goodwill created by the royal visit was by no means exhausted when the Court departed from Edinburgh on 18 July 1633. The political nation was not unaware of the discordant events leading up to the king's dissolution of the English parliament in 1629 and had no wish to tarnish the royal visit by provoking a similar constitutional impasse in Scotland. Furthermore, the disaffected element had been given a timely reminder of the military reserves available to the Crown on 29 June, when the Council converted a royal audience with highland chiefs into a general muster of the clans.[30]

Anti-Clericalism

The king's heavyhanded management of parliament nothwithstanding, the most critical mistake arising from the coronation visit was Charles I's failure to restore effective channels of communication between the Court and Edinburgh. In the wake of Menteith's political eclipse, royal government in Scotland was characterised by drift. Yet the expectation at the outset of the royal visit was that James, marquis of Hamilton, now the most influential Scotsman at Court, would emerge publicly as the manager for Scottish affairs.[31]

However, Hamilton's position at Court was neither long established nor omnipotent. He had spent little more than four years of broken service at Court since the outset of Charles's reign. Repeated royal invitations to Court were belatedly accepted in 1628, once he had accrued enough money to settle with his outstanding creditors and secured a royal bounty in excess of £60,000 to offset his anticipated lavish expenditure. Following a fifteen-month absence leading British expeditionary forces on the continent, he had returned to Court in September 1632 hardly covered in glory. His relations with his officers, particularly over pay and the deployment of troops, had not been above criticism from Charles.[32] Moreover, Hamilton did not devote himself exclusively to Scottish affairs at Court. His continental engagement led him to retain a watching brief over international relations which continued after the royal visit to Scotland. Hamilton acted as a broker for the recruitment of mercenaries from the British Isles into the service of Sweden, France and even Spain. He acted as confidant, if not unofficial ambassador, for the king's sister, Queen Elizabeth of Bohemia. From the outset of 1635, he was directly responsible for the Venetian embassy — as much to acquire art treasures as to collate political intelligence about northern Italy.[33]

Charles's delegation of Scottish affairs to Hamilton following the political eclipse of Menteith meant that shuttle diplomacy gave way to a one-way system of clientage for officials, councillors and, indeed, all members of the political nation seeking royal favour. Furthermore, Hamilton's management of Scottish affairs from Court was untrammelled by consultations with the English Privy Council. For Charles, reputedly ever-conscious if not always responsive to Scottish fears of provincial relegation, was determined that his native kingdom should 'not be dishonoured by a suspicion of having any dependence upon England'. Charles thereby isolated himself from the developing realities of Scottish politics and their British ramifications. The king's efforts to retain a measure of credibility for the Court's management of Scottish affairs were not helped by Hamilton's manifest preference for a policy of benign neglect north of the Border, a policy tantamount to the pursuit of quiescent provincialism.[34]

Within Scotland, Charles was forced increasingly to rely on the bishops to uphold the managerial interest of the Court. In turn, the estrangement of leading officials and councillors provoked by the Revocation Scheme gave way to rampant anti-clericalism.[35] Rumour, though by no means the most accurate gauge of public opinion, affords damaging evidence for the build-up of anti-clericalism since the royal visit. Rumour asserted that forty-eight abbeys and priories — in effect all temporal lordships not in episcopal hands at the outset of the Revocation Scheme — were to be restored to the clergy; an eventuality of momentous constitutional as well as political significance. For restored abbots and priors, once allied with the bishops as clerical commissioners, would compose a solid and substantial phalanx for the Court that would facilitate a royal stranglehold over future parliamentary proceedings.[36]

However exaggerated, rumours about the restoration of monastic estates to the clergy were not groundless. Since the autumn of 1634, Charles's principal counsellor in England, William Laud, archbishop of Canterbury, had been in regular contact with Scottish bishops with a view to using the king's annuity from the teinds to buy up temporal lordships. Surrendered temporal lordships had already been bestowed on bishops — notably, to endow the bishopric of Edinburgh from its creation in 1633 and to compensate the archbishopric of St. Andrews for its resultant loss of diocesan territory. Charles was now proposing to confer the abbacy of Lindores on Andrew Learmouth, minister of Liberton, presbytery of Edinburgh. This proposal was politically crass, not least because the intended beneficiary was the son of Sir James Learmouth of Balcomie, an active member of the pressure group who had supported the Revocation Scheme since 1626. Moreover, Lindores abbey was the only temporal lordship actually revoked by legal compulsion.[37]

Lindores was not only to be granted to Learmouth for life, but his tack empowered him to reduce all grants of lands and teinds made while the abbey was secularised. Writing from the political sidelines, the aged Haddington sent a *caveat* to Hamilton on 17 June 1635. The emotive revival of the term 'abbot' in connection with Lindores raised apprehensions throughout the political nation. The gentry were particularly vexed that rights of property were to be placed 'under the discretion of abbots who have but a lyfrent time to enrich their wives and children'. Any systematic restoration of monastic property to the clergy cut across the stated intent of the Revocation Scheme to enable feuars of kirklands to hold directly from the Crown as freeholders. Indeed, the resultant loss of revenue to the Crown from feu-duties and other casualties was reminiscent of the major ecclesiastical foundations of the twelfth century when David I proved 'a sore sanct to the Crowne'. Public rumours were now equating the progress of the Revocation Scheme with the reversal of the Reformation Settlement. No less damaging was the corrosive effect of adverse publicity. The printing of all major proclamations concerning the Revocation Scheme meant that criticisms of Charles I's management of Scottish affairs would not be confined to his native country. For 'Englishmen can read them and understand Scots'.[38]

It was left to Traquair to allay the apprehensions of the political nation by stopping the grant of Lindores abbey passing through the Exchequer. Much to the chagrin of the bishops, Charles's belated approval of this initiative on 24 June 1635 effectively terminated the restoration of monastic property to the clergy.[39] That the Court should have failed to anticipate the furore provoked by Lindores episode and taken no prompt action to defuse the situation not only summed up its distanced handling of the Revocation Scheme but typified its lack of political touch in governing Scotland. Denied a responsive hearing at Court and faced with mounting dissent at home, the will of lay officials and councillors to sustain absentee monarchy was being progressively undermined. Rampant anti-clericalism within the Scottish administration occasionally found expression in blatant obstruction as lay officials and councillors connived with the disaffected element. Thus Lord Advocate Hope covertly advised temporal lords that they should press for the retention of their superiorities and heritable jurisdictions under wadset (mortgage) rather than surrender them irrevocably to the Crown. During 1635, superiorities and heritable jurisdictions were regularly mortgaged back to the temporal lords pending full compensation from the Crown. This circumvention, which exploited the Crown's lack of ready cash to make immediate compensation, was essentially a legal fiction that technically deprived temporal lords of their irredeemable titles but offered them the practical benefit of an indefinite, but assuredly long-term, postponement of revocation.[40]

Lay officials and councillors colluded with the disaffected element not just to nullify projects conceived at Court, but also to check the relegation of Scotland to provincial status. For the ascendant bishops were becoming readily identified with the proposals of Archbishop Laud of Canterbury to ensure greater efficiency, probity and uniformity in royal government throughout the

British Isles: the policy of 'thorough' not only supported but anticipated by Charles I in his efforts to restructure and reorientate local government.

The Justice–Ayres

The stated intent in the king's Revocation Scheme to terminate regalities and heritable offices necessitated the overhaul of local government. The appointment of Menteith as justice-general afforded Charles the opportunity to impose a uniform system of judicial administration better suited to central control and conforming to current English practice. On 28 June 1628, he resolved to reinvigorate the commissions for circuit courts of justiciary — the justice-ayres — according to the model prescribed but never activated by his father in 1587. The kingdom was quartered, with justice-ayres being commissioned for the shires of central Scotland immediately to the south and north of the Forth-Clyde axis, for the Borders and for the north of Scotland. Each commission, headed by two senators from the College of Justice, was to tour no less than seven shires twice yearly. The function of each commission was essentially threefold: to proceed against 'all capital and odious crymes', in effect to try all criminal cases where conviction brought death or mutilation; to try all transgressors of penal statutes where conviction was met by the exaction of fines; and to oversee the competence of local government officers, a supervisory task which conformed to Charles's current deployment of judges of assize in England.[41]

Albeit Charles was not averse to exaggerating the sufferings arising from the partial administration of justice within the localities, the most demanding task of the reinvigorated justice-ayres was undoubtedly to correct if not terminate legal maintenance. Such a task, which required the reformation of customary attitudes as much as the redress of ingrained legal abuses, was demanding both mentally and physically. Charles was duly obliged to modify his extensive remit for the justice-ayres on 8 August. Priority was accorded to the holding of courts in at least two shires once each circuit commenced in October. The plan to hold biannual circuits was never implemented. When the commissions were renewed on 21 July 1629, priority was accorded to the holding of courts in shires not visited in the previous year. Only the Borders were covered fully. In central Scotland there were at least two shires on each circuit for which no provision was made. Seven out of the eleven shires remained unprovisioned on the most demanding, northern circuit.[42]

The lack of specification in the formal indictment of offenders — the uptaking of the dittays — immediately proved contentious. The justice-ayres on their inaugural circuits adhered to traditional practices in accumulating evidence and formulating charges. Following the testimony of leading landowners in every shire, dittays were drawn up citing reputed offenders to appear before the circuit courts. However, the dittays did not inform reputed offenders whether they were indicted on serious criminal charges or for breaches of penal statutes. The commissioners also adhered to the traditional practice of challenging reputed lawbreakers at the bar of the court even though they were not indicted to answer criminal charges. The resultant discontent within the localities was expressed with sufficient virulence for Charles to adopt a more measured approach for the circuits of 1629. Sudden indictments at the bar were abandoned, but dittays to reputed offenders still did not specify charges. The continuing clamour against justice-ayres was only abated temporarily when the Privy Council, on 24 November, reaffirmed its right to hear complaints from the localities.[43]

No less contentious than the uptaking of the dittays was the commissioners' remit to prosecute transgressors of penal statutes. In all there were sixty-four categories of offences liable to prosecution. The retrospective timescale for prosecutions extended in most instances to offences committed since 1621. No such time-limit applied to certain categories considered particularly heinous under James VI — notably, the sporting of firearms, exorbitant usury, the export of gold and silver, and poaching from river and loch. Two other categories were added from the outset of Charles's reign — smuggling to defraud customs and the concealment of 'lent money', the failure to disclose sums borrowed and loaned in the inventories required to calculate the extraordinary tax on annualrents. Because of the outcry over the dittays, the Council reduced categories of penal statutes liable to prosecution in the circuit-courts from sixty-four to twenty-one in July 1629 and prosecutions, other than for particularly heinous categories, were restricted to breaches committed since 31 August 1628.[44]

The Privy Council's support for moderation in dispensing justice through the circuit-courts was disregarded rather crassly by Charles on 18 September 1629. The commissioners were informed that they were to help Sir Alexander Strachan of Thornton effect his administrative patent for the recovery of Crown rents and casualties. Not only were circuit courts to be held at Thornton's convenience, but he was empowered to dispense with prosecutions and exact compositions for all breaches of penal statutes — other than the concealment of 'lent money' — prior to 30 March 1628. He was to retain half of all compositions for his own profit. Thus the judicial powers of the circuit courts were circumscribed in favour of a fiscal entrepreneur. Thornton's administrative patent was the seventeenth-century equivalent of the privatisation of public service — a process already discredited in Jacobean England.[45]

Thornton was convinced that he would treble the income currently available to the Crown from rents and casualties. In addition to the £24,000 to be exacted from all holding from the Crown by ward and relief who had either converted their feudal tenures without royal warrant or had defaulted on paying reliefs, a further £236,000 was to be realised by compositions for unpaid feudal dues, escheated goods of outlaws, rent arrears, renegotiated titles and breaches of penal statutes. Murmurings of discontent within official circles gave way to more forthright criticism once Thornton began exacting compositions in the circuit courts. So zealous was Thornton that 500 compositions were processed through the Exchequer by the conclusion of the justice-ayres for 1629. Such was the outcry from the localities, however, that his patent was suspended after several days of heated debate in the Exchequer Commission and was discreetly shelved in the wake of protests at the Convention of Estates in 1630. Its aggravation of political dissent had more than outweighed anticipated financial benefits to the Crown.[46]

Thornton's patent did provide a precedent for Charles's endeavours to finance his personal rule in England during the 1630s when, much to the consternation of English landowners, he used the court of wards to treble his income from feudal casualties. At the same time, Thomas Wentworth (later earl of Strafford), a vigorous practitioner of 'thorough' as lord-deputy of Ireland, so utilised the court of ward and liveries to augment royal revenues that he threatened to destabilise colonial no less than native Irish landownership.[47]

More immediately, the shelving of Thornton's patent prejudiced the continuance of the justice-ayres. Having been forewarned by Menteith that the circuit courts were proving exceedingly troublesome and unremunerative, Charles instructed the Convention of Estates on 28 June 1630 to grant a general indemnity for all past breaches of penal statutes except the particularly heinous. The circuit courts were also suspended for that year. Their revival in 1631 proved fitful. Priority was accorded to the exaction of compositions from those concealing 'lent money' — at the rate of one-fifth of taxation owed. After deducting legal charges, compositions yielded no more than £12,820-15/7 to the Crown and proved an inadequate check on tax evasion. Cases of tax evasion as well as serious crimes were heard in Edinburgh from 1632, with special *ad hoc* judicial commissions being warranted to curb flagrant, but localised, outbreaks of disorder.[48]

The Peace Commissions

The termination of the justice-ayres did not lead Charles to abandon his plans to make the localities more receptive to central direction. He remained adamant that peace commissions should be revived in every shire and that justices of the peace should assume greater responsibility in running local government. From the outset of his reign, Charles was determined to make the peace commissions in Scotland as effective as their counterparts in England — albeit no commissions had been issued since 1627 and justices were operative in no more than fourteen out of the thirty-three shires. The Convention of Estates in 1625 failed to respond positively to Charles's initial suggestion that a role be found for justices of peace as parochial magistrates — as secular enforcers of the disciplinary censures of the Kirk. Undaunted, Charles decided to place less stress on the judicial powers of the justices sitting in quarter sessions than on their administrative duties. Although the peace commissions where functioning were undermanned, only three justices were needed in each shire to make an administrative decision between quarter sessions.

From the spring of 1626, justices were expected to monitor price fluctuations in local markets, ostensibly to aid the Privy Council draw up guidelines for the mercantilist regulation of the Scottish economy, but primarily to maintain social stability and defuse unrest in the event of dearth. Justices, however, proved reluctant to provide statistical information on market prices, a task requiring diligent and detailed investigation. Nor did they show much enthusiasm in submitting reports to the Council's annual review of protective economic measures. Although ten shires submitted reports that autumn, only eight complied in 1627 and none the following year. Justices were no more compliant when accorded responsibility for conscripting vagrants into the British expeditionary forces during the summer of 1627. The reluctance of justices to undertake such conscription was partly in response to the public disturbances occasioned by press-gangs recruiting indiscriminately that spring. But the justices had also a financial motive — an aversion to indirect taxation. Justices in each shire were expected to draw up lists of all able-bodied men between 16 and 60, noting not only the most capable and the most dispensable but also their requirements for arms and training. The submission of composite lists of recruits threatened to become a collective assessment on peace commissions for the supply of arms.[49]

Although the Convention of Estates in 1630 supported the reinvigoration of the peace commissions in principle, the onerous and politically thankless operation of sub-commissions for the valuation of teinds in every presbytery between 1629 and 1634 prejudiced the willingness of gentry to serve as justices. Nonetheless, Charles had the coronation parliament ratify his father's enactment of 1617 detailing the judicial and administrative powers of the peace commissions. The Privy Council was also authorised 'to inlairge and amplifie' the powers of the justices. Sheriffs, stewards and bailies were duly ordered to submit lists of gentry eligible to serve on peace commissions by 19 December 1633. Less than half the requisite lists were submitted on time. Despite the threat of heavy fines and even outlawry for dilatory local government officers, the Council was still unable to provide nationwide cover when issuing peace commissions for twenty-four shires, two stewardries and three bailiaries on 18 September 1634.[50]

Nonetheless, as evident from their redefined remit and altered composition, Charles was intent on making the peace commissions integral to the running of the localities. Particular emphasis was given to the role of the justices as local informers and watchdogs on behalf of central government. Each peace commission was to act judicially as a collective sheriffship to counter legal maintenance. The sheriff was to continue merely as the electoral officer for the shire and fiscal agent of the Crown. The number of justices appointed initially for each renewed commission, no fewer than twenty and as many as fifty signified that the localities were to be supervised on the basis of at least one justice for every parish. All the convenerships were held by gentry, an affirmation that this class was expected to bear the brunt of the commissions' workload. The inclusion of nobles on most commissions was no more than a courtesy gesture. In contrast, every bishop exercised a watching brief over peace commissions within the bounds of his diocese. The English precedent for episcopal service as justices was thus expanded to cover the role exercised by lords-lieutenant. Whereas the office of lord-lieutenant was bestowed on trusted nobles to enhance their social prestige within the English shires, the Court was not prepared to dispense similar patronage in Scotland given the heritable privileges and pervasive territorial influence of the nobility. A select group of ministers, from one to six on each peace commission, were nominated by the bishops to serve as their willing allies in making the localities receptive to central direction.[51]

The major influence behind the inclusion of the clergy on the peace commissions was Archbishop Laud whose authoritarian zeal for centralisation was already evident in England. His sponsorship of the Book of Orders in 1631 initiated a decade of unremitting pressure by central government on the shires. By renewing the peace commissions according to the English model, Laud intended that Scotland should serve as an experimental area to correct English malfunctions — most notably, the declining commitment of the gentry to serve as justices. The Scottish clergy were to serve as his vanguard in the pursuit of 'thorough' north of the Border. The appointment of ministers as justices duly served as a precedent for drafting Anglican priests on to the English peace commissions to expedite the rating and collection of Ship Money — the most contentious, but remunerative, imposition of Charles' personal rule in England.[52] But the application of 'thorough' to Scottish local government was fundamentally imperialist as well as authoritarian. Laud's aggressive sponsorship of centralisation became identified with the promotion not just of efficiency and probity but of uniformity, which left little room for national diversity. The application of 'thorough' not only carried anti-clericalism into the localities, but aligned the retention of heritable jurisdictions with the defence of national diversity.

Over the next three years, the Council experienced marked difficulties in persuading gentry to serve on the peace commissions. There is limited evidence of close scrutiny being given within official circles to the past record of those nominated justices. Many of the gentry who had served on the sub-commissions in the presbyteries were nominated justices, including some actually removed from sub-commissions because of age and infirmity. In the western shires, the gentry who had served on sub-commissions became the backbone of the peace commissions only if their teind evaluation within the presbyteries had proved reasonably diligent. Although the precedent of involving yeomen on the sub-commissions was not followed, the Council invited a significant proportion of unenfranchised freeholders (35%) to serve as justices for the shires of Dumbarton, Lanark and Renfrew. In turn, the peace commissions were staffed increasingly by kinsmen and local associates of leading nobles.[53] Such staffing, however, tended to be nominal as the Council was obliged to revise and curtail drastically the size of the peace commissions from 25 November 1634, because of the refusal of gentry to serve as justices. So marked was their reluctance to serve that the Council's piecemeal attempts to name replacements included gentry who had persistently refused nomination since September 1634. By 4 July 1637 — only nineteen days before the whole structure of Scottish government was to be found wanting in the wake of the riotous reception accorded to the Service Book in Edinburgh — the Privy Council charged the justices with negligence and dereliction of duty. Service on the peace commissions 'is in effect cassin louse'.[54]

Conclusion

In essence, the failure of the peace commissions to become fully operational three years after their renewal must be seen in the context of a nationwide rejection of Charles's authoritarian designs on Scotland. The actual breakdown of the peace commissions by the summer of 1637 compounded a reaction against the style of absentee monarchy since the promulgation of his Revocation Scheme. In Scotland as in England, a decade of unremitting pressure from the Court occasioned widespread disaffection within the localities that brought about the collapse of the royal agencies for local government. Undoubtedly, the peace commissions in Scotland were relatively less well developed and less integral to local government than their English counterparts. Nevertheless, the reluctance of the gentry to serve as justices was as pronounced in Scotland as in England. Furthermore, the point of breakdown between the Court and the localities was reached three years earlier in Scotland. Indeed, the grievances of the English shires only achieved a national forum in 1640 because Charles was obliged to summon successive parliaments in an attempt to contain and suppress rebellion in Scotland.

The reaction against the restructuring and reorientation of local government, though not triggering off revolt against absentee monarchy, demonstrated the nationwide climate of dissent produced by the Revocation Scheme. In turn, the fall of Menteith, managerial overkill in the coronation parliament and the spread of anti-clericalism as well as the reaction against restructuring signposted the political nation's rejection of the Court's direction of Scottish affairs. In particular, the reorientation of local government in association with the Laudian policy of 'thorough' had endangered national diversity. The imposition of uniformity aroused fears of provincialism, fears made critical by the Crown's economic and religious policies which converted a climate of dissent into a revolt of the disaffected.

NOTES

1. HMC, Mar & Kellie, II, 238–39; HMC, Laing MSS, 172–73. Other discussions were chaired by the Anglo-Scot, James Hay, first earl of Carlisle.

2. 'The Gordon Letters', in *Miscellany of the Spalding Club*, vol. III, J. Stuart ed., (The Spalding Club, Aberdeen, 1846), 217; HUL, Maxwell-Constable of Everingham MSS, DDEV/79/H/7.

3. *The book of Carlaverock*, II, 67–68, 71–72; HUL, Maxwell-Constable of Everingham MSS, DDEV/79/H/7. By the time of his military commission in February 1627, Nithsdale had accumulated debts of £126,265–6/8 (HUL, DDEV/71/1, /78/7 & /173).

4. G. Burnet, *History of My Own Times*, (London, 1838), vol. I, 11; Napier, *Montrose and the Covenanters*, I, 80, 89; *Memoirs of Scottish Catholics during the seventeenth and eighteenth centuries*, W. F. Forbes-Leith ed., 2 vols, (London, 1909), I, 25–26.

5. RPCS, second series, I, lxxv, 507–08, 525–26, 531–32; *The Book of Carlaverock*, II, 442, 594.

6. Row, *History of the Kirk*, 343.

7. M. Lee, jr., 'Charles I and the end of Conciliar Government in Scotland', *Albion*, XII, (1980), 334–36; *The Stuart Constitution, 1603–1688*, J. P. Kenyon ed., (Cambridge, 1966), 7–86.

8. C. Russell, 'Parliamentary History in Perspective, 1604–29', *History*, LXI, (1976), 1–27; K. Sharpe, 'Parliamentary History 1603–1629: In or out of Perspective?' in *Faction and Parliament*, 1–42. The inherent vulnerability of the personal rule, attributed to the lack of a parliamentary context and a national crisis by L. J. Reeve, *Charles I and the Road to Personal Rule*, (Cambridge, 1989), was only exposed by the Scottish revolt which constituted a British crisis.

9. T. K. Rabb & D. Hirst, 'Revisionism Revised: Two Perspectives on Early Stuart Parliamentary History', *Past & Present*, 92, (1981), 55–99; P. Zagorin, *The Court and the Country: The Beginning of the English Revolution*, (London, 1969), 74–10; L. Stone, *The Causes of the English Revolution, 1529–1642*, (London, 1972), 105–08.

10. CSP, Venetian, XIX, 51, 294; XX, 102, 615; E. J. Cowan, 'The Union of the Crowns and the Crisis of the Constitution in 17th Century Scotland', in *The Satellite States in the 17th and 18th Centuries*, S. Dyrvik, K. Mykland and J. Oldervoll eds, (Bergen, 1979), 121–40.

11. NLS, Morton Cartulary & Papers, MS 81, fo. 60; Memorials of the Earls of Haddington, II, 56–57, 165–66.

12. *SR*, I, 209, 291, 296, 301, 319–20, 346, 362; II, 426–27, 505, 545, 573; *RPCS*, second series, II, 385–87, 413, 415, 418–19, 474–76; III, 384–85; C. S. Terry, *The Scottish Parliament: Its Constitution and Procedure, 1603–1707*, (Glasgow, 1905), 41–42. Charles missed a significant opportunity to build up support among the gentry by his refusal to extend the parliamentary franchise to feuars of kirklands prepared to buy out superiority and hold directly from the Crown as freeholders; a refusal which allowed a raw nerve of political frustration to fester in the localities (*RPCS*, second series, II, 419, 440–41).

13. SRO, Cunninghame–Graham MSS, GD 22/1/518; NLS, Morton Cartulary & Papers, MS 80, fo. 76; MS 81, fo. 65; *APS*, V, 208–28; *The Red Book of Menteith*, II, 31–33; HMC, Mar & Kellie, I, 173–74; Scot, *Narration*, 327–29.

14. *SR*, I, 244, 252; II, 529, 550; *The Red Book of Menteith*, I, 340; II, 3–5, 17–18, 31–32, 36–37; Lee jr., *The Road to Revolution*, 46–48, 69–71. Formal recognition of Menteith's role as an intermediary came with his appointment as a member of the English Privy Council in September 1630. Menteith's appointment as justice-general followed the surrender of the office by Archibald Campbell, Lord Lorne, whose retention of the heritable justiceship of Argyll and the Western Isles maintained the house of Argyll's territorial dominance on the western seaboard (*RMS*, VIII, no. 1253; *APS*, V, 77, c.69; 80, c.70).

15. NLS, Morton Cartulary & Papers, MS 80, fo. 68; MS 81, fo. 36, 39, 65.

16. *RPCS*, second series, I, 180, 517–18; IV, 200–04; V, 201–04; SRO, Hamilton Papers, TD 75/100/26/1592; *The Red Book of Menteith*, II, 90–91, 138; T. G. Snoddy, *Sir John Scot, Lord Scotstarvit*, (Edinburgh, 1968), 123–24, 129. Charges having first been raised in the Convention of Estates of 1625, Scotstarvit was not publicly vindicated until February 1634, following an official inquiry that upheld his claim to be restoring fees to their customary level. Chancery fees had been lowered by negligent predecessors, notably his uncle William Scot of Ardross.

17. *The Red Book of Menteith*, I, 339–79; Scotstarvit's 'Trew Relation', G. Neilson ed., *SHR*, XI, (1913–14), 284–96, 395–403; *SR*, II, 531, 649–51, 662–63; SRO, Copy Minutes taken from Exchequer Register, 1630–34, E 4/8, fo. 1, 9; *The Scots Peerage*, Sir J. Balfour-Paul ed., 9 vols, (Edinburgh, 1904–14), I, 133–35.

18. Scotstarvit's 'Trew Relation', *SHR*, XI, 287–88, 295; *The Red Book of Menteith*, I, 363.

19. Burnet, *Memoirs*, 4, 11–13; HMC, Mar & Kellie, I, 181–91; RPCS, IV, 263, 369, 387–88; V, 101; *Selected Justiciary Cases, 1624–50*, vol. I, S. A. Gillon ed., (The

Stair Society, Edinburgh, 1953), 176–77. In an affair known as the 'Incident' of 1641, Hamilton was again to be accused of treason by a Captain William Steward, son-in-law of Lord Ochiltree.

20. *RMS*, VIII, no. 1737, 1754, 2188; SR, II, 499–500, 531, 535–36, 673, 885; Guthry, *Memoirs*, 10; SRO, Miscellaneous Exchequer Papers, E 30/23/7; E 73/8/1; *The Red Book of Menteith*, II, 56–59, 154–55.

21. Lee, jr., *The Road to Revolution*, 126.

22. *APS*, V, 7–9, 11–12, 166, 208; *RPCS*, second series, V, 11–12, 45, 48, 54, 66–67, 100; SRO, Cunninghame-Graham MSS, GD 22/3/785.

23. *APS*, V, 7–8; *SR*, II, 666–67; Rait, *The Parliaments of Scotland*, 185–87. The one Englishman who did attend was Walter Ashton, Lord Ashton of Forfar.

24. Balfour, *Historical Works*, II, 193, 205–07; Row, *History of the Kirk*, 356, 379; Scot, *Narration*, 282, 329–30; SR, II, 634, 642, 648, 662, 665–66, 672; SRO, Cunninghame-Graham MSS, GD 22/1/518. The petition from the clergy was presented by Mr Thomas Hogg who had been deposed from his charge at Dysart for nonconformity by the Synod of Fife in 1620.

25. HUL, Maxwell-Constable of Everingham MSS, DDEV/79/D; D. Calderwood, *The History of the Kirk of Scotland*, vol. VII, T. Thomson ed., (Wodrow Society, Edinburgh, 1845), 488–501; *APS*, V, 6–12; Scot, *Narration*, 293–94, 337–38. The composition of the committee of articles in 1621 was marginally smaller than that of 1633, since only eight as against nine burgesses were chosen and only seven as against nine officers of state were in attendance. Moreover, the deliberations of the committee lasted only three days in 1621 as against eight in 1633.

26. Row, *History of the Kirk*, 366–67; Calderwood, *The History of the Kirk of Scotland*, VII, 492; Scot, *Narration*, 294–95, 336–38; *Large Declaration*, 10; *Memoirs of the Maxwells of Pollok*, W. Fraser ed., 2 vols, (Edinburgh, 1863), II, 232.

27. *APS*, V, 13–165; Calderwood, *The History of the Kirk*, VII, 496–97; Scot, *Narration*, 296–97, 338–39. The legislative programme of 1633 consisted of thirty-four public enactments, eight commissions deferring economic issues and diverse supplications for the consideration of the Privy Council or Exchequer Commission, and 126 private bills ratifying rights and privileges of individuals and institutions — in themselves, a useful means of ensuring that favoured nobles, gentry and burghs supported the composite agenda. In comparison, the programme of 1621 consisted of thirty-eight public enactments, five deferred commissions and seventy-one private bills (*APS*, IV, 596–97).

28. Calderwood, *The History of the Kirk of Scotland*, VII, 490–91; Row, *History of the Kirk*, 366–67; Burnet, *History of My Own Times*, 11–12; *Memoirs of the Maxwells of Pollok*, II, 235–240. *Large Declaration*, 12.

29. Balfour, *Historical Works*, II, 200; E. Hyde, earl of Clarendon, *The History of the Rebellion and Civil Wars in England*, vol. I, (Oxford, 1836), 184.

30. CSP, Venetian, XXIII, 125; *RPCS*, second series, V, 36–37; *The Black Book of Taymouth*, C. Innes ed., (Bannatyne Club, Edinburgh, 1855), 437–38.

31. Clarendon, *The History of the Rebellion*, I, 141–42.

32. Burnet, *Memoirs*, 2–3, 21, 25, 28–29; HMC, Hamilton, I, 74–76, 79–81; SRO, Hamilton Papers, TD 75/100/26/18, /97, /8164; SR, I, 111, 387. Admittedly, his military command was beset by the common ravages of pestilence and land devastation which had severely curtailed his supplies and extended his lines of communication. He was disengaged by Charles I in anticipation of Gustavus Adolphus' refusal to relieve the Palatinate.

33. HMC, Hamilton, I, 83, 91, 93; HMS, Hamilton, II, 29, 34–35, 43. Hamilton ran the Venetian embassy through his brother-in-law, Lord Basil Fielding. Their joint endeavours as art entrepreneurs had only limited success. Fielding's selection of paintings showed no great discrimination — despite an attempt to secure a Raphael for Charles I. Bulk shipments usually damaged the paintings in transit.

34. *Diary of Sir Thomas Hope of Craighall, 1634–45*, T. Thomson ed., (Bannantyne Club, Edinburgh, 1843), 5, 11–14; Clarendon, *The History of the Rebellion*, I, 149, 195.

35. Row, *History of the Kirk*, 395–96; Scotstarvit, *The Staggering State of Scottish Statesmen*, 61.

36. Sir W. Brereton, *Travels in Holland, the United Provinces, England, Scotland and Ireland, 1634–35*, E. Hawkins ed., (Chetham Society, London, 1844), 100–01. The rumours recorded by the much travelled Englishman, Sir William Brereton, were gleaned from conversations with disaffected gentry and presbyterian ministers in Edinburgh during June 1635.

37. Baillie, *Letters and Journals*, I, 429–30; *SR*, Ii, 691–92, 711, 724, 739, 795–96; *RMS*, VIII, no. 2225. Charles had already bestowed the lands and rents of the abbey of Soulseat on the newly created parish of Portpatrick, within the presbytery of Stranraer, following the admission of Mr James Blair by September 1630. Unlike Lindores, Soulseat had never been erected into a temporal lordship, being one of the two lay commendatorships still extant at the accession of Charles I. It was not until January 1632 that the Exchequer Commission confirmed that the heritors of Soulseat were to pay their feu-duties and teinds directly to Blair (SRO, Copy Minutes Taken from Exchequer Register, 1630–34, E 4/8, fo. 7; *RPCS*, second series, I, cxlvi).

38. SRO, Hamilton Papers, TD 75/100/26/315.

39. Baillie, *Letters and Journals*, I, 6–7; Spalding, *Troubles*, I, 45.   40. Scotstarvit, *The Staggering State of Scottish Statesmen*, 110; HMC, Laing MSS, I, 195–96. A rabid anti-cleric whose pension was consistently in arrears, Lord Advocate Hope was always struggling to win acceptance as a principal actor in affairs of State. He felt that his personal integrity as well as the dignity of his office was slighted by the way proceedings were conducted by the Commission for Surrenders and Teinds, which summoned him to give legal opinions but otherwise excluded him from discussions (*Diary of Sir Thomas Hope of Craighall*, 11, 22, 47, 61; *RPCS*, second series, II, 180–81; *SR*, I, 239, 275, 393; II, 725).

41. *RPCS*, second series, II, 345–47, 420–22, 434–39. James VI's model for the justice-ayres was actually based on the Elizabethan judges of assize. As the conscious expression of his desire for uniformity in both kingdoms, Charles instructed the Exchequer Commission in July 1628 that all judges on circuit were to be furnished with the same scarlet robes as the judges of assize in England. In the event, Menteith had to furnish the robes out of his own pocket (*SR*, I, 295–96, 398).

42. *RPCS*, second series, II, 434–36; III, 225–27. The right of lords of regality to repledge from circuit courts threatened the Crown with loss of income from fines for breaches of penal statutes as well as the persistence of legal maintenance with respect to serious crimes. Accordingly, the lords or their bailies were directed to sit with the commissioners on every circuit whenever their regalian rights were affected (*SR*, I, 314).

43. SRO, Cunninghame-Graham MSS, GD 22/3/787; *RPCS*, second series, II, 436–39; III, 358; *APS*, V, 219–20.

44. SRO, Cunninghame-Graham MSS, GD 22/3/579; *RPCS*, second series, II, 122–23, 137–38, 182–83; III, 257–59, 314–16; *RCRB*, Extracts, (1615–76), 235.

45. *SR*, I, 216, 318, 340, 377, 396; R. Ashton, *The English Civil War: Conservatism and Revolution 1603–1649*, (London, 1978), 44–49.

46. SRO, Cunninghame-Graham MSS, GD 22/3/582, /777; Napier, *Montrose and the Covenanters*, I, 26–32; *APS*, V, 219; *SR*, I, 318, 350–51. The reception accorded to Thornton's commission made Charles wary of further proposals to augment the income the Crown derived from casualties in Scotland. The suggestion of a former clerk in the Exchequer, Mr George Nicoll, that £360,000 could be gleaned from casualties (six times more than projected by Thornton) imputed gross mismanagement and peculation on the part of royal officials. Not surprisingly, the assessment of Nicoll's claims by

leading officials and councillors in December 1632 recommended severe censure and punishment. Condemned, but never actually tried by due process of law, Nicoll was sentenced by the Privy Council on 5 March 1633 to be pilloried, whipped and banished for life to the continent as 'ane false calumnator and liar' (*RPCS*, second series, V, 8, 21–22, 30–31, 37–39, 58; HMC, Mar & Kellie, I, 179–81).

47. Stone, *The Causes of the English Revolution*, 122; M. MacCurtain, *Tudor and Stuart Ireland*, (Dublin, 1972), 134.

48. SRO, Cunninghame–Graham MSS, GD 22/3/582. /785; SRO, Accounts of Compositions for Concealled Rents – taxation ordinary and extraordinary, 1621 and 1625, E 65/12; SR, II, 444–45, 458, 484–85; *RPCS*, second series, IV, 12.

49. *RPCS*, second series, I, 93, 160–62, 172, 178, 270–72, 276–80, 478, 507, 518, 524–25, 529–30, 537, 547–48, 658–60, 670–75, 677–78, 683–85; II, 73, 88–91, 313–14, 363, 553–57, 615–16; NLS, Morton Cartulary & Papers, MS 80, fo. 65; *The Book of Carlaverock*, II, 93–94.

50. *APS*, V, 142, c.25; 219–20; SRO, Cunninghame-Graham, GD 22/1/518; *RPCS*, second series, V, 173, 378; VI, (1635–37), 222–23. A further eighteen months were to elapse before peace commissions were finally issued for the shires of Renfrew, Kincardine and Clackmannan. There would seem to be no extant record of the remaining defaulters submitting lists.

51. *RPCS*, second series, V, 228, 378–91; SRO Hamilton Papers, TD 75/100/26/965; Ashton, *The English Civil War*, 49–54.

52. L. M. Hill, 'County Government in Caroline England, 1625–40', in *The Origins of the English Civil War*, C. Russel ed, (London & Basingstoke, 1975), 66–90; H. R. Trevor-Roper, *Archbishop Laud, 1573–1645*, (London, 1962), 231–32.

53. Macinnes, *Thesis*, II, 479–80.

54. *RPCS*, second series, V, 409, 424–30; VI, 21, 36, 56–57, 78, 175–76, 378, 426, 449, 453, 472, 481. Despite a statutory fine of £40 for every unexcused absence, no marked improvement in the willingness of the gentry to serve as justices resulted. Fines could only be levied if the absentee's excuse was not accepted by his colleagues. Central government's resort to systematic fining was ineffective against collusion on the part of justices to cover up absenteeism.

5

Economic Nationalism

Introduction

The heavy-handed maxim which guided Charles I from the outset of his reign, 'itt is better the subject suffer a little than all ly outt of ordor', was particularly applicable to his conduct of economic policy.[1] Charles I wished to promote uniformity throughout the British Isles by espousing mercantilism. Native manufactures were to be protected against rival imports and exports nourished by monopolies, commercial restructuring and tariff reform. As well as bullion, supplies of gold and silver coin were to be built up. Mercantilism — in essence, the pursuit of economic nationalism — required political muscle and was espoused primarily to promote English interests at the expense of the Dutch, whom the Scots regarded more as commercial allies than competitors. Moreover, the pursuit of uniformity, set against the Crown's failure to secure sound money in Scotland, was profoundly damaging to the economic prospects of the political nation. As well as undermining the competitiveness of Scottish goods abroad and occasioning recession at home, uniformity stimulated nationalism within Scotland when the demands of the Court were clearly seen to diverge from the national interest. The nationalistic impact of economic policy during the personal rule has hitherto been seriously underplayed.[2]

Charles I was not insensitive to the parlous state of the currency at the outset of his reign. In an effort to remedy the wholesale export of Scottish specie, the chronic shortage of native currency and the excessive reliance of foreign dollars for domestic exchange, a plethora of remedial proposals were presented to the Convention of Estates on 1 November 1625. The Estates opted to restrict exports of Scottish specie to pay for luxury goods from the continent. Because the state of the currency was a complex issues, the Estates also selected a committee — of eight nobles, eight gentry and three bishops, together with burgesses from Edinburgh, Dundee, Aberdeen and Glasgow — to recommend a definite course of remedial action to the Crown.

Despite the inclusion of nobles of the stamp of Rothes, Loudoun and Balmerino, and the prolongation of deliberations until the summer of 1627, the select committee was merely a consultative body which always met under the tutelage of the Privy Council. Nonetheless, the Council's deliberations with the select committee did serve to sharpen political awareness about the national importance of economic issues in general, not just the state of the currency. The lack of initial consensus between councillors and committee members led to deliberations being augmented from the spring of 1626 to include all interested parties among the nobility and gentry, the latter estate being represented by commissioners from fourteen shires. Simultaneously, the remit of the deliberations was broadened to cover not only the desirability of restraining unnecessary imports, but also the expediency of imposing corn laws, continuing exports of coal and salt under licence, restricting exports of livestock and monitoring prices of staple commodities in domestic markets. Deliberations were thus conducted according to a mercantilist agenda.

Support for protective measures, if not for the whole mercantilist agenda, was evident when the Privy Council was moved to impose corn laws on 20 April 1626. Corn laws, to accommodate the relative scarcity or plenty of grain supplies, not only sustained the buoyancy of landed incomes, but offset fears within official circles that the recurrence of dearth on the scale of 1623 would occasion endemic disorder, even rebellion. Official fears were fanned by vociferous petitioning by the Convention of Royal Burghs in favour of protectionist measures to preserve native manufactures, notably of woollen and leather goods.[3]

No definite action was taken to remedy the state of the currency, however. The Privy Council held no more than cursory discussions on the coinage during the summer of 1626 and repeatedly prorogued its meetings with the select committee until the spring of 1627. Following the resumption of lengthy discussions, the Council was moved to record on 16 June that it was still neither meet nor expedient to devalue the native currency, to adjust exchange rates or to restrict the circulation of foreign dollars. Over the next eighteen months, lack of official resolve on remedial action did nothing to diminish the flow of foreign dollars into Scotland or curtail their circulation at inflated rates in domestic markets. Debased and clipped dollars were imported mainly through east-coast ports, either as a direct result of trade with the German states or indirectly through the Low Countries, notably from the acceptance of German dollars in place of bullion or 'rix-dollars' by coalowners and saltmasters on the Firth of Forth. Official indignation was expressed that the additional varieties of German dollars introduced recently into Scotland abetted much dishonest dealing. Counterfeiting opportunities were increased and merchants were able to exploit lack of public knowledge about international exchange. Although it was deemed desirable to restrain future imports, there was a tacit acceptance that foreign dollars of doubtful provenance would continue to circulate surreptitiously. For the Council decreed on 17 February 1629 that the 'rix-dollar' should be taken as the international standard for allowing or discharging their circulation. All efforts to impose restraints on foreign dollars over the next twelve months duly proved ineffective.[4]

Attempted restraints on importing dollars ran counter to the interests of the main earners of foreign currency, the coalowners and saltmasters. The best-connected political lobby in the early seventeenth century was possessed of a collective determination to ensure customs rates remained unchanged in Scotland after 1612 and that attempts to place embargoes or impose exchange restrictions on overseas sales were rendered ineffectual. Obliged to export under licence from 1608, the coalowners and saltmasters were intent on maintaining the export orientation of their trade. Above all, they were adamant that no cost advantage should accrue to English competitors through the erosion of tariff differentials between both kingdoms. Thus, the Convention of Estates on 2 November 1625 was moved to reject outright a royal proposal that a discriminatory custom of 48/- should be imposed on every ton of coal exported from Scotland in foreign ships.[5]

Having petitioned the Crown to establish clear guidelines for the export of commodities under licence, the royal burghs became entangled in acrimonious discussions with the coalowners and saltmasters. Differential rates favouring Scottish merchants and domestic consumers were thrashed out during the expanded discussions between the select committee and the Privy Council on 20 April 1626. This meeting established a rapport between the coalowners and the mercantile community which was to endure for as long as the personal rule. More significantly, this meeting evinced the first traces of an accord among councillors and the lay estates that economic policies should take account of the national interest no less than that of the Crown. No action was taken to implement the king's proposal of 13 June that native traders pay an additional impost for the privilege of exporting coal under licence, an impost that was to be doubled for strangers shipping coal from Scotland. Separation of the national from the royal interest was enhanced by Charles's direct intervention in the Thirty Years' War, which led France and Spain to impose trade embargoes inhibiting imports of necessities like salt for fish-curing as well as luxuries like wine. In turn, widespread scepticism greeted Charles's claim of 18 September 1627 that national defence necessitated an impost of 2/- on every ton of exported coal and salt in order to refurbish the coastal fortifications along the Firth of Forth. Little effort was made to uplift this impost.[6]

Financial Liabilities

The strategic aims of economic policy notwithstanding, Charles I was confronted by a perennial shortage of ready cash to meet his escalating expenditure. The extensive feuing of Crown lands since the fifteenth century, allied to the continuing impact of inflation from the sixteenth century, had undoubtedly eroded the capacity of the Crown to meet routine as well as occasional expenditure out of its ordinary income. Nonetheless, while fixed monetary duties depreciated as commodity prices rose, the Crown was partly cushioned by provendar rents and the increased customs and imposts derived from the expanding volume of trade in the early seventeenth century. But the liberal, if not profligate, dispensing of patronage by James VI in his declining years compromised the capacity of the Crown to honour its financial commitments. Out of his first year's ordinary income of £223,930-7/4, Charles had inherited a recurrent commitment of £159,091-11/8 for pensions, fees and allowances.[7]

Instructions to retrench having proved of no avail over the next three years, Charles commanded Treasurer Mar on 26 November 1629 to conduct a vigorous inquiry into the management and disposal of Crown rents and revenues. Mar's investigation revealed that expenditure on pensions had risen by £11,342-13/4 and arrears had been accumulating steadily to £116,080-7/6. A sum in excess of £51,000 was outstanding for fees and allowances. Moreover, as Charles was according courtiers priority in the payment of pensions, fees and allowances, Scottish-based administrators were expected to bear the brunt of mounting arrears with little immediate prospect of remuneration. At the same time as the recurrent debts of the Crown were accumulating, its ordinary income had fallen to £196,608-13/-. Charles's declarations of war, against Spain in 1625 and then France in 1626, had led to significant losses in customs and imposts.[8]

Indeed, Charles's resolve to intervene directly in the Thirty Years' War made the Crown's perennial shortage of ready cash a chronic problem. An interim audit of the land tax of £400,00 authorised by the Convention of Estates in 1625 revealed that £384,314-4/- had already been assigned by 22 March 1628. With two years' levies still to be collected, the bulk of the land tax was committed to military expenditure. The actual revenue raised through the land tax in the previous two years amounted to no more than £243,046-18/7, the deficit being in part offset by a subvention of £53,467-9/4 from the tax on annualrents. The rest of the shortfall was met by borrowing £100,000 from William Dick (later of Braid), merchant-burgess of Edinburgh. The supply voted in 1625 was finally audited in July 1634. £579,863-10/6 had been collected from the land tax and tax on annual- rents. All but £6,060-17/- was committed to repay and service loans.[9]

The interim audit of 1628 had been occasioned by the resignation of Sir James Baillie of Lochend as collector-general of taxation in November 1627. Baillie had resigned after only nine months in office to allow his personal fortune to recuperate. Instead of his receiving prompt remuneration as the leading Scottish creditor of the Crown, the escalating costs of the military programme had served to increase his financial liabilities. Lochend's tribulations as collector-general, coupled to the partial payment of fees, pensions and allowances, demonstrate that under Charles I officeholding in general was becoming a financial liability.[10]

The traditionally hazardous post of treasurer remained particularly unrewarding. Mar relinquished office in the spring of 1630 with no more than a promissory note from the Exchequer Commission that the £120,000 he had expended in the king's service would be accorded priority over all pensions, fees and allowances. The principal drain on his finances were the sums borrowed, in anticipation of the coronation visit, to remedy the state of disrepair in which royal houses and palaces were languishing. In the event, officials were obliged to borrow a further £200,000 from merchants, principally William Dick, to finance the coronation.[11]

Having appointed the earl of Morton as treasurer in April 1630, Charles made repeated overtures on the need to cut back pensions, fees and allowances. Morton's first three years in office, however, witnessed a marked rise in recurrent expenditure. Pensions alone increased in excess of £30,000 and the total debts of the Crown accumulated to £852,870. This accumulated deficit far outstripped the ordinary revenues of the Crown. The audit of the treasury accounts in August 1634 disclosed that the king's income had more than recovered the ground lost through the disruption to trade and, with the ending of embargoes, had risen by £41,772-18/3 over the past five years to £238,381-11/3. Nevertheless, since £260,164-3/1 was committed to routine expenditure, £21,582-11/10 had been added to the Crown's burden of debt. Indeed, the Crown's accumulating deficit was only kept in check by annual subventions of around £100,000 from the taxation authorised by the Convention of Estates in 1630. Audits completed in July 1634 revealed that treasury officials received £403,269-0/6 over the previous four years to meet the most pressing needs of the Crown from the total sum of £592,411-18/2 realised by the land tax and the tax on annualrents. Of the remainder, all but £15,138-7/11 was committed to repay and service loans.[12]

Such reliance on borrowing proved an acute political embarrassment as well as prejudicial to sound financial management. Strategic objectives of economic policy were not the most pressing concern within the Scottish administration. Leading officials also accorded a low priority to the systematic recording of income and expenditure. Their main concern was to relieve themselves and their associates of debts contracted on behalf of the Crown. Because the management of royal revenues was characterised by procrastination, dilatoriness and partiality, leading officials were smeared as bankrupts or as fraudulent manipulators of the machinery of government. Moreover, the preference accorded to courtiers in the payment of pensions, fees and allowances left the Court open to charges of parasitical behaviour at the expense of the political nation.[13] At the same time, recourse to taxation subjected the king's economic policy to detailed scrutiny, notably with respect to strategic objectives as well as financial returns. Two particular projects — monopolies and the common fishing — cemented opposition among commercial and landed interests.

Monopolies

The main stimulus to solidarity among the disaffected element in the Convention of Estates in 1630 was provided by the burgh commissioners. Their claim that monopolies and patents were an insupportable burden on the nation and should be recalled elicited concerted support among the lay estates, particularly when their attack was directed against the patent for tanning leather granted to John, Lord Erskine, the eldest son of the earl of Mar, the recently retired treasurer.

Erskine's patent, granted in 1620, was intended to promote the reform of leather manufacture over the next thirty-one years. In return for an expected outlay of £20,000 to improve the tanning process and import seventeen skilled workers from England, Erskine was conceded the right to exact a stamp-duty on every hide of tanned leather marketed in Scotland, whether produced domestically or imported. This stamp-duty was set at 4/- for the first twenty–one years of the patent, falling to 1/- thereafter. Erskine was equipped with vigorous powers of enforcement.

The Convention of Royal Burghs remained unconvinced about the superiority of the new tanning process. The stamp-duty was regarded as excessive. The complaints of the burgess estate against Erskine's patent having been taken up by the gentry in the Convention of Estates in 1625, Charles conceded that trials should be conducted under the auspices of the Privy Council to establish the superiority of the new process. This task was not accomplished until March 1629, when a panel of master craftsmen (shoemakers) pronounced emphatically in favour of Erskine, who proceeded to bring a series of prosecutions against refractory native craftsmen who adhered to traditional tanning methods.[14]

Nonetheless, complaints about the excessive rates of stamp-duty continued. Its exaction affected not only the prosperity of craftsmen and merchants in royal burghs, but also squeezed the profit margins of tanners in rural commmunities, undercutting their capacity to pay rent to their landlords. Hence, the burgh commissioners were accorded a sympathetic hearing from the landed classes present at the Convention of Estates in 1630. Although the Estates recommended further review rather than outright rejection of his patent, Erskine was placed on the defensive. Despite his dogged prosecution of refractory native craftsmen over the next five years, Charles conceded in May 1634 that Erskine's patent should not be renewed. His exaction of stamp-duty was again the subject of official scrutiny in June 1635, though a further six years were to elapse before the Covenanters terminated Erskine's patent and all other contentious monopolies.[15]

Monopolies in general and Erskine's patent in particular had a more immediate constitutional significance. In response to the specific demands of the royal burghs for their recall, monopolies were referred to the scrutiny of select committees by the Convention of Estates in 1630. Service on the select committees brought together a core of disaffected activists. Of the eleven nobles, twelve lairds and seven bishops who served on the committees scrutinising monopolies, all but three were also involved in committees considering the king's controversial proposals for a common fishing. While the select committees for monopolies and the common fishing drew extensively upon the service of eight out of ten bishops and seventeen out of the thirty-four gentry attending the Convention, of greater import was the involvement of only sixteen out of the forty-eight nobles and the total absence of leading officials. In effect, the select committees became uncensored outlets for dissent, affording the disaffected among the nobility — notably Rothes, Loudoun and Balmerino — free reign to organise and exchange views with the gentry and burgesses. By propagating the distinction between the economic policy of the Crown and the national interest, the select committees began a decisive shift away from compliance with the Court towards collusion among the disaffected; a shift consolidated by ongoing discussions between the Privy Council and the committee appointed by the Estates to review the common fishing.[16]

The Common Fishing

On 30 July 1630, Secretary Alexander (later earl of Stirling) read out a missive to the Convention of Estates intimating that negotiations were to commence within Scotland, as within England and Ireland, 'to sett up a commoun fishing'. Charles I was adamant that the fishing rights 'which properlie belong to our imperiall crowne' should be exploited solely by his subjects within the British Isles. His determination to advance economic uniformity through the common fishing was mercantilist — to emulate and, above all, to replace the Dutch who dominated deep-sea fishing in the North Sea.[17]

Integral to the maintenance of Dutch supremacy was an accommodation authorised by James VI in 1594. The Dutch were granted access to Scottish waters provided their fishing busses did not intrude within a kenning (the equivalent of twenty-eight land miles) from mainland shores. The Dutch regarded the herring fishing in the North Sea as a major contributor to their national prosperity, meriting protection by as many as forty warships. Their highly capitalised and technically advanced fleet was held up as a model of enterprise, strategically and commercially, in serving as a nursery for sailors, a proving ground for navigators and a stimulus to shipbuilding. More pertinently, their deep-sea supremacy, coupled with their cavalier attitude towards territorial limits, was a constant source of friction with the English whose commercial rivalry with the Dutch extended from herring fishing in the North Sea to whaling in the Arctic.[18]

Lacking the capital or technical expertise to compete realistically with the Dutch herring busses, Scottish fishermen tended to concentrate on inshore fishing. In effect, the accommodation of 1594 placed Scottish fishing on a complementary footing to the Dutch deep-sea ventures. Scottish fishing communities, located mainly in the royal burghs of the north-east, Fife and the west, were only just beginning to exploit the hitherto untapped fishing resources of the western isles and the Minches when Dutch busses first began to appear regularly off Lewis in the 1620s. Rumours that the Dutch were intent on establishing a fishing base on the island were well founded. Colin MacKenzie, first earl of Seaforth and landlord of Lewis, was intent on promoting Stornoway as the prime fishing port on the west coast. Dutch fishermen were invited to settle in the burgh of barony, paying ground rents and landing dues to Seaforth. The deployment of superior Dutch capital and expertise in inshore waters as well as deep sea was a threatening prospect for the Scottish economy in general as well as native fishing communities in particular. No fewer than 800 and as many as 1500 boats, ranging from four to six tons and employing around 6000 men, were engaged commercially in inshore fishing during the 1620s.

By March 1629, the Privy Council had been won over by the alarmist propaganda manufactured by the Convention of Royal Burghs. Seaforth was censured for having allowed twelve Dutchmen to settle on Lewis. As neither Seaforth nor the Convention was prepared to make concessions, however, the issue was referred to arbitration at Court by a despairing Council in March 1630. At the outset of July, Charles seemed to be favouring the royal burghs by cancelling Seaforth's patent to develop Stornoway. Accordingly, the commissioners for the burghs attending the Convention of Estates at the end of that month were caught unawares by the king's detailed instructions for a common fishing.[19]

The common fishing was deliberately not promoted as a unitary joint-stock company, but as a confederation of provincial fishing associations based on the chief towns and cities in the British Isles. Each provincial association was expected to attract its own investment from local adventurers. A select group of prominent adventurers from Scotland, England or Ireland were to form a council charged with drawing up regulations governing the conduct of the provincial associations and, subsequently, with resolving any differences arising between them. This corporate structure was modelled on the College of Herring Fishing which met yearly to regulate the operations of the Dutch fleet. Since the provincial associations were to have free access to the coastal waters around the British Isles, the adventurers were all to be native or naturalised subjects of the king in Scotland, England or Ireland. In the North Sea, the herring fishing was to commence off Orkney and Shetland in June and continue along the Scottish and English coasts until late January. Herring and white fish were to be pursued continuously throughout the year around Ireland and the Hebrides.

The projected deep-sea fleet of 200 busses, ranging from 30 to 50 tons, employing around 1600 men and boys, required a massive capital outlay. The total charge to build, equip and operate 100 busses was estimated as £72,000 sterling (£864,000). But the gross profit from one year's fishing for herring and white fish was expected to realise £194,000 sterling (£2,328,000). The net profit in the first year of operations — after allowances had been made for such recurrent costs as tackle, barrels, salt, wages and victuals — was anticipated to be £82,707 sterling (£992,484). If all 200 busses were built, the net profit was expected to double. Significantly, no figures were given for the anticipated return to the Crown in royalties and customs. However, the common fishing was launched against a background of constitutional impasse between Crown and parliament in England and growing diplomatic rapprochement with Spain at the expense of the Dutch. Such a background would suggest that a substantial financial return was expected for the political capital Charles was investing in the common fishing.[20]

The Convention of Estates was not content simply to ratify the king's missive. For, the common fishing was conceived at Court, fashioned according to English mercantilist aspirations and intended to open a window of opportunity into Scottish territorial waters at the expense of the native fishing industry as much as the Dutch. The instruction that a commission should be appointed to act for Scotland in negotiating the common fishing was referred to select committees, first for deliberation and then comment after liaison with the Convention of Royal Burghs, which remained in session in Edinburgh for the duration of the Convention of Estates. The committee charged with commenting on the instruction reported on 7 August 1630 that the inshore fishing was the customary, proper and sole preserve of Scottish fishermen. Under pressure from leading officials and councillors, further liaison between the committee and the Convention of Royal Burghs produced the concession that the burghs would enter an association with the English to fish twenty-eight miles beyond mainland shores, provided they were given exclusive licence to develop new stations in the Hebrides, such as Stornoway. The Convention of Estates proceeded to appoint seven nobles, nine gentry, two bishops and ten burgesses — in effect the members of the select committees on the common fishing — to act as a committee of review for the negotiations at Court.[21]

The Council's appointment of a seven-man commission to negotiate for Scotland was not announced until 10 August, three days after the dissolution of the Convention of Estates. Its composition was loaded in favour of leading officials and courtiers. Only Mr John Hay, town-clerk of Edinburgh and the lobbyist despatched by the royal burghs to Court in July 1629, had participated in the select committees on the common fishing. During the initial round of negotiations which commenced at the end of September 1630, the Scottish commissioners did take cognisance of comments at the Convention of Estates, particularly the select committee's resolve to maintain an exclusion zone for inshore fishing. Their counterparts, however, being exclusively English officials and courtiers appointed by and answerable only to Charles, were determined to promote the common fishing to sustain the king's claims to sovereignty around the British Isles. Indeed, the English commissioners were prepared to rely on the king's prerogative to secure the proposed association of adventurers unrestricted and exclusive access to inshore as well as deep-sea fishing off the Scottish coasts.[22]

In order to ensure greater compliance on the part of the Scottish commissioners, Charles directed them on 12 October to secure plenary power from the Privy Council. In a personal postscript, he affirmed the common fishing to be 'a work of so great good to both my kingdomes' that the furthering or hindering of the venture 'will ather oblige or disoblige me more than anie one busines that hes happened in my tyme'. Over the next few weeks, councillors not noted for their diligent attendance were exhorted to turn up at the scheduled discussions between the Scottish commissioners, the Council and the committee of review.[23]

The negotiating commission was duly refashioned on 11 November. Its composition was increased to eight with the addition of another leading official

(Treasurer Morton). The committee of review, having canvassed opinion within the political nation since the dissolution of the Convention of Estates, was able to exert sufficient political muscle to ensure that the national interest should not be swamped by the king's British aspirations. In turn, the Council was persuaded that the refashioned commission should insist upon safeguards. While the 28-mile exclusion zone was still to remain in force for the Dutch and other foreign fishermen, members of the association, whether natives of England or Ireland or naturalised subjects, were to be allowed to fish up to fourteen miles off the Scottish mainland. The Council was also moved to issue a vigorous assertion of separate national identify. On their return to Court, the refashioned commission were to represent to the king 'the prejudice which this kingdome susteanes by suppressing the name of Scotland in all the infeftments, patents, writts and records thairof passing under his Majesteis name and confounding the same under the name of great Britane altho ther be no unioun as yitt with England'.[24]

Such uncharacteristic assertiveness on the part of the Council can be attributed partly to resentment simmering since the union of the Crowns about the neglect of Scottish affairs at Court, but primarily to the widespread fears within the political nation about the imposition of economic uniformity. The common fishing was the thin end of a wedge designed to relegate Scotland to the provincial status of Ireland. Indeed, Irish interests were not represented directly at the negotiations, but were encompassed within the remit of the king's English officials who exhibited little concern for their advancement.[25]

Once negotiations resumed at Court in March 1631, the refashioned commission did not interpret their instructions to insist upon specific safeguards as binding. Indeed, the Scottish commissioners were prepared from the outset to defer to the wishes of the English in redrawing Scottish territorial limits. Over the next sixteen months, Charles intervened personally and frequently to minimise concessions. Although Charles was prepared to concede that the salmon fishing should be wholly reserved for the royal burghs, the exclusion zone was reduced to two sectors of inshore waters by 31 July 1632 — namely, the firths of Forth and Clyde, encompassing the waters from St. Abb's Head to Redhead on the east coast and between the Mulls of Galloway and Kintyre on the west. The ability of the Convention of Royal Burghs to mount a rearguard action was further compromised when Mr John Hay, their lobbyist at Court, redefined his role to become the Court lobbyist to the Convention. Rewarded first with the knighthood, Sir John Hay of Lands was duly appointed clerk-register in December 1632.[26]

Charles did make one superficial concession to appease Scottish sensibilities. Two charters were drawn up on the conclusion of negotiations to allow the common fishing to be authenticated separately in Scotland and England. Niceties of protocol notwithstanding, the format of incorporation of the general association for the common fishing adhered to the structure outlined to the Convention of Estates in July 1630. The common fishing was instituted as a confederation of adventurers organised in self-financing, provincial associations subject to the common regulation of a council. Of the 152 adventurers enrolled as original members of the general association, twelve were designated councillors. The remainder composed the commonty of fellows. The governing council of twelve — on which the Scottish and English nations were represented equally — was appointed by and removable at the pleasure of the Crown. The commonty of 140 — composed of equal numbers of Scottish and English adventurers — was elected for life, but fellows could be removed and added at the discretion of the Crown and governing council.

The six Scots appointed to the governing council had all been commissioners for Scotland in the negotiations at Court. Among the Scots elected to the commonty of fellows, all but twenty were burgesses. Their election was not so much a measure of their commitment to the common fishing as a testimony of their determination to remain involved in the industry since the general association was granted a monopoly over the catching, processing and marketing of fish throughout the British Isles. A more telling indicator of Scottish commitment is the fifty nobles, gentry and burgesses appointed to the select committees on the common fishing by the Convention of Estates in 1630. Only thirteen joined the commonty.[27]

Lack of commitment to the common fishing was especially evident in the ongoing forum for discussions on economic policy afforded by the Privy Council. Plenary sessions involving the committee of review and the royal burghs had been held at Perth in September 1631, in the midst of the negotiations at Court and again at Edinburgh in November 1632, after the registration of the general association. The plenary session on 22 September 1631 was preceded by a propaganda campaign generated by the Convention of Royal Burghs — tantamount to a seventeenth-century cry of 'it's Scotland's fish' which equated the vitality of the native fishing industry with the national interest. As well as drawing on the public resentment aroused by the Crown's sponsorship of the general association of adventurers, nobles and gentry receiving ground rents and landing dues were especially targeted. Since the prime fishing grounds around the British Isles were off the Scottish coasts, there was a general antipathy to English adventurers being conceded any greater privileges than Dutch, French or Spanish fishermen.

The commissioners negotiating for Scotland attended the next plenary session in Edinburgh on 17 October 1632. No formal attempt was made to censure them for their neglect of the national interest. Nor was any attempt made to amend or reject the charter of incorporation for the general association of adventurers. Nevertheless, the contents of the charter did afford the disaffected element specific guidance on the imposition of constitutional checks on an absentee monarch. Charles had insisted that the Crown must ratify all laws and ordinances promulgated by the governing council to ensure that they 'be not contrarie nor derogatorie to the statutes, Laws, Liberteis or acts of parliament of his Majesteis kingdomes'. In turn, the governing council was to review the decisions and ordinances of the provincial associations to ensure that they 'be not repugnant and contrarie to the lawes, acts of parliament nor statutes of his Majesteis kingdomes'. This emphasis on constitutional safeguards for the national interest was to resurface as an integral component of the National Covenant of 1638.[38]

In the event, no more than three provincial associations were formed all headed by English officials who had negotiated the general association for the common fishing and were duly appointed to the governing council. All three were to be noted less for their commercial accomplishments than for their financial difficulties. Their debts consistently outstripped paid-up subscriptions. Subscriptions of venture capital amounting to £22,682-10/- sterling (£272,190) had been promised in 1633. But only £16,975 sterling (£203,700) was paid up by members of the general association by 1637, of which £2047-7/10 sterling had to be returned to offset annual losses admitted from 1635, when pressing commitments were well in excess of £13,000 sterling (£156,000). Recurrent costs on equipment and manpower — for no more than 20 busses built by the general association — necessitated borrowing in excess of £8250 sterling (£99,000). An additional assessment on members having realised only £6142-13/4 sterling, the general association was on the brink of bankruptcy by August 1638. All capital invested had been used up and a deficit of £21,070-5/- sterling (£52,843-6/-) accumulated.[29]

That the general association was on the brink of bankruptcy cannot solely be attributed to inadequate funding. Indigenous Scottish circumstances militated against its success. The separatism of native fishing communities was bolstered by the determination of the royal burghs to retain control over fish processing and marketing. The lack of wholehearted co-operation from the Scottish administration was manifest in their tolerance of inhospitable conduct by landlords and chiefs in the western isles, whose tenants and clansmen were unleashed on fishing stations and even sea lochs to disrupt the activities of the provincial associations should there be any reluctance to pay ground rents and landing dues. Seaforth was merely the foremost among landlords and chiefs prepared to harbour the Dutch and other foreign fishermen prepared to pay higher ground rents and landing dues. By March 1637 the governing council had all but abandoned fishing activities around the western isles.[30]

External factors cannot be discounted in explaining the failure of the common fishing. The herring busses of the provincial associations were subject to sporadic preying by piratical Dunkirkers as well as Dutch warships. The loss of six busses helped precipitate a financial crisis for the governing council by 1635. Continuing Dutch disregard for his claims to the seas around the British Isles led Charles to conclude, by 1636, that his imperial rights could best be enforced by licensing rather than resisting the incursion of foreign vessels. The Privy Council, however, had made no meaningful effort to implement licensing by October 1637, when Traquair, the treasurer-depute, was pressing Hamilton for a policy reappraisal at Court. Charles had at least received £1500 annually from the customs on fish exported from Scotland through the royal burghs prior to 1633. No foreseeable profit could be expected from the common fishing which 'is nou leik to cum to nothing for want of right government'.[31]

Fiscal Retrenchment

Although Traquair's office had been formally subordinate to that of Morton since 1630, the treasurer's preference for life at Court meant that his impact on the management of royal revenues was incidental rather than integral. Initially, Traquair had been content to build up his reputation at Court as an official adept at mobilising ready cash, specifically by ensuring the prompt transfer of taxation into the treasury. Following the political eclipse of Menteith in 1633, however, Traquair was intent on establishing himself as the foremost, Scottish-based administrator and second only to Hamilton in counselling the king on Scottish affairs.[32]

Far from being an exponent of greater efficiency, probity and centralisation in the management of royal revenues, Traquair was a pragmatist of limited scruples. He was not an exponent of 'thorough' in Scotland comparable to Archbishop Laud in England or Thomas Wentworth in Ireland.[33] Traquair was unable to terminate the king's dependence on taxation, far less ensure that Charles could live off his ordinary income. Indeed Laud, who interpreted his admission to the Privy Council during the royal visit of 1633 as a licence to intrude sporadically in Scottish affairs, remained unconvinced about the treasurer-depute's reliability as a financial controller. Traquair, with the assistance of Sir John Hay of Lands as clerk-register, was intent on using the judicial powers bestowed on the Exchequer Commission by the coronation parliament — to decide the validity or invalidity of charters which had formerly been regarded as the preserve of the College of Justice — to promote fiscal retrenchment and his own political aggrandisement. Ostensibly, retrenchment was to be accomplished by the rigorous application of revocation to recurrent expenditure. In practice, retrenchment enabled Traquair to pay pensions, fees and allowances selectively to extend his political patronage while irregular audits were used to embarrass rivals within the Scottish administration.[34]

Charles I had directed the coronation parliament to declare all pensions, fees and allowances void save for ten specified awards — a concession, worth around £54,0000 annually, weighted heavily in favour of courtiers. Charles subsequently conceded on 2 August 1633 that pensions, fees and allowances would be ratified after their validity had been scrutinised, a process which took over two years and generated much ill-will within the Scottish administration. The validation process served primarily to demonstrate Traquair's capacity to expedite or delay payments of arrears. Financially, the crisis of liquidity afflicting the Crown was eased only temporarily. Although no more than £109,973 of expenditure on pensions, fees and allowances had been authorised by August 1634, the Crown's recurrent commitments remained around £256,511.[35]

The promotion of fiscal retrenchment was carried a stage further in the summer of 1634 by the operation of two committees. The committee of inquiry into the running of the Exchequer (seven nobles, two gentry and four bishops) predominantly drew its membership from the committee of audit (fifteen nobles, three gentry and four bishops). Both committees were loaded in favour of the nobility as of Scottish-based officials and councillors. Under the direction of Traquair, the committee of inquiry was less intent on cataloguing managerial malpractices than on rectifying unnecessary expenditure. The committee established that recurrent expenditure actually stood at £335,159. £78,648 was required annually to service the debts of the Crown, which totalled £922,087 by August 1634. The committee of audit duly revealed that the Crown's financial managers and tax collectors were neither corrupt nor grossly inefficient — merely, that accounting procedures were slow and not markedly zealous or precise. Unrecovered taxes from the levies authorised in 1625 and 1630 ran to £100,955-7/3 (8.6% of accredited income) in July 1634 — a sum subsequently reduced, after rectifying omissions in the tax rolls, and threatening, fining and exacting compositions from tax evaders to no more than £31,597-7/7 (less than 3% of accredited income.[36]

In November 1634, Traquair deployed the judicial powers of the Exchequer Commission to reduce the tack of the customs granted six years earlier to a consortium of Edinburgh merchants and their associates in Glasgow and Aberdeen. This tack had been set for fifteen rather than the customary five years during the wars with Spain and France. Its yearly return of £54,000 was allegedly as much as £3600 below the going rate in time of peace. Accordingly, the customs' tack was reset to William Dick of Braid for an annual duty of £60,000 and an entry fee of 20,000 merks (£13,666-13/4). Despite official attestations that the five-year tack had been reset to the highest bidder, Traquair had been less concerned to maximise royal income through competitive tendering than to ensure that the customs were farmed to an individual of undoubted means with a proven record of advancing money to the Crown.

Moreover, Dick of Braid had already assented to elaborate financial negotiations masterminded by Traquair to revoke the king's gift of the impost on wines to Hamilton for sixteen years from August 1631. Hamilton was prepared to make a voluntary surrender once Traquair had convinced Charles that the gift was financially imprudent. Hamilton had been further favoured by his appointment of collector-general of the taxation authorised for six years by the coronation parliament. Compensation was not finalised until July 1634. Hamilton was authorised to lift a sum totalling £720,666-13/4 from the readiest available taxes — £480,000 for surrendering the imposts; £200,000 for taking over the king's coronation debts to Dick of Braid; and the remaining £40,666-13/4 for clearing off arrears and paying pensions. Dick of Braid, who had farmed the imposts for a yearly return of £74,666-13/4 to Hamilton, was confirmed as principal tacksman.[37]

The resultant improvement in royal revenues was more immediately discernible in managerial rather than financial terms. The confirmation of Dick of Braid as the principal tacksman of both the customs and imposts enabled the Exchequer Commission to exercise strict oversight of his sub-contracting to local mercantile consortia. The treasury also secured ready advances of cash for the routine financing of government. Nonetheless, the deficit of £21,582-11/11 recorded in the treasury accounts in August 1634 had increased to £29,652-6/11 by November 1635. Traquair's pursuit of fiscal retrenchment notwithstanding, expenditure continued to outstrip income by £7467-16/9, albeit the ordinary income of the Crown had more than doubled to £439,197-11/2 by November 1636. Moreover, Hamilton had to wait two years before he could commence recouping the sums promised him in July 1634. An interim audit of taxation in August 1636 disclosed a deficit of £124,181-12/5, even though Hamilton had been commended for his zeal by Charles in securing £733,674-8/9 from the first year's levies and advances from eight leading burghs.[38]

In the meantime, Archbishop Laud, in concert with Scottish bishops, was drawing up plans to insinuate the principle of 'thorough' to make financial management in Scotland 'conforme to that of Ingland'. The committee of audit appointed in February 1634 was purged in May 1635. The new committee — of eight nobles, eight gentry and five bishops — not only terminated the absolute majority of nobles but marked a distinctive shift away from Scottish-based administrators in favour of courtiers and Laud's supporters among the bishops. Traquair was dropped. The recasting of the Exchequer Commission in the summer of 1636 consolidated Laud's influence. Whereas two bishops and eight nobles had been appointed to the Commission in 1626, the balance was altered on recasting to four bishops and one noble.[39]

At the same time, the resignation of Morton as treasurer afforded Laud further scope for insinuating 'thorough'. Having already secured the appointment of William Juxon, bishop of London, as treasurer in England, his preferred candidate for Scotland was a leading acolyte, John Maxwell, bishop of Ross. However, lay officials and their associates at Court were becoming increasingly alarmed by Laud's episcopal vanguard. Moreover, the appointment of the aged and infirm Spottiswood, archbishop of St. Andrews, to the office of chancellor in December 1634, the first cleric to hold the post since the Reformation, had provoked a public outcry against clerical influence on civil government. Riding the rising tide of anti-clericalism, Traquair, supported at Court by Hamilton and Lennox, outmanoeuvred Laud. But his promotion to treasurer checked neither the Crown's pursuit of economic uniformity nor the growing cohesion of the disaffected element as evident from the nationwide resistance to tariff reform.[40]

Tariff Reform

Although Traquair was not personally sympathetic to the disaffected element, who regarded him with absolute distrust, he was prepared to use their platform — the need to safeguard the national interest — to counter Charles I's plan to equalise customs throughout the British Isles. When Charles recommended in April 1636 that the tariffs on all commodities exported from Scotland be increased from 5% to 7% of their rated value, Traquair demurred. Such an increase would erode the cost advantage enjoyed by staple goods in continental markets. Furthermore, tariff reform was supported by Archbishop Spottiswood and Laud's episcopal vanguard who used their influence on the Exchequer Commission to suggest that tariffs be increased by as much as 2.5% from November 1636.

To pre-empt a sharper rise, the Convention of Royal Burghs had actually accepted the 2% increase in July. Over the next four months, however, the royal burghs expeditiously mobilised support among the landed classes whose rent rolls would suffer through the loss of commercial competitiveness. The Convention affirmed that the national interest demanded no higher custom be imposed on staple commodities. Plaiding and linen cloth were the major employers of labour outwith agriculture. The poor quality of these textile products meant that their commercial viability depended on costs being kept low. Salmon and herrings already suffered from a plethora of riparian dues and petty customs compounded by the high risks of consigning this trade overseas. Hides and skins were only marketable abroad because of their cheapness. As with the other staple commodities, trade was dependent on exports because of limited domestic demand from manufacturers as well as consumers. The national interest also demanded exemption for the carrying trade, notably in hides and skins imported from Ireland pending shipment to the Baltic and eastern Europe. That the Exchequer Commission — or at least its majority lay membership — was duly persuaded by this argument was borne out on 12 December. Not only was exemption granted to staple commodities and the carrying trade, but a partial exemption was accorded to the droving trade. The customs on all beasts exported on the hoof was to rise by only 1%.[41]

On 23 December 1636, eleven days after the tack for the new augmentation of customs was put out to competitive tender, Traquair accepted the offer of Dick of Braid which promised an additional 40,000 merks (£26,666-13/4) annually for the Crown over the next three years. On paper, the qualified 2.5% rise in customs represented a 44% rise in income for the Crown. Traquair was conspicuously less successful in farming the new augmentation on the impost of wines. The augmentation of £4 on the impost of £32-8/- per tun was offered for tender at the same time as the augmented customs, but not actually set — again to Dick of Braid — until November 1637. The £102,000 promised annually over the next five years was equivalent to a 36.6% rise in income from a 12% rise in imposts. However, both augmented tacks were overtaken by the deteriorating political situation, though the Crown did secure advances of £153,000 from Dick of Braid over the next twelve months.[42]

That Charles, on 28 December 1636, should congratulate Traquair on his great care and industry in effecting tariff reform, 'without grievance to the people', underlined the absentee monarch's lack of political touch in Scotland. Not only had tariff reform threatened the competitive edge of Scottish goods in overseas markets but, in relation to the trade in coal and salt, had actually induced recession. Indeed, Traquair himself had repeatedly warned the Court of this very danger since the spring of 1634. Despite Traquair's warnings about the subordination of Scottish to English interests, his principal correspondent at Court was reluctant to intercede with the king. As well as being a prominent coalowner and saltmaster in Scotland, Hamilton had extensive coal mines and salt works in the north of England. Moreover, having exploited his position as royal favourite to further his personal and family fortune by investing in a whole range of commercial ventures in England, Ireland and the American colonies, he was reluctant to compromise his standing at Court by troubleshooting on behalf of his native country.[43]

An anonymous report circulating at Court around 1634 underscored the national importance of the interdependent trades in coal and salt. Coal and salt were worth around £650,000 annually, provided a livelihood for above 30,000 people and made a major, if incalculable, contribution to the provisioning and clothing trades. Of the 100,000 bolls of salt manufactured each year, three-fifths were exported, earning (at 40/- per boll) £160,000. A further £160,000 was realised yearly by the export (at £4 per ton) of 40,000 tons of coal, about four-fifths of total production. Although bulk exports to the United Provinces were shipped in Dutch convoys, as many as 260 ships were engaged regularly in carrying coal and salt to other continental and English markets. As each Scottish ship carried on average 100 tons of either product, carriages (at 10/- per ton) were worth £156,000 annually, a sum which more than offset the imports of the superior sea salt from France and Spain essential for fish curing. The trade was export-led because of tariff differentials between Scotland and England.[44]

As part of Charles's continuous search for income during his personal rule in England, an additional impost on coal exports (4/- sterling per chaldron) came into effect from February 1634. Because this impost ceded further cost advantage to Scottish traders, Charles came under sustained English pressure to subject Scottish coal to a like impost. Charles informed the Privy Council on 22 February that an impost equivalent to 6/- sterling per Newcastle chaldron was to replace the existing custom (10/- per chalder) on bulk exports of Scottish coal. Although there was no standard Scottish measure for coal, the Council came up with a notional equivalent of 57/8 per chalder, which amounted to a drastic sixfold reduction on the cost advantage hitherto enjoyed by Scottish traders. At the same time, concerted petitioning by coalowners, saltmasters and royal burghs led the Council to support discreet lobbying at Court which secured a modified increase. Charles conceded on 3 June that the custom on bulk exports was only to be doubled to 20/- per chalder. The cost advantage enjoyed by Scottish traders was nonetheless reduced from almost nine — to little over fivefold. The erosion of the tariff differential, coupled with the greater risk of piracy by the Dunkirkers on the longer sea voyage from the Forth, induced Dutch convoys to switch back to the Tyne. No Dutch convoys having visited the Forth since the summer of 1635, Traquair informed Hamilton that the export trade in both coal and salt had undergone 'very great decay' by October 1637.[45]

Economic recession was compounded by Charles's determination that the access of Scottish salt to English markets should be restricted. This proposal was rejected outright by the Privy Council, under sustained pressure from the coalowners, saltmasters and the royal burghs when first mooted in June 1631. On its revival in November 1635, Charles appeared to defer to Scottish sensibilities by proposing that the production and wholesale distribution of salt throughout the British Isles was to be regulated by separate Scottish and English associations of saltmasters and traders. The reluctance of Scottish saltmasters to participate in negotiations was duly confirmed by the format of incorporation despatched from Court on 21 April 1636. The proposed Scottish association was not just modelled on, but subordinate to, the English association established the previous December.

Although the Scottish association was to have exclusive rights over wholesale distribution as over the production of Scottish salt, a strict quota was placed on bulk exports to England and tariffs were equalised between both countries. Given that Dutch convoys had deserted the Forth, the quota of 8000 weys (equivalent to 80,000 bolls) sought to redirect, not expand, the volume of Scottish exports. The directing of Scottish saltmasters and traders into greater dependence on English markets was compounded by the new custom on each wey which, at 10/- sterling (£6) in both countries, eliminated the twelvefold cost advantage enjoyed by Scottish traders in continental markets. Simultaneously, the impost of 50/- sterling (£30) on every wey of salt imported into the British Isles doubled the current cost (at £3-6/8 per boll) of salt used for fish curing in Scotland.[46]

In short, the format of incorporation for the Scottish association reaffirmed that the mercantilist policy of the Crown subordinated the Scottish to the English economy. Six months were to elapse before Traquair was able to mobilise sufficient support from saltmasters and traders to launch the Scottish association as a regulated monopoly from December 1636. The English association, however, had embarked on an aggressive campaign to squeeze Scottish traders out of the lucrative wholesale market in the populous southern counties and out of London in particular. Shipments of Scottish salt were regularly refused landing facilities at Yarmouth and other southern ports. No meaningful effort was made to restrict the number of wholesale traders admitted to the English association. New members were encouraged to compete directly with Scottish traders. Traquair duly warned Hamilton on 3 January 1637 that the inchoate Scottish association was 'so much opposed and crossed be ye Inglische' that the well-established trade in Scottish salt was facing ruin. Although an attempt was made to reach an accommodation between both associations at Berwick on 28 April, the Scottish saltmasters broke off negotiations because of the 'unreasonable demandis' of the English to limit imports of Scottish salt.[47]

Unsound Money

The Court-induced economic recession, which preceded the outbreak of political troubles in Scotland, revived fears about endemic social disorder. The imminent likelihood of widespread redundancies among the native workforce coincided with the nationwide spread of plague (probably smallpox) and followed on from two years of agricultural dearth during 1635–36. Economic problems were compounded by Charles's promotion of inferior copper coin, the unwelcome transfer of Nicholas Briot from the English to the Scottish Mint and a swingeing devaluation of silver coin whose cumulative impact was to make sound money unobtainable throughout his personal rule.[48]

Following extensive submissions from the Scottish Mint and the Convention of Royal Burghs, supplemented by frequent soundings at Court, the Privy Council held plenary discussions on the state of the coinage in January 1633. No definite programme for remedial action emerged, however. The Privy Council did strive for consensus on the best way to restrain imports of foreign dollars and augment stocks of native coin with minimum disruption to the country's commerce. Charles I, for his part, was determined that discussion on the coinage should not be continued in the coronation parliament. The management of the money supply and the ordering of exchange rates were 'aspects of the prerogative royall' which did not require the consent of the Scottish Estates.[49]

Charles was particularly concerned to curtail discussion because of the outcry occasioned by inferior copper coin whose minting was first authorised in February 1629. Charles, taking advantage of Spain's temporary stop in minting which had relaxed the international demand for copper supplied mainly from Sweden, had commissioned the coining of 500 stone of copper into 1d and 2d pieces. Charles was responding to pleas from the royal burghs that the scarcity of currency for small-scale exchange required a re-issue of the traditional 'turners'. But the initial amount coined proved insufficient. At the same time, the issue of 'turners' encouraged the exodus of native silver coin from domestic markets. Rather than impose on imports of foreign dollars, Charles compounded the problem of bad money driving out good by his directive of 26 August 1631 that the amount of copper coined was to be trebled to 1500 stone. Moreover, his decision to change the denomination of the small coin to 3d — equivalent to one farthing sterling — was not made in the interests of domestic exchange but rather to promote economic uniformity. Over the next three months, the royal burghs mounted a sustained campaign in favour of traditional 'turners'. On 10 November, the Council banned imports of English farthings and other coins of dubious copper content. No more than a minuscule proportion of the new 3d pieces had been minted by 10 January 1632, when Charles conceded that the copper coinage should revert to the traditional 'turners'.[50]

The coining of 1500 stone of copper, which was actually completed by November 1633, proved no more popular with the general public. Not only were the predominant 2d pieces diminutive and inconvenient, but their minting was privatised for the benefit of Secretary Alexander (earl of Stirling), the Crown's principal creditor for the ill-fated and recently abandoned colony of Nova Scotia. Under a contract of 20 February 1632, the equivalent of £120,000-worth of copper was to be coined over the next nine years. Because Stirling was also owed £72,000 for arrears of pension, fees and allowances, Charles envisaged coining an additional 7500 stone of copper and thereafter 1500 stone annually to settle the Crown's debts to the earl from November 1634. The public outcry against the 'Stirling turners', bolstered by complaints within official circles that the king had granted a favourite courtier liberty 'to coin base money', led the Exchequer Commission to delay redrafting Stirling's contract for another four months. In the event, the coining of no more than 3300 stone of copper was warranted. It is doubtful if much more than 1500 stone was actually minted as 'turners' by the formal suspension of his contract in December 1637. Claims that Stirling had overwhelmed the nation with 'black money' relate primarily to the lax standards applied to minting and distribution which opened the floodgates to counterfeit and debased coin.[51]

Opposition within the Scottish Mint to privatisation was personalised by the importation of Nicholas Briot and workmen from London to mint the copper coin on behalf of Stirling. Briot, the chief engraver in the English Mint, was an irascible and arrogant Frenchman who had exercised a considerable influence at Court on Scottish currency matters since 1626. His submission on the coinage to the plenary session of the Privy Council in January 1633 — upholding the royal prerogative in all aspects of policy and linking a staggered devaluation of foreign dollars to a debased new issue of silver coin — certainly intensified the acrimonious conduct of debate. Briot rarely remained in Scotland for more than a month following his initial despatch north in November 1632. He made little provision for quality control, yet his generous, if not excessive fees, ensured that the initial minting and distribution of 1500 stone of copper valued at £9600 incurred a loss of £256-13/4. Briot's appointment as master-coiner in the Scottish Mint was actually held up by the Council for ten months and only ratified temporarily in June 1636. Over the next fourteen months, he demonstrated his technical expertise in a new issue of silver coin which effectively recycled two-thirds of the foreign coin circulating in Scotland. His insistence that he receive all royalties from the exchange of dollars accepted for conversion in the Mint conveyed the impression to the country at large that he exercised his calling 'insolently'. No less significant for the groundswell of disaffection building up on currency matters was that Briot's appointment as master-coiner was associated indelibly with a swingeing, if staggered, devaluation of the 'rix-dollar'.[52]

In a despairing attempt to check the excessive circulation of foreign dollars, the value of the 'rix-dollar' was reduced from 58/- to 56/- on 11 February 1636. The immediate benefit to debtors from the fall in the value of real money was more than outweighed by the deleterious impact of devaluation upon commerce, especially evident in the tightening up of credit and the erosion of landed income. During the seven months in which this 2/- reduction remained in force, the Crown lost £1446-10/- on the value of the taxation voted by the coronation parliament. The failure of this devaluation to reverse the outflow of native specie and the influx of dollars of diverse denominations led the Council on 12 September, after much fraught debate, to reduce the 'rix-dollar' to 54/-.

Implementation of devaluation was both hasty and maladroit. Instead of conserving native coin, the swingeing reduction of the 'rix-dollar' encouraged traffickers in coin to export dollars of guaranteed silver content, leaving counterfeit and debased coin to proliferate in domestic markets. Devaluation further drained the country's stock of acceptable coin by forcing up prices of necessary imports as well as luxuries. Native manufactures were generally in too embryonic a state to take meaningful advantage of the reduced cost of Scottish commodities overseas. Indeed, the accumulative reduction of 4/- in the value of the 'rix-dollar', which was tantamount to an indirect tax of 7% on all commercial transactions, could not readily be absorbed by the Scottish economy.[53]

Belatedly, Charles authorised the renewal of plenary discussions on the coinage which the Council broadened to include 'some understanding' nobles and gentry on 23 June 1637. No positive action was taken to alter interest rates or expand trade. Nor was any fresh initiative launched to clamp down on illicit trafficking in counterfeit and debased dollars. A new issue of silver and gold coin served to stimulate a fresh spate of forgeries. Moreover, the new issue afforded tangible proof that Charles was less concerned to remedy the chronic shortage of native coin than to use the country's currency to extol his prerogative and propagate economic uniformity. A Court directive of 14 December instructed that the 20d coins were to bear the inscription UNITA TUEMUR (I shall protect through unity). Coins of greater denomination were to bear the legend HIS PRAESUM UT PROSIM (I am put in authority that I may do good).[54]

Conclusion

Charles I's dogmatic pursuit of economic uniformity through monopolies, common fishing and tariff reform had entailed the subordination of the resources, institutions and aspirations of the Scottish people to the dictates of the Court. Conversely, the promotion of the national interest as pioneered by the royal burghs became a potent rallying cry for the disaffected from the Convention of Estates in 1630. Indeed, the arrestment of the country's expanding commerce does much to explain why the royal burghs were regarded within Royalist circles during 1638 as 'the greatest strength' of the Covenanting movement. Moreover, the pursuit of economic uniformity, which continued unabated regardless of fiscal constraints on the Crown and unsound money, not only induced economic recession but emphasised the relegation of Scotland to provincial status. Aversion to provincialism no less than the reality of recession spread dissent beyond the political nation. Whereas class collusion to circumvent the Revocation Scheme was confined to the political nation, entire communities expressed their contempt for the economic policy emanating from the Court by collective acts of disobedience. The circulation of banned or counterfeit coins, smuggling and the disregard for trade embargoes became commonplace and routine rather than localised or occasional occurrences during the 1630s.[55] In turn, habitual civil disobedience throughout Scotland raised national tolerance for direct political action as for organised protest by the disaffected element.

NOTES

1. HMC, *Mar & Kellie*, I, 141.

2. Lee, jr, *The Road to Revolution*, 100–08; Stevenson, *The Scottish Revolution*, 51; Donaldson, *James V to James VII*, 303.

3. *APS*, V, 178, 182–84, 187, *RPCS*, second series, I, 159–60, 170–73, 178, 269–72, 276–80, 300-02, 350–51, 418; *RCRB, Extracts*, (1615–76), 195, 213–15, 225. According to the corn laws, wheat could be exported until the price per boll reached 14 merks, bere until the price per boll reached 11 merks, meal and oats until the price reached 8 merks. Imports of victual were exempt from custom on condition the importing merchants did not sell until prices reached the levels prescribed for barring exports — that is, until wheat reached 14 merks per boll *etc.*

4. *RPCS* second series, I, 564, 628–31; II, 162, 192–93, 540–41, 545–46; III, 3, 8, 16, 19–20, 51, 457–58, 464; *Records of the Coinage of Scotland*, R. W. Cochrane-Patrick ed., vol. II, (Edinburgh, 1846), 71–75. Certain German dollars were being exchanged at rates from 4 to 29% above the intrinsic value of their Scottish equivalents. Thus, the 'lion-dollar'/'dog-dollar' was circulating at 48/- whereas its true worth was deemed no more than 46/-; the 'base-dollar' was circulating at 33/4 whereas its true worth was no more than 25/10; and the latest intruder, the 'embden dollar', was also circulating at 33/4 instead of 26/-.

5. *APS*, V, 176, 181–82, 186; Nef, *The Rise of the British Coal Industry*, II, 224–27. The yearly consumption of coal on the domestic market barely realised sufficient income to meet a month's maintenance costs for the pumping machinery used to extract water from the mines below the Forth.

6. *RCRB, Extracts*, (1615–76), 213–15; RPCS, second series, I, 269–72, 277–80, 301; II, 72–73, 146–47, 561; IV, 41, 570. Coal sold to Scottish merchants was to be retailed on the domestic market at 5/- less per chalder than the price charged to foreign shippers; that sold for export in Scottish ships now cost 2/- less per chalder.

7. SRO, Treasury Accounts, 1624–25, E 19/22.

8. SRO, Mar & Kellie Collection, GD 24/100/340; Purves, *Revenue of the Crown in 1681*, xlv–xlvi; *SR*, I, 47, 143, 347, 397, 399–400.

9. SRO, Accounts of Taxations granted in 1625, E 65/10-/11; *SR*, I, 227–28, 232.

10. HMC, *Mar & Kellie*, II, 250–51; *The Red Book of Menteith*, II, 12, 26, 37, 40; Napier, *Montrose and the Covenanters*, I, 75–76; *SR*, I, 67, 92–93. Having secured sufficient money by July 1626 to purchase three warships, two in England and one in Scotland, for the defence of coastal waters, Charles met with no success in his efforts to lay off the costs of naval supply and maintenance — estimated at £2500 monthly for a ship of 300 tons, with 28 cannons and ready to sail with 100 men — on the royal burghs. The political embarrassment caused by the size of Charles's ill-equipped Scottish navy was partially ameliorated in May 1628, when the marquis of Hamilton agree to provide and equip another five ships (*RPCS*, second series, I, 367–68, 378–79, 386–91, 408; II, 277, 324–25; *RCRB, Extracts*, (1615–76), 213–15, 218–19).

11. HMC, *Mar & Kellie*, I, 173–75; *SR*, I, 96–97, 241–42, 330, 334; II, 448–49, 614–15, 643–44, 758.

12. SRO, Salhousie Muniments, GD 45/1/120; SRO, Treasury Accounts, 1633–34, E 30/23/5; SRO, Accounts of the Taxations granted in 1630, SRO, E 65/13-/14; *SR*, II, 521, 626–27.

13. *The Book of Carlaverock*, II, 74–75; HMC, *Mar & Kellie*, I, 168, 171; Scotstarvit, *The Staggering State of Scottish Statesmen*, 60–63; Balfour *Historical Works*, II, 180; Napier, *Montrose and the Covenanters*, I, 48, 54–57, 63–65.

14. *APS*, V, 185, 219, 224–25; SRO, Cunninghame-Graham MSS, GD 22-/1/518; *RCRB, Extracts*, (1615–76), 195, 225, 249, 288, 313; *RPCS*, second series, I, 54–55, 67–68, 77, 174, 237–38; II, 101–02, 123–24, 196; III, 107–09, 359–60, 425, 611–12, 624.

15. *APS*, V, 228, 411, c.98–99; *RPCS*, second series, IV, 78–79, 162, 169, 196, 241, 281, 295–96, 443; V, 599; VI, 20–21, 61.

16. *APS*, V, 208, 219, 223–25. The other monopoly referred specifically to a select committee was the earl of Linlithgow's patent to manufacture gunpowder, granted for 21 years in June 1629. The most objectionable aspect of this patent was not Linlithgow's exclusive right to import the commodities necessary to manufacture gunpowder, but the comprehensive and draconian powers bestowed on the earl and his agents to enter any estate or building in Scotland to search out the working of saltpetre. Although the investigative scope of Linlithgow's patent remained a cause of public disquiet, its sweeping powers of search were never exercised fully.

17. *APS*, V, 220–21.

18. SRO, Seaforth Muniments, GD 46/18/147; *CSP, Venetian*, XII (1629–32), 453. J. R. Elder, *The Royal Fishery Companies of the Seventeenth Century*, (Glasgow, 1912), 7–18, 25–30. Up to 3000 Dutch busses, ranging from 70 to 120 tons and employing around 50,000 men, were reputed to be fishing off the coasts of Scotland and England — albeit the renewal of hostilities with Spain in 1621 subjected the Dutch herring fleet to sporadic, but devastating, naval engagements. Between 60 to 80 busses were sunk off Scotland in 1625 (J. I. Israel, 'A Conflict of Empires, Spain and the Netherlands, 1618–48', *Past & Present*, 76 (1977), 44–47). Moreover, the massacre of English traders at Amboyna in the East Indies, which left the Dutch in undisputed control of the lucrative spice trade, caused widespread resentment in England — particularly as the massacre remained unavenged (P. Cornfield, 'Economic Issues and Ideologies', in *The Origins of the English Civil War*, 213).

19. SRO, Seaforth Muniments, GD 46/18/147; *RPCS, second series, III, 94–96, 428–29, 479–80, 495–96; RCRB, Extracts*, (1615–76), 222–23, 243, 259–62, 277, 289–93, 300, 318–20; W. C. Mackenzie, *History of the Outer Hebrides*, (Edinburgh, 1974), 304–06, 320–21; Elder, *The Royal Fishery Companies*, 27–33.

20. *APS*, V, 220–23; Elder, *The Royal Fishery Companies*, 35–39; W. R. Scott, *The Constitution and Finance of English, Scottish and Irish Joint-Stock Companies to 1720*, 2 vols, (Cambridge, 1910–12), II, 361–63; Reeve, *Charles I and the Road to Personal Rule*, 204–05.

21. *APS*, V, 223, 225–27; *RPCS*, second series, IV, 20.

22. *APS*, V, 220, 228–29; NLS, Morton Cartulary & Papers, MS 81, fo. 78; *CSP, Domestic*, (1629–31), 450; (1631–33), 237–38; Snoddy, *Lord Scotstarvit*, 183–84. Leading officials among the English negotiators had already collated reports on the fishing resources around the Scottish coast and had been instrumental in formulating the corporate structure, commercial privileges and financial prospects of the common fishing.

23. *SR*, II, 479–80, 483; *APS*, V, 229–30.

24. *APS*, V, 231–33; *RPCS*, second series, IV, 56–57; *RCRB, Extracts*, (1615–76), 325–26.

25. A factor militating against the common fishing operating amicably as a British venture was the Crown's indifference to the hostility exhibited to Scottish whaling ventures in the Arctic and North Atlantic by vested English interests. In July 1626, the noted Scottish monopolist and entrepreneur, Nathaniel Udward, had received a patent to fish and trade in and around Greenland for 21 years, mainly to procure oils for his soapworks at Leith. However, the rival Greenland Company of London had refused

to recognise the validity of his Scottish patent. Over the next three years, his ships were subjected to continuous harassment culminating in the seizure of two whalers, the plundering of their stores and the incarceration of their crews. In November 1629, the Council had endorsed Udward's claim for £4000 sterling (£48,000) compensation. Despite an accompanying suggestion that a select number of councillors drawn equally from both kingdoms should be invited to arbitrate, no remedial action was implemented at Court (*RPCS*, second series, I, 375–76; III, 354–56; Scott, *Joint-Stock Companies to 1720*, II, 55, 70, 104, 363).

26. *APS*, V, 233–37, 244–46; *SR*, II, 544, 589, 612, 614, 627, 641; *RCRB*, *Extracts*, (1677–1711), 534–36; Elder, *The Royal Fishery Companies*, 42–50.

27. *APS*, V, 239–44; *SR*, II, 606, 613. As well as regulating membership of the commonty, the governing council was warranted to license provincial associations and to resolve differences between them; to make statutes and ordinances for the conduct of the common fishing and the fishing trade in general which were enforceable by fines and imprisonment; and to issue directives to promote speedy administration among the provincial associations. Every provincial association was to elect four judges who were empowered to issue local ordinances as well as resolve internal disputes. The judges were removable at the will and pleasure of the governing council which also served as a court of appeal. To settle controversies at sea within and between provincial associations, the masters, merchants and principal factors for each fleet were to elect four judges prior to sailing who were to serve as an arbitration panel and issue administrative orders at sea. Their appointment was valid only for the duration of each fishing voyage and their decisions were open to review by the governing council. The attendance of at least six councillors from each nation was necessary for the governing council to resolve disputes between provincial associations. Two of the four judges within each provincial association and likewise two on each arbitration panel during fishing voyages were required to be Scots.

28. *APS*, V, 237–40, 272–76; *RCRB*, *Extracts*, (1677–1711), 525–30, 532–33, 536–37; *RPCS*, second series, IV, 181, 208, 308–09, 541–42, 546–48, 551–52, 554–56. The burgesses attending the plenary session in October 1632 had admitted that there were eight 'great shippes' and possibly another 52 boats on the west coast and around 60 vessels of 20 tons or more on the east coast suitable for deep-sea fishing. In return for having their commercial privileges ratified in the coronation parliament, a ratification that entailed expenditure of £666-13/4 'for favour and kindness', the royal burghs were obliged to give an undertaking in November 1633 to have at least 60 busses in readiness for the coming herring season.

29. *APS*, V, 221–22; Elder, *The Royal Fishery Companies*, 54–55; Scott, *Joint-Stock Companies to 1720*, II, 365–71. The prominent English officials who took the lead in forming provincial associations in 1633 were the treasurer, Richard Weston, Lord Weston (later earl of Portland) and the earl marshal, Thomas Howard, earl of Arundel and Surrey; the chamberlain, Philip Herbert, earl of Pembroke and Montgomery; and the attorney-general, William Noy. All three associations were defunct by 1641.

30. SRO, Exchequer Act Book, 1634–39, E 4/5, fo. 199–203; *RCRB*, *Extracts*, (1677–1711), 541–42; *RPCS*, second series, V, 286, 414–16; Mackenzie, *History of the Outer Hebrides*, 319–22, 326; Elder, *The Royal Fishery Companies*, 54–64.

31. SRO, Hamilton Papers, TD 75/100/26/978, /1000; *RPCS*, second series, VI, 279–80, 292, 335, 346, 457; Elder, *The Royal Fishery Companies*, 65–80.

32. SRO, Exchequer Act Book, 1634–39, E 4/5, fo. 52; SRO, Miscellaneous Exchequer Papers, E 30/23; NLS, Morton Cartulary & Papers, MS 81, fo. 84; Scotstarvit, *The Staggering State of Scottish Statesmen*, 61–63.

33. Stevenson, *The Scottish Revolution*, 53; H. F. Kearney, *Strafford in Ireland, 1633–41*, (Manchester, 1959), 170; J. C. Beckett, *The Making of Modern Ireland, 1603–1923*, (London, 1978), 64–72.

34. *APS*, V, 35, c.18; 285, c.28; 605, 607, 614; *RPCS*, second series, V, 116–17; Balfour, *Historical Works*, II, 220–21; SRO, Hamilton Papers, TD 75/100/26/1379; Trevor-Roper, *Archbishop Laud*, 144, 231–33.

35. *APS*, V, 25, c.9; SRO, Exchequer Act Book, 1634–39. E 4/5, fo. 21; *SR*, II, 634, 673, 694, 696–99, 702–04, 706–07, 710–11, 720–25, 731, 738, 785–86, 798, 804, 810, 828, 830–32, 844–45, 864.

36. SRO, Exchequer Act Book, 1634–39, E 4/5, fo. 21–24; SRO, Accounts of the Taxations granted in 1625 & 1630, E 65/10-/15; *SR*, II, 719–20, 735–36; Purves, *Revenue of the Scottish Crown in 1681*, xlv–xlvi.

37. SRO, Exchequer Minute Book 1630–34, E 5/1; SRO, Accounts of the Tacksmen of the Customs, 1633–34, E 73/6; SRO, Exchequer Act Book, 1634–39, E 4/5, fo. 26–29, 34–40; Burnet, *Memoirs*, 25–26; D. Stevenson, 'The King's Scottish Revenues and the Covenanters, 1625–51', *The Historical Journal*, XVII, (1974), 20–22.

38. SRO, Exchequer Act Book, 1634–39, E 4/5, fo. 24, 32–34, 46–47, 50–52, 65–69, 95–96, 100, 132–36, 144–45, 155, 159–61; SRO, Account of the Small Customs for 1635, E 73/8/1-/2; SRO, Treasury Accounts, 1633–35, E 30/23/5, /7; SRO, Treasury Accounts, 1635–36, E 26/1/29; SRO,. Accounts of the Taxation granted in 1633, E 65/16-/17.

39. SRO, Exchequer Act Book, 1634–39, E 4/5, fo. 29, 58, 64, 142–43; SRO, Treasury Accounts, 1634–35, E 21/10; *SR*, II, 739, 813–14, 818, 840, 857, 882; Baillie, *Letters and Journals*, I, 6–7; Stevenson, *The Scottish Revolution*, 27.

40. Balfour, *Historical Works*, II, 141–42; Row, *History of the Kirk*, 385–86, 396; *Diary of Sir Thomas Hope of Craighall*, 45–46, 51, 58; SRO, Exchequer Act Book, E 4/5 fo. 148, 151; Trevor-Roper, *Archbishop Laud*, 231–33.

41. HMC, *Traquhair MSS*, 247; SRO, Hamilton Papers, TD 75/100/26/1970; SRO, Exchequer Act Book, 1634–39, E 4/5, fo. 170–72; *RCRB, Extracts*, (1677–1711), 540–41; *Aberdeen Council Letters*, 2 vols, L. B. Taylor ed., (London, 1950), II, (1634–44), 34–37.

42. SRO, Exchequer Act Book, 1634–39, E 4/5, fo. 100, 170, 172, 180, 185–88, 239–43, 245–46, 269–70; SRO, Treasury Accounts, 1635–36, E 26/1/29.

43. HMC, *Traquhair MSS*, 247; SRO, Hamilton Papers, TD 75/100/26/357, /8207; TD 76/100/5/11138, /11139; NLS, Morton Cartulary & Papers, MS 81, fo. 44; H. L. Rubinstein, *Captain Luckless: James, First Duke of Hamilton, 1606–49*, (Edinburgh & London, 1975), 45–47.

44. SRO, Hamilton Papers, TD 75/100/42/28/11; Nef, *The Rise of the British Coal Industry*, II, 222–23. Calculation and national comparisons of tariff differentials are tentative, given the lack of uniform weights and measures within Scotland. Despite the standard tariff of 5% of the rated value on all Scottish exports since 1612, and despite legislation in 1617–18 to promote national conformity in weights and measures, local particularism ensured that variations persisted with respect to districts as well as commodities throughout the reign of Charles I and well into the eighteenth century (R. E. Zupko, 'The Weights and Measures of Scotland before the Union', *SHR*, LV, (1977), 124–39).

45. SRO, Hamilton Papers, TD 75/100/26/1000; SR, II, 729–30, 732, 790; RPCS, second series, V, 217–18, 223–24; VII, 160–61; Nef, *The Rise of the British Coal Industry*, II, 227–28, 272–77.

46. *RPCS*, second series, IV, 250, 255–57; VI, 139–40, 175; HMC, *Traquhair MSS*, 247, 253; SRO, Hamilton Papers, TD 75/100/26/8165; TD 75/100/42/28/11. Alexander Bruce of Alva was duly elected by the Scottish saltmasters and despatched to Court as sole negotiator in January 1636. A prominent member of the most technically innovative family of coalowners and saltmasters in Scotland, Bruce of Alva, was the foremost tacksman of the customs on coal and salt exported form the Forth (SRO, Exchequer Act Book, 1634–39, E 4/5, fo. 65–69, 110–14).

47. HMC, *Traquhair MSS*, 253; SRO, Hamilton Papers, TD 75/100/26/357, /1000, /8165; *RPCS*, second series, VI, 256, 344, 352; Scott, *Joint-Stock Companies to 1720*, I, 208–10; II, 469–70.

48. Baillie, *Letters and Journals*, I, 5; Balfour *Historical Works*, II, 221–22; Spalding, *Troubles*, I, 39; T. C. Smout, 'Famine and Famine Relief in Scotland', in *Comparative Aspects of Scottish and Irish Economic and Social History, 1600–1900*, L. M. Cullen & T. C. Smout eds., (Edinburgh, 1972), 22–23.

49. *RPCS*, second series, IV, 63–64, 155–56, 298, 301–02, 578–82; V, 102–03; *RCRB, Extracts*, (1615–76), 329–30; *Records of the Coinage of Scotland*, II, 71–73, 80–100, *Aberdeen Council Letters*, I, (1552–1633), 351–59; *APS*, V, 49–50, c.35.

50. *RPCS*, second series, III, 47, 130–32; IV,. 323–25; E. Burns, *The Coinage of Scotland*, vol, II, (Edinburgh, 1887), 484–86; R. B. K. Stevenson, 'The Stirling Turners of Charles I, 1632–39', *British Numismatic Journal*, XXIX, (1958–59), 128–32, 134–36.

51. *RMS*, VIII, no. 1920; SRO, Exchequer Act Book, 1634–39, E 4/5, fo. 30, 58–60; J. Gordon, *History of Scots Affairs, 1637–41*, 3 vols, J. Robertson & G. Grub eds., (Spalding Club, Aberdeen, 1841), III, 87–88; Scotstarvit, *The Staggering State of Scottish Statesmen*, 75; Baillie, *Letters and Journals*, I, 77. The abandonment of Nova Scotia had been demanded by the French during their peace negotiations with Charles I that concluded in July 1631.

52. *RPCS*, IV, 323–25; V, 230–31, 488–90; VI, 98–101, 258–59, 270–71, 295–98, 323–24, 344, 360–62, 432; *Records of the Coinage of Scotland*, II, 103–05, 116; Gordon, *History of Scots Affairs*, III, 88; Burns, *The Coinage of Scotland*, II, 445–49, 488. Briot initially made use of the traditional hammer to coin 20d, 40d, and half-merk (6/8) denominations before he persuaded Charles that conversion of foreign dollars into native coin could be accomplished more efficiently by mill and press. His expertise eventually persuaded a majority in the Privy Council to ratify his appointment as master-coiner, in association with his Scottish son-in-law, John Falconer, from August 1637.

53. SRO, Account of the Taxation granted in 1633, E 65/16; *RPCS*, second series, VI, 189, 322–24; *Records of the Coinage of Scotland*, II, 109–10; *Diary of Sir Thomas Hope of Craighall*, 47; Spalding, *Troubles*, I, 40, 44; J. Brown, 'Merchant Princes and Mercantile Investment in Early Seventeenth Century Scotland', in *The Early Modern Town in Scotland*, 125–46.

54. *RPCS*, second series, VI, 2, 434, 446–47, 464–68, 477–78, 489, 505, 542, 550, 685, 691–92; *Records of the Coinage of Scotland*, II, 111–12; Burns, *The Coinage of Scotland*, II, 450–51, 476.

55. SRO, Hamilton Papers, TD 75/100/26/326; *SR*, II, 712–14; *RPCS*, second series, VII, 58–59, 103. The Convention of Royal Burghs, in July 1638, duly became the first Scottish institution to make subscription of the National Covenant compulsory for all aspiring to hold public office (*RCRB, Extracts*, (1677–1711), 543).

6

Rallying the Disaffected

Introduction

The coronation visit to Edinburgh of 1633 was to prove the critical turning point in the personal rule of Charles I as an absentee monarch. His presence provided tangible proof of not just his intransigence and ineptitude as a monarch, but also his crass insensitivity to Scottish sensibilities. The legislative programme presented before the four estates confirmed that the Revocation Scheme would be implemented relentlessly according to royal dictate; that taxation would continue on an annual basis until 1640; and that no guarantee could be given that Charles would not use his prerogative to promote religious innovations. The coronation ceremonial and other religious services conducted by bishops in the king's presence aroused universal concern. The emphasis on order and seemliness rather than scriptural warrant reeked of Anglicanism. At a stroke, innovatory religious practices were associated with the suppression of the national interest.

Despite Charles's intimidatory presence at the coronation parliament, his efforts to deny a national forum for the grievances of the disaffected enjoyed no more than superficial success. Certainly, the rigorous vetting of bills and supplications eliminated all criticism deemed inimical to the Crown. The deployment of bishops on the committee of articles ensured royal control over the composite agenda. The manipulation of voting practices to maximise support for the Court secured the block-passage of the 168 measures on the legislative programme. However, the numbers from all four estates drawn to Edinburgh for the king's visit far outstripped the sixty-five nobles, forty-five shire commissioners, fifty-one burgh commissioners, twelve bishops and nine officers of state attending the coronation parliament. No amount of royal intimidation or management could prevent informal meetings among the disaffected in the capital. In turn, the rallying of the disaffected can best be monitored not by public expressions of dissent, but by suppressed supplications and speeches critical of the direction of Scottish affairs from the Court.[1]

Targeting Constitutional Protest

A petition drawn up on behalf of nonconforming presbyterians among the clergy was presented by a deposed minister, Mr Thomas Hogg, to the clerk-register,

Sir John Hay of Lands, in May 1633. Though suppressed, Hogg's Petition articulated the constitutional justification for nonconformity, a justification rooted in the 'golden age' of presbyterianism between 1592 and 1597 — when presbyterianism was acknowledged temporarily by James VI to be the established polity for the Kirk. The representation of the clerical estate in parliament by the bishops was castigated as being 'without any authority or allowance of the generall assemblies of the Kirk'. Hence, all acts of parliament affecting the Kirk that the bishops had supported as clerical commissioners should be suspended. This demand would have reversed the gradual re-establishment of episcopacy by James VI from 1597. The acts of the general assembly of 1610 in Glasgow were allegedly tampered with pending their ratification by the parliament of 1612 in Edinburgh. A notably heinous omission was the enactment subjecting the bishops to the censure of the general assembly. Despite the tendency towards annual general assemblies from the Reformation, the cessation of this practice since 1618 had consolidated the unaccountability of the episcopate.

Strict imposition of conformity to the Five Articles was regarded as contrary to the spirit of proceedings at the general assembly of 1618 in Perth. The requirement to receive communion kneeling especially deviated from the sacramental practices professed since the Reformation and sanctioned by parliament in 1567. Nonconformists, as adherents to Reformed standards, wanted the traditional administration of the sacraments to be reaffirmed by parliament, a reaffirmation which would indemnify them for past breaches of the Five Articles. The oath of conformity to the Five Articles imposed by the bishops on all entrants to the ministry since 1626 — which upheld the royal supremacy and episcopal authority — was condemned as unwarranted by either general assembly or parliament. Particularly obnoxious was the oath's promise of passivity in Kirk affairs. Exacted under pain of deprivation and perpetual perjury, the oath was regarded as self-damning and discriminatory obligation. Whereas all entrants were bound by this oath, all incumbent ministers at the passage of the Five Articles had their scruples tolerated provided they neither preached, published nor proselytised in favour of nonconformity. Ecclesiastical censure by the Courts of High Commission, instituted by the royal prerogative in 1610, lacked constitutional warrant from general assembly or parliament relative to the presbyterian courts established by the authority 'of the countrie and kirke'.[2]

Hogg's Petition demonstrated that the association of militant presbyterianism and constitutionalism remained vibrant during the personal rule of Charles I. Revived by the implementation of the Five Articles, militant presbyterianism since 1625 had been sustained on a steady diet of fears and suspicions about the openness of the Court to Catholicism and the seemingly relentless progress of the Counter-Reformation on the continent. Despite the drastic reduction in her French attendants during the summer of 1626, the Catholic coterie surrounding Queen Henrietta Maria continued to attract suspicion as suborners of the Reformation. Nonetheless Charles, aided and abetted by the Scottish bishops, was arguably the greatest promoter of militant presbyterianism because of his equivocal treatment of nonconformists from the outset of his reign. His failure to differentiate between presbyterians and Catholics as contumacious nonconformists was interpreted by the militant faction within the Kirk as ranking 'the most precious and most gracious Christians in the land' with unrepentant and incorrigible papists.[3]

The clerical convention of 17 to 19 July 1627 enabled militant presbyterians to appear as a constitutional opposition, not just a factional interest within the Kirk. Militant endeavours to have the convention constituted a general assembly and to commence proceedings with petitions against conformity to the Five Articles failed to receive majority support. Nonetheless, the militants secured sufficient backing to persuade the convention to supplicate the Crown to license a general assembly and to ensure that the two-man delegation carrying this petition to Court included a presbyterian. The convention met in the midst of the class antagonisms arising from the first session of the Commission for Surrenders and Teinds when the bishops were criticised for their truculence, their intentional dissimulation and their disruptive influence. In order to deflect such criticism from the Crown as well as the lay estates, the bishops chose to exploit Scottish fears about Catholic expansionism by mounting a systematic campaign against recusancy. In effect, the convention was used by the bishops to launch a three-year campaign which unleashed anti-popish sentiments within the localities as within the Scottish establishment.[4]

The episcopal campaign against Catholic recusancy, which was climaxed by the strict enforcement of the penal laws from July 1629, was marked by sustained and concerted pressure on the Privy Council. Excommunication was to be complemented not just by outlawry but by the confiscation of goods and, where appropriated, by the sequestration of rents. Although a quarter of all Council business from January 1629 to July 1630 was taken up with the enforcement of the penal laws, it would be an exaggeration to suggest that the three-year campaign against Catholic clergy, their adherents and protectors, amounted to a 'storm of prosecution'.[5]

There was limited scope for sustained prosecution since Catholicism was no more than a minority pursuit in an overwhelmingly Protestant country. The one area offering the greatest prospects for Catholicism was the Highlands and Islands. Principally as the result of the missionary endeavours of Irish Franciscans there had been a limited awakening of the faith among clans from 1619. Yet, the mere handful of missionaries and their need to be continuously on the move — to spread the faith as much as to avoid detection and persecution — meant that Catholicism was only established within isolated pockets of Scottish Gaeldom during the personal rule of Charles I. In the Lowlands, only the protection afforded by the extensive regalian jurisdiction of George Gordon, marquis of Huntly, enabled Catholicism to consolidate itself as a community faith in the shires of Aberdeen and Banff. Catholicism tended to be based on households where mass was celebrated privately and irregularly — albeit Catholicism was spreading from the country seats of nobles to those of the gentry and from their town-houses to the tenements of burgesses. Unlike nonconformists, however, Catholics enjoyed a political influence out of all proportion to their position as a minority. Though only a few of the nobility on the Council were Catholics, other councillors were not unsympathetic to their interests. In addition, most leading officials saw no personal advantage to be derived at Court in advocating rigorous persecution of recusants.

Indeed, the sympathetic hearing accorded at Court to prominent Scottish Catholics like Huntly and Nithsdale ensured that the penal laws against recusancy, however intemperately their reimposition was trumpeted, were never enforced comprehensively. Even though the Council remained implacably opposed to the Crown granted individual dispensations from the penal laws to incorrigible papists, the bishops were only allowed free rein to prosecute in ecclesiastical courts. The Council adamantly retained discretionary control over civil sanctions which were imposed pragmatically. The Council's guiding spirit was the selective application of the penal laws to eradicate popery in succeeding generations rather than inflict irreparable material damage on prominent Catholic families. Thus, Catholic landowners were not expropriated though their children were removed from their households for schooling directed by the Kirk. Nor were Catholic recusants prevented from acquiring or inheriting estates. In turn, circumspection on the part of the Catholic nobility in not flaunting their faith served to dampen clerical zeal. Few contumacious recusants were prosecuted by the Council.[6]

At the same time, the upswing in Protestant fortunes associated with the Swedish intervention in the Thirty Years' War lulled Scottish apprehensions about Catholic expansionism. Notwithstanding the primacy Gustavus Adolphus accorded to his country's interests in the Baltic, the Swedish king was viewed as the saviour of Protestantism and princely autonomy within the Holy Roman Empire. The publicity accorded to the progress of Europe's first national army over the next four years remained triumphal though Gustavus Adolphus was killed while defeating Albrecht von Wallenstein, the supreme commander of the imperial forces, at Lutzen in September 1632.[7]

Apart from affirming the pervasive aversion to Catholicism throughout Scotland, the episcopal campaign was significant also in imposing a religious test for public office, a test as applicable to nonconformists as recusants. On 12 June 1629 Charles ordained that all officials, councillors and members of the judiciary, on pain of dismissal from royal service, were to receive communion quarterly in the chapel royal. In conformity to the Five Articles of Perth, communion was to be received kneeling. As to recusants, the religious test was little more than a politic gesture to appease clerical clamour. Although Huntly and Nithsdale had prudently withdrawn from the Council, two other prominent Catholics remained active councillors during the imposition of the penal laws — namely, Huntly's eldest son and successor, George, Lord Gordon, and George Seaton, third earl of Winton.[8]

Charles's directive on the religious test was supplemented by the injunction that all Scottish subjects should receive communion kneeling in their own parish church at least once a year. This injunction, designed to prevent the laity seeking communion from militant presbyterians in neighbouring parishes, was duly interpreted by the bishops as a test for nonconformity rather than recusancy. The continuing harassment of nonconformist clergy throughout and beyond the episcopal campaign against Catholic recusancy led to long debates in the Convention of Estates in 1630. Lord Balmerino protested on 31 July that the bishop's exaction of the oath of conformity from all entrants to the ministry lacked parliamentary warrant. His argument that conformity was a matter of conscience, not compulsion, was taken up by the shire commissioners on 4 August. Both protests — though suppressed rather than forwarded to Court — marked the tentative beginnings of concerted action by the disaffected element.[9]

A concerted constitutional attack on the bishops' role in Kirk and State was suggested in the speech prepared for, but — in view of no defined privilege of free speech in the Scottish Estates — prudently not delivered to the coronation parliament by Lord Loudoun. Loudoun's Speech emphasised the constitutional impropriety of Charles swearing to preserve 'all canonical privileges' in his coronation oath. This concession was an unwarrantable limitation on the royal prerogative, especially as no comparable concession was required for the maintenance of the rights and privileges of the lay estates. However, Loudon's Speech was not so much an unreserved defence of the royal prerogative as an opportunist attempt to negate any political advantages to the clerical estate in general or the bishops in particular.

As canonical privileges remained unspecified, Loudoun held that any concession beyond the existing first article of the coronation oath, 'for maintenance of the religion of Christ, now preached and professed within this realm', opened up the prospect of the bishops attempting to reclaim rights enjoyed by the clergy prior to the Reformation — notably, rights over secularised kirklands. Further concessions would be direct contravention of the 'reformed' and 'far more equitable' coronation oath approved in 1567 and subsequently ratified in 1581 and 1592. By such a selective appeal to post-Reformation constitutional precedents, Loudoun identified the bishops as the common threat to the landed privileges of the laity and, simultaneously, associated the unbounded ambition of the bishops with the spectre of popery.[10]

Religious and Materialist

The constitutional juxtaposition of religious and materialist considerations was carried a stage further by 'the Humble Supplication' formulated by commissioners from the shires and burghs and endorsed by nobles as a protest against the rumoured composite agenda prepared by the committee of articles. Although denied a hearing on 28 July 1633, the one day set aside for the four estates to assent to the entire legislative programme, the Humble Supplication formally consolidated a united movement of disaffected laity and presbyterian nonconformists to secure free assemblies in Kirk and State. The Humble Supplication accorded priority to dissuading Charles from ratifying enactments 'which have bred great division and many evils' in the Kirk, notably the imposition of religious standards 'rejected at the Reformation'. The supplicants were as concerned that Charles should not attempt any liturgical innovations until a favourable consensus had been established within the Kirk.[11]

Despite Charles's endeavours over the previous two years to promote general acceptance throughout the British Isles of *The Psalms of King David* — translated by James VI, but revised substantially by Secretary Alexander — no clerical consent had been secured in Scotland for printing and distributing copies to every parish. Presbyterian nonconformists, led by the indefatigable polemicist David Calderwood, had campaigned vigorously against their general introduction on nationalist grounds — as the thin end of a wedge for the imposition of religious uniformity; on biblical grounds — more concern seemed to have been lavished on poetical metre than scriptural warrant; and, above all, on constitutional grounds — the work had been undertaken without direction by the Kirk or approval by a general assembly.[12]

Religious priorities notwithstanding, the main thrust of the Humble Supplication was directed towards the material aspirations of the landed and commercial classes. In his effort to secure a renewal of taxation, Charles could rely on a substantial measure of public support as well as official backing, even though the levies voted by the Convention of Estates in 1630 still had two terms to run. A vote of supply by the coronation parliament was preferable to the king's unilateral resort to fiscal expedients. Moreover, there was a general inclination among the political nation not to mar the long-awaited coronation visit by appearing niggardly in voting supply. Charles, nonetheless, was intent not only on renewing but augmenting and extending taxation.[13]

On the grounds that his Scottish subjects were heavily oppressed by burdensome interest rates, Charles proposed to the committee of articles that the maximum rates of interest for all financial transactions be reduced from 10 to 8%. Any goodwill accruing to the king from this gesture was soon dissipated when it was leaked that the proposed reduction in interest was to be suspended for three years, during which time the 2% reduction was to be requisitioned as a benevolence for the Crown. This temporary tax was to differ critically from the extraordinary tax on annualrents in being applied to all monies borrowed, not just to the free income left from the surplus of money loaned as credit over money borrowed as debt.

With characteristic ineptitude, Charles further insisted that the duration of the renewed land tax should be extended from four to six years. Levies of the extraordinary tax on annualrents were likewise extended by two years. More contentiously, the rate of exaction from annualrents was increased from every twentieth to every sixteenth penny — that is, from 5 to 6.25%. Charles thus played into the hands of the disaffected who were particularly aggrieved that the extraordinary tax on annualrents, introduced in 1621 as a temporary expedient to afford relief to the Palatinate, had become an established levy. In condemning the extraordinary tax as 'an inquisition in men's estates, as is not practised in any other natione in Christendome', the disaffected element sought to capitalise politically on the requirement that all borrowers and lenders of money had to complete inventories twice a year itemising their financial standing. The biennial submission of inventories 'makes our nation contemptible by the discoverie made therby of the povertie thereof'. Moreover, the rigorous diligence employed by tax collectors, the harassment of parties failing to submit or complete inventories, together with the punitive fines and compositions imposed on those deemed tax evaders, distressed 'innumerable persons of good respect'. That Scotland was the most taxed nation in Europe could not be substantiated. What mattered politically was that the disaffected element *considered* Scotland to be the most taxed nation in Europe.[14]

The Humble Supplication also contended that the national interest had been slighted by Charles's loading of voting strength in favour of the Court. His granting of proxy votes was compounded by his summoning of five Englishmen who held Scottish honours, 'such persons as hes no interest in the good or evill of this kingdome'. No less integral to Charles's loading of votes had been his award of honours to Scottish nobles and gentry. During the seven weeks of his coronation visit, fifty-four gentry were dubbed knights and nine were created peers; ten existing peers were elevated in rank. Charles's selective award of honours was also conditional, on beneficiaries supporting the composite agenda packaged by the committee of articles. In belatedly realising that the coronation parliament witnessed the first concerted stirrings of an identifiable opposition, Charles contended that his denial or withdrawal of honours ranked third — after his promotion of revocation and his implementation of the Commission for Surrenders and Teinds — in rallying the disaffected. Such a ranking affords striking testimony that his preoccupation with his prerogative had resulted in political myopia. Of the prominent members of the disaffected element provisionally granted honours, only two — Lord Loudoun and John Lindsay, Lord Lindsay of the Byres — were penalised by having their patents to become earls withdrawn.[15]

National touchiness over the award of honours was undoubtedly aggravated by the personal remoteness of Charles during his coronation visit. Charles preferred to be phalanxed by familiar English and Scottish courtiers. Other than for ceremonial purposes, the resident nobles and gentry were excluded from the royal presence. Nonetheless, they felt obliged to provide lavish hospitality for the royal train both as a matter of individual rivalry and national prestige. Albeit twenty-seven English nobles, leading officials and ecclesiastical dignitaries had advanced a third of their annual income to accompany Charles, there was a general expectation among the 120 persons in the royal train that their expenditure would be relieved considerably if not reimbursed entirely by a generous vote of supply from the Scottish Estates. While the personal expenditure of Scottish courtiers during the royal visit was partially offset by pensions from the Crown, such favours were not regarded as benefits to the nation but merely as bounties 'cast away' upon parasitic absentees. Conversely, the unrelieved debts accruing to Scottish nobles and gentry from their conspicuous expenditure made a telling contribution to the gathering momentum of constitutional frustration.[16]

Constitutional Frustration

The most striking testimony to this gathering momentum from the summer of 1633 was provided by the supplication penned by a former Crown solicitor, Mr William Haig, to justify the conduct of the disaffected element in voting against the block passage of the legislative programme. If credence can be attached to rumours circulating at Court the following summer, Haig's Supplication was endorsed by thirty-five nobles — more than half the sixty-five votes cast on behalf of that estate at the coronation parliament and the overwhelming majority of the forty-five peers who actually attended and voted personally. In part, Haig's Supplication was a protest against Charles's management, especially his packaging of the legislative programme. But above all, Haig's Supplication was an expression of continuing dissent from specific ecclesiastical and fiscal enactments which amplified the apprehensions articulated in the Humble Supplication.[17]

Haig's Supplication itemised breaches of constitutional convention in the course of the coronation parliament. Hogg's Petition had been suppressed. No opportunity was afforded for the redress of grievances raised at, but deferred from, the Conventions of Estates in 1625 and 1630. The customary meeting of the gentry to collate grievances from the localities had been interrupted in the king's name. The nobility were prohibited to meet either as a separate estate or to discuss the legislative programme with the committee of articles. All three lay estates were denied official notice of the legislative programme until its presentation for approval on 28 June 1633. Charles's noting of the names of the disaffected who attempted to speak as well as cast their votes against its block passage was unprecedented.[18]

The bishops, deployed by Charles as his lynch-pins to secure control over the committee of articles, were attacked as suborners of free assemblies in the State as in the Kirk. Reinforcing the call for a return to the practice of 1609, when each estate chose its own representatives on the committee, was the actual selection of nobles. Of the eight chosen by the bishops, three — Lennox, Hamilton and Roxburghe — were courtiers and two — Winton and William Douglas, first marquis of Douglas — were Catholics. No more than nine of the sixty-five nobles summoned to the coronation parliament were Catholics. Leading recusants were thus accorded a disproportionate influence in blatant disregard of the penal laws against Catholics serving in public office. The deliberately bland 'ratification of the actes touching religione', which studiously avoided specifying previous enactments of parliaments or general assemblies, served not only to confirm episcopacy and the continuing enforcement of conformity, but also to underwrite royal supremacy in ecclesiastical affairs. The lack of constitutional limitations on the prerogative gave rise to 'a generall feare of some innovations intended in essential poynts of religion'. At the same time, the reputed licence afforded by the bishops to the preaching of Arminianism, if continued uncensored in Scotland, opened up the prospect that 'books full of Poperie and Arminianisme' currently circulating in England would soon be distributed north of the Border.[19]

Arminianism was no more a perceived than an actual threat to the Calvinist orthodoxy of the Kirk. Nonetheless, the charge of Arminianism provided a convenient means of abusing the Scottish bishops for their apparent doctrinal laxity. More pertinently, the association of Arminianism and Catholicism, a practice common among English Calvinists, masked a thinly veiled attack on William Laud, the religious mentor of Charles I and mainspring of the Court's growing assertiveness in ecclesiastical affairs throughout the British Isles. Yet the association of Arminianism and Catholicism in Haig's Supplication was not so much an attempt to make common cause with English dissidents as to highlight the danger to the Kirk from the wholesale importation of religious standards currently in favour at Court. Laud's insistence on the primacy of order and seemliness in religious observances reinforced Charles's fundamental belief that the Church of England was 'instituted the nearest to the practice of the apostles, and the best for the propagation and advancement of the Christian religion, of any church in the world'. Laud's stage management of Charles I's Scottish coronation on 18 July 1633 had brought home to Scottish Calvinists that the Court rather than Rome posed the more immediate threat. The archbishop of St. Andrews and the five other Scottish bishops officiating had worn rochets, a practice unwitnessed since the Reformation; likewise their seeming deference to the altar and crucifix when conducting divine service. Laud's translation from the bishopric of London to the archbishopric of Canterbury on 19 September duly served notice to Scottish Calvinists that the British drive for religious uniformity would be unstinting.[20]

The threat from the Court to the Reformed tradition in the Kirk was viewed by the disaffected as constitutional no less than religious subversion. The most contentious item within the legislative programme presented to the coronation parliament was undoubtedly the act, 'anent his Majestieis royall prerogative and apparell of Kirkmen': a reaffirmation of the enactment of 1606 acknowledging the royal prerogative in Kirk and State in association with the enactment of 1609 empowering James VI to prescribe the apparel of all legal officers as well as clergymen. Haig's Supplication condemned the 'subtill conjunction' of the prerogative with a relatively trivial enactment regarded as a personal concession to James VI, in consideration of his 'long experience and incomparable' knowledge of government in Kirk and State.[21]

Indeed Charles, by deliberate legislative association, was claiming that the right to regulate apparel — conceded personally to James VI, but never actually exercised — was vested inherently in the Crown. Hence, any rejection of his prescription of clerical dress was tantamount to defiance of his prerogative. Charles duly ensured that the relatively innocuous issue of clerical dress remained a matter of constitutional controversy when he ordered the wearing of 'whytes' by clergy from 15 October 1633. Whether attending affairs of State or officiating in the Kirk, bishops were to wear rochets, the apparel favoured in the coronation ceremony. Ministers were to continue wearing black gowns when preaching, but surplices were to be worn when administering the sacraments, reading divine service or carrying out burials.[22]

Despite the emphasis given to religious issues in Haig's Supplication, the conduct of the disaffected element, particularly of the nobles at the coronation parliament, was arguably motivated as much by politics as by piety. Indeed, the religious emphasis was by no means supported by all presbyterian non-conformists.[23] If not especially devout, the religious emphasis was tactically sound. Religious standards affected congregational activity in every parish and were therefore of concern to Scottish society as a whole. Nonetheless, Haig's Supplication was politically indiscreet. Charles's authoritarian conduct on religious issues was compared unfavourably with James VI. His fiscal demands were contrasted with the consideration for the material condition of the Scottish people shown not only by his father, but by his predecessors as far back as James I in the fifteenth century. Charles needed little reminding of his promise when launching his Revocation Scheme, that the augmentation of the patrimony of the Crown would ensure that 'your Majestie should not be burthensome to your people'. Still less was Charles receptive to complaints that the renewal of taxation in 1625, 1630 and 1633 amounted to the economic subversion of the national interest by a voracious Court.[24]

As well as protesting that the renewal of the extraordinary tax on annualrents had breached his father's promise in 1621 about its temporary nature, Haig's Supplication issued a prophetic warning that the supply voted in 1633, especially the 2% benevolence, would prove litigious and difficult to uplift. Creditors were certainly prepared to massage interest rates to avoid paying the benevolence, albeit tax evasion degenerated into open violence on only one occasion. During the Whitsum levy in 1635, a tax collector in Aberdeen was 'shamefully hounded' in a riot instigated by rival factions within the town council. However, the riot was as much a protest against royal interference in the appointment of the burgh's magistrates — because of past complicity with the disaffected element in the coronation parliament — as against the extended and augmented fiscal demands of the Crown.[25]

When news of his authorship of the Supplication reached the Court in the spring of 1634, Haig at least had sufficient foresight to be safely ensconced in the Netherlands. Charles having returned from Scotland with the firm impression that the disaffected element was 'seditiouslie disposed', he was determined that exemplary punishment should be meted out to the opposition leaders. Having perused a copy of the 'clandestine infamous Libell', Charles decided on 2 May to warrant 'some whom we spetiale trust' to investigate grounds for prosecution of the author's accessories. A nine-man investigative commission was duly designated three days later, consisting of six leading officials and three bishops. Archbishop Spottiswood of St. Andrews, who had actually despatched a copy of Haig's Supplication to the Court at the outset of March, was to preside over the investigations which commenced on 1 June. Balmerino and Rothes were the two opposition leaders summoned before the investigative commission to give an account of their involvement in the publication and distribution of what Charles was now prejudging a 'scandalous and seditious lybell'. Rothes was dismissed on 3 July, but Balmerino was detained in Edinburgh Castle pending indictment, an indictment that was to prove the single most important event transforming the disaffected element from a political faction into a national movement.[26]

Leasing-Making

Balmerino was particularly suited for Charles's prescription 'to single out one of that rank, who was most obliged to Us and Our Crowne'. As a temporal lord, he was a member of the new rather than the traditional nobility. Moreover, his father, a former secretary of state, had been forfeited for treason only to be subsequently pardoned by James VI. All investigations against other leaders of the disaffected were suspended on 24 July 1634.[27]

Over four months were to elapse from Balmerino's referral to trial to his indictment on 3 December. The legal substance of his alleged criminal activity was not easy to determine, albeit the investigative commission had subjected Balmerino and his associates to continuous interrogation between 7 June and 1 August. Having received two copies of Haig's Supplication from the author, Balmerino had revealed its contents to only two people outwith his household — the earl of Rothes and a Dundee notary, Mr John Dunmore. When Rothes returned one copy, deeming its presentation to the king inexpedient, Balmerino interlined it at three points — all minor revisions moderating its critical tone. Although the other copy was returned to Haig, three pirated copies were made — two within Balmerino's household and one by Dunmore. The latter unauthorised transcription was brought to the notice of Archbishop Spottiswood who communicated its contents to Court. The investigative commission upheld Charles's view that Haig's Supplication was libellous and 'tended to alienate the subjects from their duty to the king'. But Balmerino had neither penned the Supplication nor dispersed it widely. The only substance for criminal proceedings was that he concealed the libel by neither revealing nor apprehending the author.[28]

At the insistence of Traquair, the investigative commission was reconvened on 20 October 1634, to incorporate the interlining of a copy of Haig's Supplication in the charges against Balmerino. Three weeks later, Lord Advocate Hope publicised the Crown's intent to have Balmerino indicted for treason on the technical charge for leasing-making — stirring up enmity between the king and his subjects by false and malicious writings. Indeed, Charles had pre-empted further revision or classification of charges arising from Haig's Supplication by maintaining on 11 November that 'all our good subjects be bound in conscience, as also by the laws of this our kingdom to crush this Cockatrice in the egg and to abhor it as a pestilentious clout'. Denied access to depositions and other papers affecting his case until the formal specification of charges against him, Balmerino was given no more than three weeks to instruct legal counsel and confer with friends before his trial commenced.[29]

The initial diet of the trial, which commenced on 3 December, was spread over two weeks and comprised marathon sessions which lasted up to nine hours daily. Balmerino was arraigned before a four-man judicial commission over which William Hay, tenth earl of Errol and hereditary high constable of Scotland, presided. Errol had been admonished by Charles to be fair and just, but also to be mindful of the interests of the Crown in establishing the grounds for trial. The charges against Balmerino were found relevant in all three indictable points — his concealment of the libel; his failure to apprehend the libeller; and his association with the authorship of the libel evident from his interlined copy. Balmerino was ordained to pass to the judgement of an assize on 20 December, that the extent of his guilt might be determined by fifteen of the forty-five nobles and gentry already summoned to Edinburgh.[30]

The vehemence with which the bishops, especially Spottiswood of St. Andrews and Maxwell of Ross, sought a treasonable indictment not only aggravated tensions within the Scottish administration, but alienated moderate support among nobles and gentry not yet aligned with the disaffected element. Episcopal efforts to secure amenable assessors for Errol's judicial commission were compounded by episcopal attempts to influence the final selection of the assize. John Maitland, earl of Lauderdale, articulated the general dissatisfaction. Writing to Hamilton on 8 December, he castigated the bishops as his 'small friendes' for their design to have him nominated on the assize. He was most reluctant to condemn Balmerino, a task for which he confessed, 'I have not the courage to adventure upon the damnation of my Soul'. This standpoint was borne out of personal disinterest. Other than to exchange courteous pleasantries, he had not spoken to Balmerino for several years.[31]

The prosecution of Balmerino also provoked a public outcry demonstrated by 'the inordinat concurse of people' in Edinburgh. Indeed, the city magistrates were required to provide an armed escort between the castle and the tolbooth for both the prisoner and the judicial commission throughout the initial diet of the trial in December. After the judicial commission had found the treasonable indictment relevant, the trial was prorogued in the forlorn hope that Balmerino would submit to the mercy of the Crown and thus prevent further public disturbances. Following the impanelling of the assize on 20 March 1635, the conduct of final proceedings was marked by elements of legal chicanery as well as judicial farce. The defence counsel's objections against nine of the landowners originally selected — either for affirming prior to impannelling that Balmerino was guilty or for receiving covert solicitations to find against Balmerino — were upheld in only one instance. The notorious courtier and fiscal entrepreneur, Alexander Strachan of Thornton, was not obliged to stand down. More flagrantly, Traquair was admitted to the assize and elected to preside over its deliberations even though he had served on the investigative commission and was currently co-ordinating the king's campaign for a successful prosecution.

The assize of eight nobles and seven gentry was eventually sworn in by ten o'clock on Friday evening, 20 March. For the next eight hours, they 'spake their mynds freelie' before convicting Balmerino on the casting vote of Traquair. Lauderdale, having been impanelled despite his reservations to Hamilton, voted to acquit Balmerino on all three counts. The most impassioned and influential plea for clemency was made by the elderly John Gordon of Buckie who, forty-three years earlier, had himself been convicted as an accomplice to the murder of James Stewart, 'the bonnie earl' of Moray. William Keith, the earl Marischal, was subsequently to claim that he had been filed in favour of a conviction because he was asleep when the vote to acquit was taken. Balmerino was eventually convicted on only one charge — that of failing to reveal that the Supplication's author was Mr William Haig. Nonetheless, this conviction was sufficient to merit capital punishment.[32]

The threat that public agitation during the trial would now lead to the exaction of reprisals against himself and the seven others on the assize who had voted for a conviction, persuaded the wily Traquair to repair to Court. Charles was advised that the execution of Balmerino 'was in no sort advisable'. Though the verdict was just, the penalty was impolitic. Albeit reminded by Haig's Supplication of his unfavourable standing in comparison to his father among the political nation, Charles was not deaf to pleas for clemency. Ironically, the most influential support for the full pardon granted to Balmerino by the end of June came from Archbishop Laud, who looked to English precedent in deciding that the condemnation of a man to death by such a narrow majority was inequitable.[33]

However, the pardoning of Balmerino could not undo the crucial damage his trial had inflicted on the personal rule of Charles I. Haig's Supplication had probably been rooted more in the tradition of medieval canon law than of Roman law, in that individual conscience was not to be outweighed by a majority decision. In effect, Charles's denial of the right to appeal was a negation of the individual's freedom to oppose the policies of the Crown.[34] William Drummond of Hawthornden, a supporter of a divinely ordained, social hierarchy over which the monarch was the irremoveable head, had sought to advise Charles, prior to the resumption of Balmerino's trial before the assize, that Haig's Supplication should have been 'answered by a Pen, not by an Ax'. This conservative anti-cleric subsequently went on to affirm that the bishops, by their determination to punish Balmerino, were no less culpable as 'occasioners to have infamous Libels published'. The people having been driven towards 'a desperate carelessness' by the combination of excessive taxation and insecurity of landholding during the personal rule, public sympathy was firmly on the side of Balmerino.[35]

However unheeded, Hawthornden's admonitions to Charles I were well founded. The disaffected element had learned from the trial of Balmerino that there was a potent alternative to submission to the dictates of the Court. From its initial diet in December 1634 until its conclusion in March 1635, the trial was held against a continuous backdrop of public and private prayer meetings for the comfort of Balmerino, reinforced by tumultuous petitioning and political agitation. Indeed, the trial marked a decisive shift from reform towards revolution in exposing Charles's critical lack of effective forces of coercion and persuasion to sustain his authoritarian personal rule in Scotland.[36]

Rumours circulating during Balmerino's trial that Charles could, if necessary, call upon the support of the clans for the forcible defence of his interests were no more than fanciful Gaelic imaginings. Charles's efforts to reactivate the appointment of Alexander Lindsay, Lord Spynie, as general muster-master and colonel of trained bands throughout Scotland, were effectively blocked in the aftermath of the coronation parliament. Spynie's original patent of January 1626 to create a national militia had been forestalled by his departure overseas in October 1627 to join the British expeditionary forces engaged in the Thirty Years' War. A national militia, if co-ordinated centrally, but recruited, equipped, trained and provisioned locally, would create a standing army on the cheap without necessitating the summoning of a parliament to vote supply. Because Spynie's patent was deemed a matter of national interest, the Privy Council were not prepared to effect a militia without plenary discussions of the like held on the common fishing and the coinage. In response to the continuous presence maintained in Edinburgh by members of the disaffected element since the coronation parliament, the plenary discussions of the Council to review Spynie's patent were attended by four representatives each from the three lay estates in March 1634. Rothes and Loudoun were to the fore in resisting the creation of a national militia. The Council was persuaded to seek permission from Court to hold meetings in every shire prior to a final round of plenary discussions which were to be expanded to include commissioners from the clergy as well as greater representation for the three lay estates. Faced not with a plenary session of Council but a convention of estates whose agenda need not be restricted to Spynie's patent, the Court shelved plans for a national militia.[37]

Politicising Nonconformity

The readiness of the Privy Council to set the national interest against that of the Court was furthered by the mounting reaction against the bishops. Their manifest political ambitions served to undermine their role of apologist for the monarchy: that is, to preach obedience in matters of Kirk and State. This changing equilibrium in civil affairs exposed by the trial of Balmerino had actually been foreshadowed in ecclesiastical affairs by the further politicising of nonconformity.

The reimposition of compulsory communion for leading officials, councillors and members of the judiciary — albeit on an annual rather than a quarterly basis — from 8 October 1633 was integral to the king's drive for religious uniformity throughout the British Isles. Initially imposed in July 1629 to flush out papists within his Scottish administration, the mandatory reception of communion while kneeling in the chapel royal was now intended to eradicate presbyterian nonconformity. The accompanying directive that prayers were to be conducted twice daily according to the English liturgy, 'till some course be taken for making one, that may fit the custom and constitution of the Church', confirmed that the use of Anglican ritual during the coronation ceremonial was not an isolated occurrence. Despite a demonstrable lack of enthusiasm for his religious test for public office, Charles decided on 13 May 1634 that the first Sunday in July and December should be set aside for his Scottish administration to take communion in the chapel royal. With little evident backing from his Scottish administration, Charles extended the use of the English liturgy for daily prayers in cathedrals and universities as well as bishops' oratories and the chapel royal from 20 October.[38]

The aspersions of the disaffected element that Archbishop Laud was behind these directives were not unfounded. Despite Laud's persistent claim that he only intervened in the affairs of the Kirk at the express command of the king, he encouraged Adam Bellenden, bishop of Dumblane and dean of the chapel royal, to submit not just annual but regular reports to Court. Bellenden was left in no doubt that his advancement within the Scottish episcopate depended on his keeping non-communicants under surveillance. Laud's dismissive attitude towards the Reformed tradition of the Kirk during the coronation visit was open to exploitation, however. Suspicions were planted among the laity as well as the ministry that changes in public worship were but the first step in the Court's displacement of the prevailing Calvinist orthodoxy.[39]

The threat to Calvinist orthodoxy was seemingly underscored by the appointment of William Forbes to the newly created bishopric of Edinburgh on 28 January 1634. Not only was Forbes one of the few leading churchmen in Scotland disposed towards Arminianism, but he was the one member of the Scottish episcopate prepared to countenance an accommodation with Rome. As well as leaving presbyterians in Edinburgh 'all in a dump', news of his appointment had perplexed moderate opinion, not hitherto sympathetic to nonconformity, well beyond the bounds of the capital. The key strategic significance of the diocese of Edinburgh for the pursuit of religious uniformity was signalled by Forbes's admission to the Privy Council within three days of his consecration as bishop. Although his stint as bishop lasted barely three months, Forbes, notwithstanding his sickly constitution, sought to influence all conforming clergy in an Arminian direction. Nonconforming scruples were disregarded in his instructions to ministers for the celebration of communion on Easter Sunday, 6 April. Each minister was to set an example to his congregation by kneeling to receive the sacraments which he, in turn, was to give personally to every participant unassisted by elders. The majority of clergy within his diocese failed to comply, however. Only the death of Forbes on 12 April prevented his imposition of ecclesiastical censures for nonconformity.[40]

The Court of High Commission was confirmed as the principal agency for ecclesiastical censure by its reconstitution on 21 October 1634. Its judicial powers — over all persons scandalous in life, doctrine and religion; over slanderous preaching and libellous writing against the current establishment in Kirk and State; over all appeals from inferior ecclesiastical courts — depended solely on the royal prerogative. Unlike inferior ecclesiastical courts, the High Commission could impose civil sanctions ranging from fining to imprisonment for both clergy and laity. As well as being an alternative to the general assembly for the oversight of decisions taken in synods, presbyteries and kirk sessions, the High Commission was an alternative to the Privy Council for the civil censure of ecclesiastical transgressions — albeit the Council was required to sanction outlawry.

Intended as the main judicial weapon of the Crown against nonconformity, the High Commission in practice exhibited considerable restraint in attempting to get militant presbyterians to accept its jurisdiction. Only six ministers were arraigned before the High Commission during the thirteen-year personal rule of Charles I, as against forty-eight prosecuted in the last fifteen years of James VI. But its very existence was anathema to nonconformists fearful that the High Commission was reconstituted by Charles to undo presbyterianism. Its openness to episcopal manipulation aroused friction within the Scottish administration. Charles's appointment of 156 commissioners was a considerable enlargement on the fifty-six members of James VI's last High Commission of 1619; a markedly lower portion of clergy were appointed: sixty-one in 1634 as against thirty-seven in 1619. Nonetheless, the running of the High Commission tended to be dominated by the bishops and their adherents among the clergy, a feature presaged by the modest requirement for a quorum — seven members, a mere increase of two from 1619. No meeting was quorate unless a bishop was present. Actual clerical domination of proceedings meant that the Privy Council was not always prepared to maintain lines of jurisdictional demarcation with the High Commission.[41]

Since 1630, militant presbyterians had been increasingly aware of ecclesiastical censures exacted or threatened against Puritans in England and especially concerned about the imprisonment of polemicists opposed to prelacy and Arminianism. It cannot be demonstrated, however that disaffected elements in both countries were making common cause from around the time of the coronation visit.[42] Despite the concurrent groundswell of protest against the personal rule of Charles I in England, the rallying of the disaffected in Scotland was predominantly a self-contained political phenomenon. No united front in opposition to religious uniformity or in support of constitutional assemblies was formulated in either country prior to the termination of Charles's personal rule in Scotland. Conversely, covert communing between the disaffected should not be discounted because of the supercilious view at Court that prevented Scottish affairs being mentioned in any gazette prior to the outbreak of revolt in 1637. Balmerino's trial and the politicising of nonconformity had aggravated the dissent occasioned by the management of the coronation parliament. Perceptive voices within the Scottish administration were warning the Court from the summer of 1635 that adverse publicity generated by the king's insensitive handling of Scottish affairs could further undermine English confidence in monarchy.[43]

The Canterburians

More immediately, the monarchical position in Scotland was not just parlous but prone to paralysis. The groundswell of disaffection in the country was accompanied by the steady erosion of political will within the Scottish administration to take concerted action on behalf of Charles I. Not only was there demonstrable polarity between bishops on the one side and lay officials and councillors on the other, but the episcopates was divided between the innovatory Laudian or Canterburian faction and the erastian defenders of Calvinist orthodoxy; a division exploited by Traquair to project himself as the main check to the political ambitions of the bishops.

Traquair's strategy of exploiting episcopal divisions depended upon his retention of substantial support from the middle ground in Scottish politics, support which could no longer be guaranteed in the course of 1636 as the aggressive posturing of the Canterburians persuaded discontented lay administrators to give covert counsel to the disaffected element. In effect, Traquair's strategy left the bishops politically isolated and exposed and, simultaneously, spread public disillusionment about the capacity of the Scottish administration to prevent Charles I treating his native kingdom as a province. By the time the Crown's plans for liturgical innovation were clarified, the division within the episcopate stood in stark contrast to the cohesiveness of the disaffected element in defence of the national interest.[44]

The want of harmony among the bishops, exploited by Traquair but fostered by Laud, was primarily a matter of political style and presentation rather than the product of differing social origins or even a generation gap. Despite greater familiarity and affinity with the upper echelons of landed society enjoyed by the older erastian bishops, class antagonism occasioned by the implementation of the Revocation Scheme had nullified this advantage over the younger Canterburians. Charles pursued a policy of episcopal promotion that differed markedly from that of his father who had made appointments from short leets drawn up by the existing episcopate. All bishops appointed or translated by Charles owed their advancement to the recommendation of leading courtiers. As Court clients, the new bishops tended to form a cadre fit to act as Laud's vanguard within the Scottish administration. As the increasingly senile Archbishop Spottiswood tended to be carried along by the aggressive posturing of the five Canterburians, the erastian bishops appeared 'prudent and humble men' because of their reluctance to promote episcopal acquisition of civil offices or impose religious uniformity.[45]

Laud and the Canterburians undoubtedly shaped policy, exercising an especially decisive influence on the politicising of nonconformity and the imposition of liturgical innovations. However, that they attracted public opprobrium for their close association with experimental and innovatory policies does not necessarily mean that they devised these policies, far less that they were the main instruments of social change or even a radical force within Scottish politics during the 1630s.[46] In the adverse judicial climate following the exemplary prosecution of Balmerino, it was both necessary and prudent to blame agents enforcing the dictates of the Court rather than Charles I personally. Moreover, the main guidelines for unpopular policies were already established before the public emergence of the Canterburian faction in the course of the coronation visit.

Laud was largely content to act as a power-broker at Court in civil affairs, providing an alternative but complementary network of clientage to that provided by Hamilton. Whereas the marquis preferred a policy of benign neglect tantamount to quiescent provincialism, Laud, as evident in his application of 'thorough' to fiscal management and local government, was prepared to countenance the occasional exercise in aggressive provincialism. At no time, however, did he challenge Hamilton's paramount responsibility at Court for managing civil affairs in Scotland. But he was prepared to defer only to the king in the conduct of ecclesiastical affairs in Scotland, whose episcopate, like its Kirk, he regarded as provincial, remote and lacking adequate representation at Court. He positively encouraged the bishops not only to seek his clientage but to channel all their correspondence to Court through him. His political energy, his interminable capacity for intrigue, his sense of rightness and, above all, Charles I's reluctance to involve himself in administrative detail, established Laud as the indispensable intermediary at Court for the conduct of ecclesiastical affairs in which he brooked no interference. Thus, Laud and the Canterburians were intent on identifying and isolating opponents of liturgical innovation within the Scottish administration by the autumn of 1635.[47]

Acutely conscious that James VI had dropped his plans for further liturgical innovation as the price of public acceptance of the Five Articles, the erastian bishops were concerned about the disruptive impact of the wholesale importation of Anglican ritual, an importation signposted by the publication of three Scottish editions of the English Book of Common Prayer between the coronation visit and October 1634. While accepting the king's resolve to foist liturgical innovations on the Kirk, the erastian bishops affirmed the need to preserve a distinctly Scottish dimension for worship and religious observance. They pressed for Anglican ritual to be diluted to accord with Scottish sensibilities of which they were a better judge than Laud. Rather than regurgitate the English Book of Common Prayer, it was vital for public acceptance of liturgical innovation that some of the Scottish episcopate should be commissioned to draw up a prayer book for Scotland.[48]

Although Charles conceded Scottish authorship in May 1634, he was adamant that the want of uniformity in worship and discipline was the major defect of the Kirk and could only be remedied by the production of a book of canons as well as a prayer book. The Court was to exercise strict supervision of the production of both. All drafts and amendments were to be approved by the king in consultation with Laud and his English associates — namely, William Juxon, bishop of London, and Matthew Wren, bishop of Norwich. Archbishop Spottiswood was specially admonished on 20 October that a Scottish prayer book was to be produced 'with all convenient diligence', its format 'as neir as can be to this of England'. Nonetheless, the erastian bishops were in no haste to expedite liturgical innovation; a standpoint with which Laud concurred, not because he recognised the need to preserve a Scottish dimension in worship and discipline, but because he was averse to any concessions that would serve as precedents for moderating his uncompromising stance towards English Puritans. Although Laud was obliged by Charles to accept Scottish versions of the prayer book and the book of canons, he demanded and received regular accounts of their diligence from the Scottish bishops. He continued to commend and explain Anglican ritual as well as correct and add to Scottish revisions after the king had warranted the printing of both books in May 1635.[49]

Moreover, Laud's aversion to Scottish authorship was progressively allayed by the presence of assertive Canterburians. His leading Scottish acolyte, John Maxwell, bishop of Ross, shared the desire of the erastian bishops that liturgical innovation must accommodate Scottish sensibilities — not so much to appease nationalist sentiment, but because of scriptural unsoundness. The English Book of Common Prayer contained lessons from the Apocrypha and retained vernacular translations made anachronistic by the Authorised Version of the Bible of King James VI and I published in 1611. Maxwell's personal assertiveness and his willingness to liaise regularly with the Court ensured that there would be no drastic revision of Anglican ritual once a modified version of the English liturgy had been despatched north in September 1634. The king having inserted translations from the Authorised Version, the only significant alteration for which there was episcopal concensus over the next nine months was the universal adoption of 'presbyter' as a compromise between the Canterburian preference for 'priest' and the 'minister' of orthodox Calvinism. By the spring of 1636, Laud was prepared to endorse Scottish proposals for significant further revision of the prayer book. The proposals, initiated by a committed Canterburian, James Wedderburn, bishop of Dunblane, moved liturgical innovation firmly in the direction of sacerdotalism and more than hinted at Arminianism. The most fundamental change, in ordering and administering communion, amounted to a comprehensive rejection of Calvinist orthodoxy.[50]

Notwithstanding Laud's claims to be upholding Reformed tradition, charges from the Calvinist mainstream in both Scotland and England that the king and the archbishop of Canterbury were innovators in the pursuit of religious uniformity were irrefutable. Intended as a shift along Anglican lines in favour of sacerdotalism and Arminianism, liturgical innovations were received in Scotland as little better than a divisive sacramental exercise insinuating Catholicism, a deliberate subterfuge by a Romanised Court in conjunction with 'popishlie-affected Bishops'. Scottish Calvinists were becoming convinced that the Canterburians were intent on undermining not just received doctrinal orthodoxy but the entire Reformed tradition of the Kirk.[51]

Although not all were convinced Arminians, the Canterburians and some of the younger Scottish clergy were certainly inspired by Arminian teaching to press for the readoption of sacramental practices dormant since the Reformation. Laud, especially, was preoccupied with the view that the altar, the place for the celebration of Christ's body, was of prime importance in the church as opposed to the pulpit, the place for the preaching of God's word. The focal point of divine service should be the indiscriminate bestowal of saving grace through the sacraments administered exclusively by the priest, not the assurance of the truth of God's law and gospel which Calvinists believed the elect received from the minister's preaching of the word. Thus, the king's authorising of liturgical innovations represented a direct onslaught on established Calvinist orthodoxy; an onslaught of revolutionary potential in Scotland, where the preaching of the word had been reckoned the chief part of divine service since the Reformation and where Arminianism was popularly classed with popery.[52]

Laud personally had no intention of insinuating Roman Catholicism throughout the king's dominions. He considered Roman Catholicism a corruption of the glorious tradition of the early church, but he did not regard the faith as inherently wicked or its practitioners beyond redemption. He consistently deplored the fashionable Catholicism of the clique at Court associated with Queen Henrietta Maria. He was notably resistant to the six-year, but ultimately fruitless, scheme mooted by the marquis of Douglas in 1633 to lobby the papacy for a cardinal's hat for one of the king's Catholic subjects, preferably George Con, an expatriate Scot within the Vatican bureaucracy. Nonetheless, Laud and the Canterburians made no public effort to dispel popular identification of liturgical innovations with popish practices.[53]

Notwithstanding their defective public relations, their aggressive posturing and their inadequate accommodation of Scottish sensibilities, the most critical error of Laud and the Canterburians was their failure to realise that liturgical innovations and associated doctrinal issues could not be isolated from a political setting that was patently unwelcoming in Scotland. Contemporary accusations of popery against Archbishop Laud, which were damaging because of the close association of Protestantism and patriotism in England, were made the more heinous in Scotland by the imposition of sacerdotalism as a provincial exercise directed by the Court. The Canterburians were castigated as the 'English faction'.[54]

Conclusion

The Scottish version of the book of canons was duly published in Aberdeen at the outset of 1636 as *Canons and Constitutions Ecclesiastical*. In substance, by upholding the royal supremacy in ecclesiastical affairs, the book of canons abrogated disciplinary powers to episcopacy in terms offensive to Calvinists in general and presbyterians in particular. Episcopal government was held accountable only to the Crown; there was no future commitment to general assemblies. The bishops were to rely on the assistance of the Court of High Commission for the enforcement of discipline nationwide. At diocesan level, the bishops were expected to hold synods twice yearly for consultations with their clergy, but no disciplinary role was specified for presbyteries, kirk sessions or elders. All clergy and laity who refused to acknowledge or deemed unscriptural the king's supremacy, episcopal government or liturgical innovations in the Kirk faced excommunication — a threat which represented the ultimate politicising of nonconformity during the personal rule. At the same time the book of canons, by prescribing compulsory use of a new prayer book, forewarned the disaffected element.[55]

Indeed, the combination of impolitic delays in drafting, deliberate leakage of episcopal intentions from within the Scottish administration and wanton incompetence on the part of the principal printer afforded the disaffected ample time to mount a concerted attack on the Scottish version of the prayer book. Final instructions for drafting were not issued until 18 October 1636, when the king issued a missive commanding the conformity of all clergy and laity to the new liturgy; every parish was to be provided with at least two copies of the prayer book by Easter 1637. When the Privy Council proclaimed the king's missive on 20 December, the book was still not printed in its entirety — a task not completed for another four months. However, Traquair, in order to compromise the bishops politically and give himself a free rein in civil affairs, had already leaked a copy of the new prayer book that had been printed in London for perusal at Court. Meanwhile, Robert Young was allowing discarded leaves and sheets from his printing house to be recycled as wrapping paper for spices and tobacco purchased in Edinburgh shops.[56]

The new prayer book, published as *The Book of Common Prayer and Administration of the Sacraments*, incurred public odium as the Service Book which was 'much more Popish nor the Inglishe Book, and much less Protestant'. In calling for the nationwide rejection of the Service Book, the disaffected made great play of the sacerdotal emphasis on ritual 'urged upon the Kirk of God by antichristian prelats'. The targeting of the bishops was a deliberate ploy by the disaffected to capitalise on the widespread aversion within the political nation to episcopal advancement within the Scottish administration. In like manner, that Laud, the apostle of 'thorough', should be specifically targeted as the malicious influence behind liturgical innovation served to link public hostility to the imposition of economic and religious uniformity and, simultaneously, enabled the disaffected to make common cause with the English Puritans.

To further the association of unpopular secular policies with the suborning of the Reformed tradition, liturgical innovations were held to have emanated from the Court rather than directly from the Crown: a manoeuvre which allowed the disaffected to portray themselves as the defenders of the national interest without launching an outright attack on Charles I. Nonetheless, the tarnishing of Laud and the Scottish episcopate channelled the endemic unrest occasioned by the Court's civil and ecclesiastical dictates towards tangible limitations on the royal prerogative. Liturgical innovations were imposed 'without consent of either Generall Assemblie or Parliament, aganis the will of all men, except such as are popishlie affected'. By broadcasting that royal government in Scotland was little more than a provincial exercise in arbitrary rule, liturgical innovations rallied the disaffected nationwide in a determined drive for constitutional change in Kirk and State; a change which, in the aftermath of Balmerino's trial, would have to be accomplished by direct action.[57]

By the outset of 1637, a situation of revolutionary potential existed within Scotland. The Scottish administration was racked by internecine conflicts. The political nation regarded with mounting apprehension the policies and directives emanating from the Court. Above all, the disaffected element were resolved to utilise the religious issue to fashion a concerted movement for the accomplishment of constitutional change in both Kirk and State. This resolve, which can certainly be traced back to the coronation parliament, was reinforced by genuine religious conviction — notably, the assurance spreading among nonconformists of the imminent triumph of presbyterianism, when 'Truth in Scotland shall keep the crown of the causeway'.[58]

NOTES

1. *APS*, V, 1–165; Row, *History of the Kirk*, 362–63; Spalding, *Troubles*, I, 16–20.

2. Balfour, *Historical Works*, II, 207–14; Row, *History of the Kirk*, 357–62.

3. Balfour, *Historical Works*, II, 142–45; Row, *History of the Kirk*, 340; G. Albion, *Charles I and the Court of Rome*, (London, 1935), 78–94; 104–09.

4. *The Bannatyne Miscellany*, III, 219–24; *RPCS*, second series, II, 327–28, 334, 343–44, 392, 535–36, 596–97; III, 237–49; VIII, 366–67. The two-man delegation was composed of Bishop Patrick Lindsay of Ross (later archbishop of Glasgow), who had presided over the clerical convention in the absence of Archbishop Spottiswood, and Mr Robert Scott of the High Kirk of Glasgow, a noted nonconformist.

5. *Memoirs of Scottish Catholics during the seventeenth and eighteenth centuries*, W. F. Forbes-Leith ed., 2 vols, (London, 1909), I, 14, 22–27, 56; M. V. Hay, *The Blairs Papers*, (1603–60), (London & Edinburgh, 1929), 192–95; P. F. Anson, *Underground Catholicism in Scotland, 1622–1878*, (Montrose, 1970), 30–32.

6. The limited imposition of penal sanctions against Catholic recusants is appraised more thoroughly in A. I. Macinnes, 'Catholic Recusancy and the Penal Laws, 1603–1707', *RSCHS*, XXIII, (1987), 27–63.

7. Row, *History of the Kirk*, 353; Polisensky, *The Thirty Years War*, 194–208; Steinberg, *The 'Thirty Years War*, 53–69.

8. *SR*, I, 325, 338, 354–55, 390; II, 428; *RPCS*, second series, II, 3, 303; III, 24, 187–88, 244, 260, 316, 320–31; IV, 189–90; *Memoirs of Scottish Catholics*, I, 60.

9. SRO, Cunninghame-Graham MSS, GD 22/1/518; Row, *History of the Kirk*, 350–51.

10. Baillie, *Letters and Journals*, I, 476–78.

11. Row, *History of the Kirk*, 364–66.

12. *SR*, II, 581, 591, 605, 620–21; 'Reasons Against the Reception of King James's Metaphrase of the Psalms, 1631', in *The Bannatyne Miscellany*, vol. I, (Bannatyne Club, Edinburgh, 1827), 227–50; *Letters of Samuel Rutherford*, 2 vols, A. A. Bonar ed., (Edinburgh, 1863), I, 69–70; Row, *History of the Kirk*, 352–53; McGrail, *Sir William Alexander*, 49–51, 165–67.

13. *Memorials of the Earls of Haddington*, II, 164–65; *CSP, Venetian*, XXIII, (1632–36), 127.

14. Row, *History of the Kirk*, 365–66; *APS*, V, 13–16, c.1; 167–70, 209–12. That the benevolence was levied on all lent money was attributed to Hamilton as collector-general designate of taxation. The marquis, with the connivance of Hay of Lands, the clerk-register, reputedly had the specification that the benevolence was to be exacted from free money only omitted from the enactment as drafted by the committee of articles: an omission estimated to have cost the political nation £53,333–6/8 (Scotstarvit, *Staggering State of Scottish Statesmen*, 87).

15. Balfour, *Historical Works*, II, 202; Spalding, *Troubles*, I, 45; *Large Declaration*, 10–11, 15; *RMS*, VIII, no. 2164–65; Row, *History of the Kirk*, 366.

16. Balfour, *Historical Works*, II, 180–81, 193–95; Clarendon, *History of the Rebellion*, I, 138–43; *CSP, Venetian*, XXIII, 78–79.

17. Row, *History of the Kirk*, 376–81; *State Trials*, W. Cobbett ed., vol. III, (London, 1809), 701.

18. The managerial techniques deployed by Charles in the coronation parliament were rejected comprehensively in the first Covenanting parliament of 1639. The specific demand that parliament should henceforth consist of only three estates — the nobles, gentry and burgesses — can also be traced back to Haig's Supplication (Lennoxlove, Hamilton Papers, C 1/1071, /1073; *Aberdeen Council Letters*, II, 140–45; HMC, *Mar & Kellie*, I, 192).

19. *APS*, IV, 413; V, 8–9, 21, c.4; Row, *History of the Kirk*, 377–79.

20. Spalding, *Troubles*, I, 17, 19–20; Row, *History of the Kirk*, 351–52, 368–69; *The Works of William Laud, D. D.*, J. Bliss ed., (Oxford, 1853); W. Tyacke, 'Puritanism, Arminianism and Counter-Revolution', in *The Origins of the English Civil War*, 130–42; M. C. Kitshoff, 'Aspects of Arminianism in Scotland', (University of St. Andrews, M. Litt. Thesis, 1968), 63–69, 92–110, 140–42.

21. Row, *History of the Kirk*, 376–78; Burnet, *History of My Own Times*, I, 11.

22. *APS*, V, 20–21, c.3; Row, *History of the Kirk*, 362–63; *Memoirs of Scottish Catholics*, I, 161–66.

23. Sir John Gordon of Lochinvar, created Viscount Kenmure at the outset of the coronation visit, was convinced that the Five Articles were 'superstitious, idolatrous, and antichristian, and come from hell'. Yet, on his deathbed in September 1634, Kenmure admitted that the sin which lay heaviest on his conscience was his expeditious withdrawal from the coronation parliament without actively opposing the ecclesiastical enactments of the Crown. But he also castigated the nobility for being 'key-cold' in their resistance to alterations to the Reformed tradition in the Kirk (*Select Biographies*, W. K. Tweedie ed., 2 vols, (Wodrow Society, Edinburgh, 1845–47), I, 397, 402–03).

24. Row, *History of the Kirk*, 378–80. The strictures in Haig's supplication about taxation, as about the constriction of patronage resulting from the departure of the Court south, were highly coloured by the personal experience of the author. Mr William Haig was a disappointed placeman. Having served as a Crown solicitor specialising in fiscal policy, Haig had been commissioned in August 1629 to investigate excessive charging by tax collectors and the resultant exaction of excessive reliefs by temporal lords, barons and freeholders. His commission, which was a victim of the political fall-out from Thornton's commission to exploit feudal casualties of the Crown, established that the major discrepancy arising from the tax rolls was not excessive charging but the imbalance in monies levied from secular barons and freeholders relative to bishops, temporal lords and royal burghs. Haig was duly granted a fresh commission to review existing tax quotas in October 1630, a commission shelved by the Privy Council three months later following hostile overtures from Chancellor Hay (then Viscount Dupplin), in his capacity as collector-general of the taxation voted in 1630. In the expectation that Hamilton would be confirmed as collector-general of the taxation voted by the coronation parliament, Haig unsuccessfully importuned

the marquis for a position as clerk, promising to use his specialised knowledge of the tax rolls to increase the revenue accruing to the Crown by a third (*SR*, I, 369–70, 410–11; II, 427, 477–78, 482–83; *RPCS*, second series, IV, 65–66, 71, 109, 112, 116; SRO, Cunninghame-Graham MSS, GD 22/3/582; SRO, Hamilton Papers TD 75/100/26/258).

25. Row, *History of the Kirk*, 380; *RPCS*, second series, V, 586–90, 594–95; VI, 117, 143–45, 172–74; *Aberdeen Council Letters*, II, 24–25, 28–31, 45–46, 148; SRO, Hamilton Papers, TD 75/100/26/984. Inventive methods of eluding the benvolence were especially practised by the burgesses as foremost creditors. Acting in collusion with their debtors, burgesses antedated their financial loans charging interest at 8% (the rate exempt from the benevolence) from one to two months before the coronation parliament; some suspended payments of interest for three years from Martinmas 1633; others had interest payments incorporated within the wadsets (mortgaged capital) granted by debtors as security on their estates rather than registered separately as annualrents.

26. *State Trials*, III, 699–700, 705–06; *SR*, II, 695, 725, 734–35, 767–69; *Large Declaration*, 12–13; Row, *History of the Kirk*, 382.

27. *Large Declaration*, 13; *SR*, II, 773–74; Lee, jr., *The Road to Revolution*, 157–59.

28. *State Trials*, III, 593, 691–706; Burnet, *History of My Own Times*, I, 12–13; Row, *History of the Kirk*, 383.

29. *State Trials*, III, 593–603; Balfour, *Historical Works*, 216–18; *RPCS*, second series, V, 409–10; *SR*, II, 800–01; SRO, Hamilton Papers, TD 75/100/26/998.

30. *SR*, II, 789–92, 808–09, 823; *State Trials*, III, 689; SRO, Hamilton Papers, TD 75/100/26/8130. The decision to prosecute on all three counts was not altogether surprising. The three assessors appointed from the College of Justice to counsel Errol were all suspected of being open to Court influence. As well as being the president of the College, Sir Robert Spottiswood was the son of the archbishop of St. Andrews who was instrumental in having Balmerino investigated, imprisoned and indicted. Sir James Learmouth of Balcomie had been in the van of attempts to mobilise support among the gentry for the Revocation Scheme. The appointment of Hay of Lands had actually been contested by Balmerino's advocates on the grounds that the clerk-register had already given partial counsel in formulating charges against Balmerino as a member of the investigative commission.

31. SRO, Hamilton Papers, TD 75/100/26/8310; Row, *History of the Kirk*, 384; Spalding, *Troubles*, I, 45; *Diary of Sir Thomas Hope*, 18.

32. *State Trials*, III, 689–91, 711–12; NLS, Salt & Coal; Events, 1635–62, MS 2263, fo. 89; *SR*, II, 823, 838–39; Row, *History of the Kirk*, 384, 386–87; Burnet, *History of My Own Times*, I, 13–14. The one landowner removed from the assize was William Stewart, Lord Blantyre, who admitted under oath that he had declared Balmerino to be guilty. The members of the assize became the butt of scurrilous verse (NLS Wodrow MSS, octavo, XXVII, fo. 20–21). Traquair was to expend £800 keeping Charles up to date with procedural developments during the trial (SRO, Treasury Accounts, 1635, E 30/23/7).

33. *State Trials*, III, 595–96; 699–700; *Large Declaration*, 14; Balfour, Historical Works, II, 218–19; Row, *History of the Kirk*, 389–90; *Ancrum & Lothian*, I, 85–86. By July 1635, Balmerino had been removed from Edinburgh Castle and confined to his estates in Fife which were secured heritably in his favour by an enactment of the Exchequer Commission. By November, he was liberated unconditionally (*SR*, II, 856; SRO, Exchequer Act Book, 1634–39, E 4/5, fo. 77).

34. I am indebted for this suggestion to Dr. R. G. Cant, former Reader in Scottish History, University of St. Andrews.

35. W. Drummond of Hawthornden, 'Memorials of State', in *The History of Scotland, from the year 1423, until the year 1542*, (London, 1681), 358–67; T. I. Rae, 'The political attitudes of William Drummond of Hawthornden', in *The Scottish Tradition: Essays in*

Honour of Ronald Gordon Cant, G. W. S. Barrow ed., (Edinburgh, 1974), 132–46; I. M. Smart, 'Monarchy and Toleration in Drummond of Hawthornden', *Scotia*, IV, 44–50.

36. Burnet, *History of My Own Times*, I, 14; Lee, jr., *The Road to Revolution*, 161–62. The contention of Maurice Lee jr., however, that the aristocracy had no spokesman or place in government after the trial of Balmerino wholly ignores the role of Traquair and Hamilton.

37. J. Fraser, *Chronicles of the Frasers: The Wardlaw Manuscript, 916–1674*, W. Mackay ed., (SHS, Edinburgh, 1905), 257; Burnet, *History of My Own Time*, I, 15; *RPCS*, second series, I, 293–94, 411–12, 561–62; II, 32–34, 88–89; V, 237–38, 249–50, 280; *APS*, V, 50–51, c.37; 225–27, 231–33; *Aberdeen Council Letters*, II, 10–14.

38. SRO, Cunninghame-Graham MSS, GD 22/3/785; *SR*, I, 354–55; II, 677–80, 693, 703, 744–45, 750, 796–97; Baillie, *Letters and Journals*, I, 421–24; Row, *History of the Kirk*, 368–70; Hailes, *Memorials*, 1–2.

39. NLS, Wodrow MSS, octavo, XXVII, fo. 21–22; Row, *History of the Kirk*, 368–69; *Works of William Laud*, III, 303–07; Baillie, *Letters and Journals*, I, 431–36; Hailes, *Memorials*, 5–7, 10–12.

40. D. Laing, *Memoir of the life and writings of Robert Baillie*, (Bannatyne Club, Edinburgh, 1842), xxix–xxxi; *RPCS*, second series, V, 192–93; Row, *History of the Kirk*, 371–74; Mathew, *Scotland under Charles I*, 89–91; D. G. Mullan, *Episcopacy in Scotland: The History of an Idea, 1560–1638*, (Edinburgh, 1986), 171–72. The actual creation of the bishopric from the bounds of the overextended see of St. Andrews in September 1633, though justifiable administratively, was an immediate source of controversy and not just among presbyterians in the Kirk. The endowment of the bishopric with the estates of Holyroodhouse and New Abbey, both temporal lordships revoked by Charles I, irritated the landed classes. The town council of Edinburgh was made financially liable for the conversion of the kirk of St. Giles into a cathedral, a commitment which more than outweighed the prestigious award of city status on the capital, especially as the burgesses had already borne the main cost of entertaining the royal train during the coronation visit and were also liable for the erection of a new parliament house which was to incorporate the College of Justice. The capital committed to a building programme was in excess of £141,000 (*RMS*, VIII, no. 2225; *RPCS*, second series, V, 136–37, 340; R. K. Hannay & P. H. Watson, 'The Building of Parliament House', *The Book of the Old Edinburgh Club*, XIII, (1924), 1–78).

41. *RMS*, IX, no. 228; *RPCS*, second series, 349–50, 491–92, 658–59; Baillie, *Letters and Journals*, I, 424–29; *Works of William Laud*, III, 312; G. I. R. McMahon, 'The Scottish Courts of High Commission, 1610–38', *RSCHS*, XV, (1964–66), 198–207.

42. *Letters of Samuel Rutherford*, I, 69, 74, 109–10; Row, *History of the Kirk*, 350–51; Spalding, *Troubles*, I, 45–46; *Works of William Laud*, III, 299–300; Zagorin, *The Court and the Country*, 100.

43. SRO, Hamilton Papers, TD 75/100/26/315; Clarendon, *History of the Rebellion*, I, 195.

44. Balfour, *Historical Works*, II, 140; Baillie, *Letters and Journals*, I, 8; Carlton, *Charles I*, 189; Lee, jr., *The Road to Revolution*, 189–92.

45. *The Memoirs of Henry Guthry*, 14–16; *Memorials of the Earls of Haddington*, II, 148–51; Foster, *The Church before the Covenants*, 61–62; Mullan, *Episcopacy in Scotland*, 169–71, 173–74. Although no more than four Canterburians served concurrently on the Scottish episcopate — from February 1636 — Laud was instrumental in ensuring that co-adjutors acceptable to, if not directly appointed by, the Court were taken on by aged and infirm bishops to help run their dioceses from May 1634.

46. W. Makey, 'Presbyterian and Canterburian in the Scottish Revolution', in *Church, Politics and Society: Scotland, 1408–1929*, N. MacDougall ed., (Edinburgh,

1983), 151–66. The contention that the Canterburians, like the Melvilleans of the later sixteenth century, claimed the entire patrimony of the Kirk — temporality as well as spirituality — is erroneous. Laud specifically distanced himself from such claims in the summer of 1635. The associated contention that the Canterburians, like the Melvilleans, were intent on using the reclaimed revenue of the Kirk to sustain a large professional bureaucracy to further social welfare and educational provision is unsupported conjecture. That the Canterburians, like the Melvilleans, wanted to subordinate royal government fits uneasily with Laud's support for episcopal advancement within the Scottish administration, his endeavours to overhaul the Scottish Exchequer and his efforts to improve the material prospects of the clergy through teind redistribution. The one valid comparison with the Melvilleans was not so much that they were anti-aristocratic as that their unstinting conviction of their rightness and their dogmatic distaste for compromise isolated them and made them vulnerable to political campaigns intent on curbing their influence in Kirk and State (*Works of William Laud*, III, 311–13; Baillie, *Letters and Journals*, I, 6–7, 428–30).

47. *Works of William Laud*, III, 310–15; Baillie, *Letters and Journals*, I, 436–38; Hailes, *Memorials*, 13–17. Charles I's influence over public policy cannot be satisfactorily assessed from the published letters of the secretary of state for Scottish affairs based at Court. Although Charles personally wrote none of the 2000 letters issued on his behalf during the first decade of his reign and annotated, amended or added postcripts to a mere handful, this does not betoken an 'abysmal ignorance' of Scottish affairs, but rather a lack of inclination to involve himself in the minutiae of policy. Charles's bursts of energy, as signified by the volume of letters issued in his name, appreciated considerably in the wake of his coronation visit (Carlton, *Charles I*, 158–59).

48. Baillie, *Letters and Journals*, I, 443–44; Clarendon, *History of the Rebellion*, I, 148–49; *A List of Books Printed in Scotland before 1700*, H. G. Aldis ed., (NLS, Edinburgh, 1970), no. 798, 830–31.

49. *SR*, II, 752–53, 796–97; *CSP, Domestic*, (1635), 4; *Works of William Laud*, III, 278, 427–28. Laud even extended his supervision to cajole the principal printer commissioned by the Scottish bishops — the egregiously errant Robert Young — to attend to his business in Edinburgh instead of plying his trade in London.

50. *SR*, II, 855–56; Donaldson, *The Making of the Scottish Prayer Book*, 41–58, 127–28; W. G. S. Snow, *The Times, Life and Thought of Patrick Forbes, bishop of Aberdeen, 1618–35*, (London, 1952), 97–98. Despite the reservations of the erastian bishops, lessons from the Apocrypha were retained as were all holy days and saints' days prescribed in the English liturgy — including the feast of St. George. The feast of St. Andrew and days of other saints particular to Scotland were included as a sop to nationalist sentiment. The preface to morning and evening prayer reserved the right of the Crown to prescribe the use of ornaments in the Kirk especially, but not exclusively, during communion.

51. *Works of William Laud*, III, 372–76; Baillie, *Letters and Journals*, I, 4–5; Row, *History of The Kirk*, 392–95, 398–406; Tyacke, 'Puritanism, Arminianism and Counter-Revolution', in *The Origins of the English Civil War*, 119–21, 129–30, 142–43.

52. Donaldson, *James V to James VII*, 305–06; MacLeod, *Scottish Theology*, 24; Edgar, *Old Parish Life in Scotland*, I, 86–87.

53. *Works of William Laud*, III, 219, 341; Albion, *Charles I and the Court of Rome*, 158, 167–92, 216–31, 260; G. D. Henderson, *Religious Life in Seventeenth Century Scotland*, (Cambridge, 1937), 73, 89.

54. Baillie, *Letters and Journals*, I, 30, 113; Clarendon, *History of the Rebellion*, I, 165; C. Hill, *The Century of Revolution, 1603–1714*, (London, 1967), 60.

55. Hailes, *Memorials*, 17–18; Baillie, *Letters and Journals*, I, 438–40; Row, *History of the Kirk*, 392–95; Mullan, *Episcopacy in Scotland*, 174.

56. *RPCS*, second series, VII, 334, 336–37, 343, 352–53; Baillie, *Letters and Journals*,

I, 4–5, 440–42; Balfour, *Historical Works*, II, 223–25; Donaldson, *The Making of the Scottish Prayer Book*, 57–59, 101–02.

57. Row, *History of the Kirk*, 392, 398–406; NLS, R. Mylne's Collection, Adv. MS 31.2.1, fo. 140–47; *The Memoirs of Henry Guthry*, 19; Carlton, *Charles I*, 197–98; Lee, jr., *The Road to Revolution*, 200–01.

58. *Letters of Samuel Rutherford*, I, 161; D. Calderwood, *The Pastor and the Prelate, or Reformation and Conformitie*, (Edinburgh, 1636), 36–37.

7

The National Covenant

Introduction

The willingness of the Canterburians to provoke confrontation over religious uniformity was effectively signalled from July 1636, when Thomas Sydserf, bishop of Galloway, decided that the prosecution of noted nonconformists by the Court of High Commission should be renewed within his diocese. The refusal of Alexander Gordon of Earlston to appear before the High Commission was met by a fine of 500 merks (£333–6/8) and his banishment to Montrose. Robert Glendinning was suspended from his charge in Kirkcudbright. When the bailies of the burgh refused to enforce the High Commission's warrant for imprisonment, they were placed in custody in Wigtown. Samuel Rutherford, minister in the neighbouring parish of Anwoth and a noted critic of episcopacy, the Five Articles of Perth and Arminianism, was banished to Aberdeen.[1]

However, Archibald Campbell, Lord Lorne (later eighth earl and first marquis of Argyll) exploited the general outcry in Galloway to widen the breach between the bishops and lay councillors and officials. Concerned that the Court of High Commission was being deployed against lay as well as clerical nonconformists, the Privy Council intervened in favour of Earlston, dispensing with his banishment on condition he paid his fine. Lay councillors and officials 'were highly offended' by Bishop Sydserf's querulous acceptance of this decision, particularly as his offensive against nonconformists in Galloway had coincided with the harvest which had ensured that the High Commission was barely quorate for episcopal adherents. The confrontation engineered in Galloway was especially ominous because citations before the High Commission were issued not just to presbyterian nonconformists, but to known and admitted conventiclers.[2]

Conventicling

The maintenance of spiritual assurance among nonconforming presbyterians in the face of temporal adversity during the personal rule of Charles I was due, in no small measure to the covert growth of praying societies, known as conventicles. Following the imposition of the Five Articles, the reluctance of many bishops to publicise nonconformity by prosecution had enabled presbyterian laity, with the connivance of sympathetic ministers, either to absent themselves from communion or refrain from kneeling when receiving the sacrament. Conventicles were a radical alternative to such passive disobedience. Conventicles sought to sustain the purity of the Reformed Kirk by private meetings for collective devotion. Taking advantage of the reluctance of the Privy Council to instigate a campaign of prosecution, conventicling had spread from Edinburgh to Fife, the south-west and west-central Scotland in the last years of James VI. Invitations to assist in administering nonconforming communions — which attracted huge influxes of presbyterians from neighbouring parishes — led to the establishment of summer circuits for guest preachers.[3]

Popular support for nonconforming presbyterianism, especially in the south-west, was enhanced by the re-exportation of evangelical fervour from Ulster. The existence of preaching circuits among conventiclers facilitated occasional sorties by exiled Scottish presbyterians — notably, Robert Blair and John Livingstone, ministers in the diocese of Down. Although presbyterianism in Ulster was still at a missionary level, praying societies had been imported by Scottish colonists during the 1620s. Sympathetic ministers had been attracted from Scotland by the determination of colonists to preserve a presbyterian presence within the episcopal framework of the Church of Ireland. However, this small but zealous presbyterian vanguard composed less than a tenth of the Protestant ministry in Ulster. The vulnerability of their position to a concerted attack by Irish and Scottish bishops was demonstrated by the suspension of Blair and Livingstone in 1631, for preaching and participating in revivalist meetings on both sides of the North Channel.

The presbyterian vanguard in Ulster was acutely exposed by a new episcopal offensive promoted to coincide with the Court's first export of Laudian directives for religious uniformity: that is, the imposition of ecclesiastical canons to terminate the independence of the Church of Ireland from November 1634. Within twenty months, not only had Blair and Livingstone been excommunicated, but the remainder of the presbyterian vanguard had been deposed for their refusal to conform to Anglican standards. Blair and Livingstone, together with other members of the presbyterian vanguard and prominent conventiclers from Ulster, with a leavening from the south-west, decided to seek release, 'from the bondage of the prelates'. On 9 September 1636, 140 nonconformists embarked from Ulster with sufficient provisions to sustain their intended settlement in New England for two years. Although their ship neared Newfoundland, tempestuous weather forced their return to Scotland by November: a reversal interpreted as divine intervention, the Lord making evident 'that it was not his will that they should glorify him in America, he having work for them at home'.[4]

The influx of Ulster nonconformists to the south-west, which coincided with the imposition of the book of canons, served to harden the resolve of Scottish conventiclers to resist further liturgical innovation. Despite the vehemence of their language towards the bishops and their conviction that the political nation should atone for past sins and oppose the Service Book, the conventiclers were catalysts for rather than instigators of revolution. In essence, the conventiclers were a pressure group organised covertly throughout the Lowlands by 1637. Collective as well as personal discipline was maintained by periodic fasting. Godliness was cultivated nationally as well as individually. Their militant sense of righteousness reinforced their assurance that they were God's elect on earth. However, not all nonconforming presbyterians were committed conventiclers at the introduction of the Service Book. Moreover, the eclectic image of the conventiclers, not dissimilar to that of Puritans in New England, exposed them to charges of separatism; charges which persisted beyond the establishment of presbyterianism by the Covenanting Movement.[5]

From 1630, regular bulletins from Edinburgh had notified conventiclers about the growing involvement of bishops in civil affairs as about the sufferings of evangelical Calvinists elsewhere in the British Isles. Conventiclers were summoned to Edinburgh to comfort Balmerino through prayer as his trial was concluded before an assize in March 1635. Yet, the association of the conventiclers with the disaffected element should not be regarded as a foregone conclusion. Despite a shared distaste for liturgical innovations, conventiclers were not convinced that the nobles, as leaders of the disaffected, were intent on the pursuit of godliness. Writing from exile in Aberdeen on 9 March 1637, Samuel Rutherford cautioned against political confrontation in the name of religion: 'I am not of that mind, that tumults or arms is the way to put Christ on His throne'. For their part, the disaffected were wary of too close an association with conventiclers that would attract official surveillance of their planned opposition to the Service Book.[6]

Nonetheless, the disaffected leadership came to appreciate the ideological advantage of association with conventiclers. For the conventiclers were foremost among nonconforming presbyterians advocating communal banding in covenants as the alternative religious standard to liturgical innovations. The covenant of grace and works not only assured the righteous of their temporal as well as their spiritual calling, but affirmed the special relationship between God and Scotland whose people were heirs to ancient Israel as God's covenanted nation. As well as an elaboration of God's compact with the elect, covenanting in Scotland was a manifestation of the divine band between God and the Scottish people. The godly were bound to seek the reformation of an errant Kirk whose present corruption under 'the tyranny of prelates' was attributable to 'our breach of the covenant, contempt of the Gospel and our defection from the truth'. By March 1637, the godly were being charged to prepare for the coming of Christ, 'The Great Messenger of the Covenant'.[7]

Such purveying of apocalyptic visions undoubtedly added a sense of divine imminence to the political scene. But covenanting adherence in Scotland was not so much a decisive cause of revolt against Charles I as a means of communicating symbolically a fundamental ideological message: that opposition to the royal prerogative in defence of religious and civil liberty was divinely warranted. By identifying their cause with the covenant of grace and works, the disaffected availed themselves of the seventeenth-century equivalent of liberationist theology. At the organisational level, the covert and disciplined nature of conventicling enabled the disaffected leadership to prepare discreetly, but systematically. At the same time, the appearance of spontaneity was preserved when open demonstrations were mounted against the imposition of the Service Book.[8]

Instigating Revolution

The proclamation of 20 December 1636 commanding publication and compulsory use of the Service Book by Easter, compounded by delays in printing, had afforded the disaffected element four months to concert their campaign against liturgical innovations. On the publication of the Service Book at the end of April 1637, Alexander Henderson, minister of Leuchars in Fife, and David Dickson, minister of Irvine in Ayrshire, as national co-ordinators for nonconforming ministers, availed themselves of the cover of the spring communion season to meet Loudoun and Balmerino in Edinburgh. The leading dissident within the Scottish administration, Lord Advocate Hope, was also reported present. The probable outcome was the formulation of a strategy for public demonstrations against the imposition of the Service Book in the capital. Henderson and Dickson then proceeded to entreat prominent conventiclers in Edinburgh to give their active support.[9]

Divisions within the episcopate, which undoubtedly served to mislead the Court about the scale of anticipated opposition to liturgical innovations in Scotland, were again manifest during the half-yearly synods of late spring, when the imposition of the Service Book dominated the agenda in every diocese. Archbishop Spottiswood was content to exact a legally binding commitment from the clergy in his diocese of St Andrews that two copies of the Service Book would be purchased for every parish without insisting upon a specific date for their use. The erastian bishops were generally content to intimate that the purchase and use of the Service Book was commanded by royal warrant. The clergy in their various dioceses were given until the autumn round of synods to examine its contents. The Canterburians, however, were intent on interpreting the royal warrant of the previous December as commanding prompt use as well as purchase.[10]

Within specific presbyteries a co-ordinated campaign of resistance to the imposition of the Service Book was marked by the clandestine circulation of critically annotated copies among nonconforming ministers who used their pulpits to inveigh against its purchase and use. In a belated counter to the overt refusal of nonconforming ministers to purchase copies, the Privy Council affirmed on 13 June that it was the collective responsibility of the presbyteries to ensure that every parish was provided with two copies within fifteen days.[11]

That no official attempt was made to enforce this order exposed the lack of clear understanding between the Court and Edinburgh. The bishops made no

effort to insist upon immediate enforcement as they were intent on reasserting
their flagging political influence by throwing their weight behind an alternative
approach. An episcopal edict, issued independently of the Privy Council on 16
July 1637, served notice that the Service Book would be read in all churches
in and around Edinburgh on Sunday 23 July. Although Charles concurred with
this alternative approach, Laud took a less sanguine view. While not opposed
to exemplary readings from the Service Book, he was apprehensive that the
issuing of one week's formal notice would encourage the disaffected to stage
public demonstrations. His apprehensions were duly borne out by the hostile
reception accorded to the Service Book in the capital, particularly in St. Giles
Cathedral.[12]

The public demonstrations during divine service on 23 July were neither
spontaneous nor merely the outcome of seven days' notice, but the outcome of
three months' planning finalised by 6 July, ten days before the episcopal edict for
exemplary readings was actually issued. A meeting in Edinburgh convened by
Henderson and Dickson was attended by at least ten nonconforming ministers
drawn from eight presbyteries in west and central Scotland as well as Fife and
the Lothians. The main business of the meeting was to identify all 'corruptions' contained in the Service Book for compilation into a reasoned case that
nonconforming ministers could deploy against its imposition by the bishops.
Nonconforming brethren who were pressed hard to purchase copies of the
Service Book should prepare, severally and collectively, to petition the Council
for its suspension because it lacked warrant from a constitutional assembly, its
importation of Anglican usages was against the national interest and, above all,
its popish leanings were inimical to the Reformed tradition in the Kirk. If the
bishops ordered exemplary readings, the 'weill affected' in Edinburgh were to
stage peaceable public demonstrations by walking out during divine services
and, thereafter, absent themselves from church until the Service Book was
withdrawn. The day following this meeting, prominent conventiclers in the
city were placed on stand-by to lead public demonstrations.[13]

Clerical endeavours to read the Service Book in three churches in the capital
on the morning of 23 July duly encountered public demonstrations. Whereas the
occasion and location of the demonstrations were undoubtedly premeditated,
their scale and nature exceeded all expectations, being violent and abusive
rather than peaceable and disciplined. The political impact of the demonstration
in St. Giles was particularly significant, less on account of the celebrated
stool-throwing and the attempt to denude the bishop and dean of Edinburgh
than for the presence of the archbishop of St. Andrews, numerous bishops
and lay councillors as well as the magistrates and town council of Edinburgh.
Partly because of the violence of hostile mobs, partly because of the reluctance
of the Scottish administration to investigate the social standing of the instigators
and perpetrators of the public demonstrations — which continued outside St.
Giles during and after the afternoon service — official accounts emanating from
Edinburgh blamed the 'turbulent and mutinous carriage' of the demonstrators
on the 'meaner sort of people', especially serving women and 'rascall masterless

boyes'. In reality, Edinburgh matrons of the mercantile community, notably the 'holy and religious women' associated with conventicling in the city, were closely involved in fomenting and directing the disturbances, if not in extending the riots from verbal abuse to physical assaults on the officiating clergy.[14]

By having the political sagacity to adopt a low profile during the staging of the public demonstrations, and by remaining in the background until the rioting in Edinburgh had abated, the disaffected leadership was well placed to capitalise on the populist reaction against the Service Book. Indeed, such was the scale and violent nature of the rioting, 'as was never heard since the Reformation in our nation', that the disaffected leadership could appear as the acceptable face of protest, opposing liturgical innovations as unwarrantable, unscriptural and disruptive of public order. At the same time, the disaffected leadership could pose as defenders of the Crown, 'by whose authority abused' the bishops had imposed the Service Book. Maximum political capital was also extracted over the next month from the buck-passing of responsibility between the Privy Council and the town council of Edinburgh for apprehending instigators and perpetrators of the riots.[15]

Although the Council suspended the use of the Service Book on 29 July, bishops and lay officials were more intent on blackening each other at Court than on upholding the monarchical position within Scotland.[16] The bishops, who had suggested suspension, reversed their position on 10 August. They decided unilaterally to enforce the order of 13 July requiring presbyteries to ensure that ministers purchased two copies of the Service Book. On this occasion, the two archbishops not the Canterburians took the lead. Patrick Lindsay of Glasgow charged all the presbyteries within his diocese to comply, a directive countered by David Dickson mobilising the ministers in the presbyteries of Irvine and Glasgow to petition for the suspension of the episcopal edict of 10 August, a manoeuvre also supported by nonconforming ministers in the presbytery of Ayr. Spottiswood of St. Andrews singled out only three ministers, all in the presbytery of St. Andrews, each of whom he instructed to purchase two copies of the Service Book. Two of the three charged, Alexander Henderson and James Bruce, minister of Kingsbarns, were actually present at the final planning meeting in Edinburgh for public demonstrations against the Service Book. Although none of the ministers commissioned to petition on behalf of the three western presbyteries was actually present on 6 July, they all adhered to that meeting's exhortation for concerted action by joining up with Henderson in Edinburgh on 23 August.

The substance of the petitioners' complaints against the episcopal edict followed the guidelines drawn up on 6 July, calling on the Council to suspend the use of the Service Book. Its unconstitutional introduction and insinuation of popery were prejudicial to the national interest in undermining the doctrine, discipline and worship established at and practised since the Reformation. The presbyterian petitioners felt sufficiently confident to add a populist dimension. Even if nonconforming ministers were moved to accept the Service Book, such was the depth of commitment among the Scottish people to the Protestant teaching received since the Reformation, 'it is likely they will be found unwilling to change'.

The presbyterian petitioners also drew up an information sheet for use of sympathetic nobles and gentry prepared to write to or lobby lay councillors personally. In essence, this sheet elaborated the guidelines for opposing liturgical innovations drawn up for the nonconforming brethren on 6 July. Paying upon the probability that lay councillors, like the nobles and gentry sympathetic to the petitioners, lacked detailed knowledge of liturgical innovations, the contents of the book of canons were opportunely assimilated to justify the claim that the Service Book entailed a fundamental shift in favour of unfettered episcopacy.[17]

The danger of public demonstrations made the prosecution of the presbyterian petitioners politically inexpedient, a situation appreciated by the disaffected leadership when restricting the scale of protest against the episcopal edict of 10 August. The number of colleagues, friends and neighbours accompanying the presbyterian petitioners to Edinburgh was curtailed. Physical support from the disaffected outwith the west and Fife was not encouraged. The alternative strategy of briefing sympathetic nobles and gentry to write or lobby lay councillors struck a responsible chord. Assertion of lay influence on 24 August moved the Council to set aside a royal letter which called for the prompt apprehension of the instigators of the demonstrations in Edinburgh and the expeditious promotion of the Service Book throughout the kingdom. Instead, the Privy Council at last chose to inform Charles officially that the political state of affairs in Scotland was now critical. The Council was not prepared to countenance the compulsory imposition of the Service Book until further consultations were held at Court. Hence, all measures for imposing the Service Book should be delayed until 20 September, when the king's response to the call for consultations could be published.[18] This belated initiative by the Council set the scene for the nationwide mobilisation of the disaffected, a mobilisation whose gathering momentum has been described aptly as 'crisis by monthly instalments'.[19]

The National Petition

The four weeks that elapsed from the Privy Council's decision not to enforce the use of the Service Book were characterised by 'much trafficking throughout the country for drawing numbers to Edinburgh'. The disaffected leadership was intent on orderly and disciplined petitioning by nobles and commissioners drawn from the other political estates. At least a third of the Scottish nobility, together with a considerable number of gentry, a generous leavening of burgesses and around 100 ministers from central Scotland, were esconced in the capital by 20 September, bearing with them sixty-eight petitions from burghs, parishes and presbyteries.[20]

Protests were standardised but not stereotyped, following the format of the petition presented by presbyterian ministers to the Council on 23 August which, in turn, was based upon the guidelines drawn up for nonconforming brethren on 6 July. Petitions tended to condemn the Service Book on three grounds: its introduction was unwarranted by any constitutional assembly; its usage was prejudicial to the national interest by undermining religious standards established and practised since the Reformation; and its contents were closer to popery than to the Reformed tradition of the Kirk. All petitions did break new ground, however, in calling for the delivery of every community from the fears of further innovation provoked by the compulsory imposition of the Service Book.

The majority (35) of the 47 extant petitions came from parishes in the west and Fife. Usually drawn up by ministers and subscribed by gentry and yeomen in their capacity as heritors and elders, the petitions expressed the dissent of local congregations. Undertaken as a community not a class-based enterprise, petitioning demonstrated the growing sophistication of organised disaffection. While ministers took the initiative in standardising and drafting, nobles, gentry and burgesses gave willing support and encouragement in securing subscriptions to the petitions. Leading gentry were commissioned to carry the petitions from the parishes to Edinburgh. The galvanising of community opposition to the personal rule of Charles I demonstrated the administrative potential of the parish as an instrument of revolution.[21] Such galvanising, moreover, confounds the view that the disaffected element was essentially looking back to the restoration of aristocratic dominance in Kirk and State.[22]

The nobles did control national strategy, however. The community petitions were turned into a national petition, which was initially presented to the Council on 20 September. However, the deliberations of the Council were wholly taken up with the Court's response to its letter of 25 August. Laud was strongly disinclined to make any concessions to Scottish nonconformists that would encourage English Puritans to oppose religious uniformity. Although the archbishop of Canterbury was prepared to reprimand the Scottish bishops for acting unilaterally, he was not prepared to admit that they had acted precipitately in promoting the purchase and use of the Service Book. He contended that lay councillors, ill-disposed to liturgical innovations, had connived at its suspension. That Laud's view prevailed were evident from the king's reply. Not only were overtures for wider consultation on liturgical innovations rejected, but the Council was lambasted for its slackness. Compulsory imposition of the Service Book was to be resumed promptly and unequivocally.[23]

The Council was not prepared to comply immediately. Nine councillors were dutifully selected to serve with the chancellor and treasurer on a vacation committee for establishing the use of the Service Book nationwide. But the Council, much to the annoyance of the three bishops present, moved on to consider the national petition which was resubmitted following extensive consultations between the disaffected leadership and lay councillors. Significant redrafting attempted to make the national petition more acceptable to the Crown. All suggestions that the bishops were subverters of the discipline, doctrine and worship of the Reformed Kirk were removed. The lack of constitutional warrant for liturgical innovations was glossed over.[24]

The redrafted version, together with two sample local petitions — from the burgh of Glasgow and the presbytery of Auchterarder — and a list of the remaining sixty-six were despatched to Court with the warning that the political situation north of the Border was deteriorating critically. The 'numerous confluence of all degrees and rankes of persones' to petition the Council was accepted as evidence of a general antipathy to liturgical innovations. The Council went on to affirm that despite anticipated calumnies against its members at Court, it 'forbare to meddle' further until the king made known his response to the national petition. Moreover, the vacation committee was not intent on the intemperate application of religious conformity, especially as its first meeting on 23 September was subjected to private lobbying by the disaffected leadership reinforced by an orderly presence of supplicants. A mass lobby, mounted at the tolbooth on 26 September, forced the city of Edinburgh to fall into line with supplicants elsewhere in the kingdom. Two days later, the town council duly submitted a petition attaching Edinburgh to the list of communities opposed to the Service Book.[25]

When accepting Edinburgh's petition on behalf of the vacation committee, Archbishop Spottiswood had served notice that the king's response would be reported to the magistrates and town council by 17 October. This was the first official indication of when a general response to the national petition and the other sixty-eight local petitions could be expected from Court. No less significantly, another member of this committee, Lord Advocate Hope, established an informal liaison with Balmerino and Henderson to maintain the ongoing protest of the disaffected element within the bounds of legality.

Although many of the supplicants had already departed the city convinced that a response could not be expected from Court before November, a vigorous propaganda campaign was mounted to extend the community basis of supplication outwith the west and Fife. The rest of the country, except for the Highlands and Islands, was divided into four supervisory districts which were assigned to leading nonconformists to concert and publicise the disaffected cause. Individual ministers within these supervisory districts were encouraged to cultivate the political awareness of their parishioners by popularising the conventicling techniques of fasting and prayer meetings. Such was the success of the propaganda campaign that when the disaffected received corroboration from Court that the king's response could indeed be expected by 17 October, unprecedented numbers of nobles, gentry, burgesses, ministers and commons from all parts of the Lowlands mustered in Edinburgh. This mustering, at the finish of the harvest season, strengthened fears of an imminent insurrection north of the Border when reported at Court.[26]

The National Supplication

In order to mobilise support within the localities to attend the royal reply of 17 October, the disaffected leadership had nonconforming ministers circulate a common advertisement through the presbyteries. The formulation of this advertisement was entrusted to Archibald Johnston of Wariston, an Edinburgh lawyer of undoubted personal piety, zealously committed to the triumph of presbyterianism. Although he had decided on a vocational calling that was legal rather than clerical, Wariston was convinced he was carrying out God's work. An insomniac of prodigious energy, as well as an austere Calvinist and conventicler, Wariston had been taken into the confidence of the nonconforming coterie of ministers on 7 July, the day after their meeting to finalise strategy for public demonstrations against the Service Book.[27]

As well as commissioning the common advertisement, the disaffected leadership had written personally to sympathetic nobles to help rally support within the localities. In the event, that support exceeded their expectations. Attended by kinsmen, friends and neighbours, commissioners from over 200 parishes, as from presbyteries and burghs, supplicated against liturgical innovations. The Crown having made no real effort to diffuse unrest, the Council was instructed to issue proclamations that confirmed the lack of concern of Charles I as an absentee monarch.[28]

The meeting of the Privy Council on 17 October was dissolved. All supplicants were given twenty-four hours to quit the capital except those who could furnish the Council with 'just cause of stay for their particular affairs'. As a result of Edinburgh's belated identification with the supplicants the previous month, the Council and the College of Justice were to be removed from the capital. The council was to proceed to Linlithgow. The disaffected leadership responded by letter and supplication. Loudoun was detailed to prepare a letter affirming their right to remain in Edinburgh to settle pressing legal affairs — notably, outstanding debts to creditors. David Dickson was commissioned to draft, in the name of the commons as well as the political estates, a national supplication of grievance against liturgical innovations.[29]

The national supplication, which mounted an explicit attack on the bishops as the 'contryvers and devysers' of these innovations, marked a significant advance in three other respects from the national petition of 20 September. Although the Church of England was reputed 'bot halfe reformed', the Service Book was now attacked for imposing religious observances so abusively popish as to reverse 'the gratious intentions of the blessed reformers of religione' in England as well as Scotland. The book of canons was condemned explicitly as an unwarranted subversion of the discipline of the Reformed Kirk. Most significantly, Dickson drew on his conventicling associations to counter the threat of penal sanctions to enforce liturgical innovations. The disaffected must suffer 'the ruin of our estates and fortunes' or endure divine retribution for 'breach of our covenant with God, and forsaking the way of true religione'. This first public association of their cause with covenanting enabled the disaffected leadership to elevate their divine obligation to supplicate above their duty to obey royal proclamations.[30]

In the meantime, the citizenry of Edinburgh were reacting in a more demonstrative manner. Vociferous protests were directed initially against Hay of Lands, the clerk-register, whom Charles I had recently foisted on the city as provost. Provost Hay not only had Edinburgh's petition of 26 September suppressed, but had the magistrates pen a disclaimer to Archbishop Laud that the petition against the Service Book was merely an expedient response to populist pressure. On 18 October, the meeting of the town council 'was environed with huge numbers of all sorts of people' who threatened to burn down the city chambers should commissioners not be elected to join the supplicants. Prompted by women, this tumultuous assembly in excess of 300 people switched their attention to Bishop Sydserf of Galloway, the noted prosecutor of conventiclers and the only Canterburian remaining in Edinburgh. When Traquair and other lay councillors arrived to protect the bishop, they, in turn, were besieged in the council chambers. Traquair was obliged to seek assistance from the disaffected leadership who escorted the Privy Council to Holyroodhouse and stood watch during the resumption of business.

Although not so prolonged as the first public disturbances against the Service Book on 23 July, the rioting of 18 October was undoubtedly of greater intensity. When reports reached Court that councillors were besieged, abused and physically intimidated, the rioting was condemned as the second act of rebellion, but 'farre more seditious and dangerous' than the first public disturbances. The manifest lack of political will on the part of the Council to identify and punish the instigators and perpetrators reinforced the uncompromising stand of Laud, that the Scots should accept liturgical innovations without further equivocation.[31]

As on 23 July, the rioting on 18 October served to advance the supplicants' cause, particularly as the disaffected leadership was determined to exploit its custodial presence at Holyroodhouse to ensure that public agitation against liturgical innovations would be transformed from a party enterprise into a national endeavour. A delegation of four nobles — Rothes, Loudoun, John Gordon, thirteenth earl of Sutherland, and John Hay, Lord Hay of Yester — moved the Council to accept the 'Magna Carta' of the disaffected, the national supplication or rather a copy of the original with signatures deliberately excluded to prevent legal reprisals. The two principal targets of the mob, Provost Hay and Bishop Sydserf, were so discomfited by their morning's experience that they jointly suggested that the supplicants choose commissioners 'to wait in small numbers' on the Council pending the king's reply to the national supplication. The disaffected leadership agreed. Not only would the supplicants be spared the expense of a prolonged stay in Edinburgh, but official backing could now be claimed for a mass meeting in Edinburgh on 15 November, to establish a holding committee drawn from each political estate.[32]

Representatives from the other political estates were summoned into the presence of the disaffected nobility in the late evening of 18 October. Balmerino and Loudoun presided over a meeting which affirmed that the original national supplication should be dated 18 October, though drawn up the previous evening. This dating served to indicate that their proceedings had been authenticated by the Council which, in turn, would encourage subscriptions from the disaffected who had not yet featured among the supplicants in Edinburgh. Copies of the national supplication were duly despatched for circulation within presbyteries for return by 15 November.

Despite rumours that subscriptions had reached 800 by the dispersal of the supplicants from the capital, no more than 482 subscribers — 30 nobles, 281 gentry, 48 burgesses and 123 ministers — can be identified on the original national supplication dated 18 October. Before the original was actually lodged with the Council, the leadership had it circulated among sympathisers outwith Edinburgh in order to enhance the social standing of the supplicants as well as recruit potential paymasters for the cause. Around half the nobility subscribed — James Graham, fifth earl (later first marquis) of Montrose being the most prominent acquisition. Subscriptions were collected from all the leading burghs with the exception of Aberdeen, St Andrews and Inverness.[33]

The Tables

Charles I's decision to remove the beleaguered Scottish administration from the capital yielded a critical advantage to the disaffected element. Not only was the Privy Council denied first hand knowledge of the mobilisation and lodging of the supplicants within Edinburgh, but the disaffected leadership was able to assume political responsibility for the state of the nation from 15 November 1637. In a forlorn endeavour to dissuade the supplicants from holding public meetings in Edinburgh, Traquair had obtained authorisation from the Council at Linlithgow on 14 November to journey to the capital to confer privately with the disaffected leadership.

Accompanied by Lauderdale and Lorne, Traquair sought to persuade them not to give further offence to the king. They remained adamant, however, that the national supplication was 'verie just, warrantable and necessar'; that the present meeting of the supplicants in Edinburgh was warranted by the Council for the election of a holding committee; and that the election of this committee necessitated public convocations in the streets of the capital. Moreover, the provocative conduct of some bishops and their clerical supporters in condemning the supplicants as 'mutinous and rebellious subjects' made it imperative to protect the disaffected from judicial reprisals. Petitioning was to be extended against the Court of High Commission as well as liturgical innovations.

In the meantime, elections were proceeding among the supplicants gathered in Edinburgh, ostensibly for a holding committee to await the king's reply to the national supplication, but in reality for a consultative body to ratify the proceedings of the disaffected. As the nobility were currently engaged in the negotiations with authorised councillors, no more than 6 of the 24 lodged in Edinburgh were to serve on the committee, together with two gentry for every shire, one representative from every burgh and one minister from every presbytery. On this basis, the consultative body was to number in excess of 130 — too unwieldy for a holding function, but sufficiently broad to provide a consensus to sanction negotiations.

The commissioners for each estate met separately not collectively to await consultation by the disaffected following the initial round of negotiations with Traquair and his associates. Representatives were then elected by each estate to form a committee to continue negotiations. A committee of four nobles, three gentry, three burgesses and three ministers resumed on 16 November. Traquair and his associates — who were expanded to include David Lindsay, bishop of Edinburgh, and Lord Advocate Hope — were intent on temporising. The negotiating committee did make one significant breakthrough, however. Warrant was sought to extend the electoral process for commissioners to every locality prepared to supplicate not just those who had actually supplicated by 15 November. Much to the chagrin of Traquair, the Lord Advocate affirmed that the disaffected were legally entitled 'to choose Commissioners for Parliament, for Conventions of Estates, or for any Public business'. Indeed, all assembled were aware that Charles I had encouraged such meetings ten years earlier when seeking to rally support for the Revocation Scheme.[34]

The negotiating committee having reported, each constituent estate proceeded in separate meetings to elect four representatives to a committee charged to liaise with the Council pending notification of the king's reply to the national supplication. The liaising committee, headed by Sutherland and Balmerino, was charged on 17 November to circulate the localities once the arrival of the king's reply was confirmed officially. The outcome of the discussions with Traquair and his associates was presented as conveying warrant from the Council to extend the representation of the disaffected on the basis of every noble prepared to identify with the cause, two gentry from every shire, at least one commissioner from every burgh and one minister from every presbytery. When the expanded consultative body returned to Edinburgh, it was to assume the institutional status of the Tables and install itself in parliament house in the continuing absence of the Scottish administration.[35]

The acclaimed warrant of the Council was undoubtedly decisive in transforming the supplicants into 'an organized national party with elected national representatives and local branches'. But, to assert that the disaffected had hitherto been 'a disorganized mass of individual supplicants' is to underestimate the evolutionary nature of this party structure.[36] From the outset of the original mass meeting on 20 September, the supplicants had tended to lodge and meet separately according to their respective political estates, a practice formalised by each estate constituting a Table following the return of commissioners for the nobles, gentry, burgesses and ministers to Edinburgh at the outset of December. The disaffected leadership — that is, the nobles together with a few commissioners elected from the three other Tables — were not formally constituted as the fifth or general Table for another two months. Nonetheless, the emergence of this executive body had been foreshadowed during the second mass meeting on 18 October, when disaffected nobles met with representatives from the three other estates to collate subscriptions to the national supplication and arrange the third mass meeting for 15 November. Indeed, before this mass meeting broke up on 17 November, the twenty-four nobles active in the cause met with representatives from the three other estates to co-ordinate the forthcoming elections in the localities.[37]

The application of the term 'Tables' to the organisation of the disaffected element did not gain general currency until the promulgation of the National Covenant on 28 February 1638. Nonetheless, contemporary commentators do recognise that the organisation which came into operation from 6 December followed guidelines established at the mass meeting in November.[38] The composition of all five Tables was altered constantly, but deliberately, in order to spread the burden of political responsibility and financial commitment. The expediency of such alterations should not be confused with a want of coherence or lack of permanence in the party structure.[39] Indeed, the use of the term 'Tables' allowed the supplicants to draw upon established administrative practice to convey the image of acting formally in the national interest, without making any claim to official status. In turn, recourse to separate meetings, rather than a unicameral convention, meant that the four Tables did not abrogate the formal standing of a parliament for Scotland.[40]

The inspiration for the disaffected's organisation may have been drawn as much from incipient freemasonry as from established administrative practices. Each estate met in separate lodgings to discuss and speculate on matters of common interest during the supplicants' mass meetings. The planning caucus of 17 November to co-ordinate the election of commissioners from the localities was held in the noblemen's lodgings with rights of admission strictly reserved. The meeting was marked not only by overtures for divine assistance, but also by a divinely inspired sense of purpose for 'the restitution of the truth'. Those present were reputedly inspired by a striving for justice, a belief in constitutional perfectability and a commitment to regular fraternity in resisting the establishment of 'tirannical power' devoid of 'the warrant of God's law and the law of the land'. There is no hint among contemporary participants in the disaffected cause about the currency of shibboleths to control access to the planning caucus or, subsequently, to the fifth Table. Nonetheless, Traquair was moved to complain to Rothes in the course of private discussions on 13 November that his adversaries 'said he had the Masone word among the nobilitie'.[41]

A Provisional Government

The liaising committee having been informed of the impending response from the Court, around 140 supplicants armed with commissions from their localities arrived in Edinburgh and formally constituted themselves into four separate Tables on 6 December. A fifth Table, consisting of the gentry, burgesses and ministers, operated as the disaffected executive. Its first formal enactment was to ratify an approach made by the liaising committee to retain five advocates as legal counsel. The most notable advocate was Johnston of Wariston, destined to become clerk to and chief polemicist for the fifth Table.[42] His passionate belief, tinged with chiliasm, in Scotland's special relationship with God, led him to shape the revolt against the personal rule in a radical direction; but he never sought nor had thrust upon him radical leadership.[43]

The immediate remit of Wariston and the four other advocates, to underwrite the legal authenticity and political solidarity of the Tables, was presaged by the king's instructions delivered to the Privy Council at Linlithgow on 7 December. In keeping with the king's resolve to punish Edinburgh, the Council and the College of Justice were to meet at Stirling from the outset of February 1638. In the meantime, the Council was moved to Dalkeith. A further proclamation affirmed the king's abhorrence of popery and, in a more conciliatory vein, disclaimed innovations 'aganis the laudable lawes of this his majesties native kingdome'.[44]

That Charles's apparent conciliatory gesture was merely a stalling manoeuvre was confirmed by the Council's refusal to accord the supplicants a formal hearing until 21 December. The intervening days were used purposefully by the Tables for consultation, private negotiation with lay councillors and, above all, for refining their forces of political persuasion. Extensive discussions among the Tables upheld the paramount need for a common sense of purpose to maintain the momentum of their cause. Wariston, at the behest of the fifth Table, had actually been working from 9 December on a declinator refusing to accept any or all of the bishops as judges whenever the supplicants were granted a formal hearing. Two days later, he was commissioned to draft a composite supplication, extending protest explicitly against the Court of High Commission and maintaining the disaffected element's right to seek redress from the bishops. At the same time, the Tables were narrowing the avenues for remedial action. The clear inference to be drawn from the composite supplication was that the grievances of the disaffected must be redressed constitutionally: that is, through assemblies in Kirk and State. The Council having twice refused to accept the declinator and the composite supplication, Wariston drew up a protestation for 15 December, which emphasised that the 'redress of their just grievances' must be through accepted constitutional channels.[45]

The disaffected executive carried their campaign for constitutional redress to the country. Henderson and Dickson, the foremost ministers on the fifth Table, co-ordinated appeals through the pulpit. A day was to be set aside in each parish for public humiliation and fasting when congregations were to be acquainted how far the Service Book was contrary 'to the Confession of Faith, sworn and subscryved be all the ranks in this kingdom': that is, the King's Confession of 1581, known alternatively as the Negative Confession for its denial of 'all contrary religion and doctrine, but chiefly all kind of Papistry'. Subscribed by James VI and his household prior to its distribution nationwide for public subscription, the Negative Confession provided a precedent for banding together at the behest of the Crown against popery. Accordingly, Charles I's affirmation against popery of 7 December was interpreted as sanctioning communal banding to secure constitutional redress. At the same time, the king's affirmation was propagated as a royal admission of ignorance. The bishops had not informed Charles that liturgical innovations contained any superstition, or anything contrary 'to the established religion and lawes of the contray'.[46]

The evident willingness of the Tables to sanction further tumultuous lobbying, confirmed by the blockading of the Council in the royal palace of Dalkeith on 19 December, led to a formal hearing being accorded to a twelve-man delegation two days later. The delegation, headed by Loudoun, presented a highly selective rehearsal of events since July constructed to extol the orderliness, patience and reasonableness of the supplicants; to infer that the Tables were the custodians of the national interest; and to specify the priorities to which the supplicants were bound in the service of God, Crown and people. Loudoun then concentrated his attack upon the episcopate by enunciating the contents of the declinator which should be upheld although the bishops, following overtures for their removal from the delegation, were expediently absent from the hearing. He added another important rider. Effective remedial action required not only the trial of all the bishops, but the institution of a permanent restraining power — the clear, but unspoken, assumption being redress through constitutional assemblies not through the Council.

Loudoun's speech was seconded by an emotionally persuasive oration from James Cunningham, minister of Cumnock in Ayrshire, who warned of the nemesis that awaited councillors found wanting in their duty to God, king and people. Their manifest reluctance to remonstrate against liturgical innovations was compounded by their wanton failure to ensure the transmission of the Reformed tradition untainted by practices abjured 'in the confession of faith and covenant of the quholl land'. This latter reference to the covenant commanded by the general assembly of 1596 — for the spiritual regeneration of the nation through stricter religious observance and disciplinary standards — was the first specific indication by a member of the disaffected executive that the Negative Confession and the last national covenant were to be harnessed as precedents for their cause.[47]

At the conclusion of proceedings on 21 December, the Council agreed to communicate to Court the complaints of the supplicants as enunciated in the national petition, the national supplication of grievance and the composite supplication. By agreeing also to respect the declinator, the bishops were thus accepted by lay councillors, as by the Tables, as public enemies. Prior to their dispersal from Edinburgh on 22 December, the Tables elected a holding committee dominated by Rothes, Loudoun and Balmerino, whose principal remit was to monitor the movement of leading officials and councillors to and from the Court; a task facilitated by the offer from Lorne on 29 December to accompany Traquair and act as 'ane intelligencer for the Tables'. The holding committee was also charged to draw up a 'Historical Informatione' giving the supplicants' authentic version of events from the first tumults in Edinburgh on 23 July 1637. Johnson of Wariston readily accepted responsibility for its compilation which was ready by 15 January 1638 and duly conveyed to Court by the justice-clerk, Sir John Hamilton of Orbiston. Though a kinsman and close political associate of the marquis of

Hamilton, Orbiston was demonstrating growing sympathy with the disaffected cause.[48]

Despite Traquair's assiduous cultivation of Hamilton and Stirling and despite the private lobbying of leading Scottish courtiers by the holding committee, Charles was intent upon an uncompromising stand towards the supplicants. Indeed, Traquair was summoned to Court in late January largely to account for his close association with the disaffected leadership. Traquair found himself further compromised by his blatant antipathy to the Scottish bishops, particularly the Canterburians, whom he blamed for the current unrest north of the Border. Charles was not prepared to tolerate such criticism any more than he was willing to have Laud castigated as the instigator of disorder in Scotland. Charles was intent on suppressing bad news and discouraging discussion of the mounting crisis. Although he may not have shared Laud's belief that this crisis was part of a British Puritan conspiracy, he maintained adamantly that the situation in Scotland was under control. No encouragement was to be given to the English disaffected. Charles was convinced that by promising publicly to uphold Protestantism but making no concessions to the supplicants, he would occasion a split among the Tables. Accordingly, Traquair was despatched north on 9 February with a proclamation in which the king accepted full responsibility for the compilation and publication of the Service Book. An indemnity was offered to all who withdrew from the Tables and retired submissively to their localities. All further mass meetings were discharged under pain of treason.[49]

That Charles should make the exercise of his royal prerogative the pivotal issue of the current crisis had already been anticipated by the disaffected leadership. Having been investigating the nature and scope of the royal prerogative, Johnston of Wariston was turning his thoughts to its specific application. By 25 January, Wariston had penned a treatise against the continuance of the Court of High Commission which, in calling for fundamental checks on the prerogative, served as a test piece for the National Covenant. By drawing selectively on biblical sources, Roman law commentaries and parliamentary precedents, Wariston sought not only to repudiate the High Commission as an instrument of ecclesiastical coercion, but also to press the necessity for free assemblies both to redress past excesses of royal authoritarianism and, more positively, to provide a continual check on the king's prerogative.[50]

Forewarned of the unfavourable response from Court, the holding committee on 6 February distributed an advertisement summoning the Tables back to Edinburgh. The forthcoming proclamation, reputedly procured by the bishops to enforce the Service Book, had 'no legal force to hinder the absolutlie necessarie meitinges of all interrests in this common cause'. Within twenty-four hours of Traquair's return to the capital on 15 February, Wariston had drafted a counter-protest to the royal proclamation whose contents had been extensively leaked from Court. The Tables then assembled in Edinburgh resolved to send flying pickets to attend the Council's publication of the king's proclamation at Stirling; a task duly accomplished on 19 February, as at Linlithgow the following day. In furtherance of a mass protest against the proclamation in

Edinburgh, a second advertisement was despatched to the localities on 18 February calling for reinforcements for the Tables. By 22 February, the number of supplicants and sympathisers in the capital had swelled to around 2,000. After royal heralds had intimated the proclamation's contents at the market cross, they were surrounded by the nobles' Table and obliged to listen to Wariston read through the counter-protestation: a disrespectful gesture condemned by Charles as a 'higher act of rebellion' than either the first tumult in the capital on 23 July or the second on 18 October 1637.[51]

The demonstration on 22 February 1638 demonstrated the resolve of the Tables to offer a direct challenge to royal authority and to prepare for, but not provoke, outright confrontation. Not only was his Scottish administration in evident disarray, but the Court of Charles I was apprehensive that foreign powers, notably France under Cardinal Richelieu, were intent on making diplomatic capital out of the deteriorating political situation north of the Border and that channels of communication had been established between the Tables and English Puritans. Charles was actively preparing to extend treasonable charges to cover banding together for purposes not authorised specifically by the Crown — a monumental extension of criminal activity which would cut customary practices of early modern Scotland at the root.[52]

On 23 February, a third advertisement was despatched to nobles and gentry deemed well-affected to the cause in districts remote from the capital not hitherto involved in supplicating, notably the northern and central Highlands and the north-east. Their prompt attendance was invited at Edinburgh to participate in 'the most important business that ever concerned this natione'. The Tables proceeded to effect a revolutionary innovation in the Scottish body politic, which ended all pretence that they acted merely as delegates for supplicants from the four political estates. The decisive step in transforming a political party into a provisional government was the formal constitution of the disaffected executive as the fifth Table, consisting of the nobles' Table and four representatives from each of the other three Tables. The fifth Table assumed the responsibility 'to grow a kynde of power and judicatorye to co-ordinate and contradistinctive from the Councell': that is, to operate not as an alternative authority to the Council, but as a provisional government intent on acting as the custodian of the national interest. Henceforth, the fifth Table initiated all business which, after discussion and approval by the other Tables, was to be communicated to the localities. Members of the gentry's Table were designated to remain in the shires as a local secretariat to carry out instructions from the capital and report back 'with expeditione'.[53]

More immediately, having recalled the repeated endeavours to sow discord and division within the ranks of the supplicants not only by bishops, but by lay councillors and officials who placed their personal credit at Court above the national interest, the first executive act of the fifth Table, approved 'by unanimouse consent' of the other Tables on 23 February, was to commission 'a Band of mutuall associatione for offence and defence'; a band duly published and subscribed as the National Covenant five days later.[54]

Revolutionary Ideology

Drawn up by Johnston of Wariston with the assistance of Alexander Henderson, the National Covenant was essentially a revolutionary enterprise binding the Scottish people together to justify and consolidate the revolt against absentee monarchy. Its moderate tenor, coupled with its conservative format and appeal to precedents, has led to the National Covenant being described as 'a constitutional, and not a revolutionary document': a description which undoubtedly belies its radical nature.[55] The finalised version having been approved by all four Tables before subscriptions commenced in the Greyfriars church on 28 February, its appearance of unanimity was not deceptive. The National Covenant deliberately maintained 'a shrewd vagueness' not just to attract support from all classes and from every locality,[56] but primarily to avoid specific imputations of treason.

The National Covenant was not a private league of rebellious subjects, nor even an aristocratic reaction against the personal rule of Charles I,[57] but a nationalist manifesto asserting the independence of a sovereign people under God. The explicit intent of the fifth Table was that the National Covenant should be propagated as a tripartite public band embracing God, Crown and people, 'for the maintenance of religione and the King's Majesteis authority, and for the preservatione of the lawes and liberties of the kingdome'. Accordingly, the National Covenant can be split into three component parts demonstrating the present cause, the dual imperative and the fundamental priorities of public banding.[58]

The first component rehearsed the Negative Confession of 1581 in association with a detailed, if selective, series of parliamentary enactments perpetrated to maintain the 'true religion, and the King's Majesty'. The radical implication of this component was that loyalty to the Crown was conditional on expunging idolatrous, superstitious and popish practices from the Kirk, on protecting the purity of the reformed tradition and upholding the rights of the Scots people to be governed according to the common laws of the realm as grounded in statute. The selection of parliamentary statutes reveals the radical astuteness of the fifth Table. Precedents for the removal of erroneous doctrines and prejudicial practices culminated with the collation and codification of the penal laws in 1609, which served to press the urgency of an uncompromising Protestant crusade to ward off the unabated threat from the Counter-Reformation.[59] Precedents for sustaining the Kirk's purity of doctrine, discipline and worship did not extend beyond the era of the first presbyterian experiment during the 1590s; a calculated omission of all subsequent legislation in favour of episcopacy — but not a categorical declaration 'to extirpate the bishops'. Indeed, recourse to such erastian precedents demonstrates no convincing support for Melvilleanism nor any resolve to establish a theocracy.[60] At the same time, the intention of the fifth Table to restore a 'moderate episcopal regime', as typified by the Jacobean episcopate, cannot be sustained.[61]

The attack on episcopacy, though muted,[62] was contained within the resolve of the fifth Table to sweep away all innovations, not just religious, which had threatened national independence and the subjects' liberties since the union of the Crowns. Precedents respecting the vital importance of the 'fundamental lawes' of the kingdom drew chiefly on the legislation of the 1604 parliament, called to discuss union with England. Innovations prejudicial to parliamentary authority were deplored, 'as this Realme could be no more a free Monarchy'.[63] Constitutional tradition masked a revolutionary determination: sovereignty was to be vested in the king-in-parliament at the expense of the royal prerogative.

The statutory limitations imposed on monarchy were accepted formally in the solemn oath taken not only by Charles I in 1633, but by 'all Kings and Princes at their Coronation and reception of their Princely Authority' to preserve the 'true Religion, Lawes and Liberties of this Kingdome'. The true religion 'now receaved and preached' was Protestantism in accord with the Negative Confession of 1581 — that is, prior to the readmission of bishops and the Five Articles of Perth as well as the recent liturgical innovations. Moreover, true religion and royal authority were so linked that it was impossible to be truly loyal to the Crown without being loyal to the true religion. Although the first priority of the Crown was to rule the people according to the will of God as revealed by scripture, royal authority must respect, simultaneously, 'the laudable Lawes and Constitutions received in this Realme, no ways repugnant to the said will of God'.[64]

The second component of the National Covenant elaborated the concept of a twofold contract on which the whole life of the Scottish kingdom was based. This contract encapsulated the dual imperatives of covenanting by drawing on historical, biblical and political precepts. Opposition to the divine right of kings and absolute monarchy was inspired as much by the ideology of French Huguenots and, to a lesser extent, of Dutch Calvinists as by the Knoxian legacy of resistance to an ungodly monarch.[65] Although recourse to covenanting was justified historically in terms of past examples of religious and political banding by the Scottish people, the contents of past bands — including that of 1596, the last to receive nationwide circulation — bore little relation to the religious and constitutional imperatives of the National Covenant.[66]

The religious covenant was a tripartite compact between the king and people to God to uphold the purity of 'the true reformed religion' as expressed not only in the Negative Confession, but in the enlarged confession of faith established from the Reformation 'by sundry acts of lawful generall assemblies, and of Parliament' as by the catechisms, all being grounded exclusively in scripture. Whereas obedience to God was unconditional and irresistible, the people's obligations to the king were limited and conditional. The people stood surety for the king in defence of the true religion. But, if the king betrayed his people to God, the people were bound to hold the kingdom to its obligations: indeed, they had a positive duty to resist to avoid divine retribution. In short, the religious covenant placed the Scots, like the Israelites, in the role of the chosen people. Operating within the framework of this religious covenant was a constitutional contract between the king on the one hand and the people on the other for maintenance of good and lawful government and a just political order. In return for 'maintaining the Kings Majesty, His Person and Estate', the people laid down binding conditions on the king. If the king failed to uphold the fundamental laws and liberties of the kingdom or sought to subvert his subjects' privileges or estates, the people were entitled to take appropriate remedial action — including the right to resist.

On the grounds that government existed to further the interests of the subject spiritually and materially, the National Covenant pledged its subscribers to eradicate the 'manifold innovations and evills' mentioned in past supplications of the disaffected element. The retrospective scope of these supplications arguably extended back beyond the petitioning of the last seven months to that associated with the coronation parliament of 1633. Certainly comprehended were the petitions condemning liturgical innovations which were reaffirmed to be unscriptural, subversive of the Reformed tradition in the Kirk and leading to the insinuation not just of popery, but of tyranny on account of their unconstitutional introduction. The Court of High Commission came within the scope of evils leading to the ruination of 'the true Reformed Religion' and of our Liberties, Lawes and Estates'. Although subscribers were obliged merely to forebear rather than condemn innovations in worship, final determination of the acceptability of all ceremonies, as of the current corruptions in ecclesiastical government and the exercise of civil power by kirkmen, was to be left to 'free assemblies and in Parliaments': a clear inference that constitutional redress should not be subject to the censorious royal management evident in the coronation parliament of 1633.[67]

The emphasis laid on the importance of 'lawful generall assemblies' in upholding the purity of the Reformed tradition manifestly implied that some assemblies during the reign of James VI had been unlawful. The fifth Table insisted that the oath exacted from entrants to the ministry — to respect the Five Articles and episcopal government — was invalidated by 'the prelates turning Popish'. The disaffected executive was no less convinced that James VI's management of the general assembly in 1618, as of the parliament of 1621, had made the passage and ratification of the Five Articles 'repugnant to the fundamental lawes of the kingdom'.

In calling for free assemblies and parliaments, the intention of the fifth Table was not just to secure the redress of pressing grievances between Charles I and his Scottish subjects, but to effect a permanent check on absentee monarchy to safeguard the religious and constitutional imperatives of covenanting. Although a lawful and free general assembly was propagated as the immediate objective in order to recover the purity of the Reformed tradition, the National Covenant was concerned fundamentally with the ordering of priorities between Crown and people. Its first component prescribed that the final approval of all ecclesiatical and civil issues pertained to the king-in-parliament. The second component stressed that the dual imperatives of covenanting took precedence over the dictates of absentee monarchy. That the National Covenant necessitated constitutional monarchy in perpetuity was underscored by the third and most revolutionary component — the oath of allegiance and mutual association.[68]

Allegiance to monarchy followed allegiance to God; the former was conditional, the latter unconditional and irresistible. The oath required the subscribers to swear that they would 'to the uttermost of our power, with our meanes and lives, stand to the defence of our dread Soveraigne, the Kings Majesty, his Person and Authority, in the defence and preservation of the foresaid true Religion. Liberties and Lawes of the Kingdome': that is, the king's person and royal authority were to be defended in the course of the people's defence and preservation of religion, liberties and laws. In so far as he accepted the religious and constitutional imperatives of the National Covenant, the king was to be defended. The oath went on to require mutual assistance among subscribers 'in the same cause of maintaining the true Religion and his Majesty's Authority, with our best counsel, our bodies, meanes and whole power, against all sorts of persons whatsoever'. The oath was thus a positive act of defiance in reserving loyalty to a covenanted king.[69]

There was no necessary incompatibility in promising to defend royal authority while simultaneously promoting policies contrary to the professed interests of Charles I.[70] Nor were subscribers in a hapless position because the National Covenant seemingly ignored the potential conflict of interests in swearing to uphold the true religion and at the same time defend the person and authority of the king.[71] For the revolutionary essence of the National Covenant was its ordering of priorities: 'the true worship of God, the Majesty of our King, and peace of the Kingdome, for the common happiness of our selves, and the posterity'. Integral to the permanent achievement of constitutionalism in Kirk and State was the crucial distinction between the office of monarchy and the personal conduct of the king. Resistance to Charles I was in the long-term interests of monarchy and people if the kingdom was to be restored to godly rule.[72]

Conclusion

The National Covenant was the culmination not just of the previous seven months of supplication, but of the previous thirteen years of political frustration induced by the personal rule of Charles I. In making the crucial distinction between the monarch's office and the king's person, the disaffected executive had manifestly learned the lesson of the Revocation Scheme when Charles, from 1626, had threatened private legal means to effect the professed public ends of monarchy. Within a broader European perspective, the propagation of this distinction by the fifth Table avoided recourse to republicanism in resisting absentee monarchy.[73]

Because Charles I was no usurper but the legitimate heir of the royal house of Stewart, there was no question that the right of resistance vindicated tyrannicide by the private citizen. Instead, the oath of allegiance and mutual assistance upheld the corporate right of the people to resist a lawful king who threatened to become tyrannical. Such resistance was to be exercised by the natural leaders of society, not the nobles exclusively but the Tables as the corporate embodiment of the inferior magistrate. In effect, therefore, the revolutionary oath required the subscribers to recognise the Tables as not just the provisional government, but the divinely warranted custodians of the national interest.[74]

NOTES

1. *Letters of Samuel Rutherford*, I, 148–49, 157–62; Rowe, *History of the Kirk*, 389, 396; Baillie, *Letters and Journals*, I, 8–9, 16.

2. *Letters of Samuel Rutherford*, I, 39, 162, 164; Baillie, *Letters and Journals*, I, 8; *Memoirs of Henry Guthry*, 14; *RPCS*, second series, VI, 359; Spalding, *Troubles*, I, 46. Lorne, who was reputedly passed over for the chancellorship in favour of Archbishop Spottiswood at the end of 1634, claimed to be acting on behalf of his nephew and ward, John Gordon, second Viscount Kenmure, patron of the parish of Earlston.

3. D. Stevenson, 'Conventicles in the Kirk, 1619–37', *RSCHS*, XVIII, (1972–74), 99–114; *Autobiography and Life of Mr Robert Blair*, T. McCrie ed., (Wodrow Society, Edinburgh, 1848), 117, 136–38; *Select Biographies*, I, 134–40, 150–51. Solidarity among conventiclers was promoted by marriages linking families of sympathetic ministers to leading landed and commercial families.

4. J. S. Reid, *The History of the Presbyterian Church in Ireland*, vol. I, (Edinburgh, 1834), 94–98, 105, 110–11, 119–22, 130–37, 168–69, 173–78, 182–89, 201–05, 225–34; *Autobiography of Robert Blair*, 57–59, 64, 71, 84–86, 90–91, 101–06, 128–29, 136–37, 142–48; *Select Biographies*, I, 134–35, 141–48, 152–57, 344; Row, *History of the Kirk*, 390, 397–98.

5. *Letters of Samuel Rutherford*, I, 75, 109, 156, 160, 167–71, 195, 200, 211–14, 228–35, 285–86, 370–76; *Diary of Sir Archibald Johnston of Wariston, 1632–39*, J. M. Paul ed., (SHS, Edinburgh, 1911), 250–64; *Memoirs of Henry Guthrie*, 78–80; Elder, *Old Church Life in Scotland*, II, 300–02; Stevenson, *RSCHS*, XVII, 99–101, 112–14.

6. *Letters of Samuel Rutherford*, I, 59, 69, 102, 107, 117, 134, 148–49, 159, 167, 284–91, 332–33; *Select Biographies*, I, 157–58, 336–48; II, 5–10; *Autobiography of Robert Blair*, 147–48; *Memoirs of Henry Guthry*, 15; R. Wodrow, *Analecta: or Materials for a History of Remarkable Providences*, J. M. Leishman ed., 3 vols, (Maitland Club, Edinburgh, 1842–43), III, 2–7.

7. *Letters of Samuel Rutherford*, I, 103–05, 111, 149, 163, 214, 274, 277; *Autobiography of Robert Blair*, 130, 150; *Diary of Wariston, 1632–39*, 206, 250, 256–59, 262; *Select Biographies*, I, 158; Mathew, *Scotland under Charles I*, 39–40.

8. Burrell, 'The Covenant Idea as a Revolutionary Symbol', *Church History*, XXVII, 342–43, 349; J. B. Torrance, 'The Covenant Concept in Scottish Theology and Politics and its Legacy', *Scottish Journal of Theology*, XXXIV, (1981), 225–43; G. D. Henderson, *The Burning Bush: Studies in Scottish Church History*, (Edinburgh, 1957), 65–70; A. H. Williamson, 'The Jewish Dimension of the Scottish Apocalypse: Climate, Covenant and World Renewal', in *Menasseh Ben Israel and His World*, Y. Kaplan, H. Mechoulan & R. H. Popkin eds., (New York, 1989), 7–30.

9. *RPCS*, second series, VI, 352–53; J. Gordon, *History of Scots Affairs, 1637–41*, 3 vols, J. Robertson & G. Grub eds., (Spalding Club, Aberdeen, 1841), I, 3–7; Rothes, *Relation*, 1–3; *Memoirs of Henry Guthry*, 19–24; Baillie, *Letters and Journals*, I, 1–2,

442–43. Lee, jr., *The Road to Revolution*, 209–12, raises perceptive doubts about the extent of planning, but tends to underestimate the concerted endeavours of the disaffected leadership since the trial of Balmerino. More immediately, planning was further aided by the influx of ministers to the city in the 'mistaken' belief that the half-yearly synod of the Edinburgh diocese was due on the last Wednesday of April instead of the last Wednesday in May.

10. Baillie, *Letters and Journals*, I, 16–17; Gordon, *History of Scots Affairs*, I, 4–5; Row, *History of the Kirk*, 407; *Diary of Sir Thomas Hope*, 57, 60–61.

11. *RPCS*, second series, VI, 448–49; Clarendon, *History of the Rebellion*, I, 191–93; *Memoirs of Henry Guthry*, 19–22; Baillie, *Letters and Journals*, I, 17–18.

12. Row, *History of the Kirk*, 408; Rothes, *Relation*, 2; Baillie, *Letters and Journals*, I, 445; Gordon, *History of Scots Affairs*, I, 4; *Large Declaration*, 21–22.

13. J. M. Henderson, 'An Advertisement' about the Service Book, 1637', *SHR*, XXIII, (1925–26), 199–204; *Diary of Wariston, 1632–39*, 262; Spalding, *Troubles*, I, 47.

14. *RPCS*, second series, VI, 445–46, 483–84; *Large Declaration*, 23–26; Gordon, *History of Scots Affairs*, I, 7–13; Row, *History of the Kirk*, 408–10; Spalding, *Troubles*, I, 47–48; Rothes, *Relation*, 195–201; Wodrow, *Analecta*, I, 64; *Memoirs of Henry Guthry*, 22–23; Clarendon, *History of the Rebellion*, I, 191–93; SRO, Hamilton papers, TD 75/100/26/382. Public demonstrations during divine service were not confined to St Giles. In the adjacent Old Kirk, barracking and abuse interrupted the reading from the Service Book which was only resumed after the protesters walked out of the morning service. At Greyfriars, James Fairlie, bishop-designate of Argyll, was forced to abandon his reading by riotous behaviour. Henry Rollock, minister of Trinity, who was initially in favour of exemplary readings, was able to avert a public demonstration by delaying the start of divine service. On learning of the hostile reception accorded to the readings in the other churches, he discarded his surplice before entering the pulpit to deliver a sermon denouncing liturgical innovations.

15. *RPCS*, second series, VI, 486–90, 509; Baillie, *Letters and Journals*, I, 18–19; Rothes, *Relation*, 3–5; *Diary of Wariston, 1632–39*, 265–66; Spalding, *Troubles*, I, 48. The town council of Edinburgh was made responsible for all damages resulting from the rioting. The magistrates of the city were also charged to apprehend anyone involved in the 'bygane tumult' as in future disorders. Nonetheless, the handful of serving women and apprentices apprehended by the magistrates in the course of the rioting were, with the approval of episcopal as well as lay councillors, released from custody quit of all charges by 27 July.

16. *RPCS*, second series, VI, 483–521; Gordon, *History of Scots Affairs*, I, 12–14; Baillie, *Letters and Journals*, I, 18–19, 32; Row, *History of the Kirk*, 409–10; *Historical Collections*, J. Rushworth ed., vols I–III, (London, 1680–91), II, 387–90, 393–95.

17. Baillie, *Letters and Journals*, I, 12–13, 19, 32, 449–51; Rothes, *Relation*, 4–5, 46–47; Balfour, *Historical Works*, II, 227–31; Row, *History of the Kirk*, 484; Henderson, *SHR*, XXIII, 203–04.

18. NLS, Morton Cartulary & Letters, MS 79, fo. 56; Gordon, *History of Scots Affairs*, I, 14–16; Baillie, Letters and Journals, I, 19–20, 451–52; Rothes, *Relation*, 5–7, 17–18; *Memoirs of Henry Guthry*, 24–25.

19. Stevenson, *The Scottish Revolution*, 74; *RPCS*, second series, VI, 521, 694; Burnet, *Memoirs*, 32.

20. *Autobiography of Robert Blair*, 150–51; *Select Biographies*, I, 158–59; NLS, Salt & Coal: Events, 1635–62, MS 2263, fo. 89; Rothes, *Relation*, 7–8, 18; Baillie, *Letters and Journals*, I, 21–22.

21. *RPCS*, second series, VI, 700–09, 715–16; Rothes, *Relation*, 47–48; Baillie, *Letters and Journals*, I, 13–15; Gordon, *History of Scots Affairs*, I, 18.

22. Makey, *The Church of the Covenant*, 16, 20–21.

23. Rothes, *Relation*, 8–9; Baillie, *Letters and Journals*, I, 33, 452–53; *Historical*

Collections, II, 396–99; Balfour, *Historical Works*, II, 232–33; H. Watt, 'William Laud and Scotland, *RSCHS*, VII, (1941), 171–90.

24. Rothes, *Relation*, 9, 47; *Memoirs of Henry Guthry*, 26–27; Row, *History of the Kirk*, 384–85; Burnet, *History of My Own Times*, 15.

25. *RPCS*, second series, VI, 530–34; Rothes, *Relation*, 9–11; Balfour, *Historical Works*, II, 233–35; Baillie, *Letters and Journals*, I, 453–54; Row, *History of the Kirk*, 385.

26. Baillie, *Letters and Journals*, I, 23–25, 33; Rothes, *Relation*, 12; *Memoirs of Henry Guthry*, 26–27; Gordon, *History of Scots Affairs*, I, 19; *Large Declaration*, 31–32.

27. *Diary of Wariston, 1632–39*, 135, 262, 264; Burnet, *History of My Own Times*, 15–16; Baillie, *Letters and Journals*, I, 14; D. M. Forrester, 'Archibald Johnston of Wariston, especially as in his Diaries', *RSCHS*, IX, (1947), 127–41; Mathew, *Scotland under Charles I*, 59–69.

28. Baillie, *Letters and Journals*, I, 33–34; Rothes, Relation, 18–19; *Memoirs of Henry Guthry*, 27–28; Balfour, *Historical Works*, II, 235–37; *Miscellaneous State Papers, 1501–1726*, P. Yorke, earl of Hardwicke ed., vol. II, (London, 1778), 95.

29. *RPCS*, second series, VI, 536–38; *Historical Collections*, II, 401–02; Rothes, *Relation*, 8, 16–17, 19; Baillie, *Letters and Journals*, I, 35; *Memoirs of Henry Guthry*, 29–30. All copies of a book entitled *Ane dispute agains the English popish ceremonies obtruded upon the Kirk of Scotland* were to be seized and publicly burned. This book was the work of a zealous young nonconformist, George Gillespie, chaplain in the household of John Kennedy, sixth earl of Cassillis, a leading supplicant. Gillespie maintained that liturgical innovations were matters indifferent not fundamental; their acceptance was neither necessary nor expedient nor lawful. From an unequivocal presbyterian standpoint, he went on to suggest a markedly radical direction for the disaffected cause. Ministers, elders and deacons had the right to assemble 'for healing of the church's hurt', even if consent was not forthcoming from the Crown. Moreover, the Crown had no right to review or reverse whatever a general assembly decreed on ecclesiastical controversies or questions of faith. The disciplining of ministers pertained to presbyteries or synods, not to the Court of High Commission. The banning of this book by royal edict served to stimulate public curiosity about its contents as well as increase its covert circulation among committed opponents of episcopacy (*The Works of Mr George Gillespie*, W. M. Hetherington ed., 2 vols, (Edinburgh, 1846), I, xvi–xvii, 1–217).

30. Rothes, *Relation*, 10, 49–50; Gordon, *History of Scots Affairs*, I, 24–26; D. H. Fleming, *Scotland's Supplication and Complaint against the Book of Common Prayer (otherwise Laud's Liturgy), the Book of Canons, and the Prelates, 18th October 1637*, (Edinburgh, 1927), 59–62; 'Royal Letters and Instructions, and other Documents from the Archives of the Earls of Wigton, 1510–1650', in *Miscellany of the Maitland Club*, vol. II, (Maitland Club, Edinburgh, 1840), 409–13.

31. Rothes, *Relation*, 13–15, 17, 19–20; *Ancrum & Lothian*, I, 94–97; Baillie, *Letters and Journals*, I, 37–38; Gordon, *History of Scots Affairs*, I, 21–24; *Memoirs of Henry Guthry*, 28–29; NLS, Salt & Coal; Events, 1635–62, MS 2263, fo. 89; *Large Declaration*, 34–40.

32. *RPCS*, second series, VI, 483–84, 541–42; Rothes, *Relation*, 15–16, 19, 21–23; Baillie, *Letters and Journals*, I, 38–39; *The Government of Scotland under the Covenanters, 1637–51*, D. Stevenson ed., (SHS, Edinburgh, 1982), xii–xiii; Makey, *The Church of the Covenant*, 22–24.

33. Rothes, *Relation*, 20–21, *RPCS*, second series, VI, 709–13; HMC, *Laing MSS*, I, 198–99; *Scotland's Supplication*, 62–67; *Miscellany of the Maitland Club*, II, 409–13. Another list exists with at least 560 subscriptions, containing the names of only 19 nobles and of subscribers from 21 burghs specifically cited in the original, together with general notification of subscription by 120 ministers. The number of gentry was augmented to 400. It would seem that not only the original supplication but a master-copy was circulated prior to the dispersal of the disaffected from the capital in order to ensure

proof of subscriptions should the original be mislaid once lodged with the Council.

34. Rothes, *Relation*, 23–27, 30–32; Baillie, *Letters and Journals*, I, 40–42; Spalding, *Troubles*, I, 50. Prior to receiving the Council's approval, Traquair had actually commenced informal negotiations on 13 November with Rothes who had remained in the capital as a one-man lobby since the dispersal of the supplicants on 19 October.

35. Rothes, *Relation*, 32–33; *Memoirs of Henry Guthry*, 31; Gordon, *History of Scots Affairs*, I, 27–28; NLS, Salt & Coal: Events, 1635–62, MS 2263, fo. 89–90; Row, *History of the Kirk*, 485–86.

36. *Government under the Covenanters*, xiii–xv.

37. Rothes, *Relation*, 28; Baillie, *Letters and Journals*, I, 42; *Extracts from the Records of the Royal Burgh of Stirling, 1519–1666*, R. Renwick ed., (Glasgow, 1887), 178–79.

38. *Large Declaration*, 54; Gordon, *History of Scots Affairs*, I, 28; Clarendon, *History of the Rebellion*, I, 196–97; Lennoxlove, Hamilton Papers, C 1/1068. The practice of supplicants coming to Edinburgh was never confined to commissioners elected to the Tables. By the summer of 1638, the term 'Tables' was being used pejoratively by commentators sympathetic to Charles I attempting to dismiss the supplicants as usurpers of the public functions of royal government.

39. Stevenson, *The Scottish Revolution*, 76; Burnet, *Memoirs*, 32–33.

40. *Large Declaration*, 54; *Government under the Covenanters*, xv–xvi. The Tables were occasionally specified as 'the Green Tables' to further administrative associations.

41. Rothes, *Relation*, 28, 30. D. Stevenson, *The first freemasons: Scotland's early lodges and their members*, (Aberdeen, 1988), provides a full discussion of this topic, particularly of the Lodge of Edinburgh which was regularly admitting non-operative masons during the 1630s.

42. Rothes, *Relation*, 33–34; Baillie, *Letters and Journals*, I, 24, 42–43; Lennoxlove, Hamilton Papers, C 1/1068; *Diary of Wariston, 1632–39*, 275, 278–82.

43. Makey, *The Church of the Covenant*, 25; Cowan, *Montrose*, 45–46.

44. *RPCS*, second series, VI, 546–48; *Large Declaration*, 45–47; Balfour, *Historical Works*, II, 237–40; Rothes, *Relation*, 43–44; Lennoxlove, Hamilton Papers C 1/1068.

45. Rothes, *Relation*, 34–38, 44, 50–51; *Diary of Wariston 1632–39*, 283–84; NLS, Salt & Coal: Events, 1635–62, MS. fo. 90; Row, *History of the Kirk*, 487–88; Baillie, *Letters and Journal*, I, 26. The Council was actively considering two alternative options. Charles had privately instructed Roxburghe to offer a moratorium of at least four years on the imposition of liturgical innovations in order to contain, if not assuage, public unrest within Scotland. Traquair and the Scottish-based administrators proposed instead that the issue of the Service Book be referred to arbitration at a conference attended by equal numbers of its promoters and proposers. A national assembly might be convened to ratify the conference's findings in the event of agreement or to define points of controversy if arbitration was inconclusive (*CSP, Venetian*, (1636–39), 350, 387–88; HMC, *Traquair MSS*, 253; *RPCS*, second series, VI, 549–50; Gordon, *History of Scots Affairs*, I, 29–30).

46. NLS, Wodrow, MSS, quarto XXIV, fo. 78–79; *Memoirs of Henry Guthry*, 31–32; Baillie, *Letters and Journals*, I, 26, 43, 454; Row, *History of the Kirk*, 486–87. Subscription to the Negative Confession had become a test for public office, was incumbent upon all burgesses and entrants to the ministry and had been applied nationally, as recently as 1629 at the instigation of the bishops, to flush out suspected recusants (*RPCS*, second series, III, 237–49).

47. Rothes, *Relation*, 38–40; NLS, Wodrow MSS, folio LXI, fo. 242–43; NLS, Yester papers, MS 7032, fo. 28–29; Baillie, *Letters and Journals*, I, 455–58; Balfour, *Historical Works*, II, 240–49.

48. *RPCS*, second series, VI, 553–54; Gordon, *History of Scots Affairs*, I, 30–31; Rothes, *Relation*, 40–42, 52–53; Baillie, *Letters and Journals*, I, 46–48; *Diary of Wariston, 1632–39*, 288–90, 295–97, 304, 307–11. Rothes also had the foresight to arrange for another copy to be despatched for the private consideration of Thomas Hamilton,

second earl of Haddington, presuming correctly that Lennox, Hamilton and other leading Scottish courtiers would be informed of its contents.

49. SRO, Hamilton Papers, TD 75/100/26/394; Gordon, *History of Scots Affairs*, I, 31; Burnet, *Memoirs*, 32–34; *Large Declaration*, 48–50; *CSP, Venetian*, (1636–39), 362, 370, 3709–80, 387, 394–95.

50. EUL, Laing MSS, La.I.291; Baillie, *Letters and Journals*, I, 48–49; *Letters of Samuel Rutherford*, II, 213–15, 219–22; *Diary of Wariston, 1632–39*, 292–93, 302–03, 308.

51. Baillie, *Letters and Journals*, I, 49–51, 54–61; *Diary of Wariston, 1632–39*, 311–12, 316–17; Rothes, *Relation*, 54–67, 86–89; *Large Declaration*, 47, 50–52; Gordon, *History of Scots Affairs*, I, 32–36; *Miscellaneous State Papers*, II, 97–99; *RPCS*, second series, VII, 2–5; NLS, Salt & Coal: Events, 1635–62, MS 2263, fO. 90–92; SRO, Cunninghame-Graham MSS, GD 22/3/791; SRO, Dalhousie MSS, GD 45/1/49. In a pre-emptive move to prevent the counter-protestation being published in Stirling directly after the king's proclamation, Traquair and Roxburghe slipped out of Edinburgh at 2 a.m. on 19 February. But their party was overtaken by four pickets, a footman of the treasurer having chanced to inform a servant of Lord Linday of his master's intentions when calling on an Edinburgh hostelry for a late-night refreshment.

52. HMC, *Traquair MSS*, 248; Gordon, *History of Scots Affairs*, I, 39–42; *Diary of Wariston, 1632–39*, 282, 318–19; NLS, Morton Cartulary & Papers, MS 83, fo. 118; Carlton, *Charles I*, 199; J. Wormald, 'Bloodfeud, Kindred and Government in Early Modern Scotland, *Past & Present*, 87, (1980), 54–97. Suspicions at Court about foreign involvement were centred on two Catholic clergymen, both Scots — George Con, papal envoy to Queen Henrietta Maria and Abbé Chambre *alias* Thomas Chambers, emissary for Cardinal Richelieu. The latter certainly visited Scotland during September 1637 and possibly made another visit later that autumn, ostensibly to boost recruitment for the Scottish regiment in French service since 1633, but also to make contact with the disaffected leadership. Rewarded for his endeavours by becoming almoner to Richelieu, Chambers subsequently returned to Scotland to report on the state of affairs under the Covenanters during 1638–39. Despite his Jesuit affiliations, the Covenanters expediently made use of him as their chief contact with Richelieu during 1640, when Chambers became the unofficial Scottish ambassador to the French Court (*CSP, Venetian*, (1636–39), 273–74, 277, 291, 316; Stevenson, *The Scottish Revolution*, 184–87).

53. Rothes, *Relation*, 66–69; Gordon, *History of Scots Affairs*, I, 33–34; *Aberdeen Council Letters*, II, 85–86; *Government under the Covenanters*, xvi; *Large Declarationr*, 53–54.

54. Gordon, *History of Scots Affairs*, I, 38–39; Rothes, *Relation*, 69–70; Baillie, *Letters and Journals*, I, 50, 62–62; Row, *History of the Kirk*, 488–89.

55. *A Source Book of Scottish History*, III, 104; I. B. Cowan, 'The Covenanters: A revision article', *SHR*, XLVII, (1968), 38–39.

56. *A Source Book of Scottish History*, III, 104; G. D. Henderson, *The Burning Bush*, 64; Rothes, *Relation*, 211; *APS*, III, 376–77, c.6. Indeed, the fifth Table had the contents cleared by legal counsel to ensure that the National Covenant did not come within the scope of the enactment of 1585 against private banding without royal consent.

57. Donaldson, *James V to James VII*, 316; Ferguson, *Scotland's Relations with England*, 116; D. Stevenson, *The Covenanters: The National Covenant and Scotland*, (Saltire Pamphlets, Edinburgh, 1988), 35–44.

58. Rothes, *Relation*, 90; *APS*, V, 272–76; *A Source Book of Scottish History*, III, 95–104.

59. *Ibid.*, 95–100; Makey, *The Church of the Covenant*, 26; Ferguson, *Scotland's Relations with England*, 114–15; J. H. S. Burleigh, *A Church History of Scotland*, (London, 1973), 218.

60. Mathew, *Scotland under Charles I*, 256; Makey, *The Church of the Covenant*, 29, 31.

61. Donaldson, *James V to James VII*, 314.

62. Stevenson, *The Scottish Revolution*, 85; Mullan, *Episcopacy in Scotland*, 179–83.

63. Williamson, *Scottish National Consciousness in the Age of James VI*, 140–41. To claim that the Covenanters founded their case on this article underplays the two other components of the National Covenant — the dual imperatives and public banding — which upheld the importance of fundamental laws and overstates and significance of the proposed act of union which warned against breaches of fundamental laws but did not actually constitute or implement fundamental law (*APS*, IV, 263–64, c.1).

64. *A Source Book of Scottish History*, III, 98–100.

65. Torrance, *Scottish Journal of Theology*, XXXIV, 232–36; G. H. Sabine, *A History of Political Theory*, (London, 1968), 375–85.

66. J. K. Hewison, *The Covenanters*, 2 vols, (Glasgow, 1908), I, 19–20, 24–29, 75, 129, 135–38, 481–83; Gordon, *A History of Scots Affairs*, I, 39–42.

67. *A Source Book of Scottish History*, III, 100–02; Scott, *Narration*, 330–42; Row, *The History of the Kirk of Scotland*, 357–66, 376–81.

68. Rothes, *Relation*, 90–92, 96–98, 100–02; *A Source Book of Scottish History*, III, 102–04.

69. *Ibid.*, 102; Makey, *The Church of the Covenant*, 28; Mathew, *Scotland under Charles I*, 256.

70. Cowan, *SHR*, XLVII, 40; Cowan, *Montrose*, 46–47.

71. Donaldson, *James V to James VII*, 315; Stevenson, *The Scottish Revolution*, 85.

72. *A Source Book of Scottish History*, III, 103; A. Campbell, marquis of Argyle, *Instructions to a Son, containing rules of conduct in public and private life*, (London, 1661), 30–36.

73. Kamen, *The Iron Century*, 326–30, 362–67.

74. Sabine, *A History of Political Theory*, 382–83; Makey, *The Church of the Covenant*, 28.

8

The Triumph of Oligarchic Centralism

Introduction

As well as equipping the Tables with the rhetoric of defiance, the National Covenant provided the political will to effect a revolution. Within three years of its publication, the Tables — as the revolutionary embodiment of the Covenanting Movement — had accomplished, by persuasion and coercion, a thorough transformation of government within Scotland. No attempt was made to replace the Stewart monarchy, but Charles I was obliged to accept permanent checks on the royal prerogative in Kirk and State. Adherence to the National Covenant replaced acquiescence in the dictates of absentee monarchy as the vital prerequisite for the exercise of political power in Scotland. The implacable resolve of the Covenanting propaganda left little scope for neutrality. The pulpits warned that earthly vengeance as well as divine retribution awaited those not moved to covenant with God. Simultaneously, rumours of imminent invasion by Royalist forces from England and Ireland made the Covenanting leadership acutely aware of their need to appeal furth of Scotland.[1] In turn, the Covenanting revolution served polemically and constitutionally as a British model for terminating the personal rule of Charles I.[2]

That the nobles were in the van of the movement does not mean that the Covenanting cause was inherently conservative. In like manner, radicalism was not the preserve of the ministry.[3] Between 1638 and 1641, the Covenanting movement accorded primacy to the political process, not ecclesiastical issues, a primacy upheld by Alexander Henderson and other leading ideologues among the ministry. Respect for aristocratic privilege tempered but did not prevent the wholesale restructuring of central and local government. The radical cutting edge of the Covenanting revolution, honed by constitutional defiance and recourse to war, found expression through institutional development. This development, led by a radical mainstream of gentry and burgesses no less than nobles, can be depicted as oligarchic centralism.

Like contemporaneous revolts in Catalonia and Portugal, the Covenanting Movement was fuelled by a nationalist reaction against the pursuit of uniformity by an absentee monarch. The Iberian revolutionaries sought to guard against provincial relegation by vigorously asserting their constitutional autonomy. The Covenanters countered provincialism by revitalising their constitutional assemblies in Kirk and State. The Scottish revolutionaries reversed the contemporary European trend of subordinating constitutional assemblies to the dictates of autocratic kingship.[4]

Initiative Retained

In the nine months following the promulgation of the National Covenant, the Covenanting leadership negotiated and demonstrated for 'a free Generall Assembly and Parliaments'; promoted political solidarity through nationwide subscription of the National Covenant; and established a fighting fund through voluntary contributions from the landed classes — on the basis of one dollar for every 1000 merks of free rent.[5]

Negotiations for constitutional assemblies were conducted with the marquis of Hamilton who had been despatched north as the king's commissioner in May. News of Hamilton's impending arrival in Scotland led to the numbers attending the Tables from shires, burghs and presbyteries being doubled. In order to overawe any attempt by councillors to mobilise kinsmen, friends and followers, all supporting the Covenanting cause were invited to accompany the commissioners elected for the gentry, burgesses and ministers. Around 300 Royalists had assembled at Dalkeith on 6 June, when Hamilton made the painful discovery that the Privy Council, shorn of the bishops, was broadly in sympathy with the Covenanting cause. The commissioners and associates who attended the Tables in Edinburgh numbered thousands — albeit estimates ranging from 20–60,000 suggest rather optimistic accounting of the lodgings available in and around the capital.[6]

The refusal of the fifth Table to compromise the National Covenant obliged Hamilton to return twice to Court — in July and August — before conceding unconditionally that a general assembly would meet in Glasgow on 21 November 1638. The resolve of the fifth Table was bolstered by increased representation for the gentry. Six of their number were elected daily; four continued to sit as ordinary commissioners, the other two as assessors. The burgesses and ministers kept their existing complement of four each, though both estates appear also to have revolved their commissioners to the fifth Table. Ostensibly, restructuring was designed to share out the workload and encourage wider representation. In practice, business was transacted by a central caucus of no more than thirteen nobles, twenty gentry and seven burgesses. Although nine ministers associated with this caucus, their function was primarily to prepare protestations in conjunction with Johnston of Wariston, the clerk to the fifth Table.

The gentry's Table, ably supported by that of the burgesses, provided the most vigorous opposition to the patent delaying tactics of the king's commissioner, who was intent on buying time for the king to mobilise forces to crush the Covenanting movement. The gentry were most adamant that the persistent rumours fuelled by Hamilton of a Royalist invasion warranted the Covenanters' importation of arms. The gentry were least susceptible to Hamilton's overtures that the National Covenant should be abandoned in return for the king summoning constitutional assemblies.[7]

The fifth Table had followed up a mission to the central and northern Highlands at the end of April — reputed to have attracted support from 5000 clansmen — with another to Glasgow at the end of July that secured the commitment of ministers and academics in the city. Sandwiched between these two missions was the despatch of a delegation to Aberdeen, headed by Montrose and including Henderson and Dickson. The delegation received no more than a tepid response from the population and encountered considerable intellectual resistance from six ministers and academics, known collectively as the 'Aberdeen Doctors', who stood out against subscription to the National Covenant. They also maintained that any resort to arms against the lawful Prince was on no account lawful. In public debates, the Aberdeen Doctors argued convincingly that neither episcopal government nor the Five Articles were inimical to the Reformed tradition nor necessarily abjured by the Negative Confession of 1581. Mindful of the repercussions throughout the king's dominions if Scottish condemnations of episcopacy and ceremonies remained unanswered, Hamilton eagerly sponsored the Aberdeen Doctors. They certainly gave intellectual credibility to the Royalist cause. However, they lacked the political will either to lead or contribute to an episcopal counter-attack in the Glasgow Assembly.[8]

Nonetheless, their defence of the ecclesiastical establishment did inspire Hamilton to formulate a tangible alternative to the National Covenant. The Negative Confession of 1581 was associated with a bond of 1589 designed specifically to counter Catholicism that generally committed subscribers to take the side of the king in withstanding internal enemies as well as foreign foes. The King's Covenant was presented for subscription to the Privy Council on 22 September 1638, the same day that the Glasgow Assembly was summoned. In an effort to discredit the movement throughout the British Isles, Hamilton had leading Covenanters named in the commissions for collecting subscriptions; a manoeuvre also intended to convey their apparent acquiescence in the King's Covenant.[9]

Hamilton certainly succeeded in causing consternation within the Covenanting Movement and temporarily forced the leadership on to the defensive. Nonetheless, the King's Covenant neither regained the political initiative for the Royalist cause nor expedited the formation of a cohesive Royalist party. Although 28,000 signatures were eventually collected prior to the Glasgow Assembly, the response to the King's Covenant was particularist. The most positive response came from the north-east and the central Highlands where Huntly and his associates, not without a measure of coercion, achieved around 12,000 subscriptions. The initial degree of success in attracting subscriptions within the bounds of the presbyteries of Glasgow and Hamilton, as within the shires of Angus, Perth and Peebles, was largely confined to the respective domains of the king's commissioner and prominent councillors. Covenanters in the south-west demonstrated successfully against subscription despite the efforts of Nithsdale and his adherents to enforce the King's Covenant. In the Borders, nobles and gentry tended to reserve their position. Only in Fife and the Lowlands did Covenanters persistently discourage subscriptions by intimidation.

Intimidation notwithstanding, the prospects for the Royalists were dealt a debilitating blow on 2 November. In response to Hamilton's overture to the Council to pass a resolution upholding episcopacy without equivocation, Lord Advocate Hope made public his opinion, endorsed by four senators of the College of Justice, that episcopal government was both illegal and inconsistent with the Negative Confession of 1581; an opinion which accorded with the radical interpretation of the National Covenant favoured by the fifth Table. Whereupon the Covenanting leadership opportunely switched tack by claiming that subscription of the King's Covenant was no longer prejudicial but complementary to the National Covenant. Subscribers to both were committed to the repudiation of episcopacy and the Five Articles.[10]

Continuing reservations of an influential sector not only within the city but among landowners in the presbytery, allied to the favourable reception accorded to the proclamation of the King's Covenant in Glasgow on 24 September, had raised Hamilton's hopes that the forthcoming general assembly would not inevitably result in the establishment of presbyterianism. Indeed, Glasgow was selected as the assembly's venue on the grounds that the city's proximity to Hamilton's principal domain would allow him scope to bring his considerable landed influence into play against the Tables. Hamilton had miscalculated. Glasgow was a 'merchant city' in so far as it was the only town in the west of Scotland not beholden to nobles or gentry either for guidance in running its affairs or for clientage in promoting its interests nationally. As Hamilton was ruefully to discover, not he but his formidable mother, Anna Cunningham, the dowager marchioness and committed Covenanter, exercised the controlling political as well as financial influence over his estates. More immediately, the fifth Table, though obliged to remove from their power base in Edinburgh, had taken effective steps to control the composition, remit and proceedings of the Glasgow Assembly.[11]

Constitutional Defiance

The presbyteries were the key to managerial control over the general assembly. Since March 1638, the presbyteries had asserted their right to admit entrants to the ministry and, in the process, had dispensed with the oath upholding episcopal government and the Five Articles. Complementing the increase in ministers disposed to a presbyterian polity was the removal, suspension and disqualification of episcopal adherents. As a corollary of the denial of communion to gentry who refused to subscribe the National Covenant, prominent members of the Tables had involved themselves on kirk sessions as elders from April. Once the fifth Table had made known their intention that a general assembly should be composed of clerical and lay commissioners from presbyteries, members of the Tables serving as elders in kirk sessions were intruded onto presbyteries as ruling elders in August and September.[12]

As a courtesy to Hamilton, elections for commissioners tended not to be held in the presbyteries until the Glasgow Assembly was summoned formally on 22 September. Once held, however, the elections tended to conform to the guidelines drafted by the fifth Table and circulated to royal burghs and presbyteries by 27 August. The election of ruling elders were justified by recourse to *The Second Book of Discipline* of 1578 and a selective interpretation of an enactment of 1597, whereby the general assembly stipulated that three ministers, one noble or gentleman and one burgess be elected commissioners within every presbytery. Unsigned papers from the fifth Table instructed that the full complement of commissioners were only to be elected in presbyteries well affected to the Covenanting cause. In presbyteries sympathetic to episcopacy or where bishops could rely on powerful local backing, the endeavours of the well-affected were directed towards restricting the number of commissioners elected. Town councils were expected to consult with their kirk sessions when electing burgh commissioners.[13]

With ministerial representation notable for absences and the eldership for near-perfect attendance, the electoral process in most presbyteries was loaded in favour of the Covenanting cause. In 39 out of the 62 designated presbyteries, the guidelines of the Tables were followed and returns made to Edinburgh by 1 October — albeit elections were not completed until the week before the assembly was due to meet. Around 250 commissioners were eventually to turn up in Glasgow on 21 November, 150 ministers — including academics from four universities — and 100 ruling elders (15 nobles, 36 gentry and 39 burgesses). The commissioners were committed overwhelmingly to a presbyterian reformation. No more than three presbyteries had failed to send any commissioners. Lay participation had been challenged in eight presbyteries; but only five who sent commissioners failed to elect ruling elders. In only two instances were elections concluded in royal burghs without the consent of the kirk session and in only one instance (Aberdeen) was a commissioner despatched without the approval of the town council. Hamilton was to receive solid backing from only six presbyteries and three royal burghs — all from the north-east.[14]

The fifth Table, moreover, had pre-empted efforts by the king's commissioner and councillors to mobilise their kinsmen, friends and followers. All nobles who subscribed the National Covenant, all ministers and ruling elders commissioned from the presbyteries together with four gentlemen within the bounds of every presbytery designated as assessors, all commissioners from the royal burghs accompanied by two to six assessors, and all other associates willing to volunteer their services were instructed to converge on Glasgow. The general assembly was effectively a meeting of the Tables.[15]

Proceedings were conducted in an intimidatory atmosphere which threatened, but never produced, violent confusion.[16] At the prompting of the fifth Table, presbyteries had submitted dossiers cataloguing the personal and pastoral failings of the bishops to the presbytery of Edinburgh, acting as a preparatory committee. Charges were submitted in the name of those members of the Tables not chosen as commissioners to the Glasgow Assembly. Thus, the bishops could not claim they were to be tried by their accusers. Through privy discussions and communings between the Tables from their arrival in Glasgow, the Covenanting leadership promoted the selection of Henderson as moderator and Wariston as clerk by 19 November — two days before the assembly met in plenary session.[17]

The first five days of the Glasgow Assembly were ostensibly dominated by procedural wranglings as Hamilton unsuccessfully attempted to postpone elections for moderator and clerk and, likewise, the validation of commissioners, pending the reading of a declaration from the bishops who had prudently remained in safe custody rather than journey to Glasgow. The bishops' declinator was actually read on 27 November, when the practical substance of its complaints — against the usurped authority of the Tables in controlling the composition and remit of the assembly — had been rendered meaningless. The assembly's assertion of its right to try the bishops on 28 November prompted a walk-out by Hamilton. Next day, the king's commissioner commanded a dissolution which was peremptorily upstaged by the assembly continuing to sit: the first open act of constitutional defiance of the royal prerogative. The assembly proceeded to sweep all vestiges of episcopacy out of the Kirk and effect a presbyterian reformation before dissolving itself on 20 December.

The dominance of the Tables over the assembly's proceedings was essentially vested in committees for preparing and transacting business. On 23 November, Wariston had theatrically produced registers for the proceedings of assemblies between 1560 and 1590. More weighty and acceptable precedents in support of a presbyterian reformation were thus provided than were to be found in the extant registers for assemblies since 1590. The contents of the hitherto missing registers were authenticated by a committee of six ministers and three lawyers present as assessors for the fifth Table. A committee of assessors was appointed to assist Henderson in the preparation of daily business. Another committee, with a totally separate membership, received bills, overtures and appeals from the floor of the house. The combined membership of both committees — thirteen ministers and seventeen elders — confirmed not only a distinct bias in favour of the laity in preparing business, but also the radical direction of the assembly's agenda. All the elders — seven nobles, four gentry and two burgesses — as against only five ministers were members of the fifth Table which continued to meet nightly to arrange and review proceedings daily for the duration of the assembly.[18]

Membership of business and preparatory committees hardly supports the contention that the guiding spirit of the assembly was one of moderation driven towards radicalism.[19] The grounds for nullifying the past six, episcopally dominated, general assemblies — of 1606, 1608, 1610, 1617 and 1618 — were examined by a committee of nine ministers and fourteen elders. The committee charged to confirm that episcopal government and the Five Articles were inconsistent with the Negative Confession of 1581 consisted of nine ministers and ten elders. The committee nominated to examine the corruptions inherent in the Service Book and the books of canons as in the Court of High Commission was composed exclusively of ten ministers who were joined by another four ministers and five elders instructed to hear overtures and prepare proposals for a presbyterian polity. The committee of bills to expedite proceedings collectively and severally against the bishops, following the order for their abjuration and removal from the Kirk on 4 December, consisted of thirteen ministers and eleven elders. Less than a third of the ministers and less than half of the elders attending served on business or preparatory committees. Of the total personnel serving on both types of committee, twenty-three out of the forty-three elders as against six of the forty-nine ministers had been associated with the fifth Table.[20]

Despite the Melvillean associations of its legislative programme — which was never ratified with the official degree of unanimity recorded by Wariston — the Glasgow Assembly was not intent on presbyterian autonomy. Certainly, the prohibition on kirkmen exercising civil office had widespread constitutional ramifications — not least the abolition of the clerical estate in parliament. Despite appearing to condone the separation of Kirk and State, the assembly on 19 December also made provision for commissioners not to sit in, but to represent the interests of the Kirk to the parliament anticipated for Edinburgh in May 1639. Although its remit was restricted to pressing for the parliamentary ratification of the presbyterian reformation, this committee served as a precedent for the Commission of the Kirk established in 1641 as a pressure group for the general assembly on parliament. More immediately, with its composition made up of presbyterian activists led by Henderson, by elder sons of peers and gentry — either not eligible or not chosen to represent the shires in the forthcoming parliament — the committee was designed to replace the minister's Table, now effectively redundant.[21]

The enactments of the Glasgow Assembly cannot convincingly be depicted as merely restoring the *status quo* operating during the presbyterian experiment of the 1590s. For the final enactment of 20 December 1638 asserted the inherent right of the Kirk to warrant general assemblies at least once a year. The Glasgow Assembly was especially concerned to counter the Crown's right to appoint the time and place of general assemblies as manipulated by James VI to intrude episcopacy. Accordingly, the next general assembly was designated for Edinburgh in July 1639. This abrogation of the Crown's right constituted a second attack on the royal prerogative which Charles was not prepared to accept. War became inevitable.[22]

A National Army

The Glasgow Assembly confirmed the political dominance of the Covenanting movement in Scotland. On the day following Hamilton's walk-out, Lorne (now

Argyle), attending as one of the six assessors for the king's commissioner, declared formally for the Covenanting cause. Hamilton was a cosmopolitan figure, more at home at Court than in Scotland where he had no coherent policy and lacked the tenacity to sustain the monarchical position. Argyle, by contrast, not only gloried in the territorial acquisitiveness of his clan, but brought a purposeful devotion to Scottish politics. His astute and lucid mind allied the public promotion of the national interest to the private advancement of his house. Hamilton, though deficient in statecraft, was sufficiently perceptive to warn Charles on the eve of his departure from the assembly that Argyle, above all other Scottish politicians, must be watched 'for itt feares me he will proufe the dangerousest man in this state'.[23]

Supported by Argyle, the fifth Table authorised a fundamental restructuring of the Tables' links with the localities. Restructuring, actually based on a blueprint drawn up before the Glasgow Assembly, was underway by 10 January 1639. The gentry were to the fore in establishing committees within the shires and the presbyteries, each with a permanent covener, in order to levy, equip and train troops; to assess and uplift a compulsory contribution based on landed and commercial rents; and to propagate commitment to the cause in every parish. In effect, Scotland was placed on a war footing.

The shire committee of war, whose convener was in direct communication with the fifth Table, was composed of up to four gentry from every presbytery in the shire and operated as a local executive. The main administrative burden was carried by the presbytery committees which were expected to collate lists of potential recruits as of the financial resources at the disposal of the cause. Also assessed was the capacity and inclination of the indigenous population to provide arms and sureties for the purchase of arms. Though covering the same geographical bounds, the presbytery committee was not an ecclesiastical court by a separate civil institution composed entirely of laymen — usually the most prominent gentleman from each constituent parish. Designated the parochial commissioner, he was empowered to call upon the services of the local minister to draw up the requisite lists for military, financial and ideological commitment that were to be channelled through the committee of war to Edinburgh. The development of these new agencies for local government marked a distinct break with heritable jurisdictions and, to a lesser extent, corporate privileges. Although the town councils continued to run the royal burghs, a parochial commissioner was elected to represent each burgh on the relevant presbytery committee. Each burgh was further required to provide a commissioner to serve on its shire's committee of war.[24]

The immediate purpose of the Covenanting leadership in centrally reorientating local government was the recruitment, training and provisioning of a national army. Every able-bodied man between 60 and 16 was eligible for military service and every shire committee of war was expected to raise, equip and maintain at least one regiment of foot and a troop of cavalry. The shire regiments of foot were organised into quarterly brigades of eight to ten regiments. Sufficient cavalry were mobilised in every shire to form at least one regiment from each quarter. Regional mobilisation through the quarterly commissions promoted the formation of a Covenanting vanguard, selected from the ablest men in the shires, to resist invasion by land or sea and quell Royalist discontent within Scotland. Recruitment for the shire levies, though less rigorous than selection for the Covenanting vanguard, was based on conscription. Drawn preferentially from the landed classes, the cavalry were only volunteers in so far as nobles, gentry and yeomen expressed a willingness to serve after enlistment as fighting men.[25]

In order to secure a professional backbone for the Covenanting army, the fifth Table sought the assistance of Scottish soldiers of fortune. The main recruiting agent for the Covenanting cause was General Alexander Leslie whose services were procured by Rothes. The winning over of this experienced military commander, when he was actually attending Hamilton at Dalkeith in July 1638, represented a critical lost opportunity for the Royalists. A former military associate and occasional foreign correspondent of the king's commissioner, Leslie had returned permanently from Sweden to Scotland in November, bringing not only the commitment of a substantial body of Scottish mercenaries but also a much-needed store of arms and ammunition. The seemingly permanent impasse between the Habsburg alliance and their continental opponents made foreign employers willing to release Scottish mercenaries. Thus, while the colonel of each regiment 'may be some nobleman or gentleman of quality', the putative Covenanting army could rely on every alternate position of command among commissioned and non-commissioned officers being filled by mercenaries formerly in Swedish or Dutch service. Likewise all artillery officers, gunners and engineers were veterans of the Thirty Years' War, as were the muster-masters recruited by the committees of war to pass on the basic skills of drilling and exercising with muskets and pikes to all fighting men.[26]

The Scottish mercenaries ensured that the main advances in the methodology and technology of warfare, pioneered by the Dutch and carried on by the Swedes, were adopted by the Covenanters during the Bishops' Wars. The development of rapid-fire musketry, the linear phalanxing of pikemen by musketeers and artillery, and the deployment of cavalry troops on the flanks improved the manoeuvrability of battle formations and minimised the vulnerability of unwieldy infantry regiments to close-quarter skirmishing. The Covenanting army not only conformed to the most innovatory continental practices of warfare, but the Movement regarded armed services as a national endeavour reinforced by ecclesiastical as well as military discipline.[27]

Fines — ranging from £300 for members of war committees to £100 for parochial commissioners — and even military quartering were imposed for negligent discharge of administrative duties. Logistical difficulties hindered the expeditious mobilising of levies, supplies and funds from the shires. Desertions from the armed forces were continuous. Nonetheless, the relative efficiency of restructured local government was attested by the military supremacy the Covenanting army consistently enjoyed in the field over the Royalists, who relied predominantly on family obligation and political clientage to raise forces.

Usually a third more troops were on active service for the Covenanting cause even though the Movement was faced with engagements on four fronts during the First Bishops' War of 1639 and was obliged to maintain not only an invasion force in England but a home guard during the Second Bishops' War of 1640. As recognised by the English commanders of the Royalist forces, the supremacy of the Covenanting army was not just numerical.[28] Arguably, the Covenanting movement was second only to the Swedish Crown in possessing a standing army conscripted for national service and sustained by a centralised government — a development which anticipated the emergence of the New Model Army of the English Parliamentarians by six years.[29]

Rebellious Scots

Although the Covenanters were actively preparing for war before Charles I, news that the king had secured the backing of the English Privy Council to mobilise an army of at least 30,000 men in the north of England acted as a spur to further restructuring. A meeting of the Tables took place in Edinburgh on 14 February to hasten preparations for a defensive war. In the course of six days of intensive discussions, the fifth Table was replaced as the national executive by an embryo committee of estates, entitled diffidently 'the generall committee at Edinburgh'. The most significant change in composition was that all nobles associated with the cause were no longer automatically members. Instead, the committee at Edinburgh now consisted of a caucus of six nobles, six gentry and six burgesses elected by their respective estates.

The first executive act of the general committee was to mobilise a Covenanting vanguard of 2400 men. Alexander Leslie was commissioned as general and supreme commander of the Covenanting forces. Collectors-general were appointed to uplift and distribute monies raised or borrowed on surety within the shires. Authorisation was also given for the immediate circulation to ministers of precepts drawn up by Alexander Henderson and cleared by Lord Advocate Hope, justifying the Movement's defensive recourse to arms. Charles I was portrayed as a misinformed absentee prepared to deploy papists, rebels and mercenaries to invade Scotland. The Scottish people held fast in their allegiance to the Crown but were obliged 'to defend themselves against extreme violence and oppression bringing utter ruin and desolation upon the kirk and kingdome, upon themselves and their posteritie'.[30]

The success of the Covenanting leadership in projecting the Movement as the embodiment of the national interest was reflected in the interchangeable appellation of Covenanters and Scots in the propaganda issued by or on behalf of Charles in England and Ireland. Apart from Charles's own repeated pronouncements against rebellious Scots, the main polemical opposition to the Movement was conducted by expatriate clergy, most notably by Walter Balcanqual, dean of Rochester. His Royalist manifesto rebutting Covenanting assurances that their resort to arms was defensive, known colloquially as the *Large Declaration*, was revised and approved by the king; an editorial contribution which furthered the Movement's distrust of Charles I. At the same time, formal contacts between the opponents of the personal rule in both countries, first authorised by the general committee in February 1639, were stepped up following reports that English noblemen were reluctant to support the king's army of invasion without a parliament being called to vote supply.[31]

The Covenanters' own financial needs at the outset of the First Bishops' War met when William Dick of Braid, the former financier of the personal rule, advanced 200,000 merks (£133,333–6/8), the sum raised in sureties by the Tables, to purchase arms and ammunition overseas, principally from the United Provinces. Having seized all royal castles and palaces as well as the fortified houses of uncovenanted councillors in the Lowlands — with the notable exception of Carlaverock and Threave Castles retained by the earl of Nithsdale — the Covenanters prepared a general mobilisation on four fronts.

The threat of an invasion on the western seaboard failed to materialise. As early as June 1638, Hamilton had been prepared to back an invasion from Ireland proposed by Randal MacDonnell, second earl of Antrim and chief of the Irish branch of the ClanDonald. However, Lord-Deputy Wentworth (later earl of Strafford), though convinced of the efficacy of armed force to prevent the Covenanting 'contagion' spreading to the Scottish colonists in Ulster, gauged correctly that Antrim was primarily intent on personal aggrandisement — to recover Kintyre and Islay which his Scottish kinsmen had lost to the Campbells at the outset of the seventeenth century. His projected invasion lacked the generalship and finance to become a viable undertaking. Simultaneously, Hamilton's naval assault on the east coast achieved no more than a fitful stop to trade. The expedition that embarked from Yarmouth was unable to effect a Royalist bridgehead in either Fife or the Lothians.[32]

However, Hamilton's diversion of three warships to Aberdeen did bring fresh impetus to the Royalists resurgence in the north-east. Resistance to the Covenanting movement owed less to the innate conservatism of the region than to the polarising impact of the Peruasive house of Gordon, the Catholicism marquis of Huntly and a section of his military associates being a contributory factor. Resistance was directed against the implementation of a war committee for Aberdeenshire. The armed posturing of Royalists raised by Huntly in his capacity as king's lieutenant for the north was suppressed in April 1639, primarily by indigenous Covenanting forces led by Montrose and advised by Leslie. Renewed resistance to the establishment of a war committee, instigated by Huntly's second son, James Gordon, Lord Aboyne, was not quashed until 20 June, two days after the Covenanters concluded the Pacification of Berwick with Charles I.[33]

The support Charles had received from the English Privy Council was at best half-hearted. Royalist troops were at least a third less than the anticipated number of 30,000 and remained chronically underfunded. By 5 June, a superior Covenanting army had marched into Berwickshire and pitched camp at Duns

Law. The council of war, which advised Leslie as supreme commander, had been created to provide the requisite diplomatic standing to treat for peace. The general committee in Edinburgh remained the conduit for all instructions to the war committees for weapons, supplies and monies. Moreover, although peace negotiations were conducted under the auspices of the council of war, the general committee staged a public demonstration in name of the Tables against the Pacification when the full text was published in the capital on 24 June. Charles had assented to a general assembly meeting in Edinburgh in August — a month later than decreed by the Glasgow Assembly — to determine all ecclesiastical matters, and to a parliament that would follow for the resolution of civil affairs. The general committee remained adamant that the cessation of hostilities in no way condemned the past proceedings of the Tables as 'disorders and disobedient courses'. However, the general committee had less success in managing the parliament than the assembly, both of which were presided over by Traquair who replaced the demoralised Hamilton as king's commissioner.[34]

When the general assembly met in Edinburgh from 12 August, the Covenanters pressed home their political advantage by ratifying the presbyterian reformation enacted at Glasgow. Charles had been prepared to accept a condemnation of episcopacy as contrary to the constitutions of the Kirk. But he was opposed to its propagation lest doubts were cast on the validity of the office elsewhere in his dominions. Traquair, however, was unable to prevent the abjuration of episcopacy as both unlawful and unconstitutional.

From the opening of parliament on 26 August, Traquair was intent on delaying and frustrating radical initiatives to limit the royal prerogative by focusing debate on procedural deliberations, notably the election and regulation of the committee of the articles. In the absence of clerical commissioners, Traquair was allowed to nominate the nobles who, in turn, selected eight each from the gentry and burgess to serve with the four leading officials in attendance. In the event, the only members not associated with the Tables selected from the assembled Estates were two nobles — Huntly and Southesk. The Covenanting leadership orchestrated petitions to the committee of articles during the seven weeks it met in closed session from 6 September. The gentry and the burgesses submitted itemised programmes for the redress of constitutional, economic and administrative grievances arising from the personal rule. More positively, specific proposals sought to enhance the constitutional supremacy of parliament by emphasising the Estates' right to determine their own proceedings. While enthusiasm for wholesale radical reform was by no means universal, particularly among the nobles, Traquair was unable to heal divisions to the king's advantage prior to the prorogation of parliament for seven months on 14 November; a prorogation instigated by Charles in the conviction that he would have mobilised sufficient forces in England to suppress the Covenanting Movement in the interim.[35]

Having garrisoned the royal castles in Scotland and on the English Border, and had his navy impose a stop on Scottish trade from the spring of 1640,

Charles summoned a parliament in England on 13 April to secure financial and military backing against the Covenanters. Instead of voting supply, the parliament provided a national forum for the English disaffected to air common grievances. Accordingly, the 'Short Parliament' was dissolved after twenty days.

Prior to its summoning, the Covenanting leadership had commissioned manifestos disclaiming any intention of waging war against the English people, exhorting members of parliament to give priority to redressing English grievances and revealing the lack of substantive progress by Scottish commissioners negotiating in good faith at Court since the outset of 1640. Indeed, the four Scottish commissioners had been placed under detention two days before the commencement of the 'Short Parliament' following the revelation of a letter drafted, but never delivered, to the French Court, justifying recourse to arms by the Covenanting movement and upholding free constitutional assemblies to prevent Scotland becoming 'a conquered province, as Ireland, under subjection to England'. There was certainly no intent to renounce the Stewart monarchy, nor were the Covenanters contemplating the transfer of their allegiance to France — an option exercised by the Catalans at the outset of 1641. Loudoun, as the leading Scottish commissioner as well as a signatory to the letter, was incarcerated in the Tower of London for two months; a heavy-handed gesture which served as a precedent for the detention and interrogation of the king's leading opponents in both Houses in the course of the 'Short Parliament'.[36]

Although the 'Short Parliament' failed to vote supply, its summoning afforded the Covenanters the excuse to reassemble their army and step up military preparations for a Second Bishops' War. The Tables, meeting as a general convention on 10 March, had affirmed the compulsory subscription of general bonds to relieve the common burdens. The first national tax levied by the Covenanting Movement bound the political nation to pay a tenth of landed and commercial rents according to valuations commenced in burghs and presbyteries in 1639. The raising of standing regiments was also warranted. In essence, the Covenanting vanguard was resurrected and its strength doubled not just to provide a home guard against invasion or internal dissent, but to intimidate refractory taxpayers and offer employment for the soldiers of fortune retained since the Pacification of Berwick. The general committee was reconstituted as the 'committee of estates'. Its elected membership was increased from eight to twelve from each estate, all of whom were now regarded as permanent rather than occasional members of the central caucus. General Leslie was confirmed as the supreme commander in the following month.[37]

Despite Charles's attempt to prorogue the Scottish parliament summoned for 2 July in Edinburgh, the validity of his proclamation was rejected. The Estates declared themselves to be a legally constituted assembly. Robert Balfour, Lord Balfour of Burleigh, a longstanding opponent of the unfettered exercise of the prerogative, was elected king's commissioner in place of Traquair. Over the next nine days, the Estates — attended by 36 nobles, 43 gentry and 52 burgesses

— proceeded to carry through a constitutional revolution which confirmed the momentous rise of obligarchic centralism.[38]

The Estate's first step was to validate past proceedings of the Covenanting movement. The presbyterian reformation implemented by the general assembly at Glasgow in 1638 and endorsed by that at Edinburgh in 1639 was ratified. In keeping with the self-denying ordinance excluding kirkmen from civil office, the clerical estate in parliament was abolished. In recognition of the stalwart service of the gentry on the Tables, the voting powers of the shires were effectively doubled. Instead of one composite vote being cast for each shire, gentry summoned as shire commissioners were accorded individual votes. Following the directives to burgesses in the convention of royal burghs of 1638 and to ministers in the general assembly of 1639, subscription of the National Covenant was made compulsory for all holding public office. Parliament then asserted control over its own procedures. The committee of the articles was made optional. If deployed, the committee was to be elected by and answerable to the three Estates — the nobility, gentry and burgesses. Henceforth, business was to be initiated from the floor of the unicameral Scottish parliament, and all business devolved to preparatory committees was to be reported back for full deliberation prior to voting. A triennial act specified that parliament should meet every three years regardless of a royal summons.[39]

That the parliament of 1640 was intent upon constitutional revolution rather than the consolidation of feudal insurrection was borne out by the most radical category of enactments designed to legitimise the Covenanting leadership's exercise of executive power.[40] Ostensibly on account of the imminent danger from extraneous forces, the country was placed in a posture of defence and a committee of estates was constituted with comprehensive powers to order, direct and govern the whole kingdom. Five gentry and eight burgesses who were not members of parliament were included in this committee of forty. All were Covenanting activists, however. Equal numbers of each estate either remained in Edinburgh to sustain central government or accompanied the army whose movements were not restricted to Scotland — a clear indication that the Covenanters were prepared to go on the offensive. Each section governed autonomously within its respective sphere of influence, save for the declaration of war and the conclusion of peace which required the assent of the whole committee.[41]

The establishment of the committee of estates represented a classical, if corporate, alternative (reminiscent of the consular system of ancient Rome) to the exercise of executive power by a monarch who was patently untrustworthy, palpably reluctant to make lasting concessions and resolutely intent on reversing all constitutional restrains on the royal prerogative. Although the committee can be viewed as a 'temporary expedient' in so far as its powers were finite — until a settlement was reached with the king or until the next plenary session of parliament — the prospects of Charles I accepting the National Covenant were not even remote.[42]

Three other aspects of the legislative programme consolidated the Covenanting leadership's exercise of executive power. In the first place, restructured local government was reinforced as the principal agency for the nationwide imposition of ideological conformity, financial supply and military recruitment. Secondly, the exaction of the tenth by shire committees of war was confirmed. An additional rating, a twentieth of the valued rents, was imposed as a compulsory loan to meet the anticipated shortfall in borrowing required to cover expenditure in the First Bishops' War and increased payments and allowances to the army for the Second. Thirdly, the scope of treason was extended to all who advised or assisted policies destructive of 'the liberties of this kirke and kingdom'. The charge of leasing-making was thus placed at the disposal of the committee of estates. Waging of war on behalf of the Covenanting movement was patriotic and tax-deductable; waging of war against the Covenanting movement was treasonable.[43]

Revolting Englishmen

Before going on the offensive against the Royalist forces assembling in England, the committee of war deployed its standing armies to eradicate dissent within Scotland. All vestiges of Royalist support in the north-east were crushed by September. South of the Tay, supplies to the royal castles were cut off. The earl of Nithsdale's fortified houses were taken after sustained sieges and his estates in Dumfriesshire were devastated. At the same time, the zeal of the ministers in exhorting contributions of jewels and other valuables to the cause made the Royalists 'liken it to the Golden Calf'.[44]

In excess of 25,000 troops had assembled on the Borders by 3 August, when the committee of estates with the army unanimously resolved to carry the war into England, the resolution to extend the defensive war being justified by reported Royalist mobilisation in England and Ireland. The Covenanting army crossed the Tweed on 20 August. The numerically inferior, poorly led and chronically underfunded Royalist forces were routed at Newburn on 28 August. The Covenanting army moved vigorously into the counties of Northumberland and Durham. Newcastle was occupied two days later. Covenanting control of the vital coal supply to London served to pressurise the king into suing for peace.[45]

From the issue of the articles of war on 10 August until negotiations for a cessation of arms commenced at Ripon on 2 October 1640, the Covenanting leadership cultivated the support for their cause evident in the 'Short Parliament' and subsequently notable in the city of London. As well as justifying their move to an offensive posture to maintain the Movement's constitutional gains within Scotland, the Covenanting leadership promised that their army would observe strict military discipline in England pending the conclusion of a negotiated settlement for which the recall of the English parliament was indispensable. Moreover, the Covenanting army would remain in England until Scottish commissioners were granted a hearing by the English parliament.[46]

Harmonising with Covenanting demands was a supplication in the name of twelve peers — actually drawn up by the côteries of disaffected nobles and gentry leading English opposition to the personal rule — requesting the immediate recall of parliament to resolve indigenous grievances as well as conclude a settlement with the Scots. Charles was obliged to treat with the Covenanting movement after a council of peers, summoned to York on 24 September, affirmed that continuing English support for the Royalist cause could no longer be relied upon. Once Charles issued writs summoning a parliament at Westminster on 3 November, the council of peers assumed responsibility for the English side of negotiations. Having agreed not to advance beyond the Tees, the committee of estates with the army secured a daily allowance of £850 stirling (£102,000) which was apportioned weekly from Northumberland and Durham as well as Newcastle. The English peers, not Charles, underwrote this daily allowance pending a full settlement of reparations in the forthcoming 'Long Parliament' (that continued until the Restoration). Moreover, the committee of estates with the army, which retained strict oversight of the negotiations, envisaged reparations as but the first stage of a comprehensive treaty to secure permanent checks on the monarchy in both Scotland and England.[47]

The British significance of the impact of the Covenanting army on the constitutional crisis engulfing the Court of Charles I has tended to be understated.[48] The Scottish rebellion was undoubtedly not the cause of confrontation between the Crown and the political nation in England. But only the presence of the Covenanting army in the north of England obliged Charles to summon parliament after an eleven-year lapse. Only the security afforded by the Covenanting army allowed the English disaffected sufficient scope to press for the constitutional checks on monarchy which safeguarded the English tradition of parliamentary sovereignty. The Covenanting movement provided not just military security but a constitutional model for revolt. A triennial act and an act continuing the current assembly enabled the 'Long Parliament' to resist dissolution by royal *fiat* and, in the longer term, secure control of the apparatus of government in Church and State and, ultimately to justify defensive recourse to arms on the outbreak of civil war. Conversely, the pressure to redress grievances generated by the 'Long Parliament' meant that Charles was amenable to buying off the Scots in order to concentrate on English problems.[49]

The English parliament initially proved receptive to the total claim for reparations of £514,128–8/8 sterling (£6,169,541–4/–) submitted by the Scottish commissioners. On 6 February 1641, the English parliament offered £300,000 sterling (£3,6000,000); that is, more than half the sum claimed for reparations, but less than two-fifths of the Covenanters' estimated accumulated expenditure of £785,628–8/8 sterling (£9,427,541). The willingness of the committee of estates accompanying the army to accept this settlement was compromised when an advance instalment of £80,000 sterling (£960,000) promised as 'brotherly assistance' failed to materialise and, simultaneously, the daily maintenance or cess money was allowed to fall seriously in arrears.[50]

For their part, the Scottish commissioners had pressed charges against Laud and Strafford on 16 December 1640; a direct invitation for their impeachment willingly taken up by the English parliament. Strafford in particular was deemed a 'kindler of war' for his imposition of the 'black-oath' on Ulster Scots from May 1639, requiring public dissociation from the Covenanting movement or summary expulsion. His endeavours to utilise an army of 9000 men, predominantly Irish Catholics, against the Ulster Scots was only forestalled by the cessation of arms negotiated at Ripon. Strafford's vindictiveness notwithstanding, the main cause of his unpopularity within the Covenanting movement was his publicised intent that Scotland, like Ireland should be governed as an English province in the event of a Royalist victory. Indeed, the fear of provincialism was the main political factor motivating the Covenanters' indictment of Laud and Strafford. The charges pressed by the Scots were but a secondary aspect of Strafford's trial for treason which culminated with his attainder in the Lords on 8 May 1641 and his public execution four days later. Nonetheless, the Covenanting message that both he and Laud had subverted the fundamental laws and government of the realm was readily taken up by the 'Long Parliament' to promote their impeachment for introducing arbitrary and tyrannical government in England and Ireland.[51]

The commissioners negotiating for the Covenanting movement reputedly accorded priority to unity in religion and uniformity in church government.[52] However, the Covenanting agenda accorded priority to a lasting alliance which would serve as a permanent antidote to provincialism: that is, a defensive and offensive league between Scotland and England, not an incorporating parliamentary union. The only institutional innovation was to be the appointment to both parliaments of commissioners charged to conserve and redress any breaches in the peace. The Covenanting movement was not exclusively concerned with bilateral negotiations. At the same time as the Scottish commissioners were presenting their proposals for union, the committee of estates at Edinburgh was actively promoting a tripartite alliance — a confederation involving the Scottish Estates, the English parliament and the States General of the United Provinces.[53]

The English parliament, however, was predisposed to national considerations not internationalism. Nor were the English disaffected — whom the Scottish commissioners depicted as 'the Commonwealth's men' — able or prepared to commit parliament to a permanent alliance. The Commonwealthmen in Lords and Commons lacked the depth of support, cohesive discipline and, ultimately, the revolutionary sense of purpose possessed by the Covenanting movement. Lords and Commons were moved to countenance the abolition of episcopacy, and removal of churchmen from civil office and a puritanical overhaul of religious standards and orders for worship. But the 'Long Parliament' was no more prepared than Charles I to accept a presbyterian reformation in the interests of conformity with the Scots. Nor was any enthusiasm exhibited for closer diplomatic and commercial links.[54]

The brinkmanship manifested by the Lords and Commons during the peace negotiations threatened their political isolation within the British Isles. While Covenanting intervention in England had provided an opportunity for the Irish parliament to assert the constitutional accountability of the executive, the temporary concert between Catholics and Protestants for the prosecution of Strafford was terminated by his trial and execution. The predominantly Catholic army raised in Ireland by Strafford was leaderless but restless. Determined to prevent direct rule by the English parliament, Irish Catholics were advocating loyalty to the Crown as a rallying point to conserve their sectarian interests. Nervousness in the 'Long Parliament' about the developing Irish situation was aggravated by Charles's decision to attend the autumn session of the Scottish Estates. Hamilton had impressed upon Charles that timely concessions to the Covenanters, coupled with a royal visit to ratify the Movement's constitutional gains in Kirk and State, could serve to fend off pressure for further encroachments on monarchical authority in England.[55]

While there was no serious prospect that the royal visit would result in an alliance with the Covenanting movement, the English parliament expeditiously ratified the Treaty of London on 7 August 1641. Parliament reserved its right to determine the nature of the English reformation but duly conceded that the waging of war and the stopping of trade within the king's dominions required parliamentary approval in both countries. The English parliament assented also to the appointment of conservators of the peace. Proposals for a permanent defensive and offensive alliance were to be referred to commissioners chosen from both parliaments. The ratification of the Treaty, and the bestowal of royal assent three days later as Charles I departed for Scotland, were duly interpreted as formal recognition of the independent sovereign power of the Scottish Estates as a 'free parliament'; a recognition that laid to rest the spectre of provincialism which had haunted the nation since the union of the Crowns.[56]

The Scottish Doge

Diplomatic recognition that the Covenanting movement was in the driving seat in British politics proclaimed the triumph of oligarchic centralism; a triumph duly consummated by the Scottish Estates in the autumn of 1641. Although Charles on 17 August formally opened the final session of a parliament which had commenced on 31 August 1639, the Scottish Estates had resumed unilaterally on 15 July 1641. In the interim, the committee of estates had created a plethora of business committees to secure its control over the composition, remit and proceedings of the final session of 1641.[57]

The decision of the Scottish Estates in June 1640 to prosecute all incendiaries deemed responsible for instigating the Bishops' Wars led the committee of estates to prepare indictments against seventy-five leading officials, nobles and gentry as well as former bishops. In the event, charges were pressed against only five principals — Traquair, Lord President Spottiswood, Provost Hay, Maxwell the erstwhile bishop of Ross, and Walter Balcanqual. But a new parliamentary oath was imposed on all members of the Scottish Estates on 10 August 1641. Prior to their admission, all members were required not only to subscribe the

National Covenant, but to foreswear involvement in plots or other subversive activity prejudicial to the radical leadership of the Covenanting Movement.[58]

The nobility remained the most numerous estate in the final session with fifty-six members, only because courtiers and other pragmatic Royalists led by Hamilton had accepted the parliamentary oath in order to secure admission. Though their numbers increased by fifteen, a quarter of the nobility had been replaced since parliament commenced in 1639. Nonetheless, that thirty-nine nobles should attend continuously argues for a sustained element of support for the Movement's radical mainstream. The turnover among the gentry and burgesses was actually higher — around a third in each estate changed. Yet, the gentry and burgesses also exhibited a marked degree of continuity. More pertinently, 53 gentry from 29 shires (as against 46 from 27 shires in 1639), like the commissioners from 53 burghs, now enjoyed individual voting rights and thereby ensured a solid phalanx in favour of radicalism.[59]

The radical mainstream had been faced by a conservative element of dissent in the parliamentary sessions of 1639 and again in 1640. This conservative position, which viewed parliament as a safeguard but not a permanent check in the monarchy, was denied a national forum in 1641 partly on account of the astute management of the Covenanting leadership, but principally because of the political ineptitude of Montrose. His overriding ambition and consuming jealousy left him exposed to the superior political manoeuvrings of Argyle, his arch-rival.

Having maintained covert correspondence with Charles I since October 1639, Montrose had placed himself at the head of the conservative faction of twenty nobles with the signing of the Cumbernauld Band in August 1640, in protest at the decision to invade England. Despite the increasingly intolerant attitude of the Covenanting leadership towards dissent, despite the Covenanting army being staffed by soldiers of fortune lukewarm to radicalism, despite the mistrust and suspicion of Argyle's ambitions among other nobles and, above all, despite a growing sense of public grievance about the strict subordination of the localities to the centralist demands of the committee of estates, Montrose was all but isolated by the outset of the peace negotiations at Ripon. Unable to carry the support of influential fellow Banders, Montrose and his small circle of relatives and intimates — notably Archibald, Lord Napier, Sir George Stirling of Keir and Sir Andrew Stewart of Blackhall — were imprisoned as plotters in May 1641. Two months later, judicial proceedings were instigated against them after the execution of Mr John Stewart, younger of Ladywell. The one witness able to substantiate the plotters' apersions — that Argyle sought to depose Charles I — became the first victim of the extended Covenanting charge of leasing-making. Although Montrose was offered a judicial hearing before the Scottish Estates on 24 August, seven days had elapsed since the arrival of the king, and the remit as well as the composition of parliament had been purposely ordered to prevent conservative Covenanters allying the pragmatic Royalists.[60]

By continuing to meet covertly well into the third week of the final session, the committee of estates had ensured that parliament was controlled by the radical mainstream. A committee of bills, composed of four members from each estate, served as a clearing house for standing and *ad hoc* committees elected from each estate which recommended whether legislation should follow. The critical reading stage, for further separate consideration by each estate prior to final voting on the floor of the house, effectively reconstituted the Tables; a procedure which reasserted strict party discipline as evident from the election of Argyle on 13 August, to preside over the nobles' convention for the duration of parliament.[61]

Despite the public attention given by English newsletters in particular to the proposed trial of the incendiaries and plotters, the main objective of the radical mainstream was to perpetuate the Covenanting revolution. Priority was accorded to three issues — retaining a military presence within Scotland to enforce conformity; securing of parliamentary control over the executive and judiciary; and replacing the committee of estates by diverse agencies to govern Scotland in the interval between parliaments.

The phased withdrawal of the Covenanting army from England had been concluded and the disbanding of shire levies was well underway by the end of August. Three standing regiments of foot were retained, however. Their numbers were augmented from around 3000 to 4500 men and reinforced by a cavalry troop of 400 men. Their retention was justified principally because of the menacing presence of armed forces elsewhere in the British Isles, notably the Irish Catholics under Sir Phelim O'Neill about to rise in Ulster. News of the Irish rebellion was actually conveyed to the Scottish Estates by Charles on 28 October, along with an invitation for armed intervention by the Covenanters to protect the plantations. However, the Covenanting leadership was not prepared to intervene without the consent of the English parliament. Nonetheless, the Irish rebellion enabled the Covenanting leadership to escalate rather than scale down their military forces. The Scottish Estates duly offered the services of 10,000 troops to the English parliament on 2 November.

Indiscriminate reports of the 'creuell outrages' of the Irish rebels and the 'pitiful estate of the British in Ireland', which fuelled public demand for Covenanting intervention, afforded Charles an excuse to return to England to secure parliamentary backing for armed intervention. His endeavours to secure the commitment of Covenanting forces without waiting for the consent of the English parliament, in blatant disregard of the Treaty of London, had used up his last reserves of political goodwill in the Scottish Estates.[62]

Reserves of political goodwill had been progressively dissipated by Charles's rearguard action to reserve as 'a special part of his prerogative' the appointment and removal of officers of state, councillors and senators of the College of Justice. Charles was particularly concerned lest his concession of a parliamentary veto in Scotland might serve as another precedent to limit monarchical power in England. However, the Scottish Estates secured an effective veto over the executive and judiciary when Charles I gave a binding commitment that officials, councillors and senators would henceforth be chosen with their advice and consent. This concession, which had been on the Covenanting agenda since

1639, was seemingly made more palatable for Charles on the grounds that as an absentee he was not always informed adequately about the best-qualified candidates. In the short term, the limited parliamentary role conceived for Charles I left him ample time for his golfing engagements prior to his return south on 17 November. In the long term, Charles was obliged to accept permanent restrictions on the royal prerogative that fulfilled his own prophecy in the spring of 1638 that the triumph of the Covenanting movement would leave him with no more power than the Doge of Venice.[63]

The dominance of the radical mainstream has tended to be masked by the reconstitution of the Privy Council by parliamentary veto. The reconstituted Council of thirty-six nobles, fourteen gentry and one burgess was certainly dominated by the nobility. Moreover, twenty-three members of the last Council of the personal rule had their nominations as leading officials and councillors approved by the Scottish Estates on 16 November. Nonetheless, the constitutional settlement of 1641 neither justifies the conclusion that 'the substance of power had been restored to the feudal classes' nor supports the contention that the government of Scotland' was to revert to king and council' with the Covenanting leadership relying on their inbuilt majority to preserve the revolution.[64] The apparent compromise with pragmatic Royalists in the composition of the Council was no more than a cosmetic exercise. All leading officials and councillors, like all senators and members of the three estates, were obliged under oath not only to sustain the National Covenant, but to acknowledge the parliament of 1641 to be 'free and lawfull' and to promote the implementation and observation of its enactments. More dynamically, the radical mainstream was intent on maintaining revolutionary momentum through executive commissions composed 'of all the prime covenanters'. Although the committee of estates was not resuscitated, its past role as the national government was not only approved but continued financially and ecclesiastically, diplomatically and judicially.[65]

Financial affairs were devolved to two commissions with a common membership. The commission 'for regulating the common burdings of the kingdom' was to bring order to the financial chaos left by the Bishops' Wars. The commission 'for receiving of brotherly assistance from the parliament of England' was to collate the disburse the chief source of income still outstanding for the relief of common burdens — the sum of £220,000 sterling (£2,640,000) due to be paid in equal instalments over the next two years.

The parochial ramifications arising from the abolition of episcopacy served as the primary grounds for resurrecting the work of teind valuation and redistribution. No commissioners for the Kirk were included despite the remit of the commission to dispose of episcopal rights of patronage as well as titularship of the teinds. Any relevant motion from the general assembly was to be taken cognizance of, however. The interests of the Kirk were represented by the inclusion of its procurator, Johnston of Wariston, on the commission 'for conserveing the Articles of the Treaty': in effect, the commission for diplomatic affairs with special responsibility for conserving the peace within the king's

British dominions. Wariston was also included among the inner core of members seconded to the commission 'anent the Articles referred to consideration by the Treaty'.

Ostensibly this latter commission was charged to conclude the bilateral negotiations with the English parliament left unresolved by the Treaty of London. But their primary task was 'not so much for the perfecting of our Treatie, as to keep correspondence in so needful a tyme' with respect to the 'assistance Scotland shall give to England for suppressing of the rebellione in Ireland'. To conclude the prosecution of the leading delinquents, commissions were issued 'for trying the Incendiaries and Plotters': that is, to determine the relevance of treasonable charges against the five principal incendiaries headed by Traquair and the four designated plotters led by Montrose for presentation before an assize.

The total number of people appointed to the executive and judiciary, whether as officials, councillors, senators or members of the parliamentary commissions was 123 — the breakdown for each estate being 43 nobles, 51 gentry and 29 burgesses. But only 74 of the total number of appointees — 35 nobles, 24 gentry and 15 burgesses — actually attended the final session of parliament. Covenanting radicals account overwhelmingly for the remaining 49 appointees. Three of the parliamentary commissions were composed exclusively of Covenanting radicals. Pragmatic Royalists appointed to the Privy Council were denied membership of the commissions for financial affairs. Though appointed to the commission for plantation of kirks and valuation of teinds out of respect for their landed interests, they were excluded from the commissions for trying the incendiaries and plotters. While some courtiers were nominated as conservators of the peace to enhance the diplomatic status of that office, none were admitted to the inner diplomatic circle charged to continue negotiations with the English parliament.

The statistical evidence for the relative insignificance of Council membership was compounded by the actual practice of running national government in the aftermath of the parliament of 1641. As borne out by the procedures deployed to promote armed Scottish intervention in Ireland, effective power continued to be vested in the radical Covenanting oligarchy dominating the executive commissions. The Privy Council was merely a clearing-house for the delegation and approval of affairs of State.[66]

Conclusion

The imposition of constitutional and ecclesiastical checks on monarchy, the restructuring of local government and the creation of a standing army were integral facets of the Covenanting revolution between 1638 and 1641. In seeking to assert the national sovereignty of the Scottish state, the Covenanting Movement reacted consciously against the relegation of the kingdom to provincial status during the personal rule of Charles I. Undoubtedly, Charles had systematically distanced himself from his English and his Scottish subjects by his pursuit of order and regularity; goals which were to be achieved by proclamation rather than by consultation.[67] Nonetheless, reliance on his prerogative was especially opposed in Scotland. Charles as an absentee monarch was not only remote and unresponsive, but his drive for uniformity threatened to subvert Scottish identity — economically, religiously, politically. Accordingly, the Covenanting movement sought to reforge Scottish identity by institutionalising revolution.

The machinery of the Tables provided the nationwide consensus to effect unprecedented demands for ideological, financial and military commitment; to accomplish from below the radical centralisation of government which Charles I had failed to carry through from above. Indeed, Charles can be indicted as the architect of his own downfall on three counts.

In the first place, teind redistribution had concentrated on the parish as the basic unit for evaluating landed and commercial rents. Although far from complete and far from accurate as a result of class collusion during the personal rule, these same parochial valuations were utilised initially for exacting sureties for the purchase of arms and, subsequently, for levying the tenth as the Movement's first national tax and the twentieth as a compulsory loan. Secondly, the collation and completion of accurate valuations were tasks assigned to presbytery committees, thereby reviving the role of select gentry as sub-commissioners within the bounds of every presbytery between 1629 and 1634. Thirdly, the composite oversight of recruitment, training and equipping of troops assigned to shire committees of war from 1639 had piecemeal precedents in the duties foisted on, but resisted by, justices of the peace from the outset of the personal rule. The main precedent for the committees of war was actually the peace commissions relaunched by Charles in 1634, when numbers of justices were more than sufficient to exercise strict supervision over each parish in every shire. Closer identification with this precedent followed on from the formal constitution of the committee of estates in 1640. Parochial commissioners, renamed captains, were at least doubled in every parish and assumed, as a consequence of directions to apprehend and return runaways to the Covenanting army, magisterial duties to maintain social order. As the peace negotiations got underway first at Ripon then London, the continuing need to keep the Covenanting army provisioned, to contain internal dissent and to service public debts caused the committee of estates to expand the administrative, judicial and financial powers of the committees of war.[68]

The Covenanting Movement in war, as Charles I in peace, faced acute financial problems from the lack of ready money that necessitated heavy borrowing from the London money markets, from factors at Campvere as from William Dick and other leading Edinburgh merchants well disposed to the cause. The monies received and expended in the name of the Covenanting Movement between 1638 and 1641 totalled £5,746,351–4/3. The highest component raised within Scotland (8.9%) was that from the taxation of the tenth (£395,473–3/4) and the compulsory loan of the twentieth of valued rents (£116,475–5/4). This indigenous contribution was overshadowed by the revenue (84.5% of the total) gleaned in England from the daily cess (£3,054,900) and the brotherly assistance (£960,00). Nonetheless, the unpaid public debts of the Movement — £1,486,443–17/– — were more than covered had the English parliament not defaulted on further payments after advancing half the promised brotherly assistance.[69]

Financial difficulties notwithstanding, the radical intent of the Covenanting leadership to make the localities responsive to central demands inspired the Movement to seize and maintain the political initiative within the British Isles. The resultant triumph for oligarchic centralism was confirmed by the Scottish Estates in 1641, in the wake of Charles I and the English parliament recognising the sovereignty of the Scottish state by the Treaty of London. Although the Covenanting Movement was internally secure by the close of 1641, extraneous threats to that security remained from the insurrection in Ireland and the steady deterioration towards civil war between Crown and parliament in England. Internal security continued to require the export of revolution.

NOTES

1. *Diary of Wariston, 1632–39*, 351–52, 361, 366; A. Henderson, *Sermons, Prayers and Pulpit Addresses*, R. T. Martin ed., (Edinburgh, 1867), 358–86; *Large Declaration*, 95–100; D. Reid, *The Party-Coloured Mind*, (Edinburgh, 1982), 6–10, 37–78. Reprints of heroic epics recalling the feats of William Wallace and Robert the Bruce during the Wars of Independence helped sustain popular nationalism.

2. P. Donald, 'The King and the Scottish Troubles, 1637–41', (University of Cambridge Ph.D. thesis, 1987), provides an alternative Scottish perspective to this chapter. S. R. Gardiner, *The Fall of the Monarchy of Charles I, 1637–42*, 2 vols, (London, 1882), I, 130–44; II, 1–283, is still the most comprehensive account of the British dimension.

3. Lee, jr., *The Road to Revolution*, 223–44; R. A. Mason, 'The Aristocracy, Episcopacy and the Revolution of 1638', in T. Brotherstone ed., *Covenant, Charter and Party: Traditions of Revolt and Protest in Modern Scotland*, (Aberdeen, 1989), 7–24.

4. Kamen, *The Iron Century*, 318–21; J. H. Elliot, 'The Spanish Peninsula, 1598–1648', in *The Decline of Spain and the Thirty Years War, 1609–48/59*, 468–73; L. A. R. Myers, 'The Parliaments of Europe and the Age of the Estates', *History*, LX, (1975), 11–27; H. G. Koenigsberger, *Politicians and Virtuosi: Essays in Early Modern History*, (London, 1986), 1–25.

5. Lennoxlove, Hamilton Papers, C 1/995, /1802; Burnet, *Memoirs*, 42–93; Baillie, *Letters and Journals*, I, 78–113; *Diary of Wariston, 1632–39*, 349–404; Rothes, *Relation*, 80–83. Eight gentry in every shire assumed responsibility for uplifting the voluntary contribution. The nobles set an example by contributing 670 dollars (£1809) following the promulgation of the National Covenant.

6. NLS, Wodrow MSS, quarto xxiv, fo. 125–27; Rothes, *Relation*, 95–135; Baillie, *Letters and Journals*, I, 78–82, 464–66; Gordon, *History of Scots Affairs*, 64–65, 70–72, 80–82, 100–04, 118–22, 133–34, 183–85. The eventual arrival of the king's commissioner in Edinburgh on 9 June was stage-managed by the fifth Table. In addition to 30 nobles and around 600 ministers strategically positioned at Holyroodhouse, gentry, burgesses and commoners lined both sides of his route for up to two miles from the city gates.

7. Rothes, *Relation*, 114, 145–73; Baillie, *Letters and Journals*, I, 79–87; *Diary of Wariston, 1632–39*, 346, 351–54, 359–61; *Miscellaneous State Papers*, II, 106–12; SRO, Hamilton Papers, TD 75/100/26/555–56 & TD 76/100/5/10816.

8. Row, *History of the Kirk*, 489, 493–97; Rothes, Relation, 104–10, 184–86; Burnet, *Memoirs*, 53–54, 65–67; SRO, Hamilton Papers, TD 75/100/26/446, /546, /555–56, /564; SRO, Breadalbane Papers, GD 112/39/738; J. D. Ogilvie, 'The Aberdeen Doctors and the National Covenant', *Papers of the Edinburgh Bibliographical Society*, XI, (1919–20), 73–86; D. Stewart, 'The 'Aberdeen Doctors' and the Covenanters', *RSCHS*, XXII, (1984), 35–44.

9. SRO, Hamilton Papers, TD 75/100/26/564–65, /570; Burnet, *Memoirs*, 72–78, 85; *The Hamilton Papers*, S. R. Gardiner ed., (Camden Society, London, 1880), 26–35; *RPCS*, second series, VII, 76–67; *Large Declaration*, 134–73; *The Protestation of the Noblemen, Barrons, Gentlemen, Burrowes, Ministers and Commons*, (Edinburgh, 1638).

10. SRO, Hamilton Papers, TD 75/100/26/452, /454, /457, /536, /575, /961, /8219 & TD 75/100/42/36/8 & TD 76/100/5/10831; *The Hamilton Papers*, 36–37, 42–47, 53; Baillie, *Letters and Journals*, I, 103–04, 106–08, 112, 115–16; *Large Declaration*, 186–205.

11. A. I. Macinnes, 'Glasgow: Covenanting Revolution and Municipal Enterprise', *History Today*, XL, (1990), 10–16.

12. SRO, Hamilton Papers, TD 75/100/26/961, /972 & TD 75/100/42/36/8; Lennox-love, Hamilton Papers, C 1/995; NLS, Lee Papers, MS 3430, fo. 13–164; *Diary of Wariston, 1632–39*, 348; Rothes, *Relation*, 29, 128, 166, 169; Makey, *The Church of the Covenant*, 39–41.

13. NLS, Wodrow MSS, folio lxii, fo. 22, 25–26; NLS, Salt & Coal: Events, 1635–62, MS 2263, fo. 70; SRO, Breadalbane Collection, GD 112/39/742; Baillie, *Letters and Journals*, I, 99–101, 105–07, 469–72; *Diary of Wariston, 1632–39*, 374–78; Stevenson, *The Scottish Revolution*, 105–08. Initial reluctance of ministers to accept the participation of ruling elders in the election of commissioners by presbyteries was only overcome after considerable pressure from the other Tables to preserve a united front.

14. NLS, Lee Papers, MS 3430, fo. 13–164; NLS, Wodrow MSS, folio lxii, fo. 229–31; NLS, Yester Papers, MS 7032, fo. 32–35; *RKS*, 37–38, 109–11; N. Meldrum, 'The General Assembly of the Church of Scotland in the year 1638', (University of Edinburgh, Ph.D. thesis, 1924), 53–59, 85, 109–10; Makey, *The Church of the Covenant*, 41–47. Electoral loading was further confirmed by stereotyped commissions for ministers and ruling elders from the presbyteries as for representatives from the royal burghs and the universities.

15. SRO, Hamilton Papers, TD 75/100/26/682; *Large Declaration*, 229–33; *Memoirs of Henry Guthry*, 46–47.

16. Stevenson, *The Scottish Revolution*, 115–16, 127; Makey, *The Church of the Covenant*, 48.

17. *Diary of Wariston, 1632–39*, 393–96, 399–401; Balfour, *Historical Works*, II, 297–300; *Large Declaration*, 207–20; Baillie, *Letters and Journals*, I, 108–109, 121–22.

18. Lennoxlove, Hamilton Papers, C 1/995; NLS, Yester Papers, MS 7032, fo. 39–47; *RKS*, 43–44, 133, 138–39, 151–52, 154; Baillie, *Letters and Journals*, I, 129–30, 136–37; *Large Declaration*, 248–64. The reputedly missing registers were actually in Wariston's custody since August 1638 (*Diary of Wariston, 1632–39*, 374, 401–02).

19. Makey, *The Church of the Covenant*, 50–51.

20. *RKS*, 20–47, 128–93; Baillie, *Letters and Journals*, I, 118–76; Gordon, *History of Scots Affairs*, II, 3–187; *Large Declaration*, 234–327; Mullen, *Episcopacy in Scotland*, 190–93. Eight bishops — including St. Andrews, Glasgow and the Scottish Canterburians — were summarily excommunicated as the most reprobate; four were granted a stay of execution provided they repented for past errors in their ways and recognised the assembly as the supreme authority in the Kirk; and two were merely

suspended from the ministry of a particular congregation pending their anticipated public repentance and recognition of the assembly's authority.

21. Burleigh, *A Church History of Scotland*, 219–21; Makey, *The Church of the Covenant*, 54, 63–64; RKS, 24–40, 45–476; Baillie, *Letters and Journals*, I, 151–75; D. Stevenson, 'The General Assembly and the Commission of the Kirk, 1638–51', *RSCHS*, XIX, (1975), 57–59.

22. *A Source Book of Scottish History*, III, 105–13; *RKS*, 40; NLS, Fleming of Wigtown Papers, Acc. 3142, box xvi0/29; SRO, Hamilton Papers, TD 75/100/26/575; *RPCS*, second series, VII, 91–102.

23. SRO, Hamilton Papers, TD 75/100/26/326, /1010; *Miscellaneous State Papers*, II, 113–21.

24. SRO, Breadalbane Collection, GD 112/39/561; SRO. Airlie MSS, GD 16/50/6; SRO, Hamilton Papers, TD 75/100/26/769, /986, /1002, /1005, /1008; Lennoxlove, Hamilton Papers, C 1/996; NLS, Balcarres Papers, vo. ix, Adv. MS 29.2.9, fo. 124, 126; *CSP, Domestic*, (1638–39), 405–10; Burnet, *Memoirs*, 114–16. Other than the remote shires of Sutherland, Caithness and Orkney which elected a commissioner alternatively to represent their interests, two members of every war committee were on call in Edinburgh in shifts of three months as shire commissioners. Ministers were excluded from shire and presbytery committees.

25. NLS, Salt & Coal: Events, 1635–62, MS 2263, fo. 73–83; SRO, Leven and Melville MSS, GD 26/7/158; SRO, Elibank papers, GD 32/1/17; SRO, Supplementary Parliamentary Papers, 1640–45, PA 16/2/1/2; *Minute Book kept by the War Committee of the Covenanters in the Stewartry of Kirkcudbright in the Years 1640 and 1641*, (Kirkcudbright, 1855), 50–51; Henderson, *Sermons, Prayers and Pulpit Addresses*, 144–70. Depending on the size and indigenous resources of the shire, each regiment of foot consisted of seven to nine companies of 150 to 200 men. Each shire regiment was complemented by a troop of cavalry consisting of 150 to 200 men. Actual recruitment was decided by lots to fulfil the quotas of foot and horse apportioned to each shire. However, the landed classes enjoyed the exclusive privilege of sending a substitute if they were incapable or indisposed. In return, nobles, gentry and yeomen were expected to bear the cost of equipping themselves or their substitutes with horse and weaponry though they, like the infantry levied from the shires, were maintained at common charge for the duration of their military service.

26. *The Melvilles, Earls of Melville and the Leslies, Earls of Leven*, Sir W. Fraser ed., 3 vols, (Edinburgh, 1886), II, 77–88; NLS, Salt & Coal: Events, MS 2263, fo. 81–84; SRO, Supplementary Parliamentary Papers, PA 16/3/1/14; Sir J. Turner, *Memoirs of His Own Life and Times, 1632–70*. T. Thomson ed., (Bannatyne Club, Edinburgh, 1829), 13–16. The Covenanting leadership sought to remedy the fortuitous and transient nature of mercenary employment by maintaining differential rates of pay. Soldiers of fortune were consistently paid at rates four to five times higher than those paid to nobles or gentry serving at equivalent rank as officers.

27. NLS, Salt & Coal: Events, 1635–62, MS 2263, fo. 73–77; SRO, Supplementary Parliamentary Papers, 1640–45, PA 16/2/1/1; Baillie, *Letters and Journals*, I, 210–14; J. D. Ogilvie, 'A Bibliography of the Bishops' Wars, 1639–40', *Records of the Glasgow Bibliographical Society*, XII, (1936), 21–40. A short compendium to the basic rudiments of military discipline, commissioned to standardise drilling and exercising with the shires, was the product of the thorough training and sound tactics the soldiers of fortune acquired from their Swedish and Dutch experience. *Articles of Military Discipline*, re-issued at the outset of the First Bishops' War, placed particular emphasis on religious worship and observance. Every regiment was supervised by a kirk session and all the ministers accompanying the Covenanting forces, together with an elder from every regiment, constituted a presbytery for the army. Its further re-issue as the *Articles and Ordinances of War*, in readiness for the Second Bishops' War, promoted religious as much as military instruction. In the course of battle, morale was maintained by martial

music. Each company of foot was provided with a piper; whereas the horse troopers retained trumpeters and drummers.

28. NLS, Balcarres Papers, vol. ix, Adv.MS 29.2.9, fo. 126; *The Melvilles and the Leslies*, II, 88–89; *Minute Book, War Committee of Kirkcudbright*, 103–04, 107–08; Hailes, *Memorials*, 81–106; *Miscellaneous State Papers*, II, 151–53, 159–61, 173–75, 179–80; *Analecta Scotica: Collections illustrative of the Civil, Ecclesiastical and Literary history of Scotland*, J. Maidment ed., 2 vols, (Edinburgh, 1834–37); I, 383–89.

29. This view is developed further in E. M. Furgol, *A Regimental History of the Covenanting Armies, 1639–1651*, (Edinburgh, 1990).

30. NLS, Wodrow MSS, quarto xxiv, fo. 163–70; SRO, Leven and Melville MSS, GD 26/7/158; Baillie, *Letters and Journals*, I, 191–92; *Memoirs of Henry Guthry*, 51–52. John Smith and James Murray, merchant-burgesses of Edinburgh and Covenanting stalwarts, were duly commissioned as collectors-general when the Tables next met in convention in May 1639.

31. Baillie, *Letters and Journals*, I, 155–56, 208–09, 467–68, 475–91: II, 429–31, 435–38; Hailes, *Memorials*, 47–48. Since the propagation of the National Covenant, the Covenanting leadership had received regular, but not always reliable, intelligence from English sympathisers as well as Scottish courtiers. The principal Covenanting agent at Court was Eleazer Borthwick, formerly minister to the Scottish congregation in Sweden, who had entered the service of Hamilton at the close of 1634. A committed presbyterian, Borthwick collated subscriptions to the National Covenant at Court and helped the leadership diligently monitor the spread of anti-Court sentiment in England. Hitherto, however, covert contacts by Puritans and other English disaffected were informal and unsolicited (NLS, Salt & Coal: Events, 1635–62, MS 2263, fo. 77–78, 91, 171–72; SRO, Hamilton Papers, TD 75/100/26/985, /997; *CSP, Domestic*, (1637–38), 564–65; 593–94; *Diary of Wariston, 1632–39*, 346, 354, 371, 375, 390, 408, 410; Stevenson, *The Scottish Revolution*, 57, 84, 205–06, 213). Formal contacts did not necessarily lead to more reliable information, as was borne out by the misrepresentation perpetrated by Thomas Savile, Lord Savile, prior to August 1640, when he unilaterally invited the Covenanters into England on behalf of the disaffected English nobility. His letter served as an expedient justification for the Covenanters' recourse to an offensive posture.

32. BM, Registers of the Secretaries of State of Scotland, MS.Add. 23,112, fo. 97; SRO, Hamilton Papers, TD 75/100/26/652–53, /870, /1162, /1197, /1260; SRO, Breadalbane Collection, GD 112/39/758–59; *The Hamilton Papers*, 9–13' Burnet, *Memoirs*, 120–25; Baillie, *Letters and Journals*, I, 201–07; D. Stevenson, *Alasdair MacColla and the Highland Problem in the Seventeenth Century*, (Edinburgh, 1980), 65–72; A. Clarke, 'The Earl of Antrim and the First Bishops' War', *Irish Sword*, VI, (1962–63), 109–15. No more than 200 out of the 5000 troops despatched with Hamilton had prior military training. Though adequately provisioned, the lack of fresh supplies, compounded by the cramped conditions on ship, facilitated the spread of disease — the ubiquitous 'pox' — which totally debilitated Hamilton's command.

33. SRO, Hamilton Papers, TD 75/100/26/412; NLS, Morton Cartulary & Papers, MS 81, fo. 82; P. Gordon, *A Short Abridgement of Britane's Distemper, 1639 to 1645*, (Spalding Club, Aberdeen, 1844), 12–28; Gordon, *History of Scots Affairs*, II, 204–38, 253–82; Spalding, *Troubles*, I, 91–124, 133–56; *Historical Notices of St. Anthony's Monastery, Leith and Rehearsal of Events in the North of Scotland from 1635 to 1645 in relation to the National Covenant*, C. Rogers ed., (Grampian Club, London, 1877), 44–52; G. Donaldson, 'Scotland's Conservative North in the Sixteenth and Seventeenth Centuries', *TRHS*, fifth series, XVI, (1966), 65–79; Cowan, *Montrose*, 63–79.

34. NLS, Wodrow MSS, folio lxii, fo. 57; folio, lxiii, fo. 57, 61, 63; quarto xxiv, fo, 149–51; NLS, Salt & Coal: Events, 1635–62, MS 2263, fo. 81–84; SRO, Airlie MSS, GD 16/50/5–6; SRO, Breadalbane Collection, GD 112/39/763; Baillie, *Letters and Journals*, I, 184–224; *Fragment of the Diary of Sir Archibald Johnston of Warison, 1639*,

G. M. Paul ed., (SHS, Edinburgh, 1896), 35–97; Burnet, *Memoirs*, 112–60; Gordon, *History of Scots Affairs*, II, 204–83; III, 3–36.

35. SRO, Hamilton Papers, TD 75/100/26/809, /949; Lennoxlove, Hamilton Papers, C 1/1071, /1073; NLS, Wodrow MSS, folio xxvii, fo. 40–41; lxiii, fo. 22, 32, 44, 231; *RKS*, 205, 237–70; *APS*, V, 252–58; *Aberdeen Council Letters*, II, 140–48; Spalding, *Troubles*, I, 160–66; *Memoirs of Henry Guthry*, 50–65; Balfour, *Historical Works*, II, 320–69.

36. NLS, Wodrow MSS, folio lxiv, fo. 82; SRO, Breadalbane Collection, GD 112/39/797; *Historical Collections*, III, 1114–20; CSP, Domestic, (1640), 19–21, 29–33, 104, 118–19, 134; Gordon, *History of Scots Affairs*, III, 7–9, 32–36, 125, 133–46, 148–53; A. Stevenson, *The History of the Church and State of Scotland from the accession of Charles I to the year 1649*, (Edinburgh, 1840), 410–19; *The Short Parliament (1640) Diary of Sir Thomas Aston*, J. D. Maltby ed., (Camden Society, London, 1988), 3, 6–7, 63–64, 124–25, 131–32, 145. The ostensible purpose of this recharging of the 'auld alliance' in the spring of 1639 was to secure the services of Louis XIII as a mediator between Charles I and his Scottish subjects. A year later, this was secondary to the attainment of international recognition for the *de facto* standing of the general committee as the national executive.

37. SRO, Elibank Papers, GD 32/1/17; SRO, Supplementary Parliamentary Papers, 1640–54, PA 16/3/1/14; NLS, Salt & Coal: Events, 1635–62, MS 2263, fo. 84; *Aberdeen Council Letters*, II, 166–69, 175–83, 186–200, 266–69, 277; CSP, Domestic, (1639–40), 577–78; *The Melvilles and the Leslies*, III, 164–67. Instead of being assisted by a council of war, Leslie was to work 'with the consent of the committee which shall be with him in the armie': the first indication that the committee of estates was to be split between those members residing at Edinburgh and those accompanying the army (*Government under the Covenanters*, xx–xxi).

38. Balfour, *Historical Works*, II, 373–79; Burnet, *Memoirs*, 162–73; *Memoirs of Henry Guthry*, 67–72; Clarendon, *History of the Rebellion*, I, 512–18; Gordon, *History of Scots Affairs*, III, 100–86.

39. *APS*, V, 258–307. The Estates' ultimate control over their own meetings was demonstrated by the concluding enactment continuing parliament until 19 November; a procedure that was to be repeated on another four occasions over the next year.

40. Makey, *The Church of the Covenant*, 55–56; Ferguson, *Scotland's Relations with England*, 117–18. 41. *APS*, V, 282–84, c.24; Gordon, *History of Scots Affairs*, III, 181–84. To maintain a constant correspondence between both sections, Adam Hepburn of Humbie was appointed clerk to the committee and empowered to employ deputies to remain at Edinburgh. Wariston was also to reside at camp where, as clerk to the general assembly and procurator for the Kirk, he was to oversee the preparation of treaties, consultations and publications. The officers of the general staff were eligible to attend all meetings of the committee with the army.

42. *Government under the Covenanters*, xvii–xxvii; *Memoirs of the Marquis of Montrose*, 2 vols, (Edinburgh, 1856), I, 236, 254–61; Cowan, *Montrose 93–94; J. Willcock, The Great Marquess: The Life and Times of Argyll*, (Edinburgh & London, 1903), 112–14.

43. *APS*, V, 264, 280–82, c.23–24; 285–90, c.26–27, 29–33, 39, 41: CSP, Domestic, (1640), 331–32; Burnet, *Memoirs*, 168.

44. HUL, Maxwell-Constable of Everingham MSS, DDEV/79/F & /H/49; Gordon, *History of Scots Affairs*, III, 162–69, 251–56; Spalding, *Troubles*, I, 202, 208–32, 237–40, 249–52, 256–57; *Aberdeen Council Letters*, II, 169–73, 187–89, 212–27; *Memorials of Montrose*, I, 257–64. Licensed to harry dissidents in the central and eastern Highlands, Argyle used his military commission not only to lay waste the estates of suspected Royalists, but also to press his claims to the lordship of Badenoch and Lochaber as the principal creditor of Huntly.

45. SRO, Hamilton Papers, TD 75/100/26/1217–18; SRO, Supplementary Parliamentary Papers, 1640–58, PA 16/1/12, /15; EUL, Instructions to the Committee of Estates

of Scotland, 1640–41, Dc.4.16, fo. 1, 30; Baillie, *Letters and Journals*, I, 255–61; II, 470–71; Hailes, Memorials, 81–106; *Miscellaneous State Papers*, II, 151–53, 159–61, 173–75; *Analecta Scotica*, I, 383–89. The arrival of the Covenanting army in the north-east of England was welcomed by colliers and salters displaced from Scotland as a result of the economic recession induced by Charles during the 1630s (Nef, *The Rise of the British Coal Industry*, II, 148, 282–83).

46. *The Intentions of the Army of the Kingdom of Scotland declared to their Brethren in England*, (Edinburgh, 1640); Spalding, *Troubles*, I, 231–32, 240–49, 257–61; Gordon, *History of Scots Affairs*, III, 186–94; *CSP, Domestic*, (1640–41), 161–66; Sir J. Borough, *Notes on the Treaty carried on at Ripon between King Charles and the Covenanters of Scotland, A.D. 1640*, J. Bruce ed., (Camden Society, London, 1869), 70–77.

47. EUL, Instructions of the Committee of Estates, 1640–41, Dc.4.16, fo. 1–32; SRO, Breadalbane Collection, GD 112/39/820; Balfour, *Historical Works*, II, 383–424; Borough, *Notes on the Treaty of Ripon*, 1–69; *Miscellaneous State Papers*, II, 179–80, 190. The committee accompanying the army elected eight commissioners — two from each estate, together with Henderson and Wariston for the Kirk — to conduct negotiations at Ripon. Another three commissioners — one from each estate — were added for the conclusion of negotiations in London, which were attended by four ministers from the presbytery accompanying the army to propagate the Covenanting cause and the virtues of a presbyterian reformation.

48. The minimalist position on Scottish intervention is upheld by T. K. Rabb & D. Hirst, 'Revisionism Revised: Early Stewart Parliamentary History', *Past & Present*, 92, (1981), 51–99. A growing awareness of the British significance of the Scottish revolution is manifest in A. J. Fletcher, *The Outbreak of the English Civil War*, (London, 1981), 17–22, 408 and, more especially, C. Russell, 'Why did Charles I call the Long Parliament?', *History*, LIX, (1984).

49. EUL, Instructions of the Committee of Estates, 1640–41, Dc.4.16, fo.5, 34–107; *CSP, Domestic* (1640–41), 425–26, 513–14; APS, V, 620–33; Baillie, *Letters and Journals*, I, 271–355. His stay at York having distanced him politically as well as physically from the negotiations at Ripon, Charles was excluded from the talks between the commissioners for both parliaments and relegated to the role of third party on the resumption of negotiations in London. As negotiations dragged on for nine months, Charles sought to sow discord by treating privately with Scottish and English commissioners and to delay a final resolution by conditionally withholding consent.

50. NLS, Wodrow MSS, folio lxxiii, fo. 46, 50–51; NLS, Fleming of Wigtown Papers, Acc. 1342, box v/D/14; EUL, Instructions to the Committee of Estates, 1640–41, Dc.4.16, fo.60–63; *The Great Account Delivered to the English Lords by the Scottish Commissioners*, (London, 1641); *Miscellany of the Maitland Club*, II, 417–23. The total claim was made up of two distinct components. Military engagements during the Bishops' Wars, together with payments to mercenaries and the maintenance of fortifications in the interim, accounted for £410,128–8/8 sterling the remaining £104,000 sterling being the estimated cost of the stops on trade in 1639 and 1640. In addition, the Covenanters had further incidental common burdens totalling £271,5000 sterling (£3,258,000) arising from the servicing of public debts, supplying the armed forces and commercial disruption.

51. Lennoxlove, Hamilton Papers, C 1/1034; Spalding, *Troubles*, I, 275–84; *Historical Collections*, I, 70–71, 133–34, 722–27, 749–50, 769–72; M. Perceval-Maxwell, 'Strafford, the Ulster Scots and the Covenanters', *Irish Historical Studies*, XVIII, (1972–73), 524–51; C. Carlton, *Archbishop William Laud*, (London, 1987), 168–71, 192, 200–03.

52. Levack, *The Formation of the British State*, 110, 130–31; C. L. Hamilton, 'The Anglo-Scottish Negotiations of 1640–41', *SHR*, XLI, (1962), 84–86.

53. EUL, Instructions of the Committee of Estates, 1640–41, Dc.4.16, fo. 75–78, 82–85, 88–96; NLS, Wodrow MSS, folio lxiv, fo. 114–16; folio lxxiii, fo. 63; *CSP, Domestic*, (1640–41), 513–14. Moves for a confederation were stimulated by the marriage

alliance Charles I concluded with the house of Orange in February 1641, with a view to extricating himself from constitutional restraints within the British Isles (Carlton, *Charles I*, 223).

54. EUL, Instructions of the Committee of Estates, 1640–41, Dc.4.16, fo. 101, 105, SRO, Hamilton Papers, TD 75/100/26/1397, /8276; Spalding, *Troubles*, I, 291–94, 303–05, 325–26, 342–43; *Eight Articles of the Scots Demands*, (London, 1641); Stevenson, *The Scottish Revolution*, 132, 220–22.

55. NLS, Wodrow MSS, folio lxxiii, fo. 106; SRO, Hamilton Papers, TD 75/100/26/1322, /1378, /1386; Burnet, *Memoirs*, 81–84; Fletcher, *The Outbreak of the English Civil War*, 47–51, 72, 76; A. Clarke, 'Ireland and the General Crisis', *Past & Present*, 48, (1970), 79–99.

56. SRO, Hamilton Papers, TD 75/100/26/1688, /1742–43, /1782, /1808, /1846, /1887; *APS*, V, 335–45, c.8; *Memoirs of Henry Guthry*, 96–97, 100; Stevenson, *The History of the Church and State of Scotland*, 464–67.

57. *APS*, V, 308–30, 624–43; SRO, Hamilton Papers, TD 75/100/26/1386; Balfour, *Historical Works*, III, 4–45; Baillie, *Letters and Journals*, I, 377–85; II, 469.

58. EUL, Instructions of the Committee of Estates, 1640–41, Dc.4.16, fo. 97–98, 103; NLS, Yester Papers, MS 7032, fo. 49; Balfour, *Historical Works*, II, 403–04; Spalding, *Troubles*, I, 331, 337–38.

59. SRO, Supplementary Parliamentary Papers, 1639–41, PA 7/25/1/2; SRO, Hamilton Papers, TD 75/100/26/904; *APS*, V, 251–53, 258–59, 308–09, 330–32; *The Nicholas Papers, Correspondence of Sir Edward Nicholas, Secretary of State*, G. F. Warner ed., 2 vols, (Camden Society, London), I, 24–25, 27.

60. NLS, Wodrow MSS, folio lxxiii, fo. 54; SRO, Hamilton Papers, TD 75/100/26/326, /1315, /1378, /1386 & TD 75/100/42/1/3; *Memoirs of Henry Guthry*, 65, 87–98; *Memorials of Montrose*, I, 254–55, 264–316, 319–63; *Certain Instructions Given by the L. Montrose*, L. Napier, *Lairds of Keir and Blackhall, with a True Report of the Committee for this New Treason*, (London, 1641); Cowan, *Montrose*, 96–101, 108–18; Stevenson, *The Scottish Revolution*, 206–07, 225–32.

61. *APS*, V, 312–22, 318, 328–588, 643–722; SRO, Supplementary Parliamentary Papers, 1606–42, PA 7/2/74, /78, /106; Balfour, *Historical Works*, III, 22, 27, 32, 35, 37–39, 45. Balmerino, the longstanding opponent as well as victim of the unfettered exercise of the royal prerogative, presided over the last session of parliament in which the Estates approved 145 enactments, of which all but 20 concerned public affairs.

62. *APS*, V, 334–35, 346–50, 364, 369, 376–78, 400, 429–30; SRO, Supplementary Parliamentary Papers, 1606–42, PA 70/20/74; 1641–45, PA 140/1; 1640–54, PA 16/3/5/3; *The Nicholas Papers*, I, 25, 33–34, 58–59; *Questions Exhibited by the parliament Now in Scotland Assembled concerning the Earl of Montrose His Plot*, (London, 1641); Balfour, *Historical Works*, III, 64, 92, 125, 128–30, 134–35, 143–46; D. Stevenson, *Scottish Covenanters and Irish Confederates*, (Belfast, 1981), 43–45, 95–102; Becket, *The Making of Modern Ireland*, 82–86. Charles's limited capacity to influence parliamentary proceedings was critically undermined when he appeared to condone the tumultuous lobby on parliament of 12 October. 'The Incident', the rumoured assassination of Argyle and Hamilton as a prelude to the public rupture of the Scottish Estates by an armed force well in excess of 500 militant Royalists, sympathisers of Montrose and disgruntled mercenaries, was forestalled by the flight of the intended victims from the capital and the arrest of ringleaders, actions which Charles interpreted as a personal affront. His insistence upon a public investigation to embarrass the Covenanting leadership as well as his former favourite served to hasten the political rapport with pragmatic Royalists which obliged Charles to accept the constitutional dictates of the radical mainstream (SRO, Hamilton Papers, TD 75/100/26/1440–41, /1544; *The Truth of the Proceedings in Scotland containing the Discovery of the late Conspiracie*, (Edinburgh, 1641); Stevenson, *The Scottish Revolution*, 391–94).

63. *APS*, V, 354–55, c.21; 356–57, 368, 655–56, 666; Burnet, *Memoirs*, 46, 184–87; Baillie, *Letters and Journals*, I, 389–98; Balfour, *Historical Works*, III, 58–59, 64–69; *A Declaration of the Proceedings of the Parliament of Scotland*, (London, 1641).

64. Makey, *The Church of the Covenant*, 56–58; *Government under the Covenanters*, xxvii–xxxix.

65. HUL, Maxwell-Constable of Everingham MSS, DDEV/76/10; *The Dissolution of the Parliament in Scotland*, (Edinburgh, 1641); *Memoirs of Henry Guthry*, 99–109; *APS*, V, 505–07, c.89. Charles's formal acceptance of the realities of political power in Scotland was manifest by his liberal bestowal of honours and pensions on the Covenanting leadership who had masterminded his defeat, militarily and constitutionally, over the previous three years. Thus, Argyle was promoted to marquis, General Leslie became earl of Leven, Loudoun and Lindsay belatedly received the earldoms which had been suspended for their opposition in the coronation parliament, Wariston was knighted and Henderson appointed to the chapel royal.

66. *APS*, V, 391–96, c.76–77; 400–03, c.85; 404–05, c.87–88; 408–09, c.92; SRO, Supplementary Parliamentary Papers, 1641–45, PA 14/1, fo.12; 1640–54, PA 16/3/5/3; SRO, Hamilton papers, TD 75/100/26/1458, /1472, /1488; *RPCS*, second series, VII, 149–55, 163–64, 170–72; Baillie, *Letters and Journals*, I, 397.

67. J. Richards, "His Nowe Majestie' and the English Monarchy: the Kingship of Charles I before 1640', *Past & Present*, 113, (1986), 70–96.

68. NLS, Salt & Coal: Events, 1635–62, MS 2263, fo. 79, 82–84; NLS, Wodrow MSS, folio lxii, fo. 246–51; quarto xxiv, fo. 149–51; NLS, R. Mylne's Collection, Adv. MS 31.2.1, fo. 193–94; SRO, Airlie MSS, GD 16/50/5; SRO, Elibank papers, GD 32/1/17; SRO, Leven and Melville MSS, GD 26/7/158; *APS*, V, 280–84, c.23–24; *Minute Book, War Committee of Kirkcudbright*, 9–10, 26–28, 40–41, 48, 51–55, 78, 84–89, 95–96, 112–15, 136–37, 145–47, 156–58.

69. SRO, Supplementary Parliamentary Papers, 1606–42, PA 7/2/62; 1641–45, PA 14/1, fo. 4–12; 1640–54, PA 16/3/4/1 & PA 16/3/5/1–3; SRO, Breadalbane Collection, GD 112/39/844; NLS, Fleming of Wigtown Papers, Acc.3142, box v/D/14; *The Journal of Thomas Cunningham of Campbere, 1640–54*, E. J. Courthope ed., (SHS, Edinburgh, 1928), 38–56; D. Stevenson, 'The financing of the cause of the Covenants, 1638–51', *SHR*, LI, (1972), 89–123. The sums raised in taxation by the Covenanting movement stand in favourable comparison to those raised during the personal rule. Of the total taxation levied in 1625 and 1633 (£1,172,275–9/2), audits, which were not completed for eleven and six years respectively, revealed that less than 3% remained unrecovered. Audits of the public accounts of the Covenanting movement, completed after three years, revealed an evasion rate for the tenth of less than 4% when allowance was made for £41,388–1/4 written off locally (SRO, Accounts of the Collectors of Taxation, 1625–30, E 65/10–15).

Bibliography

I. Original Sources
   (i) *Manuscripts*
   British Museum
Registers of the Secretaries of State of Scotland, MS.Add. 23,112.
   Edinburgh University Library
Instructions to the Committee of Estates of Scotland, 1640–41, Dc.4.16.
Laing MSS, La.I.
   Glasgow University Archives
Beith Parish MS, P/CN, II.
   Hull University Library
Maxwell-Constble of Everingham MSS,
                        DDEV/76/10
                        DDEV/79/D, /F & /H.
   Lennoxlove
Hamilton Papers, C 1.
   National Library of Scotland
Wodrow MSS, folio xxvii, lxi-iv, lxxiii.
               octavo xxvii.
               quarto xxiv.
Fleming of Wigtown Papers,
Acc. 3142, box v/D, box xvi.
Balcarres Papers, vol. ix, Adv. MS 29.2.9.
R. Mylne's Collection, Adv. 31.2.1
Morton Cartulary & Papers, MS 79–81, 83.
Kirklands; Laws, MS 1943.
Salt & Coal: Events, 1635–62, MS 2263.
Teinds, MS 2708.
Yule Collection, MS 3134.
Lee Papers, MS 3430.
Yester Papers, MS 7032.
   Scottish Record Office

Church
Synod Records of Moray, (1623–44), CH 2/271/1.
Register of the Presbytery of Lanark, 1623–57, CH 2/234/1.
Paisley Presbytery Records, 1626–47, CH 2/294/2.
Miscellaneous Ecclesiastical Records, CH 8/83.

Exchequer
Exchequer Responde Book, 1623–38, E 1/11.
Exchequer Act Book, 1634–39, E 4/5.

Exchequer Minute Book, 1630–34, E 5/1.
Copy Minutes taken from Exchequer Register, 1630–34, E 4/8.
Treasury Accounts, 1624–25, E 19/22.
Treasury Accounts, 1634–35, E 21/10.
Treasury Accounts, 1635–36, E 26/1.
Treasury Accounts, 1633–35, E 30/23.
Annuity of Teinds, 1632–42, E 50/1–2.
Annuity Accounts & Papers, 1632–36, E52/3, /10.
General Tax Rolls, 1625–33, E 59/7–9.
Accounts of the Collectors of Taxations granted in 1625, 1630 & 1633, E 65/10–17.
Inventories given up for Taxation, 1625 & 1630, E 61/6, /34, /41, /46, /49.
Accounts of the Tacksmen of the Customs, 1633–34, E 73/6.
Account of the Small Customs for 1635, E 73/8/1-/2.
Southesk Miscellaneous Papers, RH 2/8/13.

Gifts & Deposits
Airlie MSS, GD 16/50.
Cunninghame-Grahame MSS, GD 22/1, /3.
Leven and Melville MSS, GD 26/7.
Elibank Papers, GD 32/1.
Mar & Kellie Collection, GD 124/10.
Dalhousie Muniments, GD 45/1.
Seaforth Muniments, GD 46/18/147.
Breadalbane Papers, GD 112/39.
Hamilton Papers, TD 75/100/3, /5, /26, /42.
TD 76/100/5/.

Parliament
Supplementary Parliamentary Papers, 1606–42, PA 7/2. 1639–41, PA 7/25.
1641–45, PA 14/1.
1640–58, PA 16/1.
1640–45, PA 16/2.
1640–54, PA 16/3.

Teinds
Sederunt Books of the High Commission of Teinds, 1630–50, TE 1/1–2.
Notes from the Sederunt Book of the Teind Commissioners, 1633–50, TE 1/4.
Reports from the Sub-Commissioners of the Presbyteries of Argyll, Dumbarton and
Lanark, TE 2/1, /5 &/13.
    Strathclyde Regional Archives
Glasgow Presbytery Records, (1628–41), CH 2/171/3A-B.
    (ii) *Pamphlets & Broadsheets*
A Declaration of the Proceedings of the Parliament of Scotland, (London, 1641).
Calderwood, D. *The Pastor and the Prelate, or Reformation and Conformitie*, (Edinburgh, 1636).
Certain Instructions Given by the L. Montrose, L. Napier, Lairds of Keir and Blackhall, with a True Report of the Committee for this New Treason, (London, 1641).
Drummond of Hawthornden, W. 'Memorials of State', in *The History of Scotland, from the year 1423, until the year 1542*, (London, 1681).
Eight Articles of the Scots Demands, (London, 1641).
The Great Account Delivered to the English Lords by the Scottish Commissioners, (London, 1641).
Guild, W. *The Humble Address, Both of Church and Poore*, (Aberdeen, 1633).

Questions Exhibited by the parliament Now in Scotland Assembled concerning the Earl of Montrose His Plot, (London, 1641).

'Reasons Against the Reception of King James's Metaphrase of the Psalms, 1631', in *The Bannatyne Miscellany*, vol. I, (Bannatyne Club, Edinburgh, 1827).

The Dissolution of the Parliament in Scotland, (Edinburgh, 1641).

The Intentions of the Army of the Kingdom of Scotland declared to their Brethren in England, (Edinburgh, 1640).

The Protestation of the Noblemen, Barrons, Gentlemen, Burrowes, Ministers and Commons, Edinburgh, 1638).

The Truth of the Proceedings in Scotland containing the Discovery of the late Conspiracie, (Edinburgh, 1641).

    (iii) *Printed Texts*

A Source Book of Scottish History, vol. III, (1567–1707), W. C. Dickinson & G. Donaldson eds., (Edinburgh, 1961).

Aberdeen Council Letters, vols 1–2, (1554–1644), L. B. Taylor ed., (London, 1950).

Acts of the Parliament of Scotland, T. Thomson & C. Innes eds., vols II–VI (ii), (1414–1660), (Edinburgh, 1814–72).

Analecta Scotica: Collections illustrative of the Civil, Ecclesiastical and Literary history of Scotland, J. Maidment ed., 2 vols, (Edinburgh, 1834–37).

Autobiography and Life of Mr Robert Blair, T. McCrie ed., (Wodrow Society, Edinburgh, 1848).

Ayr Burgh Accounts, 1534–1624, G. S. Pryde ed., (SHS, Edinburgh, 1937).

Baillie, R. *Letters and Journals, 1637–62*, D. Laing ed., 3 vols, (Bannatyne Club, Edinburgh, 1841–42).

Balcanqual, W. A. *A Declaration concerning the Late Tumults in Scotland*, (Edinburgh, 1639).

Balfour, Sir James. *Historical Works*, 4 vols, J. Haig ed., (Edinburgh, 1824–25).

Borough, Sir John. *Notes on the Treaty carried on at Ripon between King Charles and the Covenanters of Scotland, A.D. 1640*, J. Bruce ed., (Camden Society, London, 1869).

Brereton, Sir William. *Travels in Holland, the United Provinces, England, Scotland and Ireland, 1634–35*, E. Hawkins ed., (Chetham Society, London, 1844)

Burnet, G. *History of My Own Times*, 2 vols, (London, 1838).

Burnet, G. *The Memoirs of the Lives and Actions of James and William, Dukes of Hamiltons and Castleherald*, (London, 1838).

Calderwood, D. *The History of the Kirk of Scotland*, T. Thomson ed., 8 vols, (Wodrow Society, Edinburgh, 1845).

Calendar of State Papers and Manuscripts relating to English Affairs existing in the Archives and Collections of Venice, and in other Libraries of Northern Italy, A. B. Hinds ed., vols XIX–XXIV, (1625–39), (London, 1913–23).

Calendar of State Papers Domestic Series, of the reign of Charles I, J. Bruce & W. D. Hamilton eds., 17 vols, (1625–41), (London, 1858–82).

Calendar of State Papers relating to Ireland, of the reign of Charles I, 1625–32, R. P. Mahaffey ed., (London, 1900).

Campbell, Archibald, marquis of Argyle. *Instructions to a Son, containing rules of conduct in public and private life*, (London, 1661).

Connell, J. A. *Treatise on the Law of Scotland respecting Tithes*, 3 vols, (Edinburgh, 1815).

Correspondence of Sir Robert Kerr, first earl of Ancrum and his son William, third earl of Lothian, D. Laing ed., 2 vols, (Edinburgh, 1875).

Dalrymple, Sir David, Lord Hailes. *Memorials and Letters relating to the History of Britain in the reign of Charles I*, (Glasgow, 1766).

Diary of Sir Archibald Johnston of Wariston, 1632–39, J. M. Paul ed, (SHS, Edinburgh, 1911).

Diary of Sir Thomas Hope of Craighall, 1634–45, T. Thomson ed., (Bannatyne Club, Edinburgh, 1843).

Dumbarton Common Good Accounts, 1614–60, F. Roberts & I. M. M. Macphail eds, (Dumbarton, 1972).
Extracts from the Records of the Convention of Royal Burghs, J. D. Marwick ed., 2 vols, (1616–1711), (Edinburgh, 1880–98).
Extracts from the Records of the Royal Burgh of Stirling, 1519–1666, R. Renwick ed., (Glasgow, 1887), 178–79.
Fife Fiars, 1619–1815, (Cupar, 1846).
Fleming, D. H. *Scotland's Supplication and Complaint against the Book of Common Prayer (otherwise Laud's Liturgy), the Book of Canons, and the Prelates, 18th October 1637*, (Edinburgh, 1927).
Fragment of the Diary of Sir Archibald Johnston of Warison, 1639, G. M. Paul ed., (SHS, Edinburgh, 1896).
Fraser, J. *Chronicles of the Frasers: The Wardlaw Manuscript, 916–1674*, W. Mackay ed., (SHS, Edinburgh, 1905).
Gordon, J. *History of Scots Affairs, 1637–41*, 3 vols, J. Robertson & G. Grub eds., (Spalding Club, Aberdeen, 1841).
Gordon, P. *A Short Abridgement of Britane's Distemper, 1639 to 1645*, (Spalding Club, Aberdeen, 1844).
Henderson, A. *Sermons, Prayers and Pulpit Addresses*, R. T. Martin ed., (Edinburgh, 1867).
Historical Collections, J. Rushworth ed., vols I–III, (London,, 1680–91).
Historical Notices of St. Anthony's Monastery, Leith and Rehearsal of Events in the North of Scotland from 1635 to 1645 in relation to the National Covenant, C. Rogers ed., (Grampian Club, London, 1877).
HMC, Eleventh Report, appendix, *The Manuscripts of the Duke of Hamilton*, (London, 1887).
HMC, *Manuscripts of the earls of Mar and Kellie*, (London, 1904).
HMC, Ninth Report, part ii, appendix, *Traquhair Muniments*, (London, 1887).
HMC, *Report of the Laing MSS preserved in the University of Edinburgh*, (London, 1914).
HMC, *Supplementary Manuscripts of the earls of Mar and Kellie*, (London, 1930).
HMC, *Supplementary Report on the Manuscripts of the Duke of Hamilton*, (London, 1932).
Hyde, Edward, earl of Clarendon. *The History of the Rebellion and Civil Wars in England*, vol. I, (Oxford, 1836).
Laing, D. *Memoir of the life and writings of Robert Baillie*, (Bannatyne Club, Edinburgh, 1842).
Leslie, John, earl of Rothes. *A Relation of Proceedings Concerning the Affairs of the Kirk of Scotland, from August 1637 to July 1638*, J. Nairne ed., (Bannatyne Club, Edinburgh, 1830).
Letters of Samuel Rutherford, 2 vols, A. A. Bonar ed., (Edinburgh, 1863).
Memoirs of Scottish Catholics during the seventeenth and eighteenth centuries, W. F. Forbes-Leith ed., 2 vols, (London, 1909).
Memoirs of the Marquis of Montrose, 2 vols, (Edinburgh, 1856).
Memoirs of the Maxwells of Pollok, W. Fraser ed., 2 vols, (Edinburgh, 1863).
Memorials of the Earls of Haddington, Sir W. Fraser ed., 2 vols, (Edinburgh, 1889).
Minute Book kept by the War Committee of the Covenanters in the Stewartry of Kirkcudbright in the Years 1640 and 1641, (Kirkcudbright, 1855).
Miscellaneous State Papers, 1501–1726, P. Yorke, earl of Hardwicke ed., vol. II.
Napier, M. *Montrose and the Covenanters*, 2 vols, (London, 1837).
Ogilvie, J. D. 'A Bibliography of the Bishops' Wars, 1639–40', *Records of the Glasgow Bibliographical Society*, XII, (1936).
'Proceedings of the Commissioners of the Kirk at a Meeting held in Edinburgh in July 1627', in *Bannatyne Miscellany*, III, (Bannatyne Club, Edinburgh).

Purves, Sir William. *Revenues of the Scottish Crown in 1681*, D. M. Rose ed., (Edinburgh and London, 1897).

Records of the Coinage of Scotland, 2 vols, R. W. Cochrane-Patrick ed., (Edinburgh, 1846).

Records of the Kirk of Scotland, containing the Acts and Proceedings of the General Assemblies, 1630–54, A. Peterkin ed., (Edinburgh, 1843).

Records of the Privy Council of Scotland, D. Masson & P. H. Brown eds., first series, vols VI–XIV, (1599–1625), (Edinburgh, 1884–98); second series, 8 vols, (1625–60), (Edinburgh, 1899–1908).

Registrum Magni Sigilli Regum Scotorum, J. M. Thomson ed., vols VIII–IX, (1620–51), (Edinburgh, 1894–97).

Renaissance and Reformation 1300–1648, G. R. Elton ed., (New York, 1968).

Reports of the State of Certain Parishes in Scotland, 1627, A. MacGrigor ed., (Maitland Club, Glasgow, 1835).

Row, J. *The History of the Kirk of Scotland 1558–1637*, D. Laing ed., (Wodrow Society, Edinburgh, 1842).

'Royal Letters and Instructions, and other Documents from the Archives of the Earls of Wigton, 1510–1650', in *Miscellany of the Maitland Club*, vol. II, (Maitland Club, Edinburgh, 1840).

Royal Letters, Charters and Tracts relating to the Colonization of New Scotland and the Institution of the Order of Knight Baronets of Nova Scotia, 1621–38, D. Laing ed., (Bannatyne Club, Edinburgh, 1857).

Scot of Scotstarvit, Sir John. 'Trew Relation of the Principal Affaires concerning the State', G. Neilson ed., *SHR*, XI, (1913–14); XII, (1914–15); XIV, (1916–17).

Scot of Scotstarvit, Sir John. *The Staggering State of Scottish Statesmen, from 1550 to 1650*, C. Rogers ed., (Edinburgh, 1872).

Scott, W. *An Apologetical Narration of the State and Government of the Kirk of Scotland since the Reformation*, D. Laing ed., (Wodrow Society, Edinburgh, 1846).

Select Biographies, W. K. Tweedie ed., 2 vols, (Wodrow Society, Edinburgh, 1845–47).

Selected Justiciary Cases, 1624–50, vol. I, S. A. Gillon ed., (The Stair Society, Edinburgh, 1953).

Spalding, J. *The History of the Troubles and Memorable Transactions in Scotland and England, 1624–45*, 2 vols, J. Skene ed., (Bannatyne Club, Edinburgh, 1828–29).

State Trials, W. Cobbett ed., vol. III, (London, 1809).

Stevenson, A. *The History of the Church and State of Scotland from the accession of Charles I to the year 1649*, (Edinburgh, 1840).

The Acts of Sederunt of the Lords of Council and Session, 1628–1740, (Edinburgh, 1740).

The Black Book of Taymouth, C. Innes ed., (Bannatyne Club, Edinburgh, 1855).

The Book of Carlaverock, W. Fraser ed., 2 vols, (Edinburgh, 1873).

The Court Book of the Burgh of Kirkintilloch, G. S. Pryde ed., (SHS, Edinburgh, 1963).

The Earl of Stirling's Register of Royal Letters, Relative to the Affairs of Scotland and Nova Scotia from 1615 to 1635, C. Rogers ed., 2 vols, (Edinburgh, 1885).

'The Gordon Letters', in *Miscellany of the Spalding Club*, vol. III, J. Stuart ed., (The Spalding Club, Aberdeen, 1846).

The Government of Scotland under the Covenanters, 1637–51, D. Stevenson ed., (SHS, Edinburgh, 1982), xii–xiii.

The Hamilton Papers, S. R. Gardiner ed., (Camden Society, London, 1880), 26–35.

The Journal of Thomas Cunningham of Campvere, 1640–54, E. J. Courthope ed., (SHS, Edinburgh, 1928).

The Melvilles, Earls of Melville and the Leslies, Earls of Leven, Sir W. Fraser ed., 3 vols, (Edinburgh, 1886).

The Nicholas Papers, Correspondence of Sir Edward Nicholas, Secretary of State, G. F.

Warner ed., 2 vols, (Camden Society, London).
The Party-Coloured Mind, D. Reid ed., (Edinburgh, 1982).
The Red Book of Menteith, W. Fraser ed., 2 vols, (Edinburgh, 1880).
The Short Parliament (1640) Diary of Sir Thomas Aston, J. D. Maltby ed., (Camden Society, London, 1988).
The Stuart Constitution, 1603–1688, J. P. Kenyon ed., (Cambridge, 1966).
The Works of Mr George Gillespie, W. M. Hetherington ed., 2 vols, (Edinburgh, 1846).
The Works of William Laud, D. D., J. Bliss ed., (Oxford, 1853).
Turner, Sir James. *Memoirs of His Own Life and Times, 1632–70*, T. Thomson ed., (Bannatyne Club, Edinburgh, 1829).
Wodrow, R. *Analecta: or Materials for a History of Remarkable Providences*, J. M. Leishman ed., 3 vols, (Maitland Club, Edinburgh, 1842–43).

II. Secondary Sources
    (i) *References*
A List of Books Printed in Scotland before 1700, H. G. Aldis ed., (NLS, Edinburgh, 1970).
An Introductory Survey of the Sources and Literature of Scots Law, H. MacKechnie ed., (The Stair Society, Edinburgh, 1936).
Chalmers, G. *Caledonia: An Account, Historical and Topographic, of North Britain*, 3 vols, (London, 1824).
Donaldson, G. *The Sources of Scottish History*, (Edinburgh, 1978).
Duncan, J. M. *Treatise on the Parochial Ecclesiastical Law of Scotland*, (Edinburgh, 1869).
Dunlop, A. *Parochial Law*, (Edinburgh, 1841).
Fasti Ecclesiae Scoticanae, H. Scott ed., 8 vols, (Edinburgh, 1915–50).
Handbook of British Chronology, Sir F. M. Powicke & E. B. Fryde eds., (Royal Historical Society, London, 1987).
Stevenson, D. & W. B. *Scottish Texts and Calendars: An Analytical Guide to Serial Publications*, (SHS, Edinburgh & Royal Historical Society, London, 1987).
The Scots Peerage, Sir J. Balfour-Paul ed., 9 vols, (Edinburgh, 1904–14).
Thomas Thomson's Memorial on Old Extent, J. D. Mackie ed., (The Stair Society, Edinburgh, 1946).
    (ii) *Theses*
Brown, J. I. 'The Social, Political and Economic Influence of the Edinburgh Merchant Elite, 1600–38',
    (University of Edinburgh, Ph.D. thesis, 1985).
Donald, P. 'The King and the Scottish Troubles, 1637–41',
    (University of Cambridge Ph.D. thesis, 1987).
Fallon, J. A. 'Scottish Mercenaries in the Service of Denmark and Sweden, 1626–32',
    (University of Glasgow, Ph.D. thesis, 1972).
Kitshoff, M. C. 'Aspects of Arminianism in Scotland',
    (University of St. Andrews, M.Litt. Thesis, 1968).
Macinnes, A. I. 'The Origin and Organization of the Covenanting Movement during the reign of Charles I, 1625–41; with a particular reference to the west of Scotland', 2 vols,
    (University of Glasgow, Ph.D. thesis, 1987).
Meldrum, N. 'The General Assembly of the Church of Scotland in the year 1638',
    (University of Edinburgh, Ph.D. thesis, 1924).
    (iii) *Commentaries*
Abel, W. *Agricultural Fluctuations in Europe*, London, 1980).
Aikman, J. A. *An Historical account of Covenanting in Scotland from 1556 to 1638*, (Edinburgh, 1848).

Albion, G. *Charles I and the Court of Rome*, (London, 1935).

Anson, P. F. *Underground Catholicism in Scotland, 1622–1878*, (Montrose, 1970).

Ashton, R. *The English Civil War: Conservatism and Revolution 1603–1649*, (London, 1978).

Aston, T. ed. *Crisis in Europe 1560–1660*, (London, 1974).

Barrow, G. W. S. ed. *The Scottish Tradition: Essays in Honour of Ronald Gordon Cant*, (Edinburgh, 1974).

Beckett, J. C. *The Making of Modern Ireland, 1603–1923*, (London, 1978).

Blum, J. *Lord and Peasant in Russia*, (Princeton, 1972).

Brotherstone, T. ed. *Covenant, Charter and Party: Traditions of Revolt and Protest in Modern Scotland*, (Aberdeen, 1989).

Brown, K. M. 'Aristocratic Finances and the Origins of the Scottish Revolution', *English Historical Review*, CIV, (1989), 46–87.

Brown, K. M. *Bloodfeud in Scotland 1573–1625: Violence, Justice and Politics in Early Modern Scotland*, (Edinburgh, 1986).

Burleigh, J. H. S. *A Church History of Scotland*, (London, 1973).

Burns, E. *The Coinage of Scotland*, vol. II, (Edinburgh, 1887).

Burrell, S. A. 'The Covenant Idea as a Revolutionary Symbol: Scotland, 1596–1637', *Church History*, XXVII, (1958).

Carlton, C. *Archbishop William Laud*, (London, 1987).

Carlton, C. *Charles I: The Personal Monarch*, (London, 1984).

Clarke, A. 'Ireland and the General Crisis', *Past & Present*, 48, (1970), 79–99.

Clarke, A. 'The Earl of Antrim and the First Bishops' War', *Irish Sword*, VI, (1962–63), 109–15.

Cooper, J. P. ed. *The Decline of Spain and the Thirty Years War 1609–48/59*, (Cambridge, 1970).

Cormack, A. A. *Teinds and Agriculture: an historical survey*, (London, 1930).

Cowan, E. J. *Montrose: For Covenant and King*, (London, 1977).

Cowan, I. B. 'The Covenanters: A revision article', *SHR*, XLVII, (1968).

Cowan, I. B. 'The Development of the Parochial System in Medieval Scotland', *SHR*, XL, (1961).

Cullen, L. M. & Smout, T. C. eds. *Comparative Aspects of Scottish and Irish Economic and Social History, 1600–1900*, (Edinburgh, 1972).

Davidson, J. & Gray, A. *The Scottish Staple at Veere*, (London, 1909).

Davis, R. *The Rise of the Atlantic Economies*, (London, 1973).

Devine, T. M. & Lythe, S. G. E. 'The Economy of Scotland under James VI: A revision article', *SHR*, L, (1971).

Dietz, F. C. *English Public Finance, 1558–1641*, (London, 1964).

Donaldson, G. 'Scotland's Conservative North in the Sixteenth and Seventeenth Centuries', *TRHS*, fifth series, XVI, (1966).

Donaldson, G. *Scotland: James V to James VII*, (Edinburgh & London, 1965).

Donaldson, G. *The Making of the Scottish Prayer Book of 1637*, (Edinburgh, 1954).

Drummond, A. L. *The Kirk and the Continent*, (Edinburgh, 1956).

Dunbar, J. G. *The Historic Architecture of Scotland*, (London, 1960).

Dunlop, I. 'The Polity of the Scottish Church, 1600–37', *RSCHS*, XII, (1956).

Dyrvik, S., Mykland K. & Oldervoll J. eds. *The Satellite States in the 17th and 18th Centuries*, (Bergen, 1979).

Edgar, A. *Old Church Life in Scotland*, 2 vols, (Paisley, 1886).

Elder, J. R. *The Royal Fishery Companies of the Seventeenth Century*, (Glasgow, 1912).

Ferguson, W. *Scotland's Relations with England: a Survey to 1707*, (Edinburgh, 1977).

Fischer, T. A. *The Scots in Germany*, (Edinburgh, 1902).

Fletcher, A. J. *The Outbreak of the English Civil War*, (London, 1981).

Forrester, D. M. 'Archibald Johnston of Wariston, especially as in his Diaries', *RSCHS*, IX, (1947), 127–41.

Foster, W. R. *The Church before the Covenants*, (Edinburgh & London, 1975).

Furgol, E. M. *A Regimental History of the Covenanting Armies, 1639–1651*, (Edinburgh, 1990).

Galloway, B. *The Union of England and Scotland 1603–1608*, (Edinburgh, 1986).

Gardiner, S. R. *The Fall of the Monarchy of Charles I, 1637–42*, 2 vols, (London, 1882).

Hamilton, C. L. 'The Anglo-Scottish Negotiations of 1640–41', *SHR*, XLI, (1962).

Hannay, R. K. & Watson, P. H. 'The Building of Parliament House', *The Book of the Old Edinburgh Club*, XIII, (1924).

Hay, M. V. *The Blairs Papers*, (1603–60), (London & Edinburgh, 1929).

Henderson, G. D. *Religious Life in Seventeenth Century Scotland*, (Cambridge, 1937).

Henderson, G. D. *The Burning Bush: Studies in Scottish Church History*, (Edinburgh, 1957).

Henderson, J. M. 'An 'Advertisement' about the Service Book, 1637', *SHR*, XXIII, (1925–26).

Hewison, J. K. *The Covenanters*, 2 vols, (Glasgow, 1908).

Hill, C. *The Century of Revolution, 1603–1714*, (London, 1967).

Hoszowski, S. 'Central Europe and the Price Revolution', in *Economy and Society in Early Modern Europe*, P. Burke ed., (London, 1972).

Israel, J. L. 'A Conflict of Empires: Spain and the Netherlands 1618–1648', *Past & Present*, 76, (1977).

Kamen, H. *The Iron Century, Social Change in Europe, 1550–1660*, (London, 1971).

Kaplan, Y., Mechoulan, H. & Popkin, R. H. eds. *Menasseh Ben Israel and His World*, (New York, 1989).

Kearney, H. F. *Strafford in Ireland, 1633–41*, (Manchester, 1959).

Kirk, J. 'The Politics of the Best Reformed Kirks: Scottish achievements and English aspirations in church government', *SHR*, LIX, (1980).

Koenigsberger, H. G. *Politicians and Virtuosi: Essays in Early Modern History*, (London, 1986).

Lee, jr., M. 'Charles I and the end of Conciliar Government in Scotland', *Albion*, XII, (1980).

Lee, jr., M. 'James VI's government of Scotland after 1603', *SHR*, LV, (1976).

Lee, jr., M. 'Scotland and the 'General Crisis' of the Seventeenth Century', *SHR*, LXIII, (1984).

Lee, jr., M. *The Road to Revolution: Scotland under Charles I, 1625–37*, (Urbana & Chicago, 1985).

Levack, B. P. *The Formation of the British State: England, Scotland, and the Union 1603–1707*, (Oxford, 1987).

Lynch, M. ed. *The Early Modern Town in Scotland*, (London, 1987).

Lythe, S. G. E. *The Economy of Scotland, 1550–1625*, (Edinburgh & London, 1960).

MacCurtain, M. *Tudor and Stuart Ireland*, (Dublin, 1972).

MacDougall, N. ed. *Church, Politics and Society: Scotland, 1408–1929*, (Edinburgh, 1983).

McGrail, T. H. *Sir William Alexander of Menstrie*, (Edinburgh, 1940).

Macinnes, A. I. 'Catholic Recusancy and the Penal Laws, 1603–1707', *RSCHS*, XXIII, (1987).

Macinnes, A. I. 'Glasgow: Covenanting Revolution and Municipal Enterprise', *History Today*, XL, (1990), 10–16.

Mackay, P. H. R. 'The Reception Given to the Five Articles of Perth', *RSCHS*, XIX, (1977).

Mackenzie, W. C. *History of the Outer Hebrides*, (Edinburgh, 1974).

Maclean L. ed. *The Seventeenth Century in the Highlands*, (Inverness Field Club, Inverness, 1985).

Macleod, J. *Scottish Theology*, (Edinburgh, 1974).

McMahon, G. I. R. 'The Scottish Courts of High Commission, 1610–38', *RSCHS*, XV, (1964–66).
Makey, W. *The Church of the Covenant, 1637–51*, (Edinburgh, 1979).
Malcolm, G. A. 'The Office of Sheriff in Scotland', *SHR*, XX, (1923).
Marshall, G. *Presbyteries and Profits*, (Oxford, 1980).
Mathew, D. *Scotland under Charles I*, (London, 1955).
Mitchison, R. *Lordship to Patronage: Scotland 1603–1707*, (London, 1983).
Mitchison, R. 'The Making of the Old Scottish Poor Law', *Past & Present*, 63, (1974).
Mullan, D. G. *Episcopacy in Scotland: The History of an Idea, 1560–1638*, (Edinburgh, 1986).
Myers, L. A. R. 'The Parliaments of Europe and the Age of the Estates', *History*, LX, (1975).
Nef, J. U. *The Rise of the British Coal Industry*, 2 vols, (London & Edinburgh, 1966).
Ogilvie, J. D. 'The Aberdeen Doctors and the National Covenant', *Papers of the Edinburgh Bibliographical Society*, XI, (1919–20).
Paton, G. C. H. ed. *An Introduction to Scottish Legal History*, (The Stair Society, Edinburgh, 1958).
Perceval–Maxwell, M. 'Sir William Alexander of Menstrie (1567–1640)', *Scottish Tradition*, XI/XII, (1981–82).
Perceval-Maxwell, M. 'Strafford, the Ulster Scots and the Covenanters', *Irish Historical Studies*, XVIII, (1972–73).
Perceval-Maxwell, M. *The Scottish Migration to Ulster in the Reign of James I*, (London, 1973).
Polisensky, J. V. *The Thirty Years War*, (London, 1971).
Prestwich M. ed. *International Calvinism, 1541–1715*, (Oxford, 1985).
Rabb, T. K. & Hirst, D. 'Revisionism Revised: Two Perspectives on Early Stuart Parliamentary History', *Past & Present*, 92, (1981).
Rait, R. S. *The Parliaments of Scotland*, (Glasgow, 1924).
Reeve, L. J. *Charles I and the Road to Personal Rule*, (Cambridge, 1989).
Reid, J. S. *The History of the Presbyterian Church in Ireland*, vol. I, (Edinburgh, 1834).
Richards, J. '"His Nowe Majestie" and the English Monarchy: the Kingship of Charles I before 1640', *Past & Present*, 113, (1986).
Rooseboom, M. P. *The Scottish Staple in the Netherlands*, (The Hague, 1910).
Rubinstein, H. L. *Captain Luckless: James, First Duke of Hamilton, 1606–49*, (Edinburgh & London, 1975).
Russell, C. 'Parliamentary History in Perspective, 1604–29', *History*, LXI, (1976).
Russell, C. 'Why did Charles I call the Long Parliament?', *History*, LIX, (1984).
Russell, C. ed. *The Origins of the English Civil War*, (London, 1975).
Sabine, G. H. A History of Political Theory, (London, 1968).
Sanderson, M. H. B. *Scottish Rural Society in the sixteenth century*, (Edinburgh, 1982).
Scott, W. R. *The Constitution and Finance of English*, Scottish and Irish Joint-Stock Companies to 1720, 2 vols, (Cambridge, 1910–12).
Sharpe, K. ed. *Faction and Parliament*, (Oxford, 1978).
Shaw, D. ed. *Reformation and Revolution*, (Edinburgh, 1967).
Smart, I. M. 'Monarchy and Toleration in Drummond of Hawthornden', *Scotia*, IV, (1980).
Smith, A. G. R. ed. *The Reign of James VI and I*, (London, 1977).
Smith, C. T. *An Historical Geography of Western Europe before 1800*, (London & New York, 1978).
Smout, T. C. *A History of the Scottish People, 1560–1830*, (London, 1970).
Snoddy, T. G. *Sir John Scot, Lord Scotstarvit*, (Edinburgh, 1968).

Snow, W. G. S. *The Times, Life and Thought of Patrick Forbes, bishop of Aberdeen, 1618–35*, (London, 1952).

Steinberg, S. H. *The 'Thirty Years War' and the Conflict for European Hegemony 1600–1660*, (London, 1966).

Stevenson, D. *Alasdair MacColla and the Highland Problem in the Seventeenth Century*, (Edinburgh, 1980).

Stevenson, D. 'Conventicles in the Kirk, 1619–37', *RSCHS*, XVIII, (1972–74).

Stevenson, D. *Scottish Covenanters and Irish Confederates*, (Belfast, 1981).

Stevenson, D. 'The financing of the cause of the Covenants, 1638–51', *SHR*, LI, (1972).

Stevenson, D. *The first freemasons: Scotland's early lodges and their members*, (Aberdeen, 1988).

Stevenson, D. 'The General Assembly and the Commission of the Kirk, 1638–51', *RSCHS*, XIX, (1975).

Stevenson, D. 'The King's Scottish Revenues and the Covenanters, 1625–51', *The Historical Journal*, XVII, (1974).

Stevenson, D. *The Covenanters: The National Covenant and Scotland*, (Saltire Pamphlets, 1988).

Stevenson, D. *The Scottish Revolution, 1637–44*, (Newton Abbot, 1973).

Stevenson, R. B. K. 'The Stirling Turners of Charles I, 1632–39', *British Numismatic Journal*, XXIX, (1958–59).

Stewart, D. 'The Aberdeen Doctors' and the Covenanters', *RSCHS*, XXII, (1984).

Stone, L. *The Causes of the English Revolution, 1529–1642*, (London, 1972).

Tawney, R. H. *Religion and the Rise of Capitalism*, (London, 1969).

Taylor, W. 'The King's mails, 1603–25', *SHR*, XLII, (1963).

Terry, C. S. *The Scottish Parliament: Its Constitution and Procedure*, 1603–1707, (Glasgow, 1905).

Torrance, J. B. 'The Covenant Concept in Scottish Theology and Politics and its Legacy', *Scottish Journal of Theology*, XXXIV, (1981).

Trevor-Roper, H. R. *Archbishop Laud, 1573–1645*, (London, 1962).

Watt, H. 'William Laud and Scotland', *RSCHS*, VII, (1941).

Wedgwood, C. V. 'Anglo-Scottish Relations, 1603–40', *TRHS*, fourth series, XXXII, (1950).

Whatley, C. A. *The Scottish Salt Industry 1570–1850*, (Aberdeen, 1987).

Whyte, I. D. *Agriculture and Society in Seventeenth Century Scotland*, (Edinburgh, 1979).

Willcock, J. *The Great Marquess: The Life and Times of Argyll*, (Edinburgh & London, 1903).

Williamson, A. H. *Scottish National Consciousness in the Age of James VI*, (Edinburgh, 1979).

Wormald, J. 'Bloodfeud, Kindred and Government in Early Modern Scotland', *Past & Present*, 87, (1980).

Zagorin, P. *The Court and the Country: The Beginning of the English Revolution*, (London, 1969).

Zupko, R. E. 'The Weights and Measures of Scotland before the Union', *SHR*, LV, (1977).

Index